Behavioral Evidence Analysis

Behavioral Evidence Analysis

International Forensic Practice and Protocols

Edited by

Brent E. Turvey
Forensic Solutions LLC,
Sitka, Alaska, United States;
Institute of Forensic Investigation and
Criminal Profiling, Juarez, Mexico

Manuel A. Esparza
Institute of Forensic Investigation and
Criminal Profiling, Juarez, Mexico

ELSEVIER

AMSTERDAM • BOSTON • HEIDELBERG • LONDON
NEW YORK • OXFORD • PARIS • SAN DIEGO
SAN FRANCISCO • SINGAPORE • SYDNEY • TOKYO

Academic Press is an imprint of Elsevier

Academic Press is an imprint of Elsevier
125 London Wall, London EC2Y 5AS, UK
525 B Street, Suite 1800, San Diego, CA 92101-4495, USA
50 Hampshire Street, 5th Floor, Cambridge, MA 02139, USA
The Boulevard, Langford Lane, Kidlington, Oxford OX5 1GB, UK

British Library Cataloguing-in-Publication Data
A catalog record for this book is available from the British Library

Library of Congress Cataloging-in-Publication Data
A catalog record for this book is available from the Library of Congress

ISBN: 978-0-12-800607-8

For information on all Academic Press publications
visit our website at https://www.elsevier.com/

Publisher: Sara Tenney
Acquisitions Editor: Elizabeth Brown
Editorial Project Manager: Joslyn Chaiprasert-Paguio
Production Project Manager: Lisa Jones
Designer: Matthew Limbert

Typeset by TNQ Books and Journals
www.tnq.co.in

Contents

List of Contributors

D.M. Cardona
Policía Nacional de los Colombianos, Directorate of Criminal Investigation and Interpol (DIJIN), Bogota, Colombia

W.S. Crowder
Kennesaw State University, Kennesaw, GA, United States

M.A. Esparza
Institute of Forensic Investigation and Criminal Profiling, Juarez, Mexico

J. Freeman
Forensic Solutions LLC, Sitka, Alaska, United States;
University of Western Ontario, London, ON, Canada

T. Konvalina-Simas
Psychotherapist at Sala de Estar, Azores, Portugal;
Investigative Consultant at FSI Brazil

M. McGrath
Unity Healthy Systems, Rochester, NY, United States

S. Mikulay
Elgin Community College, Elgin, IL, United States

B.E. Turvey
Forensic Solutions LLC, Sitka, Alaska, United States; Institute of Forensic Investigation and Criminal Profiling, Juarez, Mexico

Author Biographies

ABOUT THE EDITORS

Brent E. Turvey, PhD, D-ABP Brent E. Turvey received a BS from Portland State University in psychology, with an emphasis on forensic psychology, and an additional BS in history. He went on to receive his master's of science in forensic science after studying from University of New Haven. He has also earned his PhD in criminology from Bond University.

Since 1996, Brent has consulted with many organizations, attorneys, and law enforcement agencies in the United States, Australia, Scotland, China, Canada, Barbados, Singapore, Korea, Guatemala, Colombia, Ecuador, Spain, and Mexico on a range of rapes, homicides, and serial/multiple rape death cases as a forensic scientist and criminal profiler. In 2002 and then again in 2005 he was invited by the Chinese People's Public Security University (CPPSU) in Beijing to lecture before groups of detectives at the Beijing, Wuhan, Hanzou, Shanghai, and X'ian police bureaus. Subsequently, the second edition of his textbook *Criminal Profiling* was translated into Chinese for the University. In 2007, he was invited to lecture at the First Behavioral Sciences Conference at the Home Team (Police) Academy in Singapore, where he also provided training to their Behavioral Science Unit. In 2010, he examined a series of sexual homicides for the solicitor–general of the Crown Office and Procurator Fiscal Service in Edinburgh, Scotland.

From 2013 to 2014, Brent was the sponsor for the Criminal Profiling and Behavioral Analysis Unit of the Forensic Laboratory in Cd. Juarez in Chihuahua, Mexico—certifying members of that unit through the IAFC. Starting in 2014, he also began working closely as an advisor to the Behavioral Analysis and Criminal Profiling Unit for the Colombian National Police. As a representative of the IAFC, he directly administered their certification training in early 2015.

Brent has been court qualified as a forensic expert in the areas of criminal profiling, victimology, crime scene investigation, sex crimes investigation, false reports, crime scene analysis, forensic science, and crime reconstruction in many courts and jurisdictions (state and federal) around the United States, in both civil and criminal matters—but most often in capital murder cases.

Brent has published in numerous peer-reviewed encyclopedias and journals, and is the author of *Criminal Profiling: An Introduction to Behavioral Evidence Analysis*, first, second, third, and fourth editions (1999, 2002, 2008, 2011), *Forensic Victimology* (2012), and *Forensic Fraud* (2013). He is also a coauthor of *Rape Investigation Handbook*, first and second editions (2004, 2011); *Crime Reconstruction*, first and second editions (2007, 2011), *Forensic Victimology* (2009), *Forensic Criminology* (2010), *Ethical Justice* (2012), *Miscarriages of Justice* (2014), and *Anabolic Steroid Abuse in Public Safety Personnel* (2015)—all with Academic/Elsevier Science.

Brent is currently a diplomate and board member of the International Association of Forensic Criminologists/Academy of Behavioral Profiling (IAFC/ABP); a distinguished member and vice-president of the Academia Internacional de Investigadores Forenses; a full partner, forensic scientist, criminal profiler, and instructor with Forensic Solutions, LLC; affiliate faculty in the Criminology Department at Regis University in Denver, Colorado; and is a director at The Institute of Forensic Investigation and Criminal Profiling in accusation with the Instituto Superior De Ciencias De Ciudad Juárez, in Juarez, Mexico.

He can be contacted via email at bturvey@forensic-science.com.

Lic. Manuel Adolfo Esparza, D-ABP Manuel Esparza was a prosecutor and investigator at the Chihuahua Attorney General's Office from November 1992 to November 2004 and is a director at The Institute of Forensic Investigation and Criminal Profiling in accusation with the Instituto Superior De Ciencias De Ciudad Juárez, in Juarez, Mexico. He also headed the Organized Crime Homicide and Women's Homicide Investigation Units between 1998 and 2004 in Juarez, Mexico. He was assigned to Special Investigations by the Attorney General, focusing on sexual homicide, domestic homicide, multiple homicide, serial rape, and homicide where case linkage and crime analysis was required. He also handled missing persons cases and headed the Violent Criminal Apprehension Program Initiative in coordination with the FBI.

He worked as a private defense attorney from 2006 to 2010, both in the Inquisitorial and Adversarial Judicial Systems. He handles cases in State, Federal, and Juvenile Court. He also worked on appeals and in the habeas corpus process when required.

He is a diplomate of The IAFC/ABP; the President of the Academia Internacional de Investigadores Forenses; and is currently a junior partner in Forensic Solutions, LLC involved in research, instruction, and casework.

ABOUT THE CONTRIBUTORS

W. Stan Crowder, PhD, D-ABP Stan Crowder is a retired US Army Military Police Colonel, and holds a PhD, an MBA, and a BS. During his military career, Stan served in numerous positions including MP Commander, Chief of Investigations for the Inspector General of Georgia, Counter-drug Commander, Battalion Commander, and Chief of Personnel. He served 7 years as a civilian police officer. He teaches at Kennesaw State University, Kennesaw, Georgia, USA, where he has been teaching since 1999 and was selected as the 2007 recipient of the Betty Siegel teaching award. He is also a coauthor of the textbook *Ethical Justice* (2012) and *Anabolic Steroid Abuse in Public Safety Personnel* (2015).

Stan is currently the President of the IAFC/ABP.

He can be contacted at: scrowder@kennesaw.edu.

Jodi Freeman, MCrim, D-ABP Jodi Freeman holds an honors bachelor degree in Health Sciences from the University of Western Ontario, Canada with a double major in health sciences and criminology. She recently graduated from Bond University, Australia with a masters degree in criminology.

During her masters program, Jodi completed an independent study under Brent Turvey, in the area of behavioral evidence analysis. Between 2010 and 2014, Jodi completed a crime scene analysis internship with Forensic Solutions. Since 2011, she has served as a liaison between the law enforcement community and the student body at the University of Western Ontario, where she has investigated criminal cases that include sexual assaults, drug dealing, and domestic violence.

In 2015, she was invited to speak on the subjective of case linkage analysis in Bogota at the 1er Encuentro Internacional de Colombia y la Direccion de Investigación Criminal e Interpol, hosted by the Policia National, DIJIN; the Colombian Ministry of Justice; and the United Nations.

Since 2014, Jodi has been a junior associate with Forensic Solutions, LLC, and continues to assist with research, casework, and workshop facilitation.

Jodi can be contacted at: jodi.freeman@rogers.com.

Tânia Konvalina-Simas, MA Tânia Konvalina-Simas received her BS in clinical psychology from the University of Porto (2000) in Portugal, her PGT (postgraduate degree) in forensic sciences from the Portuguese Institute of Legal Medicine (2001) and her MA in Integrative Psychotherapy and Counseling from Regent's College School of Psychotherapy (2008) in the United Kingdom. Currently she is at the end of her PhD in criminology and sociolegal research with Essex University (UK).

Ms. Konvalina-Simas was formerly a guest lecturer in criminology for 5 years at Instituto Superior Universitário da Maia—ISMAI. Currently she is guest lecturer and scientific coordinator of the postgraduate degree in investigative psychology and criminal profiling for the Instituto Paulista de Estudos Bioéticos e Jurídicos—IPEBJ in Brazil and for the postgraduate degrees in criminal investigation and forensic criminology at the Instituto Português de Psicologia e Outras Ciências—INSPSIC in Portugal.

Ms. Konvalina-Simas is the founder of profiling criminal—Formação e Consultoria (www.profilingcriminal.com) a Portuguese company specializing in teaching and consulting in forensic criminology and criminal profiling. Ms. Konvalina-Simas is also a consultant and lecturer for the behavioral laboratory of Forensic Sciences Investigation—FSI Brazil, a new company specializing in providing investigative support and expert witnesses in Brazil.

Her research interests are, specifically, psychopathy, deviant behavior, etiology of human behavior, psychodynamics of violent crime, and, generally, the most extravagant, creative, and unexpected manifestations of the human experience, an existential anthropologist at heart.

Ms. Konvalina-Simas can be reached at: profilingcriminal@gmail.com.

Michael McGrath, MD, D-ABP Michael McGrath, MD, is a Board-certified forensic psychiatrist, licensed in the state of New York. He is a clinical professor in the Department of Psychiatry, University of Rochester School of Medicine and Dentistry, Rochester, New York, and Medical Director and Chair, Department of Behavioral Health, Unity Hospital, a division of Rochester Regional Health, Rochester, New York.

Dr. McGrath divides his time between administrative, clinical, research, and teaching activities. He has lectured on three continents and is a founding member and past president of the IAFC/ABP. His areas of expertise include forensic psychiatry, criminal profiling, false allegations of sexual assault, and false confessions.

He can be contacted at: mmcgrath@profiling.org.

Deimer Melendez Cardona, D-ABP Deimer Melendez is an intendent with the National Police of Colombia and technical professional in Criminal Investigation. He was worked as an investigator at the Directorate of Criminal Investigation and INTERPOL—DIJIN since 1996, specializing in the management of homicides, sexual offenses, human trafficking, illegal migrants trafficking, drug trafficking, and transnational organized crime.

Deimer has also worked as a consultant and investigator with international law enforcement agencies, including the Police from Netherlands and Canada. His experience in these crimes led him to be appointed as a member of the Special Unit of the Analysis of Criminal Behavior from the Attorney General's Office for 2 years. In 2011 he was called to create the Behavioral Science and Criminal Profiling Group within the DIJIN, in which he structured the basic course in criminal profiling accompanied by the School of Criminal Investigation. He also teaches at the School of Criminal Investigation; supports investigators and prosecutors nationwide in complex cases requiring the use of criminal profiling, crime scene analysis, behavioral analysis, and linkage of cases. In 2015, he was certified as a criminal profiler with the Academy of Criminal Profiling and the IAFC.

Deimer can be reached at: deimer.melendez@correo.policia.gov.co.

PART

Limits of Profiling Methodologies

1

CHAPTER

Applied Criminal Profiling: An Introduction

1

B.E. Turvey

Forensic Solutions LLC, Sitka, Alaska, United States;
Institute of Forensic Investigation and Criminal Profiling, Juarez, Mexico

CHAPTER OUTLINE

As discussed thoroughly in Turvey (2011), modern criminal profiling owes itself to a diverse history. Researchers have determined that is grounded in the study of crime and criminal behavior (criminology); the study of mental health and illness (psychology and psychiatry); and the examination of physical evidence (the forensic sciences). However, regardless of its many forms, it must necessarily involve the inference of criminal characteristics for investigative and judicial purposes. Otherwise it is not criminal profiling, but something else.

The reasoning used to support a given criminal profile is not universal; methodological consistency is often elusive. It ranges from a basis in statistical argumentation, to examining specific criminal behaviors, to subjective intuitive opinions based on personal belief and experience. In other words, profiling methods have only ever been as informed, applicable, and accurate as the professionals behind them.

Some believe that profiling is only statistical analysis, which it is not. Some confuse it for the psychological assessments conducted on defendants by forensic mental health professionals, which is a completely different skill set. Some confuse profiling and risk assessment. Some think profiling is the strict province of law enforcement, or a particular law enforcement agency, for which there is no legitimate basis (rather this is a narcissistic myopia that ensures practitioner isolation and ultimately ignorance). And then there are the outright frauds who purport to have almost psychic abilities (discussed in the chapter: Criminal Profiling: Fraud and Failures).

The variety of profiling methods used around the world, across agencies and analysts, has resulted in a state of professional confusion. Criminal profilers are often poorly educated in the forensic and behavioral sciences (if at all), and consequently they are confused about who they are and where they fit within the criminal justice system. Other criminal justice professionals recognize and are confused about the same things,

Behavioral Evidence Analysis. http://dx.doi.org/10.1016/B978-0-12-800607-8.00001-X

resulting in more than a little skepticism and even some animosity. The media add to existing myths by portraying criminal profilers as supercops; and the general public often views profilers as a more specialized form of psychic. Ultimately, many inept and uneducated profilers are benefiting from this lack of professional cohesion and the ignorant misperceptions it allows to persist—and the justice system is being duped.

As set forth in Turvey (2011), if criminal profilers are to be taken seriously in the 21st century, as professional forensic operatives with substantive contributions to offer the justice system, then there are areas in which reforms must be made. Education and training must be the first. This means comprehending a methodology, expressing its limits, and being competent to the task of conveying it all in a written forensic report.

REPORT WRITING

When the *Academy of Behavioral Profiling* was formed in 1998, an explicit section of the practice standards that we eventually published and embraced (Baeza et al., 2000) covered the issue of report writing.[a] Specifically, we made it clear that profiles must be written documents. If it was not written down, then it did not happen. Such practice ensures a reliable record of expert opinions for internal and external evaluation. This is in accordance with just about every basic scientific practice standard mandating peer review, replication of findings, data integrity, and overall transparency (Edwards and Gotsonis, 2009; NAS, 2002, 2009).

This declarative effort was in response to a few of issues. First, there were many profilers at the time who either did not write reports or put disclaimers on their reports barring them from ever seeing the light of day. Second, many of those claiming to be criminal profilers have not actually written a criminal profile report in the course of their work—making it impossible to gauge their competence. Third, the criminal profiles that did exist read like they were written by high school dropouts with no sense of grammar, citation, or the relevant existing literature. A brief discussion is warranted.

THE IMPORTANCE OF WRITTEN PROFILES

Many profilers, even at the turn of the century, did not believe that their criminal profiles should be prepared as written reports. This is a belief and practice that continues even now, for many. It is an institutional problem reflecting bias for some. The author, for example, received an email from Gregg O. McCary, an FBI profiler (discussed in the chapter: Criminal Profiling: Fraud and Failures). He explained, in essence, that FBI agents and their progeny are the only true profilers, and that written profiles were something that only a "neophyte" would want because they help the defense. Specifically, McCrary wrote (1998), "Most current and past FBI profiles,

[a]The Academy of Behavioral Profiling was absorbed as a certification board within the International Association of Forensic Criminologists in 2010. This is discussed at length in the chapter: The IAFC Criminal Profiler Professional Certification Act.

including many of detailed and in-depth works prepared by Hazelwood, myself, and other FBI profilers consisted of absolutely no pages. There is sound legal reasoning for minimizing written documents which you (the author) are either unwilling or unable to understand."

McCrary further explained (1998), "Any detective who is 'dying to have things in writing' is a neophyte and will learn a painful lesson along the way if he does so. A written analysis tends to create many more problems than it solves...." In other words, the defense will have a field day if you write down opinions that turn out to be wrong later. If you do not write them down, you can pretend to have gotten it right in your analysis regardless of whether or not you did, because the lack of documentation allows for facile interpretations.

This becomes important because the author has had selections from Mr. McCrary's (1998) emails read to him in open court at least twice. The suggestion from opposing counsel being that this condemnation of the author's practice by a retired FBI agent amounts to a refutation of the author's overall capability and expertise. When the emails are read in their entirety, the truth becomes evident. The old FBI, through the voice of Mr. McCrary, is revealed as an agency fraught with narcissism, jealousy, and zero appreciation for transparency; all of which is bad for science and works against professionalism—not in its favor.

Consequently, the IAFC/ABP has been forced to lead the way on this issue—with the only written practice standards and ethical guidelines for criminal profilers engaged in active casework. The discussion in Turvey (2011), specifically the section on Practice Standards is worth repeating here (*Practice Standard* #5, pp. 135–136).

> *Criminal profiling, crime scene analysis, and victimology conclusions, and their basis, must be provided in a written format.*
>
> *Hans Gross referred to the critical role that exact, deliberate, and patient efforts at crime reconstruction can play in the investigation and resolution of crime. Specifically, he stated that just looking at a crime scene is not enough. He argued that there is utility in reducing one's opinions regarding the reconstruction to the form of a report in order to identify problems in the logic of one's theories (Gross, 1924, p. 439):*
>
>> *So long as one only looks on the scene, it is impossible, whatever the care, time, and attention bestowed, to detect all the details, and especially note the incongruities: but these strike us at once when we set ourselves to describe the picture on paper as exactly and clearly as possible... The "defects of the situation" are just those contradictions, those improbabilities, which occur when one desires to represent the situation as something quite different from what it really is, and this with the very best intentions and the purest belief that one has worked with all of the forethought, craft, and consideration imaginable.*
>
> *Moreover, the criminal profiler, not the recipient of the report (i.e., investigators, attorneys, and the court), bears the burden of ensuring that conclusions are effectively communicated. This means writing them down. This means that the profiler*

> *must be competent at intelligible writing, and reports must be comprehensive with regard to examinations performed, findings, and conclusions.*
>
> *Orally communicated conclusions should be viewed as a form of substandard work product. They are susceptible to conversions, alterations, and misrepresentations. They may also become lost to time. Written conclusions are fixed in time, are easy to reproduce, and are less susceptible to accidental or intentional conversion, alteration, and misrepresentation. An analyst who prefers orally communicated conclusions to written conclusions reveals a preference for conclusive mobility.*
>
> *Apart from their relative permanence, written conclusions also provide the criminal profiler with the best chance to document methods, conclusions, arguments, and the underlying facts of the case. This includes a list of the evidence examined, when it was examined, and under what circumstances. Generally, a written report should include, but need not be limited to, the following information:*
>
> - *A preliminary background section, describing the profiler's involvement in the case.*
> - *A chain of custody section, describing and detailing the evidence that was examined or included in the profile.*
> - *A descriptive section, in which the profiler thoroughly describes the examinations performed (eg, forensic analysis, victimology, crime scene analysis), with consideration of the facts and evidence.*
> - *A results section, in which the profiler lists any results and conclusions, including their significance and limitations.*
>
> *The intended users of the end result include detectives, judges, and jurors: The report should be worded so that there is no question in the reader's mind about what is being said. If a crime scene analysis or criminal profile cannot be written down in a logical form and easily understood by its intended user, then, apart from having no value, it is also probably wrong.*

These notions comport with the congressionally funded report on the forensic science community in the United States by the National Academy of Sciences (Edwards and Gotsonis, 2009). It found, after an exhaustive investigation, that the majority of the forensic science community lacks standardized terminology and report writing requirements. The result has been forensic reporting that is unclear and, in many cases, incomplete. It found that (p. 21):

> *The terminology used in reporting and testifying about the results of forensic science investigations must be standardized. Many terms are used by forensic scientists in scientific reports and in court testimony that describe findings, conclusions, and degrees of association between evidentiary material (e.g., hairs, fingerprints, fibers) and particular people or objects. Such terms include, but are not limited to "match," "consistent with," "identical," "similar in all respects tested," and "cannot be excluded as the source of." The use of such terms can*

> *and does have a profound effect on how the trier of fact in a criminal or civil matter perceives and evaluates scientific evidence. Although some forensic science disciplines have proposed reporting vocabulary and scales, the use of the recommended language is not standard practice among forensic science practitioners.*
>
> *As a general matter, laboratory reports generated as the result of a scientific analysis should be complete and thorough. They should contain, at minimum, "methods and materials," "procedures," "results," "conclusions," and, as appropriate, sources and magnitudes of uncertainty in the procedures and conclusions (e.g., levels of confidence). Some forensic science laboratory reports meet this standard of reporting, but many do not. Some reports contain only identifying and agency information, a brief description of the evidence being submitted, a brief description of the types of analysis requested, and a short statement of the results (e.g., "the greenish, brown plant material in item #1 was identified as marijuana"), and they include no mention of methods or any discussion of measurement uncertainties.*

Consequently, the NAS Report recommends that standardized forensic terminology and reporting thresholds must be developed and mandated at a national level.

THE ABSENCE OF WRITTEN PROFILES

As mentioned, many of those claiming to be criminal profilers have not actually written a criminal profile report in the course of their work—making it impossible to gauge their competence.

Evidence of this exists in two forms. First, the number of written profiles that have been made public (outside of the IAFC membership) can be counted on maybe two hands. As an ancillary, just ask any criminal profiler, regardless of where they work, to provide a copy of a written report. Most will be unable or unwilling to do so. If they are working on a regular basis, most of their reports will be confidential. This is as it should be. However, there will be some that can be made public because of their disclosure in court or to the media.

The inability of any criminal profiler to provide even one sample of competent work product is a red flag. What most mean when they say that they are a criminal profiler is—either they study crime in some fashion (and are a criminologist or mental health professional); or they like being called a criminal profiler but really have not ever done that work directly. Most fall into the second category, enjoying what people think they do without ever really having done it.

Succinctly, real criminal profilers examine evidence for clients; they do so with expectation of giving evidence in court, no matter the circumstance (because if they are any good at what they do, it is going to wind up in court whether they like it or not); and they write clear, well-cited reports based upon their examinations. They do not confuse reading the newspaper for conducting research—because they know the newspaper is not a reliable source for data; they do not confuse themselves for mental health professionals and attempt to "diagnose" the crime scene (unless they have those credentials and have conducted the proper assessments—in which case they are not profiling a crime scene but assessing a subject); they know their methods, and any inherent limitations, as they can be distinguished from the methods of others; and they do not play on the ignorance of the public or other professionals when doing their work. And this is all made painfully clear by virtue of the nature, quality, and existence of their written findings.

RATIONALE

The author has literally traveled the world, by invitation, to give education and training to government agencies and universities in the area of crime scene analysis and criminal profiling. Since 1996, this has been done in concert with colleagues now associated with the IAFC, to include Dr. Stan Crowder (former Colonel with the Army Office of the Inspector General); Michael McGrath, MD (forensic psychiatrist); Dr. Shawn Mikulay (psychologist); Lic. Manuel Esparza (retired criminal prosecutor); Hector Hawley (crime scene investigator for the Attorney General's Femicide Unit in Chihuahua, Mexico); Jodi Freeman, MCrim (Forensic Criminologist); Dr. Changwon Pyo (former Police Officer and Instructor for the Korean National Police University); and many more. Together, we have given training to major law enforcement agencies, policed academies, and sometimes their university counterparts, in the United States, China, Korea, Singapore, Mexico, Colombia, Guatemala, Ecuador, Spain, and the United Kingdom. Consequently, our textbooks have also been translated into related languages (eg, Chinese and Spanish) to facilitate these efforts.

Ultimately, we encounter the same problem in every country, at every agency and institution: students and professionals have read the books and understand the basics, but they have no idea how to write a criminal profile for lack of ever having seen or read one in person. Any independent effort on their part tends to be a copy and paste job done without understanding what is being examined, answered, or why. It is an easy enough problem to fix, and we have had great success with those that have sought our assistance. But not everyone that needs it can ask for it.

This work is written as a teaching companion to any edition of Turvey's *Criminal Profiling*. In other words, it is meant to be assigned as required reading along with any course that is tough with that book. Ultimately, it is designed to help solve the problem of inadequate access to written criminal profiles, so that students can see how reports have been written in the past in order to shape their own report writing efforts in the future. It also shows the value of standardized terminology in actual case practice. Better reports lead to more informed findings, and this leads to more competent testimony along with more informed legal outcomes.

This work is offered to help satisfy the practice standards set forth for certification in criminal profiling by the IAFC (Turvey, 2011); the requirements for sound forensic practice set forth by the NAS Report (Edwards and Gotsonis, 200); and the mandates of good scientific culture and practice in general (Cole, 2010; Judson, 2004; NAS, 2002, 2009).

REFERENCES

Baeza, J., Chisum, W.J., Chamberlin, T.M., McGrath, M., Turvey, B., January, 2000. Academy of behavioral profiling: criminal profiling guidelines. Journal of Behavioral Profiling 1 (1).

Cole, S., 2010. Acculturating forensic science: what is "Scientific culture," and how can forensic science adopt it? Fordham Urban Law Journal 38 (2), 435–472.

Edwards, H., Gotsonis, C., 2009. Strengthening Forensic Science in the United States: A Path Forward. National Academies Press, Washington DC.

Judson, H., 2004. The Great Betrayal: Fraud in Science. Harcourt, New York.

McCrary, G., May 14–15, 1998. Personal Email Communications to Brent E. Turvey (gom1@email.msn.com to bturvey@corpus-delicti.com).

NAS, 2002. Integrity in Scientific Research: Creating an Environment that Promotes Responsible Conduct, National Academy of Sciences Committee on Assessing Integrity in Research Environments. National Academies Press, Washington, DC.

NAS, 2009. On Being a Scientist: A Guide to Responsible Conduct in Research, third ed. National Academy of Sciences Committee on Science, Engineering, and Public Policy. National Academies Press, Washington, DC.

Turvey, B., 2011. Criminal Profiling: An Introduction to Behavioral Evidence Analysis, fourth ed. Elsevier Science, London.

CHAPTER

Criminal Profiling: Fraud and Failures

2

B.E. Turvey

Forensic Solutions LLC, Sitka, Alaska, United States;

Institute of Forensic Investigation and Criminal Profiling, Juarez, Mexico

CHAPTER OUTLINE

...the scientist who declines to practice his or her profession by the rules of science will soon find that he or she has earned only the derision of his or her colleagues, and eventually finds that he or she cannot continue to practice at all.

Dr. John I. Thornton – Criminalist (1994, p. 483)

The term *forensic examiner* generally refers to any professional that examines and interprets physical evidence with the expectation—though not necessarily the continuous reality—of courtroom testimony.[a] As this would suggest, forensic examiners are responsible for the scientific investigation that is meant to take place within the context of a criminal investigation or a court proceeding. They are ostensibly expected to analyze evidence in a scientific manner, to interpret the results objectively, and to report their findings faithfully (Chisum and Turvey, 2011). This makes them feared by superiors and attorneys alike, as they are not allowed to be swayed by political or financial considerations.

[a] Some portions of this chapter have been adapted from writing originally prepared for Crowder and Turvey (2013) and Turvey (2013).

Behavioral Evidence Analysis. http://dx.doi.org/10.1016/B978-0-12-800607-8.00002-1

Make no mistake: criminal profilers and crime scene analysts are forensic examiners. It is not possible to do this kind of work in an official capacity without considering the eventuality of presenting and defending one's work in a courtroom. Pretending otherwise is not only ignorant, but negligent. Those who fail to acknowledge this obligation are either not doing the work in any official capacity, and therefore need have no real concern about going under oath[b]; or they work for a government agency that is in some fashion concealing their work product from exposure to the discovery process (perhaps legitimately, perhaps not—see Brady v. Maryland, 1963).

Consequently, those criminal profilers not being called to present and defend findings in court are not operating at the same level as those that are. This statement is not intended as an insult. But it is a fact. Unless you live every day with the reality that you could be charged with perjury for giving evidence, you really cannot appreciate the gravity of what it is that happens once you raise your right hand and swear to tell the truth, the whole truth, and nothing but the truth. Your work is, ultimately, conducted without consequence.

Additionally, despite the many misinformed fictional portrayals to the contrary, forensic examiners are not intended to be decision makers in the criminal justice system. For instance, they do not generally have the authority to make arrests or take life; they do not rule on the admissibility of evidence in court proceedings; and they do not get to decide whether a defendant is guilty or innocent (Crowder and Turvey, 2013). This is intentional, as the goals of the forensic examiner must remain ideologically separate from those of the police, the prosecution, and the courts to maintain scientific impartiality (Edwards and Gotsonis, 2009).

And on that note, forensic examiners are also not supposed to be incompetent or dishonest, though far too many are. The professional criminal profiling community holds these responsibilities close—carrying them and other professional obligations forward to meet the cause of justice with an unwavering commitment to education, training, and ethics. The persistent community of forensic frauds, however, can be regularly found ignoring the public trust by virtue of doing the exact opposite.

This chapter, much to the chagrin of those hard at the work of pretending to be something that they are not, is intent on exploring the issues of fraud and negligence. It will, as is required, name names. It will be unflinching. And it will be painful for those who hate facts and evidence. For the rest of us, it will be the tonic that we need to keep our integrity while working in a community awash with professional counterfeits and mimics; a community that has the responsibility to know the difference, and to make that difference known to others.

---

[b] This is the case with those who write "true crime" novels and memoirs, adopting the moniker of "profiler" to sell books; and it is often the case with those who do statistical analysis in an academic setting, referring to that as profiling when it is actually just compiling crime stats.

THE PROBLEM

Employment within the criminal justice system provides even the freshest professionals with access to confidential personal data; access to privileged evidence and information; varying levels of authority; and often the presumption that one has a higher level of access and authority than truly exists. The problem, as a consequence, is the kind of "professional" that this work can attract. Some are solid individuals with character and integrity geared toward public service. Some are not.

It has become painfully apparent that the criminal justice professions can attract those with psychopathic and narcissistic traits—and eventually what we will refer to as professional mimics. To those of us working within the system on a daily basis, this has become a self evident and undeniable reality. We all know that professional mimics are among us and some, being incapable of casework, wind up being promoted into supervisory positions.

The *professional mimic* is a pseudoprofessional. They are a low-quality copy, or counterfeit, comprised of fictional caricatures, emulating traits, and jargon found in film and on television. Though in possession of some basic information, they possess no actual knowledge, can offer no meaningful insights, and demonstrate little or no actual ability. They will work hard to look the part, while being wholly incapable of living the part. Some of them also find work in government service.

These individuals want to be perceived as powerful, all knowing, and even heroic—in accordance with a propensity for grandiosity. Because of fictional media portrayals, as well as the exaggerated portrayals of real life figures, there is a widely held belief that certain criminal justice professionals necessarily embody all of these qualities. To be blunt, the fraud believes that if they fake it, they will make it—with respect to fame or fortune.

The forensic examiner accepts these realities and does their best to avoid being abused by either side of the courtroom. In doing so, they would do well to heed the following cautionary from Thornton and Peterson (2007, p. 4): "Forensic science is science exercised on behalf of the law in the just resolution of conflict. It is therefore expected to be the handmaiden of the law, but at the same time this expectation may very well be the marina from which is launched the tension that exists between the two disciplines." To be clear, acting as a handmaid is not necessarily a corrupted role, so long as the correct priorities are being attending. While some jurists will still seek to manipulate the findings of the ethical forensic examiner, at least there will be something scientifically competent of use to those who would defend against such manipulations. Otherwise, science abandons the courts to themselves—and this is no good solution.

SCIENTIFIC MISCONDUCT

Forensic examiners must do their best to avoid abuses of their work and findings, intentional or otherwise. There is no better way than by learning and adhering to practices that ensure scientific integrity (Gardenier, 2011). Therefore, regardless of their employment circumstances and the strain placed on the forensic examiner by those around them, scientific integrity must be the first priority. This demands that the forensic examiner be knowledgeable, competent, and ethical; that they remain impartial in their work despite their employer's needs; and that they seek to avoid cultural strain, pressure, or incentives to engage in deliberate misconduct (Chisum and Turvey, 2011; Crowder and Turvey, 2013; Edwards and Gotsonis, 2009; NAS, 2002; Turvey, 2013). Failure at any of these is not acceptable, as explained in Thornton (1994, p. 483): "the scientist who declines to practice his or her profession by the rules of science will soon find that he or she has earned only the derision of his or her colleagues, and eventually finds that he or she cannot continue to practice at all."

The literature is clear with respect to the obligations of scientists and their institutional employers to uphold values that promote scientific integrity. This includes acknowledging that there are those operating within different scientific communities who recklessly or intentionally fail to understand, uphold, and promote these obligations (Judson, 2004; Martinson et al., 2005; Sovacool, 2008; Titus et al., 2008). This is in part because of human error, and the fact that (Anderson et al., 2007, p. 3): "[scientific] norms represent ideal behavior, and so it is to be expected that scientists' actual behavior will fall short of perfect adherence to the norms." This is also, in part, owing to acts of fraud (McDowell, 2010).

The most serious violations of scientific integrity are referred to by the Office of Research Integrity (ORI) as *scientific misconduct*, which is defined as "fabrication, falsification, or plagiarism (FFP) in proposing, performing, or reviewing research, or in reporting research results" (NAS, 2009, p. 3). As described, scientific misconduct is a reference to *fraud*; it involves intentional misrepresentations by scientists designed to secure an unfair or unlawful gain. In fact, the literature treats the terms *scientific fraud* and *scientific misconduct* as essentially interchangeable. However, the term *fraud* is fraught with legal implications. As not all research violations involve a crime, the term *misconduct* has been adopted by the scientific community as the official substitute when dealing with actionable allegations in the context of internal institutional investigations (Catano and Turk, 2007; Resnick, 2003; Reynolds, 2004).

The major forms of scientific misconduct are operationalized in the ORI's "Policies on Research Misconduct" (ORI, 2009, p. 5).

1. Fabrication is making up data or results and recording or reporting them.
2. Falsification is manipulating research materials, equipment, or processes, or changing or omitting data or results such that the research is not accurately represented in the research record.
3. Plagiarism is the appropriation of another person's ideas, processes, results, or words without giving appropriate credit.
4. Research misconduct does not include honest error or differences of opinion.

These concepts are further described in Reider (2010, p. 445): "The colloquial term for fabrication is 'dry-labbing,' making up results for experiments or trials that never occurred.... The term falsification is applied when research actually took place, but the results have been manipulated, modified, or edited so that the published work no longer accurately reflects the scientific findings." Though not listed by the ORI in a pedantic sense, it has been demonstrated that scientific misconduct also includes *ghost authorship, suppression of unfavorable results, the falsification of researcher credentials, and sexual harassment*—when these actions have the potential to affect the results or interpretations of scientific inquiries (Krimsky, 2007; Parrish, 1996).

DIFFERENTIATING FRAUD AND NEGLIGENCE

Having defined fraud, it is immediately necessary to distinguish the concepts of fraud and error.

NEGLIGENCE

Negligence is defined as "the failure to use such care as a reasonably prudent and careful person would use under similar circumstances" (Black, 1990, pp. 1032). In a professional context, it is: "conduct which falls below the standard established by law for the protection of others against unreasonable risk of harm… it is characterized chiefly by inadvertence, thoughtlessness, inattention, and the like" (Black, 1990, pp. 1032).

Consider the following case example:

CASE EXAMPLE: OKLAHOMA v. RICHARD TANDY SMITH

Examiner: Tom Bevel, Bloodstain Pattern Analyst

One of the authors (Turvey) examined a postconviction case out of Oklahoma. The defendant, Richard Tandy Smith, was accused of the July 1986 murder of 28-year-old John David Cederlund. Prosecutors argued that Mr. Smith shot Mr. Cedarlund to rob him of money and illegal drugs (meth). Mr. Smith was convicted at trial in 1987, based on circumstantial evidence and the testimony of two female police informants.

A trial, a highly regarded police bloodstain analyst (Tom Bevel) testified that he found what he thought was high-velocity blood spatter on a car, which was thought to be associated with the murder. Mr. Bevel, who routinely testifies for the police (and that he is not a scientist), determined that the bloodstains on the car door almost certainly came from a shooting incident and were most likely associated with a homicidal death. Note that this occurred in the pre-DNA era, so this opinion was offered without any concern that it might be checked against conclusive evidence. Essentially, Mr. Bevel, as a forensic examiner, gave the opinion that the vehicle and all associated evidence (specifically high-velocity blood spatter) fit the profile of a shooting-related homicide crime scene.

Years later, DNA testing proved that the substance on the car door was indeed blood. However, the blood did not match the homicide victim that Mr. Smith was convicted of killing—or any known homicide victim for that matter. The bloodstain was unrelated to the homicide, and its actual origins have been lost to time.

Continued

CASE EXAMPLE: OKLAHOMA v. RICHARD TANDY SMITH—cont'd

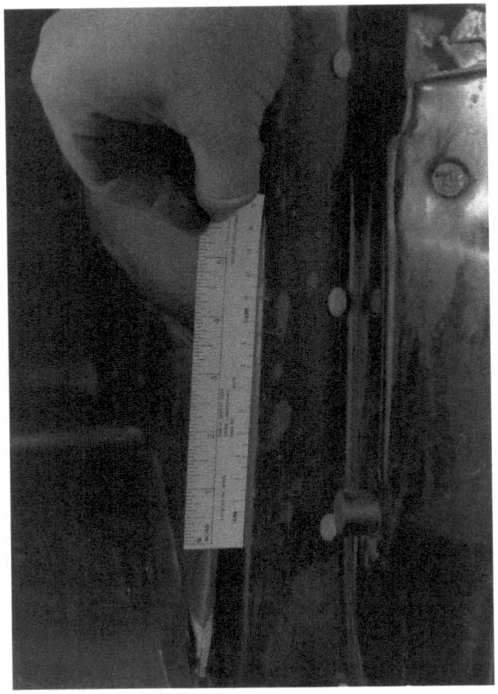

Photo taken by police investigators of this inside door from a 1979 Thunderbird. In 1987, these patterns were interpreted as shotgun-related bloodstains from a homicide victim, John Cedarlund, as reported by eyewitness testimony from female police informants. DNA testing later proved that this was not the blood of John Cedarlund.

Excerpted from the reported prepared in this case, Turvey (2005):

The testimony of Sgt. Bevel, related to the interpretation of the bloodstain pattern on the door of the 1979 Ford Thunderbird, misrepresents the evidence and fails to adequately explain or exclude alternate sources.

On March 12, 1987, Sgt. Bevel testified under direct examination that (p. 14–15):

I measured the majority of these stains over here and all of them were either one millimeter in diameter or less, which would fall into the high velocity impact, which is almost always associated -- not always -- but almost always associated with a gunshot, when you're dealing with a violent crime.

He further testified (p. 16):

In the absence of [atomized blood], it would not necessarily mean that it was not a gunshot, but when you find it, there's no question, unless there's something else that may be around. For example, if blood was poured onto an oscillating fan blade that obviously is traveling well above this 100 feet per second that could produce what we're looking at here.

In this case, I certainly, obviously, for a lot of reasons, lean towards a gunshot, unless we're able to find some fan that's directed a specific direction at a specific angle.

CASE EXAMPLE: OKLAHOMA v. RICHARD TANDY SMITH—cont'd

According to the literature, high-velocity bloodstain patterns can result from gunshot wounds, or wounds associated with an explosion, or injury caused by high-velocity machinery. While [he] did suggest one of these possibilities in a very limited and dismissive fashion, he did not explain that his examinations could not confirm the association of the bloodstain with the death of John Cedarlund. In fact, he testified in precisely the opposite direction. His testimony all but conclusively associated the bloodstain on the vehicle with violent crime, and left the strong impression that the bloodstain must be related to the death of John Cedarlund. The nature of this testimony utterly misrepresents the evidence. Again, with bloodstains of this size there are several possible origins that include

1. Accidental discharge of a firearm.
2. Intentional discharge of a firearm.
3. Explosive force.
4. High-velocity machinery.
5. Blood dripping into a pool of blood on a nearby surface.
6. A sneeze with blood in the mouth or a bloody nose.
7. Purposefully applied with an atomizer.

Sgt. Bevel did not indicate that he performed any directed experiments or investigation that might include or exclude any of these origins as a possibility (like investigating the history of the vehicle—its accident history and its involvement in criminal or injurious activity unrelated to the homicide). Consequently, his testimony on this issue is overly certain, resulting in helpful speculation for the prosecution's theories. However, it is not supported by the published forensic science literature or the scientific method.

This omission and inappropriate certainty on the sergeant's part becomes significant in light of the results of recent DNA testing. The report by Huma Nasir of *Reliagene* dated September 30, 2005 reveals that the blood collected from the door of the 1979 Thunderbird does not match the known STR DNA profile of the decedent, John Cedarlund. Mr. Cedarlund is the only alleged injured party this case. This report demonstrates that the bloodstain pattern interpreted by [the] sergeant was not actually associated with this case. It also proves that no blood or bloodstain evidence associates the 1979 Thunderbird with this case.

The issue of guilt aside (which is not the issue for any forensic examiner to address), the physical evidence in this case is problematic at best, and was interpreted based, in part, on faulty assumptions. Namely, that the car associated with Mr. Smith was also associated with the homicide.

Sgt. Bevel also testified in this case that cold water removes blood from clothing to such an extent that even chemical testing would not reveal its presence.[c] In a related issue, Mr. Bevel also withheld potentially exculpatory findings from Luminol testing that he conducted on suspect clothing in concert with now defamed Oklahoma City Police Department forensic scientist Joyce Gilchrist. Finally, he testified under oath that he was an expert in serology.

Negligence in this case is demonstrated by overzealous opinions offered outside of the forensic examiner's areas of expertise (eg, serology and profiling), in concert with believing that it is acceptable to withhold potentially exculpatory findings from a forensic report. Additionally, it is demonstrated by the ignorance revealed in the opinions offered. While it is clear that Mr. Bevel believed all of the things that he testified

[c]This assertion is demonstrably false, which anyone routinely familiar with trying to get blood out of clothing understands, given the extreme sensitivity of Luminol testing.

to (eg, that he was an expert in these areas and that the scene was associated with the homicide in question), it is also clear that he was wrong almost across the board.[d]

Just to be clear, it is also negligent for an agency to retain an incompetent, unethical, or fraudulent examiner. Obviously this is because doing so can incur future liability and might willfully contribute to miscarriages of justice. This is why forensic quality assurance management exists, and why random audits of forensic testimony are a basic standard of care adopted by forensic agencies holding themselves out as scientific.

FRAUD

Fraud is distinguished from negligence, ignorance, and error by virtue of the fact that it is intentional, involving some level of calculation (Albrecht and Albrecht, 2003). Fraud is not accidental in nature, nor is it unplanned (Albrecht et al., 2011; Black, 1990; Lord, 2010). Those who commit fraud know what they are doing and are deliberate in their efforts. They are also aware that it is unethical, illegal, or otherwise improper.

Those interested in protecting the guilty will complain that establishing fraud is difficult if not impossible explaining that intent is entirely subject without a confession. This is a ridiculous suggestion and speaks to the desire to sweep things under the rug. In the most general terms, fraudulent intent is easily established by examining the documentation and behavior associated with those under suspicion. As explained in Coenen (2008, p. 8): "Manipulation of documents and evidence is often indicative of such intent. Innocent parties don't normally alter documents and conceal or destroy evidence." Other indicators can include obstructing a fraud investigation by lying or concealing pertinent information, a known history of fraudulent behavior, and being the direct recipient of benefits from suspected fraudulent acts (Coenen, 2008). This means an investigation is required, which most would rather avoid as the results will require taking responsibility and then action.

Consider the following case example of overt fraud by a criminal profiler, mentioned briefly in Turvey (2011):

CASE EXAMPLE: ESTATE OF ELIZABETH GARCIA v. ALLSUP'S CONVENIENCE STORES, INC. (2008)

Examiner: Gregg O. McCrary, Massachusetts—Pseudoexpert, Dissembler

This case involves the abduction, rape, and murder of 26-year-old Elizabeth Ann Garcia, in the early morning hours of January 16, 2002, from her place of work at Allsup's Convenience Store located at 5312N, Lovington Hwy, Hobbs, New Mexico. She was working alone when she was abducted, and her body was found later that day in a field, with evidence of sexual assault and having suffered 57 stab wounds. The cause of death was provided as "multiple stab wounds of head, neck, and torso." Paul Lovett was arrested for Elizabeth Garcia's murder in 2003, after he was first connected to the murder of another woman almost a year later (35-year-old Patty Simon). He has been convicted of both homicides.

[d]It should be noted that at the time of his testimony in this case, Tom Bevel was the President of the International Association of Bloodstain Pattern Analysts. Similar professional negligence by Tom Bevel is detailed in the chapter: Applied Case Linkage Analysis, where he offers explicit criminal profiling conclusions with respect to his first ever forensic examination and testimony of offender modus operandi behavior. This in order to establish the admissibility of similar fact evidence for the state of Nebraska when there is no physical evidence to support it.

CASE EXAMPLE: ESTATE OF ELIZABETH GARCIA v. ALLSUP'S CONVENIENCE STORES, INC. (2008)—cont'd

The family of Elizabeth Garcia filed a lawsuit against the convenience store chain that she had worked for, alleging their negligence contributed to her death. The Defense hired retired FBI profiler Gregg O. McCrary as a security expert to evaluate the offender behavior, and the offense, in the light of those claims.

Mr. McCrary testified pretrial that Elizabeth Garcia was preselected as a target by Paul Lovett, and therefore undeterrable by any security measures. This despite the fact that they did not know each other, had never met, and did not have a preexisting relationship. In his deposition, McCrary also strayed wildly into profiling-related areas while claiming that he was not, and claimed expertise that he does not actually possess.

Mr. McCrary also failed to give his clients damaging impeachment information regarding prior cases in which his testimony had been excluded, fabricated a degree on his resume (not for the first time), and generally misrepresented his education, training, and experience under oath. The plaintiff in this case retained the services of one of the authors (Turvey), and these facts were brought to light in a subsequent expert declaration. As provided in an excerpt from that declaration (Turvey, 2008):

1. I [Brent E.Turvey] have been asked by Allegra C. Carpenter, an attorney for The Estate of Elizabeth Garcia, to examine the deposition testimony of Gregg O. McCrary in *Estate of Elizabeth Garcia v. Allsup's Convenience Stores, Inc.* I was asked to evaluate soundness of his methodology and findings with respect to the current state of forensic practice and literature.
2. This case involves the abduction, rape, and murder of 26-year-old Elizabeth Ann Garcia, in the early morning hours of January 16, 2002, from her place of work at Allsup's Convenience Store located at 5312N, Lovington Hwy, Hobbs, New Mexico. She was working alone when she was abducted, and her body was found later that day in a field, with evidence of sexual assault and having suffered 57 stab wounds. Cause of death was provided as "multiple stab wounds of head, neck, and torso." Paul Lovett was arrested for Garcia's murder in 2003, after he was first connected to the murder of another woman almost a year later, 35-year-old Patty Simon. He has been convicted of both homicides.
3. In rendering my opinions, I have examined the transcript of Mr. McCrary's deposition (Second Judicial District Court, County of Santa Fe, State of New Mexico, No. D-0101-CV-2005-00,045, December 12, 2007), and reviewed CV that he provided in this case. I have also examined the autopsy report of Elizabeth Garcia by Ross Zumwalt, MD (February 12, 2002) and related reports documentation, to include trauma-grams, notes, toxicology report, and investigative notes and reports.

Findings

1. Mr. McCrary has provided false information on his CV in this case. The undated McCrary CV provided to this examiner, which appears to have been updated through at least July 2006, provides on page 1 under EDUCATION "Master of Arts in Psychology, Marymount University Arlington, VA 1992." This would suggest that Mr. McCrary holds a graduate degree in psychology from Marymount University through their School of Psychology, received in 1992. This is false information. As provided to Ms. Carpenter, this examiner has examined this issue with respect to Mr. McCrary on a previous occasion, as a consultant to the defense in the *US v. O.C. Smith* (2005). Consistent with a previous version of Mr. McCrary's CV obtained by this examiner when consulting on the *Estate of Sam Sheppard v. Ohio* (2000), Mr. McCrary actually a holds Master of Arts in Professional Psychological Services from Marymount University—obtained through their school of education. In *US v. O.C. Smith*, Mr. McCrary provided a similar false CV to the court and was removed as an expert witness from the case by the prosecution when this information was disclosed to them. That Mr. McCrary has continued to provide this same false information on his CV subsequent to the Smith case removes the possibility of it being a typo or similar error.
2. Mr. McCrary has offered himself as an expert in behavioral science without demonstrable behavioral science qualifications (eg, deposition testimony at p. 7 "deterrability occurs in only one place, and that is in the mind of a would-be offender"). His undergraduate degrees are in

Continued

CASE EXAMPLE: ESTATE OF ELIZABETH GARCIA v. ALLSUP'S CONVENIENCE STORES, INC. (2008)—cont'd

music and criminal justice, and his graduate degree is related to guidance counseling. One could argue that as an FBI agent he accrued knowledge in the behavioral sciences, but there is no evidence of this. His experience and training appears to be that of an analyst or investigator preparing investigative findings—not forensic ones—without completing formal education in any of the behavioral sciences (psychology, sociology, criminology, or even anthropology). Moreover, his CV provides no peer reviewed research or publications in this subject area. On his CV, there are three publications listed. The first involves his contributor status to the Crime Classification Manual—as one of more than a hundred law enforcement contributors with no specific showing of his contribution to the text; the second involves a five page paper on stalking (Journal of Interpersonal Violence, Vol. 11, No. 4, pp. 487–502, 1996) with five other contributors; and the final publication is a coauthored, true crime, trade-oriented, memoir style book of no professional merit or value. This lack of demonstrable expertise in the behavioral sciences may explain why false information is provided on the CV.

3. Mr. McCrary did not prepare written findings in this case. As provided in Chisum and Turvey's Crime Reconstruction (2006; pp. 120–121), the employment of verbal opinions alone is a substandard practice:

Hans Gross referred to the critical role that exact, deliberate, and patient efforts at crime reconstruction can play in the investigation and resolution of crime. Specifically, he stated that just looking at a crime scene is not enough. He argued that there is utility in reducing one's opinions regarding the reconstruction to the form of a report in order to identify problems in the logic of one's theories (Gross, 1924, p. 439):

> *So long as one only looks on the scene, it is impossible, whatever the care, time, and attention bestowed, to detect all the details, and especially note the incongruities: but these strike us at once when we set ourselves to describe the picture on paper as exactly and clearly as possible… The "defects of the situation" are just those contradictions, those improbabilities, which occur when one desires to represent the situation as something quite different from what it really is, and this with the very best intentions and the purest belief that one has worked with all of the forethought, craft, and consideration imaginable.*

Moreover, the reconstructionist, not the recipient of the reconstructionist's opinions (i.e., investigators, attorneys, and the court), bears the burden of ensuring that her conclusions are effectively communicated. This means writing them down. This means that the reconstructionist must be competent at intelligible writing, and her reports must be comprehensive with regard to examinations performed, findings, and conclusions.

Verbal conclusions should be viewed as a form of substandard work product. They are susceptible to conversions, alterations, and misrepresentations. They may also become lost to time. Written conclusions are fixed in time, easy to reproduce, and are less susceptible to accidental or intentional conversion, alteration, and misrepresentation. An analyst who prefers verbal conclusions as opposed to written conclusions reveals his preference for conclusive mobility.

Though speaking of reconstructionists specifically in this section, the authors were referring to forensic examiners in general when rendering these practice standards from the available literature.

4. On p. 56 of his deposition, Mr. McCrary testifies regarding deterrability: "That is the humbling reality of violent crime, is that, like I say, not all crime is evenly distributed by place—type of crime or place of occurrence. And we don't really know why that is. There are lots of theories

CASE EXAMPLE: ESTATE OF ELIZABETH GARCIA v. ALLSUP'S CONVENIENCE STORES, INC. (2008)—cont'd

about this. Criminologists have a lot of theories. Law enforcement has theories. We try different things. Some things seem to work better than other things. In the long run, sometimes we find out, well, it was just a coincidence that that worked. It really didn't have any—you know, it was a correlation rather than a causation, so bottom line is, we really don't know why that is." This position would seem to preclude offering opinions about what may or may not deter any criminal from committing any given offense. However, Mr. McCrary has given the opinion that Mr. Lovett was not deterrable because he went to the convenience store for the specific purpose of killing the victim, making the crime "target-oriented."

5. Mr. McCrary has provided no research or authority, other than his own unqualified experience, that "target-oriented" offenders are any more or less deterrable than other offenders. When asked directly he evades the issue and argues experience—of which he has none as it relates to convenience store crime. Experience is not meant to be a shield. As explained by Dr. John I. Thornton, the dishonest forensic examiner exploits the ignorance of their audience by citing experience rather than demonstrating knowledge. Taken from Thornton, John I., 1997. The general assumptions and rationale of forensic identification. In: Faigman, David L., Kaye, David H., Saks, Michael J., Sanders, Joseph (Eds.), Modern Scientific Evidence: The Law And Science Of Expert Testimony, vol. 2:

   Experience is neither a liability nor an enemy of the truth; it is a valuable commodity, but it should not be used as a mask to deflect legitimate scientific scrutiny, the sort of scrutiny that customarily is leveled at scientific evidence of all sorts. To do so is professionally bankrupt and devoid of scientific legitimacy, and courts would do well to disallow testimony of this sort. Experience ought to be used to enable the expert to remember the when and the how, why, who, and what. Experience should not make the expert less responsible, but rather more responsible for justifying an opinion with defensible scientific facts.

   Equally important are the words of Dr. Paul L. Kirk from his text *Crime Investigation* (1953; pp. 17–18):

   The question of what constitutes adequate experience for the expert witness is a critical one in court procedures, and appears to be poorly understood in many quarters. It is quite common for the witness to be interrogated as to the number of years during which he has worked in a field, and the number of cases he has handled, the number of pieces of evidence he has examined, and similar quantitative matters. It must be apparent that the amount of his experience is not important beside the question of what he has learned from it.

   The summoning of experience in this context is a red herring that moves attention away from matters of science, objectivity, and sound methodology. This is not a legitimate forensic practice.

6. When pressed, Mr. McCrary concedes his opinion that the offender is "target-oriented" who is actually based on one of several possible scenarios—none of which he has investigated or reliably established. As shown in the exchange on p. 158 "A: Well, he certainly could have stumbled into her. He could have wanted to kill her and then just stumbled into her. That is a possibility. But I think it's more likely that he went there with the intention of killing her and did. Q: Even though you have no evidence that he knew she was working there? A: That never came out. That wasn't an issue in the criminal trial that I could see." See also p. 185 "I have no evidence that she knew him. I have no evidence that she did not know him. I have no evidence one way or the other." This testimony suggests that Mr. McCrary has assumed knowledge of the victim by the offender for the purpose of his analysis. This is not a legitimate forensic practice.

Continued

CASE EXAMPLE: ESTATE OF ELIZABETH GARCIA v. ALLSUP'S CONVENIENCE STORES, INC. (2008)—cont'd

7. On p. 112 of his deposition, Mr. McCrary testifies that part of his opinion regarding the Paul Lovett's individual deterrability is that "there is profound pathology here." Presumably, this refers to some disease on the part of Mr. Lovett. Mr. McCrary is neither a mental health professional, nor a behavioral scientist, nor has he interviewed and evaluated Mr. Lovett. Furthermore, I could find no evidence that Mr. Lovett had been examined in a forensic context, or diagnosed with any mental disorders. This inference by Mr. McCrary seems to overstep his expertise by a wide margin, as well as not being based on any known mental health evidence.
8. Based on his deposition, Mr. McCrary's opinions in this case are not based on the necessary victimological information required to make assessments about victim–offender interactions, and whether or not the offense could have been planned (eg, p. 157–159; McCrary concedes not gathering information relating to victim's work habits, schedule, and other related information—he did not know which stores she worked at, when, who had knowledge of this schedule, or if the offender actually knew the victim or her schedule). As explained in Mr. McCrary's own text on the subject (*Crime Classification Manual*, Burgess et al., 1992, p. 7) "Victimology is often one of the most beneficial investigative tools in classifying and solving violent crime. It is also a crucial part of crime analysis. Through it, the investigator tries to evaluate why this particular person was targeted for a violent crime." Failure to perform a complete victimology before offering an opinion about whether or not the victim was targeted is not a legitimate forensic practice.
9. Mr. McCrary testified that he is an expert in general security, and therefore to a degree in convenience store security, despite no experience working or researching cases involving convenience stores. (See p. 56 "Q: You're not an expert in convenience store security, are you? A: I think security, in general, and to the degree it carries over to a convenience store, I would say, yes. Q: Yes, you are an expert in convenience store security? A: Security, in general. And, certainly, security at a convenience store would be the same security issue you face in any workplace. Q: Yes, sir. You have never done an analysis of any convenience store chain? A: No.") Suggesting that general knowledge is equal to specialized knowledge is a non sequitur. Moreover, that Mr. McCrary believes convenience store security involves the same issues as any workplace belies his expertise on this subject. That he does not know enough to know that he is inexpert on this issue, given the facts and circumstances of this particular case, is problematic at best.
10. Mr. McCrary came to his opinions in this case without having read the whole law enforcement investigative file. (See p. 61 "A: Well, again, I don't know exactly what the police did. I have some idea from reading the trial transcript of what the investigation was, but, you know, I haven't seen the whole investigative file.") The investigative file often contains victimological detail, forensic information, and a behavioral indicator about the crime that is not available elsewhere. Failing to avail oneself to this, prior to rendering court-worthy behaviorally oriented conclusions, is not a legitimate forensic practice.
11. P. 188–194 of Mr. McCrary's deposition involves an exchange regarding Mr. McCrary's known error rates. He testifies that he and other FBI profilers were routinely "tested" while at the FBI, and that he is or has been in charge of testing analysts for the IACIAF. However, paradoxically, he claims to be unaware of his error rate, and then claims that there is no way to really know whether or not conclusions are truly accurate. This testimony does not seem consistent.
12. Mr. McCrary's testimony in this case regarding his error rates may be at odds with his previous testimony in *Estate of Sam Sheppard v. Ohio* (2000). As reported in McKnight, K., "Expert's Opinion Challenged," *Ohio Beacon Journal*, April 1, 2000:

> *An ex-FBI agent who said he hasn't been wrong yet in his analyses of crime scenes, was prepared to testify for the state yesterday that the long-debated 1954 bludgeoning death of Marilyn Sheppard was the result of a "staged domestic homicide."*

CASE EXAMPLE: ESTATE OF ELIZABETH GARCIA v. ALLSUP'S CONVENIENCE STORES, INC. (2008)—cont'd

But ready or not, Gregg O. McCrary -- like many of the state's witnesses in the Dr. Sam Sheppard wrongful imprisonment civil trial -- spent the bulk of the day being challenged by Sheppard attorney Terry Gilbert over whether he was enough of an expert to make such a determination.

Though I have not read the transcript, my information from counsel Terry Gilbert is that this characterization of his testimony is accurate.

13. One test of FBI profiling methods that may cast some light on the error rate issue is provided by Howard Teten (the very first FBI profiler). In an FBI study of 192 cases where profiling was performed, 88 cases were solved. Of those 88 cases, the profile helped with the identification of the suspect only 17% of the time (15 cases). So the known efficacy rate for FBI profilers (using criminal investigative analysis) is 15 out of 192. Taken from Teten, H. "Offender profiling" in Bailey, W. (Ed.) (1995) *The Encyclopedia of Police Science*; p. 45.

Subsequent to the disclosure of findings by the author, the plaintiffs in this case filed a motion to exclude the testimony of Mr. McCrary. Upon consideration of these findings, incorporated into the motion and cross-examination of Mr. McCrary at a hearing, the judge issued the following order (*Garcia* et al. *v. Allsup's Convenience Stores Inc.*, 2008):

ORDER

THIS MATTER having come before the Court on the plaintiff's Daubert/Alberico Motion to Exclude Defense Expert Gregg McCrary and the Court having reviewed the briefing, heard the arguments of counsel and the testimony of Mr. McCrary and Dr. Ross Zumwalt on February 13, 2007.

FINDS, as follows:

1. Crime scene analysis and criminal profiling related to the motives of a killer do not meet the standards for expert testimony in Daubert v. Merrell Dow Pharmaceuticals or State v. Alberico;
2. The methodology used by Mr. McCrary is:
   a. Not able to be tested by experiments, research, or otherwise;
   b. Not based upon or is not capable of scientific analysis;
   c. Not reproducible;
   d. Not reviewable for any rate of error.
3. The opinions of Mr. McCrary related to the motives of Paul Lovett, whether described as "victim-targeted" behavior, deterrability, or foreseeability, are not reliable;
4. The opinions of Mr. McCrary related to "crime scene analysis" whether described as "victim-targeted" behavior, deterrability, or foreseeability, do not comply with New Mexico Rule of Evidence 11-702 in that they will not materially assist the trier of fact to determine facts in issue in this case.

It Is Ordered:

1. The testimony of Gregg McCrary on crime scene analysis and any issue related to the motives of Paul Lovett, whether described as "victim-targeted" behavior, deterrability, foreseeability, or some other heading, is excluded at trial;
2. Based on his law enforcement background, Mr. McCrary may testify about the best practices to prevent crime and the adequacy of security at this Allsup's store, provided he does the following:
   a. Within 10 days of the date of the hearing (by February 23, 2009), Mr. McCrary produces to the plaintiff all documents, studies, training materials, guidelines, and other materials he has used or uses when providing security advice to other companies; and
   b. Mr. McCrary makes himself available for deposition at least 20 days before trial.

Continued

CASE EXAMPLE: ESTATE OF ELIZABETH GARCIA v. ALLSUP'S CONVENIENCE STORES, INC. (2008)—cont'd

RAYMOND Z. ORTIZ
DISTRICT JUDGE RAYMOND Z. ORTIZ

Approved as to Form:

Randi McGinn
MCML, P.A.
Attorneys for the Plaintiff

Approved Telephonically 2/19/08

Tom Outler
RODEY, DICKASON, SLOAN, AKTN & ROBB, P.A.
Phil Krehbiel
Chris Key
Attorneys for the Defendant

Subsequent to this decision by Judge Ortiz, Mr. McCrary was not called to testify when the case went to trial. Instead, the defense relied on the testimony of Dr. Merlyn Moore.[e] Dr. Moore is a former Naval Intelligence officer with a strong academic background, and a professor in the College of Criminal Justice at Sam Houston State University. As reported in Sharpe (2008a):

> *The defense called security expert Merlyn Moore, who said having two clerks on duty could increase the potential for an injury because the clerks might confront a robber. Bullet-proof enclosures, he said, suggest a high-crime area, inhibit communication between clerks and customers, and even cause criminals to turn on customers. Moore said alarms can endanger clerks if a robber sees them activating one. "It might be valuable as a last resort if someone is forcing you out of the store," he added. He said video surveillance can assist police after the fact, but "I don't know if it would have deterred Paul Lovett."*

The jury did not agree with Dr. Moore's assertions. The case ultimately settled for an undisclosed amount during jury deliberations, just as a verdict was about to be returned. As reported in Sharpe, (2008b):

> *Lawyers in the case of an Allsup's clerk murdered during her graveyard shift settled her estate's wrongful-death lawsuit Tuesday, minutes before a Santa Fe jury was to return a $51.2 million verdict.*
>
> *Jury forewoman Jean Lehman said jurors had decided to assess Allsup's Enterprises $21.2 million in compensatory damages and $30 million in punitive damages.*
>
> *But when they told the bailiff they were ready to deliver a verdict about 4:30 p.m., she said, the bailiff told them they were to return to court, where state District Judge Raymond Ortiz informed them the case had been settled.*
>
> *Allegra Carpenter, one of three Albuquerque lawyers representing the three minor children of Elizabeth Garcia, 26 — who was abducted from an Allsup's in Hobbs, raped and stabbed to death Jan. 16, 2002, on just her fourth day on the job — said she could not reveal the amount of the monetary settlement. During closing arguments Monday, plaintiffs' lawyers suggested jurors award the estate $60 million.*

[e]Dr. Moore holds a PhD from Michigan State University in Criminal Justice and Criminology; an M.S. in Criminal Justice; and a BA in Police Administration, both from Indiana University.

CASE EXAMPLE: ESTATE OF ELIZABETH GARCIA v. ALLSUP'S CONVENIENCE STORES, INC. (2008)—cont'd

Carpenter said the settlement includes a promise from Allsup's that it will never again challenge state regulations requiring convenience stores open between 11 p.m. and 7 a.m. to put at least two clerks on duty, station a guard with one clerk or put clerks in bulletproof enclosures.

Garcia's death spurred efforts to boost security at convenience stores, and Carpenter said Allsup's lobbyists or the Petroleum Marketers Association, to which Allsup's belongs, have challenged the rules every year since they were passed. A jury verdict could not have included such an assurance, and the settlement would not have been possible if not for the pressure of the lawsuit, she said.

"There was a little bit of talk (with lawyers for Allsup's) back and forth, but none of it was very serious until today," Carpenter said.

Lehman, a real-estate agent, said jurors were heavily influenced toward the plaintiff when they learned Allsup's successfully sued its previous insurance company over how to make its stores safer, yet never implemented any of the suggestions. "That was a huge inconsistency," she said.

Lehman said jurors also were curious why so little information was provided about Paul Lovett, the man convicted of abducting, raping and killing Garcia. Last year, Lovett was sentenced to life in prison for murdering Garcia and another woman. Although defense attorneys called Lovett's ex-wife and her father, they did not call Lovett or present a deposition from him during the two-week trial. Lehman and another juror, Elaine Lucero, said it seemed Allsup's provided little information on past crimes at its stores. Attorneys for Garcia's estate said they had to do much of their own research to prove, for example, that 12 Allsup's clerks have been murdered in 30 years, making the near-minimum-wage jobs the most dangerous in the state.

To the author's knowledge, Mr. McCrary continues to be hired as a security expert by civil attorneys despite his established history of unreliable, biased, and ultimately false testimony regarding the reliability of his methodology and the extent of his experience.

FALSE TESTIMONY

Part of their job is to ensure that all examinations and results are wholly and effectively communicated to the intended recipients, including investigators, attorneys, and the court (Gannett, 2009). This means that the ethical forensic examiner will refrain from making any false or misleading statements. They will also refrain from false or misleading testimony. This includes statements and testimony regarding education, training, experience, and credentials. As will be discussed in the next section, it also includes testimony regarding the occurrence of examination and testing; the results of examination and testing; and the meaning of those results.

It is important to understand that the law does not always prohibit or penalize false testimony—unless it qualifies as perjury. It must therefore be prohibited by professional organizations and employers. Otherwise, false testimony can go unpunished—which it often does.

CASE EXAMPLE: CALIFORNIA v. CALEB MADSEN

Examiner: Mark Safarik—Pseudoexpert

Mark Safarik is a retired FBI agent, formerly a senior criminal profiler with their Behavioral Analysis Unit. Over the years, this author had occasion to examine numerous criminal profiles prepared by Mr. Safarik on behalf of the FBI. They varied with respect to quality and content, but more than anything else they were heavy with regurgitations from other forensic reports, vague statistical references (to nonexistent research), and laced with predetermined law enforcement opinions that offered little or no genuine insight into the criminal mind.

In 2009 this author was hired by the defense to evaluate the work of Mr. Safarik in California v. Caleb Madsen. This was the third retrial of a young man for the murder of one of his friends. Safarik's report offered a reconstruction of the crime that showed little understanding of the physical evidence, and offer a profile that was tailor made to fit Mr. Madsen, comporting with law enforcement and prosecutorial theories. This had become Mr. Safarik's modus operandi—no profiles written until a suspect had been arrested.

Mr. Safarik was cut from the same cloth as Mr. McCrary, discussed in the prior example. He knowingly used a profiling methodology that had been disproved in the literature; testified outside of his area of expertise on a regular basis (see the discussion of Safarik's involvement in the *Yates* case in the chapter: Applied Case Linkage Analysis); and he did not seem to ever think he could be wrong—refusing to change his opinion even when key evidence dictated it (see: California v. Jennifer and Matt Fletcher, 2004).

On Mr. Safarik's resume submitted in *Madsen*, as per usual, he listed his Bachelors of Science in "Human Physiology." He used the achievement of this degree to suggest, in court, his extensive knowledge of human anatomy on par with medical examiners. Routinely, it was offered as the basis for his opinions given in the areas of wound pattern analysis and crime reconstruction. But this time the defense did their due diligence and checked.

The attorneys for Mr. Madsen pulled Mark Safarik's college transcripts. They discovered that he did not have a degree in human physiology from a biology department as would be expected. Rather, his degree was simply in "physiology," and from the school of agriculture—with classes in animal physiology. Mr. Safarik had been providing a false degree title on his resume for years, and using that to suggest expertise that he simply did not have.

Ultimately, and based in no small part on this revelation, Mr. Safarik was pulled from the *Madsen* witness list and never testified in court again to this author's knowledge. Though his did go on to have a brief stint on television with his own true crime reality show, where he alleged to have what can only be described as psychic tremors in association with his profiling efforts. Caleb Madsen, however, was tried for first degree murder, and subsequently found not guilty.

Perjury, it must be appreciated, is a strict criminal charge. It is the act of lying or making verifiably false statements on a material matter under oath or affirmation in a court of law or in any sworn statements in writing (Black, 1990). A violation of specific criminal statutes which vary from region to region, it is not sufficient for a statement to be false to meet the threshold of perjury. It must be intentionally false, and it must be regarding a *material fact*—a fact relevant to the case at hand. Consequently, not all intentional lies under oath are considered by the court to be perjury.

For example, in Title 18 of the U.S. Code of Laws, §1621 "General Perjury" provides that perjury involves a person "having taken an oath before a competent tribunal, officer, or person, in any case in which a law of the United States authorizes an oath to be administered, that he will testify, declare, depose, or certify truly, or that any written testimony, declaration, deposition, or certificate by him subscribed, is true, willfully and contrary to such oath states or subscribes any material matter which he does not believe to be true."

As a consequence of this reality, not all intentionally false statements made under oath by a forensic examiner are considered perjury—nor are all forensic examiners who give false testimony under oath charged with a crime. The decision to bring such charges is made at the discretion of the District Attorney's Office in the jurisdiction where the false testimony occurred.

Consider the following case example, in which the statute of limitations ran out well before "expert" perjury was revealed:

CASE EXAMPLE: NEW YORK v. ROBIE DRAKE

Examiner: Richard Walter, Massachusetts—Pseudoexpert

In a 1982 case, the defense discovered and a federal appeals court has agreed that a prison therapist, and self-described criminal profiler, perjured himself in regard to his qualifications during sworn expert testimony in a double homicide shooting case. Richard Walter, a fellow of the American Academy of Forensic Sciences who regularly refers to himself as a forensic psychologists and criminal profiler, in fact, lacks the credentials to be either.

Richard Walter, MA, was determined to have perjured himself across the board with respect to his employment and experience in the area of criminal profiling. Specifically, he claimed to be employed as a criminal profiler with publications, profiling experience in over 5000 cases, and a history of expert testimony. None of this was actually true at the time of his testimony in Drake.

Continued

CASE EXAMPLE: NEW YORK v. ROBIE DRAKE—cont'd

During the 1982 trial, Mr. Walter claimed that he was an adjunct lecturer at Michigan State University; that he had examined over 5000 cases while employed at the Los Angeles County Medical Examiners Office; that he had testified as an expert in hundreds of criminal trials in both Los Angeles and Michigan. This testimony was entirely false and ultimately amounted to "perjury," according to the judicial rulings in Drake v. Portuondo (2003, 2006). Mr. Walter was not employed by Los Angeles County other than as a lab assistant (certainly not as a profiler); he was never employed by Michigan State University; and he had not testified in any cases in Los Angeles as an expert witness of any kind.

FORENSIC FRAUD AND CRIMINAL PROFILERS

As suggested by the definitions in the prior sections, *forensic fraud* may be used to describe a scenario in which forensic examiners provide sworn testimony, opinions, or documents (eg, affidavits, reports, or professional resumes) bound for court that contain deceptive or misleading information, findings, opinions, or conclusions, deliberately offered in order to secure an unfair or unlawful gain.

Researched and discussed at length in Turvey (2013), forensic fraud is no small problem for the justice system. It results in the conviction of innocents, destroys careers, and creates immense financial liability for law enforcement agencies, individual examiners, and the municipalities that employ them. It also creates incalculable expense for the justice system in general. Forensic fraud is therefore not something to be disregarded, minimized, or otherwise ignored. It is a serious concern that requires the close attention of any professional community intersecting with the forensic sciences.

Adapted from, and consistent with, typologies provided in Babbage (1830), NAS (2002), ORI (2009), and Turvey (2003), forensic examiners can be cross-categorized as having used one or more of three general approaches to committing fraud, referred to as *Simulators, Dissemblers,* and *Pseudoexperts* (Turvey, 2013).

Simulators are those examiners who physically manipulate physical evidence or related forensic testing[f]. This means that they physically fabricate, tamper with, or destroy evidence. As the name suggests, they are trying to create the appearance that something happened when it did not, or create the appearance that nothing happened at all when in fact it did. This approach to fraud also describes those examiners engaging in evidence suppression by concealing its existence (eg, hide it in a desk drawer, hide it on the evidence shelf, remove it from the evidence log).

Dissemblers are those examiners who exaggerate, embellish, lie about, or otherwise misrepresent findings[g]. They are not tampering with the evidence; they are simply not telling the truth about it. *Dissemblers* exist on a continuum from those who lie outright about the significance of examination results to those who intentionally present a biased or incomplete view.

[f]Also referred to as *forging* (Babbage, 1830) or *fabrication* (ORI, 2009).

[g]Also referred to as *trimming* and *cooking* (Babbage, 1830), or *falsification* (ORI, 2009).

Pseudoexperts are those examiners who fabricate or misrepresent their credentials. They are also referred to as fakes, phonies, charlatans, and mountebanks[h]. Pseudoexperts exist on a continuum of severity as well, from those with valid credentials who misrepresent a credential or an affiliation, to those with no valid credentials at all.

Original research regarding forensic fraud was published in Turvey (2013); it analyzed data collected from 100 forensic examiners in the US that had committed fraud related to the examination of physical evidence between 2000 and 2010. This research also employed the typology above, and reported the following major findings with respect to fraudulent forensic examiners:

1. 23% (n=23) of the forensic examiners in this study were determined to have a history of addiction; 21% (n=21), a history of fraud; and 17% (n=17), a history of other criminal convictions.
2. 27% (n=27) of forensic examiners in this study were found to have been lying about some or all of their education, training, and experience. They were subsequently classified as pseudoexperts.
3. 82% (n=82) of the forensic examiners in this study were determined to be involved in an ongoing pattern of fraud within their agency, often involving multiple examiners, prior to discovery. In context, this finding generally points toward the contribution of systemic and cultural factors.
4. 78% (n=78) of the forensic examiners in this study were employed directly by law enforcement agencies. This finding supports the assertion that those working on behalf of the police and the prosecution (though not necessarily the government, in general) are responsible for a substantial amount, if not the majority, of the known cases of forensic fraud.
5. 37% (n=37) of the fraudulent examiners in the present study were initially retained by their respective employers without severe consequences despite their misconduct; of these, the weightiest involved examiners that were reassigned or temporarily suspended.

As described in this chapter, the vast majority of criminal profilers are *pseudoexperts*. That is to say, they tend not to fabricate psychical evidence, but rather they tend to lie about the nature (or existence) of their education, training, and experience. Some lie about having degrees; some lie about the type of degree they have; and a lot of them lie about how many cases they have worked to seem more authoritative.

A close second are those profilers that lie about the reliability and certainty of their methods or findings. Specifically, they claim that they are always right despite having no mechanism for evaluating the accuracy of their findings, and they continue to use outdated or disproved methodology with little respect for professional development or new research. This is not professionally defensible, as intentional use of a method that has been disproved is negligent, and claiming 100% accuracy in findings lacks scientific credibility (Edwards and Gatsonis, 2009).

---

[h]Also referred to as *falsifying credentials* (ORI, 2009).

REFERENCES

Albrecht, W.S., Albrecht, C.O., 2003. Fraud Examination and Prevention. South-Western Educational Publishing, Mason, Ohio.
Albrecht, W.S., Albrecht, C.O., Albrecht, C.C., Zimbelman, M.F., 2011. Fraud Examination, fourth ed. South-Western, Cengage Learning, Mason, Ohio.
Anderson, M., Martinson, B., De Vries, R., 2007. Normative dissonance in science: results from a national survey of U.S. scientists. Journal of Empirical Research in Human Research Ethics 2 (4), 3–14.
Babbage, C., 1830. Reflections on the Decline of Science in England, and on Some of its Causes. B. Fellowes Publisher, London.
Black, H.C., 1990. Black's Law Dictionary, sixth ed. West Publishing Co, St. Paul, MN.
Burgess, A.N., Burgess, A.W., Douglas, J., Ressler, R. (Eds.), 1992. Crime Classification Manual. Lexington Books, New York, NY.
Brady v. Maryland, 1963. U.S. Supreme Court (373 U.S. 83).
California v. Jennifer, Fletcher, M., 2004. Superior Court, Case No. PA 040748-01. Los Angeles County, CA.
Catano, V., Turk, J., 2007. Fraud and misconduct in scientific research: a definition and procedures for investigation. Medicine and Law 26, 465–476.
Chisum, W.J., Turvey, B., 2011. Crime Reconstruction, second ed. Elsevier Science, San Diego.
Coenen, T., 2008. Essentials of Corporate Fraud. John Wiley & Sons, Inc., Hoboken, NJ.
Crowder, S., Turvey, B., 2013. Ethical Justice: Applied Issues for Criminal Justice Students and Professionals. Elsevier Science, San Diego.
Drake v. Portuondo, 2003. Docket No. 01–2217, January 31 (321 F.3d 338); argued: September 9, 2002, decided: January 31, 2003.
Drake v. Portuondo, 2006. United States District Court, Western District of New York, 99-CV-0681E(Sr), Memorandum and Order, March 16.
Edwards, H., Gotsonis, C., 2009. Strengthening Forensic Science in the United States: A Path Forward. National Academies Press, Washington, DC.
Estate of Elizabeth Garcia, et al., 2008. Plaintiffs v. Allsup's Convenience Stores Inc., Defendant. Case no. D-010 1–CV-20050 0045, First Judicial District Court, County of Santa Fe, State of New Mexico, Order dated February 22.
Gannett, C., 2009. I don't need no stinkin' ethics code! CAC News, Second Quarter, 23–28.
Gardenier, J., 2011. Data integrity is earned, not given. Office of Research Integrity Newsletter 19 (3), 3.
Judson, H., 2004. The Great Betrayal: Fraud in Science. Harcourt, Inc., New York.
Krimsky, S., 2007. Defining scientific misconduct: when conflict-of-interest is a factor in scientific misconduct. Medicine and Law 26, 447–463.
Lord, A., 2010. The prevalence of fraud: what should we, as academics, be doing to address the problem? Accounting and Management Information Systems 9 (1), 4–21.
Martinson, B., Anderson, M., de Vries, R., 2005. Scientists behaving badly. Nature 435 (9), 737–738.
McDowell, R., 2010. Fat finger, falsification, or fraud? Spectroscopy 25 (12), 15–18.
NAS, 2002. Integrity in Scientific Research: Creating an Environment that Promotes Responsible Conduct, National Academy of Science Committee on Assessing Integrity in Research Environments. National Academies Press, Washington, DC.

NAS, 2009. On Being a Scientist: A Guide to Responsible Conduct in Research, National Academy of Science Committee on Science, Engineering, and Public Policy, third ed. National Academies Press, Washington, DC.

ORI, 2009. The Office of Research Integrity Annual Report 2009, Office of Research Integrity. U.S. Department of Health and Human Services, Washington DC. http://ori.hhs.gov/documents/annual_reports/ori_annual_report_2009.pdf.

Parrish, D., 1996. The scientific misconduct definition and falsification of credentials. Professional Ethics Report 9 (4), 1–5.

Reider, B., 2010. Fabrication, falsification et al. American Journal of Sports Medicine 38 (3), 445–447.

Resnick, D., 2003. From Baltimore to Bell labs: reflections on two decades of debate about scientific misconduct. Accountability in Research 10 (2), 123–135.

Reynolds, S., 2004. ORI findings of scientific misconduct in clinical trials and publicly funded research, 1992–2002. Clinical Trials 1 (6), 509–516.

Sharpe, T., April 8, 2008a. Allsup's Settles with Family of Slain Clerk: Jurors Say They Were Ready to Award Estate $51.2 Million. The New Mexican.

Sharpe, T., April 7, 2008b. S.F. Jurors Weighing Allsup's Culpability in Worker's Rape, Slaying. The New Mexican.

Sovacool, B., 2008. Exploring scientific misconduct: isolated individuals, impure institutions, or an inevitable idiom of modern science? Bioethical Inquiry 5 (4), 271–282.

Thornton, J.I., 1994. Courts of law v. Courts of Science: a forensic scientist's reaction to daubert. Shepard's Expert Scientific Evidence Quarterly 1 (3), 475–485.

Thornton, J., Peterson, J., 2007. The general assumptions and rationale of forensic identification. In: Faigman, D., Kaye, D., Saks, M., Sanders, J. (Eds.), Modern Scientific Evidence: The Law and Science of Expert Testimony, vol. 1. West Publishing Group, St. Paul, MN.

Titus, S., Wells, J., Rhoades, L., 2008. Repairing research integrity. Nature 453 (19), 980–982.

Turvey, B., 2003. Forensic Frauds: A Study of 42 Cases. Journal of Behavioral Profiling 4 (1).

Turvey, B., November 5, 2005. Signed Affidavit in Oklahoma V. Richard Tandy Smith.

Turvey, B., January 9, 2008. Expert Declaration. Estate of Elizabeth Garcia V. Allsup's Convenience Stores, Inc.

Turvey, B., 2011. Criminal Profiling: An Introduction to Behavioral Evidence Analysis, fourth ed. Elsevier Science, London.

Turvey, B., 2013. Forensic Fraud: Evaluating Law Enforcement and Forensic Science Cultures in the Context of Examiner Misconduct. Elsevier Science, San Diego.

CHAPTER

3

Behavioral Evidence Analysis: Basic Protocols for the Criminal Profiler[a]

B.E. Turvey
Forensic Solutions LLC, Sitka, Alaska, United States;
Institute of Forensic Investigation and Criminal Profiling, Juarez, Mexico

CHAPTER OUTLINE

[a] Some of this chapter has been adapted from interrelated works prepared by IAFC/ABP founding members and Diplomates over the past 15 years. See generally Baeza et al. (2000), Chisum et al. (2011), and Turvey, (2011).

Behavioral Evidence Analysis. http://dx.doi.org/10.1016/B978-0-12-800607-8.00003-3

In 1998, *The Academy of Behavioral Profiling* (ABP; www.profiling.org) was formed as an interdisciplinary professional organization, dedicated to the development of investigative and forensic protocols related to evidence-based criminal profiling. This also meant establishing, for the very first time, a code of ethics for criminal profilers. The ABP's first meeting was held in March of 1999, in Monterey, California, and the founding members included a retired FBI profiler, two forensic scientists, a forensic psychiatrist, and an NYPD sex crimes detective. Over the course of 2009–2010, the ABP became a credentialing board within the *International Association of Forensic Criminologists* (IAFC).

The IAFC/ABP continues to be the cooperative work of forensic, behavioral, and investigative professionals. In its time, it has drafted, adopted, and refined the first professional code of ethics for criminal profilers; the first written criminal profiling guidelines; and the first profiling general knowledge exam. It has also passed a Professional Certification Act, which will be discussed in the next chapter. Efforts to improve these protocols are an ongoing commitment within the IAFC/ABP, as experience, research, and legal standards force continuous evolution.

This chapter will explore those practice standards, and also discuss their international investigative and forensic utility.

DISCUSSION AND RATIONALE

Criminal profiling involves making inferences about the physical, habitual, emotional, psychological, and even vocational characteristics of criminals. However, there are many different methods of criminal profiling, and all vary with respect to the soundness of underlying protocols, theory, logic, and even insight[b]. Some methods are abstract, general, and trait predictive; others are concrete, specific, and state descriptive. Some rely on offender group statistics; some rely solely on experience; and some rely on examining case-specific behavioral evidence.

As has been discussed previously (Turvey, 2011), the variety of profiling methods used around the world, across agencies and analysts, has resulted in a state of professional confusion. In other words, a number of analysts have no idea how to do their job, let alone how to do it well. Profilers are often poorly educated in the forensic and behavioral sciences and consequently are confused about who they are and where they fit within the criminal justice system; other criminal justice professionals recognize and are confused about the same things, resulting in more than a little skepticism and even animosity; the media adds to myth by portraying profilers as ball-gazing supercops; and the general public views profilers as a more specialized form of psychic. And too many inept and uneducated profilers are benefiting from this lack of professional cohesion and the ignorant misperceptions that are allowed to persist.

The professional criminal profiler understands this problem well. They deal, however, with facts and evidence, not assumptions and emotional hyperbole. They seek to educate, not advocate. A profiler's methods and protocols will therefore be objective,

[b] Some aren't even methods at all; some are prejudice and ignorance propped up by good PR or adventitious employment in a position of authority.

informed, and necessarily rooted in the tenets of the scientific method. Learning what these are, and why they are important, is vital to staying on a professional path.

If criminal profilers are to be taken seriously in the 21st century as professional operatives with a substantive contribution to offer the criminal justice system, then there are areas to which career-long commitments must be made. Having a sound foundational education is the first. Without it, misunderstanding, ignorance, and disaster are just as certain as the likelihood that the profiler will be oblivious when these things are happening. The second area is the development, understanding of, and adherence to competent protocols.

Behavioral evidence analysis (BEA) is an evidence-based form of criminal profiling that requires analysis of forensic evidence, victimology, offender modus operandi, and offender motive in each individual criminal incident. Proficiency therefore requires the development of knowledge and skills related to these and other profiling related subject matter. It is also improved by adherence to certain foundational protocols. Certification advances professional development further, and that will be discussed in the next chapter.

BEHAVIORAL EVIDENCE ANALYSIS BASICS

BEA, as described thoroughly in Turvey (2011), is a criminal profiling method that requires three steps: examining the physical evidence to establish offense behavior (crime reconstruction); crime scene analysis to establish and characterize the choices made by the offender in relation to the offense (modus operandi and signature behavior); and forensic victimology, to establish and understand the role of the victim in the crime.

Without these three initial assessments, it is not possible to render a complete or fully accurate profile. You need to examine the evidence to know what behaviors occurred, and you need to know how and why the offender chose the victim. Those offering profiling advice or insights without this information are just plain guessing.

BEA necessarily requires a multidisciplinary approach. Either the profiler must have a strong background that includes a meld of behavioral and forensic sciences, or they have an obligation to work as a team among others that do. Operating without this background, the profiler will lack the metacognitive dexterity to know when they are uninformed or making mistakes. They will also lack respect for reading, research, and writing, which are all necessary for competent scientific casework.

SKILL IDENTIFICATION AND DEVELOPMENT

Particular to BEA, the following knowledge, skills, and abilities are of benefit to the criminal profiler. Without these, the criminal profiler is in peril, as is the quality of their findings and anyone who relies on them.

1. Knowledge and understanding of the criminal justice system within which they work
2. Knowledge and understanding of the various methods and types of criminal investigation

3. A working knowledge and understanding of the scientific method
4. A working knowledge and understanding of the science of logic
5. Knowledge and understanding of forensic science and the various methods of physical evidence collection and examination
6. A working knowledge and understanding of victims, crime, and criminals
7. A working knowledge and understanding of human sociology in relation to the study and examination of victims, crime, and criminals
8. Knowledge and understanding of human psychology in relation to the study and examination of victims, crime, and criminals
9. Knowledge and understanding of mental illness in relation to the study and examination of victims, crime, and criminals
10. Knowledge and understanding of drugs and alcohol in relation to victims, crime, and criminals
11. Knowledge and understanding of human anatomy and physiology
12. Knowledge and understanding of human sexuality in all of its contexts and incarnations
13. Proficient reading, comprehension, and research skills
14. Proficient writing skills
15. Proficiency in the construction of findings and opinions based on rational logic and reasoning
16. Proficiency in report writing that meets judicial standards
17. Proficiency in art of courtroom testimony
18. The ability to travel
19. The ability to examine evidence relating to the violent, the sexually graphic, the bizarre, and the grotesque without becoming overwhelmed by personal feelings
20. The ability to meet deadlines
21. The ability to recognize bias, and work toward maintaining objectivity
22. The ability to keep a confidence and to maintain confidential information
23. The ability to remain honest and ethical despite any potential rewards for professional dishonesty and unethical practice

Any reading, research, training, or professional experience that enhances the above considerations is of high professional value to the criminal profiler. Those that leave these areas unattended will be tested by the work, their peers, and the justice system—and they will ultimately be found wanting.

ACADEMY OF BEHAVIORAL PROFILING CRIMINAL PROFILING GUIDELINES—BACKGROUND

On December 15, 1999, the Board of Directors for the ABP approved the guidelines outlined herein by a unanimous vote. In the development of these guidelines, it should be noted that several publications played a significant reference role for board members, informing the decision-making process.

It should also be noted that these are the first written guidelines for those directly involved in the criminal profiling process by an independent professional organization. The ABP criminal profiling guidelines were designed collaboratively for use by its membership. However, they are intended to be useful to anyone involved in the process of evidence-based criminal and behavioral profiling, regardless of their capacity. They are a much-needed resource for the multidisciplinary professional community involved in criminal profiling and its related processes, created to ensure and maintain quality, as well as to decrease the chance for examiner error.

They were disseminated to the ABP membership along with the following quotation (Thornton, 1997, p. 17):

> *Experience is neither a liability nor an enemy of the truth; it is a valuable commodity, but it should not be used as a mask to deflect legitimate scientific scrutiny, the sort of scrutiny that customarily is leveled at scientific evidence of all sorts. To do so is professionally bankrupt and devoid of scientific legitimacy, and courts would do well to disallow testimony of this sort. Experience ought to be used to enable the expert to remember the when and the how, why, who, and what. Experience should not make the expert less responsible, but rather more responsible for justifying an opinion with defensible scientific facts.*

ACADEMY OF BEHAVIORAL PROFILING CRIMINAL PROFILING GUIDELINES

Forensic examiners and their methods cannot be viewed solely in terms of their products. In other words, just because they offer a finding that people like does not mean that they have done a good job. They must be judged by the legitimacy of the processes by which their evidence is examined and interpreted. Any opinion rendered by a forensic examiner in a written report, or in court testimony, must have a basis in fact and theory. Without such a basis, any conclusions reached are bereft of validity and should be treated with derision.

This passage expresses a significant part of the doctrine that was considered in the design of the ABP profiling guidelines, and the philosophy they are intended to engender.

More than simply a checklist, these guidelines impart a professional forensic philosophy of case examination that is logical, informed, and thorough. They also presuppose a measure of examiner enthusiasm for objectivity and attention to detail. At their core is the ideal, expressed by Peter Novick in his work on professionalization, *That Noble Dream*—that the value of any interpretation should be judged by how well it accounts for the facts; if contradicted by the facts it should be abandoned.

In as much as all of these things are true, the development of these guidelines is a necessary step in the direction of professionalization, helping to provide a sturdy platform for caseworkers in this field to stand upon.

NOTES

In all casework where examiners participate as investigative support, crime analyst, or criminal profiler, examiners are expected to keep and maintain reasonably detailed notes documenting their examination of case materials.

WRITTEN REPORTS

Investigative support

In all casework where examiners participate as investigative support, examiners are expected to make written reports of their findings in the form of a *threshold assessment*, a *crime analysis*, or a *criminal profile* as appropriate. It is understood that these are investigative documents only, and do not necessarily represent expert findings.

Expert examination for trial

In all casework where examiners expect to present expert findings before the court, it is preferable that the examiner should make written reports of their findings in the form of a *crime analysis*, or a *criminal profile* as appropriate. It is understood that the client or agency retaining the examiner reserves the right to request a report which includes only those conclusions that may be the focus of testimony or decline a written conclusions entirely. It is further understood that this should in no way effect the examiner's overall methods of examination, conclusions, or notes.

Depositions and testimony

In all casework where examiners present expert findings to the court, it is understood that they will testify in a clear and consistent fashion. It is also understood that examiners will not offer opinions on matters outside of their areas of knowledge or expertise, as well as follow the other ethical guidelines of the ABP. It is further understood that any opinions given by the examiner will be predicated upon evidence from the case at hand, and that the sources of that evidence will be made clear to the court upon request.

OBJECTIVITY AND BIAS

In all casework where examiners participate as investigative support, crime analyst, or criminal profiler, examiners are expected to maintain an attitude of objectivity, and guard against bias, personal, or otherwise

It is understood that bias may not be removed completely from the examination process, but that efforts can be made to minimize its effects.

Guidelines

In order to guard against bias, and maintain an attitude of objectivity, examiners should

1. strive to avoid, when feasible, suspect information when rendering a threshold assessment or criminal profile.
2. strive to avoid preconceived theories of the crime.
3. not conceal or ignore evidence that detracts from or falsifies a particular theory of the crime.
4. seek out the advice of colleagues as needed.

THRESHOLD ASSESSMENT

A *threshold assessment* is an investigative report that reviews the *initial* physical evidence of crime-related behavior, victimology, and crime scene characteristics for a particular unsolved crime, or a series of potentially related unsolved crimes, in order to provide immediate investigative direction. It should include what is generally known of events, what is not, and suggestions regarding any means by which the former may be established. It is not to be confused with, or presented as, a *criminal profile*.

Guidelines

A *threshold assessment* should include the following elements:

1. Overview of the established facts of the case relevant to crime-related behavior as appropriate.
2. Overview of the established facts of the case relevant to victimology as appropriate.
3. Overview of the established facts of the case relevant to crime scene characteristics as appropriate, with supporting argumentation.
4. Initial hypothesis regarding potential motivational behaviors and aspects, as appropriate, with supporting argumentation.
5. Initial hypothesis regarding potential offender characteristics, as appropriate, with supporting argumentation.
6. Suggestions regarding further facts that need to be determined or established in order to address logical breaks in the sequence of events surrounding the crime, including suggestions regarding additional forensic analyses that may be performed on available physical evidence.
7. Suggestions regarding further victimological information gathering.
8. Investigatively relevant suggestions regarding potential strategies or avenues for suspect development.

VICTIMOLOGY

Victimology is a thorough study of all available victim information. This includes items such as sex, age, height, weight, family, friends, acquaintances, education, employment, residence, and neighborhood. This also includes background information on the history and lifestyle of the victim such as overall personal habits, hobbies, criminal history, and medical histories. Establishing victimology is a necessary part of determining the context of some crimes. It is understood that some of the elements of a crime analysis and/or a criminal profile may be dependent upon this information.

The purpose of establishing the victimology in a particular case is to enable the examiner to make an informed assessment of that victim's risk of becoming a victim of a particular type of crime in regards to their overall lifestyle, as well as during the events preceding their demise. It may also facilitate case linkage assessments.

CRIME ANALYSIS

A *crime analysis* is a report that examines and interprets the behavioral evidence for a particular crime or a series of related crimes.

It is understood that a *crime analysis (aka, crime scene analysis)* should be based upon victim behaviors, offender behaviors, and environmental circumstances that are directly observed by the examiner, logically inferred from the case documentation, or reconstructed by the appropriate forensic specialists. Crime-related behaviors and circumstances should not be assumed for the purpose of performing the *crime analysis*. Appropriate references should be made to the established case facts to support interpretations made by the examiner.

Guidelines

A *crime analysis* should include the following elements, with references when appropriate:

1. Overview of the established facts of the case relevant to crime-related behavior.
2. Overview of the established facts of the case relevant to victimology.
3. An opinion as to the lifestyle risk of each victims when possible, with supporting argumentation.
4. An opinion as to the situational risk of each victim, when possible, with supporting argumentation.
5. An opinion as to the risk taken by the offender to acquire each victim, when possible, with supporting argumentation.
6. An analysis of the scene characteristics for each crime, when possible, with supporting argumentation. To include consideration of, at the minimum:
   - Location and scene types
   - Point of contact
   - Offender method of approach
   - Offender method of attack
   - Offender methods of control
   - Offender use of weapons
   - Offender use of force
   - Victim resistance

- Sexual acts
- Precautionary acts
- Contradictory acts
- Evidence of planning
- Offense skill level
- Items taken by the offender
- Items left behind by the offender
- Verbal behavior
- Modus operandi behavior
- Motivational behavior

7. Opinions as to the motivation evidenced by the crime-related behavior, when possible, with supporting argumentation.

CRIMINAL PROFILE

A *criminal profile* is a report that describes the investigatively relevant and/or probative characteristics of the offender responsible for a particular crime or a series of related crimes based on a thorough *crime scene analysis*. It should include the crime analysis and victimological information as a foundation, as well as logical, evidence-based arguments for each offender characteristic elicited from that foundation.

It is understood that the *criminal profile* is actually comprised of any offender characteristics elicited from the *crime analysis* or victimology. It is subsequently understood that a *criminal profile* cannot be rendered without first performing a *crime analysis* and/or victimology.

Offender characteristics

Offender characteristics include any attributes that the examiner ascribes specifically to the unknown person or persons responsible for the commission of particular criminal acts, including those that are physical, psychological, social, geographical, or relational. They can also include predictions about likely offender behavior before, during, and/or after a crime. One type of physical attribute is offender height. One type of psychological attribute is an offender's state of mind before, during, and/or after the crime. One type of a geographical attribute is where an offender lives. One type of a social attribute is the type of relationship partner that is preferred. One type of a relational attribute is the nature of an offender's relationship with their victim. One type of prediction about likely offender behavior is whether or not the offender will return to a crime scene.

Guidelines

A *criminal profile* should include the following elements, with references when appropriate:

1. Overview of the established facts of the case relevant to crime-related behavior.
2. Overview of the established facts of the case relevant to victimology.

3. An opinion as to the lifestyle risk of each victim, when possible, with supporting argumentation.
4. An opinion as to the situational risk of each victim, when possible, with supporting argumentation.
5. An opinion as to the risk taken by the offender to acquire each victim, when possible, with supporting argumentation.
6. An analysis of the scene characteristics for each crime, when possible, with supporting argumentation. To include consideration of, at the minimum:
   - Location and scene types
   - Point of contact
   - Offender method of approach
   - Offender method of attack
   - Offender methods of control
   - Offender use of weapons
   - Offender use of force
   - Victim resistance
   - Sexual acts
   - Precautionary acts
   - Contradictory acts
   - Evidence of planning
   - Offense skill level
   - Items taken by the offender
   - Items left behind by the offender
   - Verbal behavior
   - Modus operandi behavior
   - Motivational behavior
7. Opinions as to the motivation evidenced by the crime-related behavior, when possible, with supporting argumentation.
8. Opinions as to investigatively relevant and/or probative offender characteristics, when possible, with supporting argumentation. These can include, but are by no means limited to, characteristics such as
   - knowledge of/familiarity with victim
   - knowledge of/familiarity with location
   - evidence of criminal history
   - evidence relating to state of mind
   - evidence of psychopathic characteristics such as superficiality, deceitfulness, impulsively, lack of empathy, lack of remorse, egocentricity, or a need for excitement.
   - evidence of personal or sexual conflict
   - evidence of sexual fantasy

These guidelines were written with the understanding that members would also commit to staying current with the most recent editions of instructional texts prepared in relation to BEA profiling methodology. For example, use of *Criminal*

Profiling, 1st Edition (Turvey, 1999) as a reference text is not the best practice in 2015, when that text is in it's 4th Edition. They are also written with the notion that these protocols are the beginning of the knowledge, not the end of it. Members therefore have an obligation not to follow the lists provided in a pedantic fashion; not to be trapped by them. To deviate when necessary, but to be capable of understanding and explaining why.

THE INTERNATIONAL UTILITY OF BEHAVIORAL EVIDENCE ANALYSIS

Because it fully embraces the complexity of idiographic case analysis, and the reliability of the scientific method, BEA enjoys an international reputation for relevance to investigative and forensic casework. This is detailed throughout the remainder of this text, as subsequent chapters chronicle the casework and courtroom testimony of ABP-certified criminal profilers from around the world. Acceptance from the international and investigative legal communities has been hard earned.

ABP-trained criminal profilers have testified in courts across the United States, in Mexico, China, Singapore, Korea, Colombia, and Portugal. They are admitted into the courts because of their reliance on information from the crime scene as opposed to subjective external considerations; their adherence to the scientific method and a corresponding commitment to education and training; and their adherence to written practice standards and ethical guidelines. Such professionals make it easy to discriminate between themselves and frauds, or so-called "whores of the court" (Hagen, 1997) by virtue of the demonstrable hurtles they have cleared before ever putting pen to paper in any given case. And by virtue of the fact that anyone who can read is fully capable of evaluating whether or not the proper ethics and procedures were attended to in their work-product—because all of these requirements are written and public.

But most important, the requirements of BEA organize casework in a way that no other method demands. It fully expects examiners to spend hours reading and researching the particulars of their cases, and then to prepare written findings that address the same issues each time in a comprehensive yet plainly structured fashion. This is in order to educate investigators, attorneys, judges, and any other decision-maker that encounters the report through its journey within the slow but staggering maze that can be the criminal justice system. The result being a unifying structure for case analysis and a criminological language that transcends borders.

No other profiling method has done this. No other method has even tried. And that is why the rest of this book is so important. It will provide those with limited experience a glimpse of what actual reports look like, as well and a general sense of the great consequence that can flow from the work when it is done by those with ability tempered by ethics.

Presenters assembled for the 1er Encuentro Internacional de Colombia y la Direccion de Investigación Criminal e Interpol in October of 2015. This first of its kind international event was hosted by the Colombian Policia National, DIJIN; the Colombian Ministry of Justice; and the United Nations. This group was comprised of criminal profilers from all over the world, including Colombia, Mexico, the United States, Canada, Korea, and China. All pictured are ABP certified or trained.

REFERENCES

Baeza, J., Chisum, W.J., Chamberlin, T.M., McGrath, M., Turvey, B., January 2000. Academy of behavioral profiling: criminal profiling guidelines. Journal of Behavioral Profiling 1 (1).

Chisum, W.J., Freeman, J., Turvey, B., 2011. Forensic examination reports. In: Chisum, W.J., Turvey, B. (Eds.), Crime Reconstruction, second ed. Elsevier Science, San Diego.

Hagen, M., 1997. Whores of the Court: The Fraud of Psychiatric Testimony and the Rape of American Justice. Harper-Collins Pub, New York, NY.

Novick, P., 1988. That Noble Dream. Cambridge University Press, New York, NY, p. 46.

Thornton, J.I., 1997. The general assumptions and rationale of forensic identification. In: Faigman, D., Kaye, D., Saks, M., et al. (Eds.), Modern Scientific Evidence: The Law and Science of Expert Testimony, vol. 2 (West St. Paul, MN).

Turvey, B., 1999. Criminal Profiling: An Introduction to Behavioral Evidence Analysis, first ed. Elsevier Science, London.

Turvey, B., 2011. Criminal Profiling: An Introduction to Behavioral Evidence Analysis, fourth ed. Elsevier Science, London.

PART

2

Student and Professional Development

CHAPTER

The IAFC Criminal Profiler Professional Certification Act

4

B.E. Turvey
Forensic Solutions LLC, Sitka, Alaska, United States; Institute of Forensic Investigation and Criminal Profiling, Juarez, Mexico

W.S. Crowder
Kennesaw State University, Kennesaw, GA, United States

M. McGrath
Unity Healthy Systems, Rochester, NY, United States

S. Mikulay
Elgin Community College, Elgin, IL, United States

CHAPTER OUTLINE

It is important to understand that *professionalization* is the process by which any trade or vocation becomes professional, characterized by a high degree of competence with respect to domain-specific knowledge, skills, and abilities. Ideally, professional societies, associations, and organizations are intended to assist with the professionalization of the fields they serve. This generally involves the education, support, and oversight of a given membership.

Behavioral Evidence Analysis. http://dx.doi.org/10.1016/B978-0-12-800607-8.00004-5

In fulfillment of this broad-ranging responsibility, everything that a professional organization does should generally contribute to the guidance and mentoring of students and the professional maintenance or advancement of regular members. When managed responsibly, these efforts also serve another equally important function. They provide a level of protection for the discipline, and the rest of society, from unqualified, unethical, and incompetent practitioners.

Professional certification refers to the process of establishing that a practitioner has achieved a particular level of knowledge, skill, and ability as demonstrated by coursework, instruction, and/or supervised experience. This fact is attested by a signed document from the organization facilitating or providing the certification.

A discussion regarding the value of professional certification, and its absence in the forensic sciences, is provided in the NAS Report (National Academy of Sciences, 2009, p. 208):

> *The certification of individuals complements the accreditation of laboratories for a total quality assurance program. In other realms of science and technology, professionals, including nurses, physicians, professional engineers, and some laboratories, typically must be certified before they can practice. The same should be true for forensic scientists who practice and testify. Although the accreditation process primarily addresses the management system, technical methods, and quality of the work of a laboratory (which includes the education and training of staff), certification is a process specifically designed to ensure the competency of the individual examiner.*

Professional certification, therefore, refers to a course of training that results in an endorsement from a particular agency, school, or professional group. Certification programs are meant to involve an express course of study, experience, and testing. Depending on the quality and independence of a given certification program, those who pass are known to have demonstrated a specific array of professional knowledge, skills, and abilities. Legitimate professional certification is also an ongoing commitment—it requires timely reevaluation through continued education and testing.

However, as discussed in Giannelli (2007), not every organization cares about quality or competence, many care only about the ability of members to pay fees and dues (p. 227):

> *A number of organizations offer examiner certification programs. Some certifying organizations, however, appear to lack stringent requirements. Instead, they issue what are reported to be "checkbook credentials." Rigorous certification standards should be instituted for examiners in order to ensure competence. Demanding written examinations, proficiency testing, continuing education, recertification procedures, an ethical code, and effective disciplinary procedures should form the basis of such a program.*

In the criminal justice community, for example, many states require their law enforcement agents to be certified by a state agency, much like teachers. In this way, their law enforcement credentials can be suspended or revoked should they engage in unethical behavior, misconduct, or criminal activity. However, the value of such credentialing is equal only to the character of those who offer it and it is meaningless when presiding state agencies refuse to revoke it when misconduct occurs.

In short, without professional certification, there is no independent demonstration and assessment of professional ethics, knowledge, skills, or abilities. There is also no oversight with respect to professional competence and character. That is to say, those without certification have no way of knowing whether or not they are actually competent, and neither does anyone else nor is there any external incentive for behaving like a professional should.

THE INTERNATIONAL ASSOCIATION OF FORENSIC CRIMINOLOGISTS

In June of 2013, the International Association of Forensic Criminologists (IAFC) voted to pass the Criminal Profiler Professional Certification Act (CPPCA). It is the first and only independent certification available in the discipline of criminal profiling. In the past, there have been agencies that have trained their own people in house, while on the job. The result has been cronyism, and a general lack of competence and growth, within the profession. The IAFC has ever sought to address and change this persistent reality through international membership and the appreciation of multiple contributing disciplines.

Brent Turvey holds a BS in Psychology, an MS in Forensic Science, a PhD in Criminology, and is the author of *Criminal Profiling: An Introduction to Behavioral Evidence Analysis*, currently in its fourth edition. He is also founding member of the Academy of Behavioral Profiling (ABP)/IAFC. As a court-qualified expert in criminal profiling and other related forensic disciplines, he makes the following observations: "From news coverage of major cases to court proceedings, criminal profilers can be found giving their opinions. Often these are accepted based on trust and even a little ignorance without any real scrutiny of professional credentials. But a close look at even those from federal agencies reveals an absence of relevant education. Profilers can often be found with no formal education, online degrees from diploma mills, or degrees in subjects such as music and animal physiology. Frankly, it's professionally embarrassing, or at least it should be." The CPPCA argues it is necessary to cleave the qualified professional from those who simply hold a job title or perform research without doing casework.

Dr. Shawn Mikulay, a PhD-level psychologist and the current vice president of the IAFC, is in agreement. Having testified as an expert in the area of criminal profiling, he warns that: "As the field of forensic criminology and criminal profiling becomes increasingly accepted by the courts, it is critical a standard be put forth to identify those individuals who have been appropriately trained, educated, and mentored. With an increasing awareness of wrongful conviction, practitioners need to demonstrate that they have the ability to do their job and the ethical standards to do it correctly." The CPPA, he argues, is a major step toward accomplishing this.

Dr. Stan Crowder, a retired US Army Military Police Colonel and former Chief of Investigations for the Inspector General of Georgia, is the current President of the IAFC. He made the following statement: "The Diplomate status afforded to IAFC members by the CPPA is designed to reveal the knowledge, skills, and abilities of hard working, evidence-based investigators. Not only does the credential requires higher education, experience, and tenacity of purpose, it requires proofs of ability, an understanding of the scientific method, and a peer-reviewed process that rivals intensive academic gauntlets." Dr. Crowder, impatient with the fraudulent credentials and weak training requirements that mark much of government service, went on to observe: "The bottom line is: this credential cannot be purchased; it must be earned via intensive learning, proven ability, and peer-approved reviews."

The Diplomate credential ratified by CPPCA is available exclusively to members of the IAFC. The entire Act is provided herein and can also be found online at: http://profiling.org/CPPCA-2013.pdf.

Currently, there are more than 100 criminal profilers certified under the IAFC's CPPCA in the United States, Canada, Mexico, and Colombia. This includes Criminal Profiling and Behavioral Analysis Units within the Colombian Federal Police, and the Office of the Attorney General in Chihuahua, Mexico. It also includes a broad cross section of law enforcement investigators and private practitioners working as psychologists, criminologists, forensic scientists, and criminal investigators.

INTERNATIONAL ASSOCIATION OF FORENSIC CRIMINOLOGISTS CRIMINAL PROFILER PROFESSIONAL CERTIFICATION ACT OF 2013

Ratified June 23, 2013

SECTION 1: THE ABP BOARD OF EXAMINERS

There is created within the IAFC, an ABP Board of Examiners. This ABP Board of Examiners will be comprised of three Full Members of the IAFC serving at the pleasure of the IAFC Board of Directors.

SECTION 2: DIPLOMATE STATUS

There is created within the IAFC a terminal membership status: Diplomate of the ABP (D-ABP). D-ABP membership status shall serve as professional acknowledgment from the IAFC and The ABP Board of Examiners that a member has achieved an advanced level of knowledge, skill, and ability in the subject and practice of criminal profiling as demonstrated by satisfaction of the requirements outlined in this Act.

SECTION 3: D-ABP MEMBERSHIP REQUIREMENTS

To achieve D-ABP membership status, applicants must satisfy the following requirements:

Section 3.1—IAFC membership

All applicants must be members of the IAFC in good standing.

Section 3.2—Education requirement

All applicants must satisfy the requirements set forth in at least one of the following educational tracks:

Section 3.2.1—Track 1: Degree requirement

Applicants must hold an undergraduate major or a graduate degree in the Behavioral or Social Sciences from an accredited institution of higher education, in any the following subjects:

a. Psychology
b. Mental health[a]
c. Sociology
d. Social work
e. Behavioral science
f. Criminology
g. Some anthropology[b]
h. Some criminal justice programs (transcript required)[2]

Note: Education, business, justice administration, and public administration degrees do not meet the D-ABP education requirement. Degrees received based on instruction, that is, entirely without direct professor–student classroom interaction do not meet the D-ABP education requirement.

Section 3.2.2—Track 2: Research requirement

a. Applicants must complete 63+ undergraduate credit hours from an accredited institution of higher education (approximately the number associated with associate's degree requirements).
b. Complete a written thesis comprised of original research in an area of behavioral evidence analysis (eg, victimology, crime scene analysis, or criminal profiling) as it relates to criminal investigation, forensic examination, or legal issues. This thesis must be at least 30 pages in length with at least 15 peer-reviewed references (eg, textbooks and professional journals; not popular media, true crime, or Wikipedia).

---

[a] Degrees from a school of education, or which focus on guidance counseling or school counseling, do not meet this requirement.

[b] Acceptable Anthropology and CJ Degrees must be augmented with core behavioral science subjects.

c. Prior published dissertations and research, with the applicant as sole author, may be considered by The ABP Board of Examiners for satisfaction of this requirement.

Completed thesis projects are subject to evaluation and approval by The ABP Board of Examiners.

This track allows for the entry of applicants with any formal educational background to demonstrate both their scholarship and commitment to the field. This is made evident by virtue of contributing to the field's development in a quantifiable manner, while also demonstrating academic prowess and attendance to individual professional betterment through focused research.

Section 3.3—Training requirement

All applicants must complete a minimum of 40+ hours of BEA-oriented workshops from IAFC-approved instructors.

Section 3.4—Examination requirement

All applicants must satisfy the following examination requirements:

a. Successful completion of the Profiling General Knowledge Exam (the PGKE).
b. Successful completion of The ABP Board Examination (a comprehensive examination covering advanced forensic science, victimology, crime scene analysis, and offender character inference issues).
c. Those individuals appointed to committees associated with the creation of either exam are exempt from completing the requirements associated with that particular exam.

Section 3.5—Experience requirement

All applicants must satisfy at least one of the following two requirements:

a. Submission of two completed criminal profiles;
b. Submission of one completed criminal profile and two completed threshold assessments;
c. Submission of three completed threshold assessments;

These completed reports must comport with IAFC report writing guidelines and IAFC guidelines for ethical behavior.

Completed reports are subject to evaluation and approval by The ABP Board of Examiners.

SECTION 4: PROFESSIONAL CERTIFICATION AS A CRIMINAL PROFILER

Achievement of D-ABP status, once conferred by The ABP Board of Examiners, shall serve as the IAFC's highest credential for criminal profilers within the organization.

SECTION 5: IAFC-APPROVED INSTRUCTORS

Once a member of the IAFC has achieved D-ABP status, he/she is eligible to teach in IAFC-approved seminars and workshops. Specifically, IAFC members with D-APB status shall be considered "IAFC-approved instructors," in comportment with the *Section 3.3—Training Requirement,* and the provisions therein.

SECTION 6: REVOCATION

The ABP Board of Examiners may suspend or revoke a member's D-ABP status if that member violates any of the IAFC Ethical Guidelines for Professional Conduct.

THE GLOBAL FORENSIC ALLIANCE INITIATIVE

The IAFC has also joined the Global Forensic Alliance, along with dozens of other professionals, agencies, institutes, and professional groups.

The Global Forensic Alliance is a strategic alliance intended to convey a commitment to ethical forensic practice among like-minded professionals, organizations, and institutions. It arises out of necessity to identify the principled and law abiding among an ever growing global community of forensic opportunists and frauds. It will serve as a unifying symbol for students and professionals seeking education, training, and certifications, to help prevent what has become a pattern of exploitation and abuse by those operating outside of the law, offering phony credentials and without an enforced code of ethics (see generally Turvey and Crowder, 2014).

A strategic alliance is an agreement between two or more parties to pursue a set of agreed-upon objectives needed while remaining independent organizations.

Participation by any individual or organization in this strategic alliance is free. Those interested need only to submit a signed individual or agency agreement to the provisos listed below, on official letterhead.

The applicant agrees to participate in the Global Forensic Alliance by virtue of an unwavering commitment to the following:

1. Establishing clear guidelines for professional and ethical conduct rooted in scientific values;
2. Working to achieve and maintain professional and ethical conduct;
3. Unequivocal identification of, and corrective action in response to, those that demonstrate negligence or incompetence;
4. Unequivocal sanctions for those who engage in unethical behavior;
5. Intolerance for deception or criminal behavior in any form;

Upon approval by the Global Forensic Alliance Directorate, strategic partners may be approved, suspended, or expelled.

CONCLUSION

Professional certification, tethered to a clear and enforced code of professional ethics, is one of the most important ways that a discipline can self-regulate. Failing this, it becomes unclear how the profession defines itself and those practicing within it as either reliable or responsible. Just as important, unless a certification can be revoked it has no value to anyone, symbolizing only membership within a social club run by one's cronies. The IAFC has shown genuine leadership in this regard with respect to the criminal profiling community, and will continue to do so in the years to come while partnering with other professional organizations embracing the same mission.

REFERENCES

Giannelli, P., 2007. Wrongful convictions and forensic science: the need to regulate crime labs. North Carolina Law Review 86, 163–236.

National Academy of Sciences, 2009. Strengthening Forensic Science in the United States: A Path Forward. National Academy of Sciences Committee on Identifying the Needs of the Forensic Sciences Community. National Academies Press, Washington, DC.

Turvey, B., Crowder, S., 2014. Ethical Justice. Elsevier Science, San Diego.

CHAPTER

Using a Cold Homicide Case to Teach Criminal Profiling

5

W.S. Crowder[a]
Kennesaw State University, Kennesaw, GA, United States

CHAPTER OUTLINE

The success of American television programs such as *Criminal Minds* by Columbia Broadcasting System, *Profiler* by National Broadcasting Company, FOX's *Crime Scene Investigator*, and the UK television series *Wire in the Blood* and *Cracker* has captured the interests of students in criminal justice classes. They want to gain more insight into the behaviors of criminals. How does a professor harness the excitement and interest in such television and cinema projects and use it in the criminal justice classroom?

Students want to learn through the application of information they have discovered in the classroom. It is important to coach or mentor learners while helping them develop critical thinking skills and the ability to solve problems. This is best accomplished by engaging them with a question that gives purpose and direction to their work. Problems are naturally motivating. Using a cold, or unsolved, homicide case in teaching criminal profiling has proven to be a successful methodology. An example is the shortest bridge between theory and reality (Hodnett, 1955).

The application of the ACETS model developed by Abaidoo and Wachniak (2007) that addresses Academic knowledge, Collaborative learning, Experiential learning, and Technological Savvy, results in students gaining practical understanding of criminological theory, research methods, and academic knowledge applied to the real world problem of the unsolved homicide. The synergy of group learning is

[a]This work was originally published as Crowder, S., 2008. International Journal of Learning 15 (5), p. 25–28.

Behavioral Evidence Analysis. http://dx.doi.org/10.1016/B978-0-12-800607-8.00005-7

garnered in dialogic exchange outside the classroom that involves small group interaction and discussion.

This article reflects how critical thinking rooted in problems may evoke students' natural curiosity and stimulates both learning and critical thought (Bean, 2001). Creating a course that challenges students to question assumptions and explore logic and the scientific method may require creating a collaborative effort. Linking academic learning outcomes to a problem may create surprising erudition. The significance of this article shows presenting students with a challenging and complex problem may tap into the innate desire for learning.

CREATING THE COURSE

The pedagogical transition from topic-centered assignments to problem-centered assignments began with the course *Profile of the Serial Offender*, the precursor course to *Criminal Profiling and Analysis*. In the course, *Profile of the Serial Offender*, the student is introduced to learning that will test and reinforce previous learning from the *Criminal Investigations* course. The students gain exposure to the nature of violent serial offenders through the most up-to-date theories and research on victimology; typologies, characteristics, and statistical data about perpetrators; and investigation through profiling. Students are taught the inductive method of criminal profiling which is the statistical and correlational analysis of serial offenders (Turvey, 1999).

The *Criminal Profiling and Analysis* course was developed to build on previous learning in *Profile of the Serial Offender*. The assessment and understanding, and the resolution of real homicide investigative challenges had never been attempted in the major program. Academic knowledge, step one of the ACETS model, evolved after a search of the literature on profiling as a process while concurrently applying criminological theory. A "cold" or unresolved homicide case analysis component of the class was developed to improve students' critical thinking skills. These skills include generating data for analysis and decision making. Step two of the model, collaborative learning, was accomplished by utilizing the assigned cold case detective as a guest lecturer about the known facts of the case and mentor for student understanding of the task, conditions, and standards of homicide investigations. The reasoning derived from diverse backgrounds, interests, and understanding led to a critical examination in all phases of the cold case analysis. Step three of the ACETS model, experiential learning, emerged as the students attempted to solve the cold case. The "technological savvy" aspect of the course is linked to the introduction of the geographical profiling model of serial offenders as developed by Rossmo (1999).

The *Criminal Profiling and Analysis* course clarifies the deductive criminal profiling method which involves the analytical process of forensic evidence and the development of offender characteristics.

"A deductive criminal profile is a set of offender characteristics that are reasoned from the convergence of physical and behavioural-evidence patterns within a crime or series of related crimes," (Turvey, 1999, p. 28). "The general purpose of the deductive method of criminal profiling is to use behavioural-evidence analysis to assist in an investigation, at any phase, in moving from that universal set of suspect characteristics to a more discrete set of suspect characteristics," (Turvey, 1999, p. 34).

Specific course objectives include identifying the relationship between physical evidence, behavioral evidence, and criminal profiling; inspecting crime scene photographs; recognizing offender behavior; performing wound pattern analysis; and matching behaviors of serial rape or homicide to a crime scene. Students perform a case assessment and write a threshold assessment of the cold homicide case.

CREATING THE COLLABORATIVE EFFORT

Having students research to solve a real cold homicide engages them in answering the legendary question: "Who did it?" However, obtaining support from a law enforcement agency to provide the case can prove challenging. The author, having been a police officer for seven years, returned to his previous law enforcement agency with a proposal to provide a case for examination by students that would lead to 80 new examinations of the evidence. Obtaining "buy-in" from a police department is not without objections.

Law enforcement agencies are not proud; there are unsolved cases remaining in their files. The vision by the public of an incompetent or inefficient agency may be quickly denoted from the term "unsolved case." The idea of providing case materials, including crime scene photographs and autopsy photographs of a sexual homicide, made the trek for approval similar to navigating a minefield. The Chief of Police envisioned possible overzealous students contacting witnesses, subjects, a suspect, or the family of the victim.

Providing the students with over 150 pages of incident reports unnerved the Chief of Police. The answer was that students receive redacted copies. The reports were redacted so students could only use the first names of witnesses, subjects, or suspects. All addresses, phone numbers, and other personal identifying information were also withheld from the files. Only the first names of previous investigators were included in order to protect their identities.

The victim in the case selected for review has living relatives, so obtaining consent from the family was required. The cold case detective contacted the oldest sibling of the victim and explained the course objectives, methodology, and use of the cold case. The sibling, representing the family, provided an enthusiastic approval. The family opined that as long as 80 students per year were examining the case, the victim would not be forgotten and the case may one day be solved.

Motivating the assigned cold case detective was surprisingly easy; he wants to solve the case. The cold case detective inherited the case in 1990 after it remained unsolved since the homicide discovery in 1984. Having numerous active homicide cases to work, the detective understood having unbiased and motivated students examine this case might uncover something missed over the years.

COURSE DEVELOPMENT: LINKING ACADEMIC LEARNING OUTCOMES TO A COLD HOMICIDE CASE

The bridge to a path of learning was built by Brent Turvey's seminal work, *Criminal Profiling: An Introduction to Behavioral Evidence Analysis* (1999) which became the backbone for the development of the course. Turvey's work, now in the third edition, centers on the deductive criminal profiling methodology and "fact finding in a criminal investigation for the purpose of servicing justice" (Turvey, 1999, p. 28). Turvey's work offers an in-depth examination of other areas important to cold case analysis including case assessment—determining and organizing case information; equivocal forensic analysis—a critical examination of all assumptions, conclusions, and evidence; victimology—a detailed history of the victim; crime scene characteristics—the location, type, and indicators; behavioral motivational typologies—the needs and behavioral classifications of criminals and understanding modus operandi—method of operation; and signature—distinctive evidence that reveals and satisfies emotional or psychological needs of offenders.

Upon initial examination of case materials, a student's perplexity motivates his or her interest. Students become aware of the problem they face: someone is dead and the offender is unknown. As students conduct the analysis and clarification of offender and victim actions, different solutions or working hypotheses begin to develop. As the class and learning proceeds, the verification or rejection of each student's chosen solution develops (Hodnett). This reflects the critical thinking learning curve.

The cold case examined is the 1984 sexual homicide of Jane Doe (pseudonym), a flight attendant for a regional airline. The body was discovered in the master bedroom of her condominium after supervisors, where the victim worked, became concerned about her absence. The victim had suffered from battery and died of ligature strangulation.

Students are provided over 150 pages of incident reports ranging from the first responding officer to the currently assigned cold case detective. Students receive a compact disc with over 150 photographs: half of the photos are from the crime scene and half of the photos are from the autopsy of the victim. Additional documentation provided includes a copy of the victim's activity calendar, the victim's job application packet, the law enforcement agency sketch of a possible suspect, various newspaper articles, medical examiner's report, death certificate, two distinct and different profiles developed by Federal Bureau of Investigation agents, the Violent Criminal Apprehension Program analysis report (prepared 6 years after the death of the victim), and supplemental reports from law enforcement and the security team from the victim's employer.

"Real world" investigative frustration begins when students learn that all physical evidence in the case was lost when the supporting crime laboratory moved from one location to another. Students soon realize that large problems are settled by solving the smaller problems of which they are composed.

The logical flow of using the cold homicide case as a learning tool was to introduce the student to the case as he or she studies the chapters of the text. When Turvey (1999) explains case assessment in the chapter: Using a Cold Homicide Case to Teach Criminal

Profiling the students begin their assessment of the cold homicide case. The realization that they (the students) must become "all-knowing" in a real unsolved homicide case can be overwhelming; yet, the methodical process of read, discuss, learn, apply, and write soon evolves. When Turvey's chapter on crime reconstruction is reviewed, the students reconstruct the actions, as they believe they occurred, between the victim and offender. When the chapter on wound pattern analysis is reviewed, autopsy photographs of the victim are discussed in small group–learning circles to determine how and why the wound occurred to the victim. When the chapter on understanding offender signature is discussed, crime scene photographs are reviewed to determine the actions between the victim and offender. Students apply the knowledge gained in each text chapter to the case and provide their analysis and direction to the cold case detective in the form of a threshold assessment. "A threshold assessment is an investigative document that reviews the initial physical evidence of behavior, victimology, and crime-scene characteristics for a particular case, or series of related cases, in order to provide immediate direction. It makes assessments of what is currently understood to be fact," (Turvey, 1999, p. 42).

To ensure a wide lens for case examination and understanding, another case is concurrently reviewed. A solved homicide of three children is utilized to indicate other challenges that develop in solving crimes. The case, popularly known as the *West Memphis Three*, is scrutinized in two documentary films that reveal the evidence or lack thereof, subjects, suspects, the convicted criminals, and law enforcement officials. Lecture in the scientific method, solvability factors, and erotophonophilia supplements the case examination. The case was selected because it highlights the lack of a detailed forensic analysis, wound pattern analysis, and basic investigator practices such as securing the evidence and therefore scrutinizes the errors to avoid in homicide cases.

OUTCOMES

The prospect of making inferences about a crime and defense of the analysis alerts students that one day they may have to testify about their investigative analysis in front of a judge and jury. Thus, the task of writing a threshold assessment can be stressful for the student. This is the opportunity for the student to analyze the case and to provide investigative direction to the assigned cold case detective. Essentially the student reveals his or her critical thinking skills by linking concepts to case analysis, inferences, and problems or puzzles encountered. Students do not form absolute conclusions, but they do offer opinions based on critical analysis. This threshold assessment includes an equivocal forensic analysis of the case, a detailed victimology, a 24-h timeline of the victim's actions before death, an analysis of the crime scene characteristics, inferences on offender characteristics, and an investigative strategy.

Unexpected opportunities for learning often occur during an investigation. Several years ago students were discussing the case in the student center during an informal small learning circle. Being careful not to use the victim's name and referring to her only as "our victim," the group members were overheard by an older student. The student approached the group and asked if the victim the group was discussing was Jane Doe, an airline flight attendant murdered in 1984. "Yes!" was the immediate answer of the group. The student informed the group that she worked with the victim at the airline for many years. The student, desiring to help solve the murder mystery, agreed to be a part of the class investigation and to be interviewed by the professor and/or the cold case detective. The interview notes are used as a part of the case analysis today.

Linking the cold homicide case to other similar transaction murders has also produced learning opportunities. One student remembered a murder of an airline flight attendant in her hometown of Romulus, Michigan. She contacted an old high school friend employed by the Romulus Police Department. The student soon made a victimology link from the Romulus murder to the cold case. Another student later made a victimology link to another murdered flight attendant in Austin, Texas.

CONCLUSION

The application of the ACETS framework of teaching required an innovative approach to instruct *Criminal Profiling and Analysis.* The analysis of a "cold case" became the experiential learning path to success in teaching criminal profiling. The technique has proven to be a sterling motivational method that taps into the multimedia exploitation of criminal investigative curiosity.

Students learn much more than investigative technique, challenges, and mistakes because they soon realize that the most common errors for failing to see the real problem are those noted by Hodnett (1955) including emotional bias, prejudice, fear, conceit, and preconceived notions or partisan loyalty.

The course, *Criminal Profiling and Analysis*, has been amazingly successful. Each spring, 80 new learners dive into the murky waters of criminal profiling and analysis. Is this cold case solved? No. Is the case solvable? Yes. But students realize that with all the physical evidence lost, solvability depends on the confession of the offender…if that person is still alive. The critical and ongoing analysis provided by students may lead to a clue that was overlooked and assists in determining investigative direction. The local police department receives a copy of each threshold assessment written and has over 500 assessments. Learning through the mistakes of the original investigators and the elucidation of how homicides should be examined, neophyte investigators leave the university a little more prepared for the challenging task of homicide investigations.

The challenges of using a cold homicide case to teach criminal profiling and analysis are numerous. Creating support from a law enforcement agency, peers, and administrators may appear daunting; however, the excitement created by students' learning is well worth the effort to overcome critical challenges. The link between writing and critical thinking is established as a crucial step in preparing criminal investigators. Misconceptions about crime solving verses a 40-minute television show are clarified. The process and purpose of critical thinking provide the students the meaning when a real problem is in the scale of justice.

REFERENCES

Abaidoo, S., Wachniak, L., 2007. Re-thinking graduate education: an imperative for a changing world. The International Journal of Learning 14 (5).

Bean, J.C., 2001. Engaging Ideas: The Professor's Guide to Integrating Writing, Critical Thinking, and Active Learning in the Classroom. John Wiley and Sons, Hoboken, NJ.

Hodnett, E., 1955. The Art of Problem Solving: How to Improve Your Methods. Harper and Row, New York.

Rossmo, K., 1999. Geographic Profiling. CRC Press, Boca Raton, FL.

Turvey, B.E., 1999. Criminal Profiling: An Introduction to Behavioral Evidence Analysis. Academic Press, San Diego, CA.

CHAPTER

Mexico: Criminal Profiling and Forensic Criminology

6

M.A. Esparza
Institute of Forensic Investigation and Criminal Profiling, Juarez, Mexico

B.E. Turvey
Forensic Solutions LLC, Sitka, Alaska, United States; Institute of Forensic Investigation and Criminal Profiling, Juarez, Mexico

CHAPTER OUTLINE

It's difficult to remember the specifics about crimes that happened when I was a child. And today, good records just aren't available. One case sticks out, however, but all I know for sure is the victim's name. She was a little girl named Nubia. I also remember that her murder brought the City of Juarez together.

Not a lot of people remember Nubia's case. It was one of the first times that the Mexican authorities in Juarez realized, and publicly acknowledged, that they needed help. Something more than just routine police work was necessary to figure out what had happened - and what type of person would commit such a terrible crime. The case was solved when a relative was arrested and later confessed to killing the little girl. The community was in shock. And things were not going to get better.

Manuel Esparza, retired Prosecutor and former Director of the Attorney General's Women's Homicide Unit

Juarez is a city of more than 1.5 million people on the border of Mexico, sharing its skyline with the Texas City of El Paso. And its people have been through a great deal over the past 25 years. Much of this is related to the drug trade, the influx of guns from the United States, the related killings, and the related public corruption; but not all.

Behavioral Evidence Analysis. http://dx.doi.org/10.1016/B978-0-12-800607-8.00006-9

Juarez, Mexico is on the border across from El Paso, Texas. The cities share commerce, language, and even people. But while El Paso thrives, Juarez has long suffered economically—for a variety of reasons.

In the 1990s, Juarez became known for an unnerving increase in its number of female murder victims. Many of those killed were young, and many of them were also sexually assaulted in some fashion. As the volume of female homicides increased, so did the media coverage. Eventually the public became aware, and the police were forced to admit that there were multiple serial killers operating in the city. Predators at work are beyond those already associated with human trafficking or the drug cartels.

The public had a hard time coming to grips with it; the police were not trained to handle it; and the cases continue to pile up even to this day—too many of them going cold without a proper investigation.

Accepting this harsh reality led the primary author of this work (Esparza) to seek out new investigative tools, and to bring modern forensic thinking, into Mexico. That effort began in the late 1990s, while he was working for the Attorney General's (AG) office in the state of Chihuahua. His work in that regard continues to this day, through caseworks and involvement in higher education. This chapter will explore an abbreviated history of that effort as it relates to criminal profiling.

THE "DECADE OF LOST WOMEN"

In criminological circles, Juarez is understood to suffer one of the highest rates of female-related serial murder in the world. It is a place where young women simply disappear, and where their cases have not always received the attention necessary to learn the truth, let alone identify those responsible. In particular, the 1990s created what one author referred to as "The Decade of Lost Women." She offers a useful and critical history relevant to this painful designation (Paniaga, 2010).

...as industry brought prosperity to dust-laden Ciudad Juárez, an increase of murders related to drugs and human trafficking occurred. However, in 1993 the pattern of murders changed drastically—there was a dramatic upswing in the number of young women found slain throughout the outskirts of the city. These women had been "raped, mutilated, crushed, strangled...some were even dismembered or burned alive," (Washington). Their skin was marred with bite marks & they had deep slashes across their breasts. Bound with their own shoelaces & partially clothed, their shoes would be placed almost sentimentally beside their corpses—occasionally just bones, after desert jackals picked the flesh from their fragile bodies. "If you want to rape and kill a woman, there is no better place to do it than in Juárez," said Esther Chávez Cano, founder of 8 de Marzo, *in an opinion column during the fall of 1995.* 8 de Marzo *is a Juárez-based woman's advocacy organization dedicated to rousing awareness of not only the killings, but also the corrupted officials (Rodriguez 72).*

*Alma Mireya Chavirria Farel's name rings in infamy just across the southern border. Her tiny, brutalized body was discovered on January 23, 1993, making her the first documented victim of the Juárez serial murders (Newton 4). Alma was a 5-year-old child, found in the Campestre Virreyes district of Ciudad Juárez with deep slashes across her chest, evidence of sexual assault, and severe strangulation. The people of Juárez were so aghast at the brutality of the crime, that the authorities were essentially forced to acknowledge the presence of a "predator"—*El Depredador Psicópata, *who would become known as the "Juárez Ripper" (Newton 4). Twenty-one other women and young girls would meet their end that year, including a young woman who was set on fire and left to die (Valdez Appendix 2).*

In 1994, police claimed there were eight murders in Ciudad Juárez with a similar modus operandi, and advised local women not to venture out alone (Newton 5). Just as had occurred during the previous year, an unidentified victim's smoldering body was discovered semi-nude and strangled. Her shoes were placed "tenderly" beside her charred remains. The families of the murdered women were incredulous that authorities were not taking the cases more seriously. When a woman would go missing, the police would simply ask the family to come back in forty-eight hours and fill out paperwork...the investigations largely "concluded" at that point and the families were left to their own devices. Even after Chihuahuan officials were warned by their very own criminologist, Oscar Maynez Grijalva, that a group *of serial killers were responsible for the slayings, police refused to take direct action. Between March and September of 1995, nineteen young women were found brutally raped and mutilated; consequently, the police department and Federal prosecutors came under extreme scrutiny from local families for "brushing off" the cases as the numbers continued to rise (Newton 5). Oscar Maynez Grijalva, who previously warned of the danger in ignoring the "signs" of serial murder, began to notice a distinct pattern in the bodies of the victims he was examining—in eight of the nineteen cases prior to September of that year, the victims' right breast was removed and their left nipple bitten off (Newton 3). In the remaining months of 1995, another twenty-nine women would be murdered, bringing the grand total to forty-eight. As of July 2009, eight of the victims from 1995 remain buried in graves simply marked "Unknown," ("2009-Femicides...").*

As pressure mounted, authorities made a stunning announcement in December 1995, sending a ripple of relief, although short-lived, through the communities of Juárez. Officials boasted to news outlets that an Egyptian-born scientist had been arrested for the murder of young Elizabeth Castro whose body had been found on August 19 alongside the Casas Grande Highway, just outside of Lote Bravo. They would subsequently name him as the "intellectual author" of at least thirteen other slayings (Rodriguez 43). Seventeen-year-old Elizabeth Castro's autopsy revealed wounds congruent with the previous victims' injuries, as well as ligature marks from being bound with her own shoelaces. Sharif was charged with Castro's rape and murder—authorities would announce that the female slayings were "solved." Unfortunately, less than a month after "solving" the case of the Juárez Ripper, a stunning statistic was released to the media: in the past eleven months, 520 people had vanished from Juárez and an alarming, yet "important percentage of them [were] female adolescents," (Newton 4).

By April 1, 1996 at least fourteen more girls were slain, including a fifteen year-old, again with identical injuries to those of the previous victims: a right severed breast, bitten-off left nipple, and a broken neck which had literally been yanked apart (Valdez 11). Police scrambled for answers as the people of Juárez grew impatient and they soon opted for placing additional blame on Abdel Latif Sharif, implying that he was the "mastermind" behind the murders. Curiously enough, a young woman identified merely as "Blanca" came forward to accuse Sharif of raping her in his home and threatening to "dispose of her corpse in Lote Bravo," (Rodriguez 44). Unfortunately for Sharif, Lote Bravo was the "dumping ground" for multiple mutilated women in 1995, forty-five to be precise (Valdez 11). "Blanca" stood before the media and claimed to have been held hostage in Sharif's home for at least three days. She described being raped repeatedly and later escaping through an upstairs window to contact authorities from a neighbor's home (Rodriguez 13). Her story was never verified. Evidence against the Egyptian-national continued to mount when another woman, Erika Fierro, told police she'd introduced Sharif to nine of her girlfriends and hadn't seen or heard from any them in months. Fierro would go on to claim that Sharif later told her he'd murdered them all, burying their bodies at Lote Bravo and threatening to do the same to Fierro if she disclosed his secret…(Valdez 215). Both women would "disappear" within a few weeks of releasing their statements, never to be heard from again.

…On April 8, 1996, Rosario Garcia Leal was found raped, strangled, and mutilated in a vacant lot. During the course of the investigation, Hector Olivares Villalba, a member of the local street gang Los Rebeldes, *was brought in for questioning. Within a few short days Olivares Villalba would confess to the young woman's murder. Only later would it come to light that rather than endure the "torture" that ran rampant through the police forces, Olivares would confess and claim that six other Rebels helped him "dispose of her body," (Rodriguez 60). His confession would ultimately land* El Diablo, *the leader of the Rebels, in Mexican Federal prison. Sergio Armendariz Diaz,* El Diablo, *would remain in police custody for almost nine years, "awaiting trial" (Rodriguez 122). Eventually, two of the eight Rebels were released and in January of 2005, the six who remained were convicted of the*

> *murders of eight women who had been found in 1995 (Newton 8). The authorities also informed the media that Armendariz, whose bite impressions matched those found on multiple victims, plotted and conspired with the imprisoned Sharif to make it seem as if the Juárez Ripper was still at large (Rodriguez 123).*
>
> *With the help of local women's groups, poor practices in evidence collection were exposed and the Mexican government writhed under the pressure, blaming anyone they could. As the brutal killings continued, news outlets found their hands "tied" when they covered the murders and they were ultimately forced to report lower body counts for fear of retaliation by high-ranking members of the Mexican government (Newton 8). The media published each story with a statement declaring that an "unspecified number of women were still missing," affectionately naming them* Los Desaparecidos, *or the disappeared (Newton 8–9). Officials, thoroughly defensive, refused to allow the families of the* Desaparecidos *into view the bodies and identify their loved ones… Meanwhile the "corpses continued to pile up like cordwood," (Rodriguez 69).*
>
> …
>
> *The young victims of Juárez were all petite and pretty with full lips and flowing dark hair. Their abductions, some during broad daylight, continued to frighten the people of Mexico's leading industrial city. As investigators and families began to search for more distinct patterns in the disappearances, they noticed additional similarities between the cases…A sizable amount of the victims had been abducted from the* lines of workers *waiting to gain entrance to the* maquiladoras. *So was the case with a 22-year-old mother of two, Silvia Guadalupe Díaz (Rodriguez 69). She left her home on March 7, 1997, never to be heard from again. While her young husband tried desperately to involve authorities in her disappearance, four young girls were found raped, beaten, and strangled in the following ten days. Then, on March 29th, an agricultural worker discovered Díaz's body just beside the Juárez Porvenir Highway in the Lote Bravo area. An autopsy would reveal that she had been dumped just a few hours after disappearing from her new job at a local* maquiladora *(Rodriguez 70). Unlike past months, the women found in March of 1997 all were found to have multiple puncture wounds across their necks; subsequently, investigators would begin to notice the already horrendous violence, escalate.*

The public and media attention related to these tragedies, and others like them, created a demand that something be done by the authorities. At the very least, there needed to be an official acknowledgment that these crimes were occurring on a regular basis, and that special investigative attention was required. The formation of the Woman's Homicide Unit was formed in response.

THE WOMAN'S HOMICIDE UNIT

The year 1998 was a landmark for the AG's office in Juarez. In February, it officially formed the Special Prosecution Unit for Women's Homicide. This was a first, and the initiative was full of promise. That same year, the primary author was made the lead investigator of that unit.[a]

Manuel Esparza, c. 1998, working as the lead investigator for the Attorney General's Women's Homicide Unit.

As mentioned in the prior section, an Egyptian citizen by the name of Abdel Latiff Shariff Shariff had been arrested on charges of kidnapping and rape. Investigators were able to verify that the victim had indeed escaped by jumping naked out of a second story window from Shariff's home. She had then sought help from police officers nearby.

Abdel Latiff Shariff Shariff

[a]From 1998 to 1999, Manuel Esparza (the primary author of this chapter) served as lead investigator for the Chihuahua Attorney General's Special Prosecution Unit on Sexual and Gender Crimes (the Women's Homicide Unit). Subsequently, he worked as a criminal prosecutor and then returned again to head the same unit from 2002 to 2004.

The Chihuahua State AG's Office handed the primary author the task of investigating Shariff Shariff's violent past. That investigation revealed criminal records from New Jersey, Florida, and Texas. This required travel to Gainesville, Florida, where Capt. Sadie Darnell of the Gainesville Police Department provided a copy of the Violent Criminal Apprehension Program (ViCAP) form what they had sent to the FBI. This form contained more information about Shariff. She also provided the name of a former FBI profiler who might be willing to help the Chihuahua AG's office with their unsolved cases: Robert Ressler.

CRIMINAL PROFILING COMES TO MEXICO: WORKING WITH THE FEDERAL BUREAU OF INVESTIGATION

The FBI is synonymous with criminal profiling worldwide. Films and television have made this true, whether it is or not. In Juarez, at the AG's office, the prevailing wisdom echoed what happened on TV—FBI profilers solve cases. Consequently, when given the chance to get the help of an FBI profiler, especially one of Robert Ressler's standing, it was welcomed.

This was the first time that any form of criminal profiling would be introduced to the often political realm that is law enforcement investigation in México. It was no small undertaking. The primary author of this work reached out to Mr. Ressler and struck up a relationship. Eventually, Mr. Ressler traveled to Chihuahua on three separate occasions, during one of which he was afforded the opportunity to interview Mr. Shariff Shariff in prison.

Manuel Esparza and retired FBI Profiler Robert Ressler, 1998.

The most important part of Mr. Ressler's visits to Juarez was not his interview of Mr. Shariff Shariff, which bore no real fruit or insight. Rather, it was the training seminars that Mr. Ressler gave. None of the investigators that he spoke to had any idea what was happening in Juarez; they had never seen anything like these kinds of killings before. Any insight was better than nothing. Just being given the ability to understand and identify the different motives that are possible in a homicide, was a breakthrough.

It should be noted at this point that Mr. Ressler was brought to Juarez with the expectation that he would provide training to Mexican investigators and teach them how to develop criminal profiles. In essence, Mexican investigators and officials were led to believe that they would be trained to become criminal profilers. However, it was soon learned from Mr. Ressler that FBI profilers do not actually teach profiling. They teach a few techniques and typologies to outsiders. That is it. Mr. Ressler explained that investigators needed to turn to Quantico for any real assistance with profiling the Juarez cases. Disappointment in the FBI profiling unit, and Mr. Ressler, was not small.

Our very own "Criminal Minds" moment came when a group of FBI profilers led by Gerard Downes (then of the Child Abduction and Serial Killer Unit) came to Juarez to assist on our cases. They knew we had been working with the ViCAP forms and also brought the new ones with them (they were longer and much more intensive). Mexican investigators learned about timelines and translated the new ViCAP form into Spanish for them. They were also able to obtain access to Law Enforcement Online and ViCAP Online (proprietary law enforcement databases).

However, Mexican investigators also soon learned about the problem of human error with respect to the use of law enforcement databases. The Female Homicide Unit in Juarez got a call from Quantico explaining that there were multiple cases involving explosives, and that we should link those and start working on them as a possible independent series. Here is the problem: explosives were not used in any of the Juarez case submitted to ViCAP. An investigator had made mistakes on several forms and the wrong information had been entered into the database.

The FBI's involvement, and Mr. Ressler's work, in Juarez was widely covered by the American press at the time, culminating in the following media account from Holguin (1999).

> *In an unprecedented collaboration, a team of FBI profilers is in El Paso, Texas, to help Mexican authorities investigate the unsolved killings of scores of women in neighboring Ciudad Juarez - a string of deaths that has plagued the border city for six years…*
>
> *"We asked for their help because we recognize that they are very good at what they do," said Juan Carmona, a spokesman for the Chihuahua State Police.*
>
> *Since August 1993, Juarez officials have been baffled by the growing number of girls and young women whose bodies have been left in the desert along the city's outskirts. Mexican authorities estimate the number of unsolved cases to be somewhere around 80. Victims' advocacy groups have pegged it closer to 150.*

At least 30 victims were raped and strangled in a pattern that has fueled theories of serial killers and gang-initiation rituals. Despite several arrests and one conviction, the killings continued. The most recent victim was found last month in a soccer field near the local penitentiary.

"The government says they're doing the best they can, but meanwhile there are more bodies and more bodies," said Vicky Caraveo, who founded the advocacy group Mujeres por Juarez (Women for Juarez.)

More than 600 people attended a street rally in Juarez two weeks ago to draw more attention to the deaths. Meanwhile, frustrated Mexican authorities in this city of 2 million say they are hampered by an overwhelming caseload and a lack of resources.

The FBI's involvement came after months of meetings between Chihuahua state officials and bureau officials in El Paso, said FBI spokesman Al Cruz. While FBI profilers have worked regularly with Canadian authorities, the bureau's assistance in the Juarez killings is the first time federal agents have been asked to assist in Mexico…

The FBI's involvement in Juarez is only the latest chapter in the bizarre saga. Since last year, Chihuahua authorities have worked with Robert Ressler, a retired FBI agent who helped pioneer criminal-profiling techniques and who has twice traveled to Juarez, training police officers and helping organize the investigation.

Chihuahua Attorney General Arturo Chavez said his office sought Ressler's help because "we have no one with that kind of experience" in Mexico…

During his first visit to Juarez last year, Ressler said he sorted through dozens of unsolved homicides. He arrived at 76 victims who seemed to fit a pattern: Most were women between the ages of 17–24, most had been raped and strangled in a similar fashion, more than a dozen had disappeared going to or from work at the city's assembly plants.

"I determined that it wasn't one person who was responsible," said Ressler, who heads the Virginia-based Forensic Behavioral Services, a private company that focuses on profiling, investigations and law-enforcement consultation. "It's not one serial killer. I think it's probably two or three." Earlier this month, Egyptian national Sharif Halil Sharif was convicted of killing one woman after his arrest in 1996. "But he's not the end of it," Ressler said.

This account is, at best, a mild exaggeration. The FBI's involvement in casework was much more limited than the article implies. Moreover, it suggests more training and access than was actually afforded in either direction.

In the end, Mexican investigators were given the basics of FBI profiling, but they had insufficient time and experience to put together an actual criminal profile. Worse still, there was interference from the newly appointed AG at that time. She decided that outside help was neither necessary nor appropriate, and subsequently cut the training budget and any existing ties with respect to assistance from the United States. Her work was, by any account, disastrous to the cause of just investigations and prosecutions, to say nothing of undermining US–Mexico law enforcement relations.

STRUCTURAL CHANGES IN THE ATTORNEY GENERAL'S OFFICE

By September of 1998, there had been structural changes made to investigative practices within the state AG's office in Chihuahua. In order to achieve and maintain control of criminal case investigation, and to preserve their integrity for trial, prosecutors would be present at crime scenes. In essence, they were charged with directing the investigation and ably guiding it to the courtroom.

As a consequence, prosecutors were given the training and authority to manage crime scenes and criminal investigations. This afforded them the capability to identify evidence, along with the capacity to understand that there might be behavioral links between physical evidence, the victim's body, and its placement or disposition. By virtue of this structural change, crime scene investigation efforts in Juarez were taken to the next level.

This new structure was quickly put to the test.

In late 1998, there were more cases of murdered women. One of these victims had been raped, beaten, and then dumped and left to die. She woke up and got help at a home nearby. She eventually identified her attacker as Jesus Manuel Guardado Marquez, aka "El Tolteca." He was subsequently arrested, and several other arrests of additional suspects followed until the entire gang, mostly comprised of bus drivers, was in prison. The new structure proved effective in the successful investigation and prosecution of this case, the details of which are reported in Lubbock (2005):

> *A federal judge Thursday sentenced five leaders of a criminal gang jailed since 1999 to 113 years in prison each for their roles in the killings of eight women in this border city infamous for hundreds of slayings against female victims over more than 11 years.*
>
> *Five key leaders of a criminal gang known as "Los Toltecas" were sentenced to consecutive sentences ranging from 24 to 40 years behind bars for premeditated homicide, aggravated rape and criminal association in the slayings of eight women, whose bodies were discovered around a local ranch in 1999.*
>
> *The gang members, originally arrested after those bodies were discovered, all received a total of 113 years behind bars, though Mexican law prohibits any inmate from serving more than 40 years. Los Toltecas is a gang named for its alleged leader, Jesus Manuel Guardado, alias "El Tolteca," who was among those sentenced Thursday.*

> *According to government tallies, more than 300 women have been killed in this city across from El Paso, Texas, since 1993, though human rights leaders say the number is much higher. At least 100 of those slayings appear to fit a pattern where a young, slender woman was sexually abused, strangled, and dumped in the desert outside Juarez.*
>
> *Many of those cases remain unsolved and only two men have been convicted for nine of the slayings. The first person found guilty was Abdel Latif Sharif, a U.S. resident and Egyptian-born chemist, who was sentenced to 20 years in prison.*
>
> *Women continued to turn up dead in and around Juarez after Sharif's 1996 arrest, and police alleged he paid members of another gang known as "Los Rebeldes" to continue raping and killing other women to deflect suspicion away from himself.*
>
> *Victor Garcia Uribe, a bus driver, was sentenced to 50 years in October for the deaths of eight women whose bodies were found in a vacant lot in Ciudad Juarez in 2001.*

This article repeats a generic profile that has become all too familiar in the media: the victims are slender, dark brown hair, brown eyes, poor, and most of them worked in the factories of Juarez. The investigators in the Women's Homicide Unit decided to make a real effort to determine an exact profile of each victim. No hype, no media influence, just the verifiable facts. The goal was to find out what, if anything, these victims actually had in common. In other words, what distinguished them from the characteristics just mentioned—characteristics so general that they can be applied to many of the women that live in Juarez.

The investigators in the Women's Homicide Unit developed a victimological questionnaire to accomplish this goal. It was intended to reveal, in no small measure, what these victims had in common, what they did not, and their lifestyle and risks. It was an introductory effort to develop very basic forensic victimology.

BEHAVIORAL EVIDENCE ANALYSIS: PROFILER CERTIFICATION IN MEXICO

Between 2004 and 2011 the drug violence in Juarez increased, and then peaked. Homicides were at an all time high, people were scared, and law enforcement investigators across the board were working under nearly the worst conditions imaginable.

However, in 2012, the Chihuahua AG's office started the Behavioral Analysis Unit in the Juarez Crime Lab. It was designed in compliance with the model suggested by the International Association of Forensic Criminologists (IAFC) in Turvey (2011). Members of the AG's Behavioral Analysis Unit from the Juarez Crime Lab, all of whom were crime scene investigators, were subsequently taught the basics of behavioral evidence analysis.

In March 2013, the AG's Behavioral Analysis Unit from Juarez was introduced to the public. The members of that unit traveled to a professional forensic conference held in Mexico City. Subsequently, they received direct training from Brent Turvey of the IAFC, at which point he became their committed mentor and advocate. They were also awarded certificates of training from the Mexican Academy of Forensic Investigators (AMIF, now AIIF).

Members of the Attorney General's Behavioral Analysis Unit from the Juarez Crime Lab stand with Brent Turvey (third from the left), holding their training certificates, in Mexico City—March, 2013.

In December 2014, after working closely with the IAFC and AMIF, a 40-hour certification course was held in El Paso, Texas. This training was organized to accommodate the needs of the Behavioral Analysis Unit from Juarez, but to ensure that the training occurred in the United States. Consequently, multiple professionals from Mexico and the United States were certified in El Paso that week, in compliance with the IAFC's Criminal Profiling Professional Certification Act.

After successfully completing all requirements, including completion of a board exam and an oral presentation of case findings, the following unit members achieved a Diplomate status in the IAFC's Academy of Behavioral Profiling (ABP): Ana Lorena Gonzalez, Ricardo Soto, Cristina Covarrubias, Francisco Javier Garcia, Alfredo Velazco, and Julio Cesar Rojas. At the same time, the first independent criminal profilers in Mexico were also certified. This included Jesus Vaca, Mitzy Matamoros, Maria Patricia Lopez, and the primary author of this chapter (Manuel Esparza).

Criminal profilers from the United States and Mexico, including those from the Attorney General's Behavioral Analysis Unit from the Juarez Crime Lab, achieve IAFC Certification in El Paso, Texas—December, 2014.

Unfortunately, not all of the Mexican profilers would keep their IAFC profiler certification. Consistent failure to maintain the IAFC/ABP ethics guidelines forced Alfredo Velazco to resign from both the IAFC and AMIF. By doing so, he also voluntarily resigned his certification. This is an important lesson, because the only thing that gives any certification value is the possibility that it can expire or be revoked for cause.

It should be mentioned at this point that, as the result of involvement in multiple courses, conferences, and events over the past three years, Brent Turvey has become the IAFC/ABP Ambassador for Criminal Profiling in Mexico. He currently works hand in hand with International Academy of Forensic Investigators (AIIF, formerly AMIF), delivering the message that ethics and professionalism are a must for professional forensic practice in Mexico's newly adopted adversarial court system.

CRIMINAL PROFILING AS EVIDENCE IN MEXICAN COURTS

Behavioral evidence analysis (BEA), the method of criminal profiling developed and taught by the IAFC, was first introduced to the Mexican Criminal Court System 2015. This historic event occurred when Cristina Covarrubias, Diplomate of the Academy of Behavioral Profiling (D-ABP[b]), took the stand in what has been called *The Trial of the Century* in Juarez, and in Mexican women's homicide cases. She gave evidence regarding BEA-related findings in a case where six men were being tried for their involvement in the murders of 11 women whose bodies were found in a desert area known as the "Navajo Stream." As described in Paterson (2015):

[b] D-ABP means Diplomate of the Academy of Behavioral Profiling. The ABP Board is the certifying body within the IAFC, and this designation indicates that the professional with this credential has certified in the area of criminal profiling.

...in an event dubbed "The Trial of the Year" by the local press. In a judicial proceeding also termed "historic" by some, the Chihuahua State Prosecutor (FGE) is seeking the maximum sentence of life in prison plus an additional 261 years for crimes allegedly committed by Vital, Edgar Jesus Regalado Villa, Cesar Felix Romero, Esparza, Jose Gerardo Puentes Alba, Jesus Hernandez Martinez, and Jose Antonio Contreras Terrazas. The men were arrested in 2013.

Recovered from the rural Juarez Valley, the victims included Maria Guadalupe Perez Montes, Lizbeth Aviles Garcia, Perla Ivonne Aguirre Gonzalez, Idaly Juache Laguna, Beatriz Alejandra Hernandez Trejo, Jessica Leticia Pena Garcia, Deisy Ramirez Munoz, Andrea Guerrero Venzor, Monica Liliana Delgado Castillo, Jessica Terrazas Ortega, and Jazmin Salazar Ponce.

The remains of several other women were also recovered from the Navajo Arroyo, the same spot where most of the 11 victims at the center of the Juarez trial were likewise found, but until now the defendants have not been charged with the additional slayings.

Essentially, the six men are accused of participating in an organized criminal network that utilized false employment fronts to lure and kidnap young women between 2009 and 2011, work their captives as prostitutes and drug vendors and then finally kill them.

Prosecutors have implicated the transnational Aztecas gang in the murder spree. Originating in the Texas prison system and later spreading to El Paso, Juarez and New Mexico, the underworld group was a principal protagonist in the so-called narco war in Juarez between 2008 and 2012 that left more than 12,000 people slain.

In addition to the gender nature of the Juarez Valley crimes, the systematic abduction and slaughter of young women smacked of class femicide since the victims hailed from low-income families desperate for work. No female victims of wealthy or upper middle class families were found in the hidden graveyards of the Juarez Valley.

After a three month trial, Víctor Manuel Vital Anguiano, Edgar Jesus Regalado Villa, César Félix Romero Esparza, Jesus Hernández Martinez, and José Antonio Contreras Terrazas were sentenced to 697 years and 6 months in prison for the murders of Jessica Terrazas Ortega, Daisy Ramirez Muñoz, Jazmin Salazar Ponce, Lizbeth Aviles Garcia, Monica Liliana Castillo, Beatriz Alejandra Hernández Trejo, Maria Guadalupe Pérez Montes, Perla Ivonne Aguirre González, Andrea Guerrero Venzor, Idaly Jauche Laguna, and Jessica Leticia Peña Garcia. This successful prosecution was achieved in no small part because of the competence of the evidence given by Ms. Covarrubias. Her work continues to be a credit to her unit in Juarez.

CRIMINAL PROFILING IN MEXICO: THE FUTURE

Efforts to certify criminal profilers in Mexico are planned well into the foreseeable future, through the cooperative efforts of the IAFC, the AIIF, and their partner institutions around the world.

For example, in September of 2015, a group of professionals educated in criminal profiling through the National University of Forensic Investigation (UNIF) participated in a 40-hour certification course with IAFC/ABP held in Juarez. Hector Hawley (Head of Crime Scene Investigation from the Women's Homicide Unit) and Aurelio Coronado Mares (a private forensic psychologist, and an expert in government torture) were also certified during this session.

Other professionals are slated to be certified through the year-long diplomate program in criminal profiling being taught by the Institute of Forensic Investigation and Criminal Profiling based in Juarez. This program will conclude in February 2016, when another group of profilers will be certified in Guadalajara.

These efforts are just the beginning. And they are vital to professionalizing not just criminal profiling, but criminal investigation across Mexico. This is in order to be compliant with the new adversarial system. Not only to ensure that those who testify in court have the appropriate expertise, but also so that the courts can arrive at just verdicts while maintaining the confidence of the public they are meant to serve.

REFERENCES

Holguin, R., March 16, 1999. FBI Helping Mexico Investigate Serial Killings in Border City. Gannett News Service.

Lubbock, January 07, 2005. Five gang members sentenced for killing women in Juarez. Lubbock-Avalanche Journal. http://lubbockonline.com/stories/010705/upd_075-4377.shtml.

Paniagua, D., March 20, 2010. Ciudad Juárez: an untold history of femicide and violence in the western hemisphere. Reno Conservative Examiner. http://www.examiner.com/article/ciudad-ju-rez-an-untold-history-of-femicide-and-violence-the-western-hemisphere.

Paterson, K., May 1, 2015. Will Juarez murder "Trial of the Year" bring justice to families? Counterpunch. http://www.counterpunch.org/2015/05/01/will-juarez-murder-trial-of-the-year-bring-justice-to-families/.

Turvey, B., 2011. Criminal Profiling: An Introduction to Behavioral Evidence Analysis, fourth ed. Elsevier Science, London.

CHAPTER

Portugal: Applications of Behavioral Evidence Analysis and Forensic Criminology

7

T. Konvalina-Simas

Psychotherapist at Sala de Estar, Azores, Portugal; Investigative Consultant at FSI Brazil

CHAPTER OUTLINE

Behavioral Evidence Analysis. http://dx.doi.org/10.1016/B978-0-12-800607-8.00007-0

"Man is a powerful weapon, loaded by genetics, aimed by the mind and fired by society"

Jason Gideon is a fictional character who depicts an FBI profiler in the TV show Criminal Minds.

More often than not, our views of the world are shaped by our expectations, desires, fantasies, and goals; and this is especially true when teaching. In the classroom, getting everyone on board and on the same page can be an epic achievement that will carry on throughout the time one is lecturing. Having said this, it is quite wonderful to stand witness to little buds of curiosity that appear and blossom into real interest and sometimes even hard work, so, setting out, one must find a harmonious and balanced place for one's own expectations as a lecturer.

It is equally important to keep in mind, that not everyone will perform the same, or care the same, but it has been our experience that focusing on the small percentage of students who might, one day, become profilers and investigators, and the responsibility that we play in making sure that they have their basic knowledge in place, is the most motivating way forward.

In the classroom, with young undergraduates, one is dealing with potential future investigators, researchers, consultants, advisors, who are still at a very early stage of a very long road. Learning about such a compelling, yet intricate, form of behavioral analysis as criminal profiling, demands a rather vast array of specific theoretical knowledge and quite a lot of self-awareness and good sense, which pose several teaching obstacles and challenges and will rely greatly on students' aptitude for personal development.

Most students arrive very excited, starry eyed, and with a head full of *Criminal Minds* episodes which they master fully and project completely onto what they expect to learn. This is the first of many challenges such as deconstructing criminal profiling and putting it into perspective, going over the basic cornerstones of human behavior, conveying the importance of a multidisciplinary perspective, teamwork and social, as well as, personal awareness. No small task, especially when not everyone is motivated equally or equally inclined to such subjects. It is also possible that many will arrive in the classroom and not know what the subject is about, even though they are criminology students.

It is usually a fair assumption that the cornerstones of psychology, sociology, and biology, in general, and how they relate to criminal profiling, in particular, are virtually unknown and that this should be the place to begin with undergraduates. Students at the undergraduate level arrive from very different academic backgrounds, and we have found that it is important to review many of the basics, especially psychological speaking. At times students may have heard some of the material before in other classes but, because in our class it is being repeated in an applied context, it comes across as less random and less abstract. Students mostly seem to find the topics engaging as they are learning fundamental information about abnormal human behavior which they should have as criminologists, whether or not they become profilers.

In regards to the major theoretical approach to teaching this subject, no matter how much one pulls and picks and tugs on the nature versus nurture debate, the fact remains that it is exceptionally seldom for human behavior to result strictly from one or the other.

Human beings as a species do not exist in a biopsychosocial neutral environment, existential zero gravity as it were. We are all the result of powerful forces that are at play, even before we are born. Throw in some all too important psychological traits and human mechanisms such as rationality and motivation, and anything could happen, anything at all. Nonetheless, our take on teaching criminal profiling tends to be quite psychological, also because we are aware that criminology students are bombarded with classic sociological theory, particularly regarding deviance and deviant behavior.

Our overall aim in teaching criminal profiling and behavioral evidence analysis (BEA) is to get the basic underlying psychological knowledge settled and to develop reflective and analytical skills which include concepts and terminology utilized by profilers. Our time span is short for the task, as we only have 15 classes (each 3h long) spread over a 4months period. As a result we have developed a small, yet comprehensive, teaching program, which we find has fulfilled its purpose in informing the students of the principles and scope of criminal profiling, in general, and BEA, in particular, its methods and terminology. As we see it, our approach equips students with the necessary tools to pursue the subject more thoroughly in the future and build on a solid foundation.

We also make it clear to our students that we are not training them to become profilers at the end of the semester, but rather aiming at giving them skills to make informed career choices and, eventually, professional and ethical decisions in the future.

Although we chose not to go in to great theoretical depth on most items, some are more extensive than others. Our main criterion was to list, albeit synthetically, all the key ideas that we hope our students will take away with them. We also included footnotes which may serve as clues to deepen the readers understanding and research (if using this text to prepare classes).

The directionality of our program is from broad theoretical knowledge to specific knowledge, to practical knowledge. This is intentional because we are trying to mirror the profiling process in itself, and the transition that occurs from using nomothetic knowledge to using ideographic knowledge.

Another significant choice was giving BEA special attention. It is our belief that one cannot be honest about teaching criminal profiling and not do so. If one were to approach the subject of criminal profiling from an unspecific, generalist, standpoint, this would do the students a huge disfavor. In reality BEA works. It is comprised of a comprehensive and effective methodology based on the scientific method and this, in our view, puts it at the forefront when laying the foundation for serious investigation and litigation. Also its ideo-deductive approach to evidence analysis is clear and objective, leaving little room for error and/or fraud. Because we strongly believe in applying offender profiling in an ethical and serious manner, we have to endorse the theoretical model which better suits this goal in our teaching, and that is BEA without a doubt.

Having said this, we take in to consideration that students will find different uses for the knowledge we give them throughout the semester, and that often they come from diverse cultures and their take on offender profiling will reflect their own views and preferences. To this end we ensure that they have a sound knowledge of all other nomothetic models of profiling, and we provide an eclectic reading list which includes authors from different methodological standpoints as well as different continents and professional backgrounds.

Throughout this chapter we will review our teaching program by summarizing the contents and ideas that we relay to the students. In doing this we hope that the reader will understand how each component contributes to achieving our goals.

It is also our concern that the reader finds our organization of contents logical and helpful in educating others. Our teaching program is structured as follows:

1. Definition and Scope of Criminal Profiling
   a. Applied Criminology
   b. Critical thinking and deductive versus Inductive reasoning
   c. Ideographic versus Nomothetic methodologies
   d. Types of profiling according to method
   e. Generating a profile

   - f. Critical questions in an investigation
   - g. Primary and secondary variables
   - h. Problems with profiling
2. Brief Etiology of Human Behavior
   - a. Personality Theory and Traits
   - b. Major Theories in Behavior Etiology
      - i. Evolutionary Theory
      - ii. Psychodynamic Theory
      - iii. Behaviorist Theory
      - iv. Social Cognitive Theory
      - v. Humanistic Theory
      - vi. Biopsychosocial Theory
         1. Genetic Bases for Personality
         2. Neurobiology
   - c. Human Motivation
      - i. Intrinsic and Extrinsic Motivation
   - d. Theories and Models of Human Motivation
      - i. Drive Theory
      - ii. Maslow's Hierarchy of Needs Theory
      - iii. The Behavioral–Motivational Typology Model
      - iv. Motivational Model for Sexual Homicide
3. The Behavioral Evidence Analysis Model
   - a. The Principles of Behavioral Evidence Analysis (BEA)
   - b. BEA Aims and Contexts
   - c. The Components of BEA
4. Other Important Analytical Parameters in Criminal Profiling
   - a. Crime Reconstruction
   - b. Forensic Victimology
   - c. Modus Operandi
   - d. Signature
   - e. Case Linkage Analysis
5. Applying Learned Concepts
   - a. Group project, presentation structure, and research
6. Reading List

CRIMINAL PROFILING AND OFFENDER PROFILING: DEFINITION AND SCOPE

AIMS

- Locate criminal profiling as a form of applied criminology in forensic criminology;
- Understand the definition of criminal/offender profiling;
- Understanding the applicability and limitations of offender profiling;

- Distinguish between deductive reasoning and inductive reasoning, and know importance of critical thinking in the profiling process;
- Comprehend to different methodological perspectives, and to distinguish between nomothetic profiles and ideographic profiles;
- Know that there are several approaches to criminal profiling stemming from methodology;
- Comprehend the main components of a psychosocial profile;
- Know the critical questions in an investigation.

APPLIED CRIMINOLOGY

"Forensic Criminology is the scientific study of crime and criminals for the purpose of addressing investigative and legal questions" (Turvey and Petherick, 2010). Forensic criminology is a *behavioral* and *forensic* science, characterized by an integration of material from many subdisciplines including forensic science, criminal investigation, criminalistics, forensic psychology, victimology, crime reconstruction, criminal event analysis, criminal profiling, practical experience, and more. Criminal profiling is essentially an investigative methodology in applied criminology, more specifically, forensic criminology, which can also be used more broadly, eg, in crime analysis[a] and criminal proceedings.

A forensic criminologist has a particular examination to perform or set of questions to answer. As a forensic expert, he conducts a rigorous, skeptical analysis of the entire body of evidence that objectivity demands, comprehensively comparing case facts and circumstances to each piece of evidence. A rigorous analysis of evidence, both by itself, and also, in context to other evidence, can reinforce or refute its relationship to a case, or it may be inconclusive. It may reveal indicia of guilt, or expose inaccuracies and inconsistencies. Objectivity is key to this work and demands a dispassionate, skeptical approach toward a case or set of circumstances.

Offender profiling, also known as criminal profiling, is a form of behavioral analysis which is used as an investigative tool intended to help investigators profile the characteristics of unknown criminal subjects to either create a suspect pool or narrow one down. Criminal profiling is essentially an investigative methodology in applied criminology, more specifically, forensic criminology, which can also be used more broadly, eg, in crime analysis[a] and criminal proceedings. The primary goals of criminal profiling include the reduction of the viable suspect pool in a criminal investigation, assistance in the linkage of potentially related crimes, assessment of the potential for escalation of criminal behavior, provision of relevant leads and strategies, and keeping the investigation on track.

The criminal profiler is not preoccupied with specifically naming the offender. Criminal profilers are advisors, while detectives and investigators solve cases; also,

---

[a] **Crime analysis** is the process of using systematic analytical methods to acquire timely and pertinent information on crime patterns and trend correlations.

not all cases are appropriate for profiling. Appropriate cases for profiling will meet certain criteria including (1) a violent crime has been committed, (2) there is forensic evidence available to be reviewed, (3) the offender has displayed some form of psychopathology during the commission of the crime, and (4) all other investigative leads have been extinguished.

Offender profiling is mostly utilized with crimes such as rape, murder, kidnapping, terrorism, and serial crime. Also profiling may be used to guide interviews and redirect investigations which have come to dead ends. Holmes and Holmes (1996) outlined the three main goals of criminal profiling:

- The first is to provide law enforcement with a social and psychological assessment of the offender;
- The second goal is to provide law enforcement with a "psychological evaluation of belongings found in the possession of the offender";
- The third goal is to give suggestions and strategies for the interviewing process

CRITICAL THINKING AND DEDUCTIVE VERSUS INDUCTIVE REASONING

Critical thinking[b] is a way of deciding whether a claim is always true, sometimes true, partly true, or false; and it is at the core of the profiling behavioral analysis. Criminal profiling also relies on deductive and inductive thought as part of its essential analytical process. Deductive reasoning or "top-down" logic is the process of reasoning from one or more general statements (premises) to reach a logically certain conclusion. Deductive reasoning links premises with conclusions. If all premises are true, the terms are clear, and the rules of deductive logic are followed, then the conclusion reached is *necessarily true*.

Inductive reasoning or "bottom-up" logic is a kind of reasoning that constructs or evaluates general propositions that are derived from specific examples. Inductive reasoning contrasts with deductive reasoning, in which specific examples are derived from general propositions. Inductive reasoning is probabilistic; it only states that, given the premises, the conclusion is *probable*.

Deductive reasoning (top-down logic) contrasts with inductive reasoning (bottom-up logic) in the following way: In deductive reasoning, a conclusion is reached from general statements, but in inductive reasoning the conclusion is reached from specific examples.

IDIOGRAPHIC VERSUS NOMOTHETIC METHODOLOGY

"In terms of the study of crime and criminals, or any subject for that matter, there are two major approaches to research and subsequent knowledge building. The first is

[b] Critical thinking can be traced in the West to ancient Greece with its Socratic method and in the East to ancient India with the Buddhist kalama sutta and abhidharma literature.

nomothetic knowledge, referring to the study of the abstract: examining groups and universal laws. The second is *idiographic* knowledge, referring to the study of the concrete: examining individuals and their actual qualities. Idiographic study concentrates on specific cases and the unique traits or functioning of individuals" (Turvey and Petherick, 2010).

When it comes to profiling, there are essentially two types of profiles, inductive or deductive in essence, which reflect the profilers' theoretical affiliation, both types are necessary and useful:

1. **Nomothetic Profiles** are developed by studying groups of offenders which do not represent actual offenders in existence, but represent different degrees of theory and possibility, so essentially they are abstract in nature. This approach to profiling is useful and necessary, especially in constructing knowledge regarding different types/categories of crime and groups of criminals.
2. **Idiographic Profiles** are characteristics developed by studying or examining one single case, therefore the ascertained traits represent an offender that exists in reality, this is to say that idiographic profiles are concrete. Profilers who use this method also integrate nomothetic knowledge; however, they use it in theory generation rather than to present deductive conclusions.

TYPES OF PROFILING ACCORDING TO METHOD

In discussing and learning about different approaches to profiling, it is important to locate them within the nomothetic/idiographic paradigm. Ainsworth (2001) identified four main approaches to offender profiling which are nomothetic in nature.

1. **Geographic Profiling:** Kim Rossmo[c] is generally associated with the development of this type of investigation which relies on concepts from environmental criminology. Geographic information system software provides the capability to superimpose different types of data on a map. Geoprofiling/GP is an investigative strategy that uses the locations of a series of crimes to determine the most probable area of the offender's residence. GP does not "solve" crimes; it does prioritize suspects and their likely addresses, thereby allowing investigators to focus their resources and strategies, eg, saturation patrol, surveillance, and neighborhood canvasses, where they have the highest probability of being successful.
2. **Investigative Psychology:** This approach focuses on the study of psychological aspects of offender behavior which might be relevant to criminal and civil investigations. Although more than a few psychologists and psychiatrists are involved in profiling, investigative psychology is associated with the work of Englishman

---

[c] **Kim Rossmo** is a Canadian criminologist specializing in geographic profiling. He joined the Vancouver Police Department as a civilian employee in 1978 and became a sworn officer in 1980. In 1987 he received a Master's degree in criminology from Simon Fraser University and in 1995 became the first police officer in Canada to obtain a doctorate in criminology. Rossmos' dissertation research resulted in a new criminal investigative methodology called geographic profiling.

David Canter[d], an environmental psychologist, who was asked by New Scotland Yard in 1985 to integrate investigative and psychological concepts into his work. The model he developed rests on five factors:

a. **Interpersonal Coherence** assumes that offenders will deal with their victims in a manner similar to the way they treat people in their day-to-day lives.
b. **The Significance of Time and Place** may provide analysts with clues about the offender's mobility and even his residence.
c. **Criminal Characteristics** are used by researchers and analysts to place offenders into broad categories, from which subcategories can be selected or developed.
d. **Criminal Career** is an assessment as to whether the offender may have engaged in criminal activity before, and what type of activity it most likely was.
e. **Forensic Awareness** draws in part from Step 4 above, criminal career. It is an assessment of the scene and evidence to determine if the offender has any special knowledge of evidence gathering procedures used by the police.

3. **Criminal Investigative Analysis:** An investigative typological approach that aims to identify the offender's personality and behavioral traits by categorizing the crimes committed and the MO; developed by the FBI Behavioral Analysis Unit[e]. The FBI's terms of organized and disorganized are often used in the literature to describe crime scene behaviors and correlating characteristics of an offender when creating a profile. Based on the dichotomized FBI

---

[d] **David Canter** is a British psychologist. He began his career as an architectural psychologist studying the interactions between people and buildings, publishing and providing consultancy on the designs of offices, schools, prisons, housing, and other building forms as well as exploring how people made sense of the large-scale environment, notably cities. He set up the Journal of Environmental Psychology in 1980. His work in architecture led to studies of human reactions in fires and other emergencies. He pioneered Investigative Psychology in Britain. He helped police in 1985 on the Railway Rapist case. He was the Professor of Psychology at the University of Surrey for 10 years, where he developed Investigative Psychology described in detail in *Investigative Psychology: Offender Profiling and the Analysis of Criminal Action* and a course curriculum. He was Director of the Center For Investigative Psychology which is based at the University of Liverpool. Since 2009 he has been at the University of Huddersfield. At Liverpool University, Canter developed the MSc program in Investigative Psychology which he directed until 2007. He no longer directs this program which has consequently changed to reflect the wider arena of Forensic Psychology and a more balanced view of the field. He is the founder and director of the International Academy for Investigative Psychology, a professional academy for researchers seeking to apply social science to investigative and legal processes.

[e] The **Behavioral Analysis Unit (BAU)** is a component of the United States Federal Bureau of Investigation's National Centre for the Analysis of Violent Crime (NCAVC) that uses behavioral sciences to assist in criminal investigations. The mission of the NCAVC and the BAUs is to provide behavioral based investigative and/or operational support by applying case experience, research, and training to complex and time-sensitive crimes, typically involving acts or threats of violence. Four BAUs constitute the NCAVC: Behavioral Analysis Unit-1 (Counterterrorism/Threat Assessment), Behavioral Analysis Unit-2 (Crimes Against Adults), Behavioral Analysis Unit-3 (Crimes Against Children), and the Violent Criminal Apprehension Program (VICAP). The NCAVC in turn forms part of the FBI's Critical Incident Response Group. The headquarters for the BAU is located in Quantico, Virginia (USA).

typology organized offender versus disorganized offender. While many offenders may fit neatly into the organized or disorganized pattern, some crimes may reflect aspects of both patterns for a number of reasons, and these offenders are referred to as mixed organized–disorganized. The organized/disorganized offender dichotomy has a strong crime scene focus which is the foundation for its methodology:

a. **Stage 1:** Collecting inputs, which are essential for accurate profiling (forensic and others);
b. **Stage 2:** Using decision process models, which is the process of organizing and arranging the inputs into meaning patterns;
c. **Stage 3:** Crime assessment, which is the reconstruction of the sequence of events and the behavior of both the victim and the offender;
d. **Stage 4:** Developing the criminal profile, a process which addresses the type of person who committed the crime and that individual's behavioral organization in relation to the crime, including background information, physical characteristics, habits, beliefs, values, preoffense behavior leading to the crime, and postoffense behavior;
e. **Stage 5:** Continuing the ongoing investigation by those assigned to it, with the profiler making adjustments in the profile if fresh information warrants it and being available to discuss the case with those assigned on an as-needed basis;
f. **Stage 6:** Following the apprehension, reviewing the agreement between the outcome and the various stages of the profiling process are examined.

4. **Diagnostic Evaluations:** A clinical approach to offender profiling in which, mainly, clinical and/or forensic psychiatry and psychology are used to determine whether the offender is suffering from mental illness of various psychological abnormalities and provide opinions about offenders, crime scenes, or victims.

At the other end of the methodological spectrum are idiographic methodologies, very specifically BEA developed by Brent Turvey, which we look at more closely in module 3.

1. **BEA**: It is "an ideo-deductive method of crime scene analysis and criminal profiling that requires the examination and interpretation of individual case–related physical evidence, victimology, and crime scene characteristics" (Turvey, 2009).

GENERATING A PROFILE

A profile is a document that is used in conjunction with a thorough investigation to help identify the offender responsible for a violent crime, through identifying his personal traits. This is not to say that a profile cannot be a very effective tool in an investigation because in many cases an accurate profile is able to refocus an investigation and create a fresh perspective and additional leads. Profiling when done accurately is also an effective tool of narrowing down the list of possible suspects, which will also further focus the investigation.

Generating a profile entails six procedural steps:

1. A thorough analysis of the type/nature of the criminal act is made, and it is then compared to the types of people who have committed similar crimes in the past;
2. In-depth analysis of the crime scene is made;
3. Studying forensic reports;
4. Researching the victim's background and activities looking for possible motive and connections;
5. Analysis of possible factors for motivation;
6. Assembly and triangulation of all pertinent and related information to derive offender traits.

A common misconception about profiling is that investigators will be able to walk to the front door of the unknown offender when a profile is created. This is a belief that most students hold and which is very hard to correct. In fact, the author usually begins lectures by showing a Criminal Minds episode ("101-Profiling," season 7) and then deconstructing it as an example of what profiling is *not*.

CRITICAL QUESTIONS IN AN INVESTIGATION

There are four critical questions to ask and answer when creating a profile, which reflect the investigative process, and therefore there are several steps to be taken, which need to be completed in a methodical manner to arrive at the end point. The end point in this case being the creation of a profile of an unknown offender based upon forensic and behavioral evidence.

1. **What?** What happened at the scene of a violent crime? The answer to this question will come by reconstructing the crime and is done so with a thorough observation of all the evidence and the creation of a timeline of events leading up to the crime, if available during the crime, and after the crime. One of the first steps to be taken during this aspect of developing a profile is studying the victimology of the victim of the violent crime. Along with the physical evidence, the profiler will be noting all the behavioral evidence present at the crime scene.
2. **Why?** Why did the particular crime happen? Why to this particular victim? Why at this time? Why at this location? Why in this manner? Answering these questions will help determine the motivation for the crime and provide important clues regarding the suspect pool.
3. **How?** Reconstructing how the crime was committed is very important and can provide valuable information about the offender by recognizing the level of offender sophistication, level of risk taken by the offender, and actions that took place that were not necessary to complete the intended outcome of the crime, like, for example, signature behavior.
4. **Who?** The answer to this will be based upon a thorough examination of all the evidence and depending on whether one has used a nomothetic approach or an ideo-deductive approach, the profile generated will be either probable or concrete.

Although a profile will not name an offender, it can assist in identifying the *type* of offender one is looking for. Below is a list of variables that may become part of a criminal profile:

Offender Profile	
Age: Sex : Race: Marital Status:	Other information:
Education History:	
Military History:	
Employment History (including current profession):	
Criminal History (previous offenses, incarcerations, and level of experience):	
Mental Health History:	
General Physical Appearance:	
Intelligence:	
Lifestyle:	
Social Ability and Adjustment:	
Residence (proximity to crime scene and general appearance):	
Type of Vehicle:	
Motivation:	

PRIMARY AND SECONDARY VARIABLES

Primary variables are aspects of the offender that can be interpreted directly from the crime scene behavior or from forensic evidence left at the scene. An example of a primary variable might include evidence of bondage and torture performed upon the victim, which would lead a profiler to state that the offender is a sexual sadist.

Secondary variables are those that can be inferred to also describe the unknown offender based upon the criminal behaviors of similar offenders. Taking from the previous example of the sexual sadist, a secondary variable would state that this type of offender would collect sadistic pornography.

PROBLEMS WITH PROFILING

- Most problems surrounding the use of criminal profiling can be traced back to profilers themselves and other investigators, mainly due to their theoretical orientation as far as methodology is concerned and their personal ethical inclinations. For example, incorrect information from profiling can lead to *false positives* or *false negatives* and investigators, eager to find a suspect, may quickly apprehend someone who *appears* to fit the profile and ignore or stop investigating other leads.
- Psychologists have also questioned the basic presumption that one can draw conclusions about a person from a single instance of behavior under such special circumstances. In this respect, the notion that particular configurations of demographic features can be predicted from assessing particular configurations of specific behaviors occurring in short-term, highly traumatic situations seems an overly ambitious and unlikely possibility. Indeed it is a valid argument that such inferential processes should be reliably verified, and treated with great caution in investigations.
- Despite its successes, profiling as a field is not without criticisms. Included in these criticisms are untrained or inadequately trained profilers, promising too much and delivering too little, relying on inadequate or dated databases, overstating the meaning of physical evidence. Popular use of the term *criminal profiler* has led to the proliferation of many self-described profilers offering their purported expert opinions which is inappropriate and could jeopardize an entire investigation.

Nonetheless, when offender profiling is put to use within serious and ethical boundaries by competent professionals, it can be an excellent investigative aid.

BRIEF ETIOLOGY OF HUMAN BEHAVIOR

AIMS

- Understand the construct "personality" and its impact on behavior;
- Understand that personality can be construed according to different conceptual outlooks;
- The study of personality and human behavior has a broad and varied history in psychology with an abundance of theoretical traditions

- Understand that behavior tends to be the direct result of complex biological, psychological, and social forces at play together and/or separately;
- Comprehend that motivation is an inner drive to behave or act in a certain manner;
- Understand that all humans are motivated and driven by similar and distinct goals at the same time;
- Comprehend the complexity of offender motivations through crime scene behavior analysis;
- Comprehend that extreme homicidal behavior can result from powerful interacting psychosocial factors.

Psychologists use theories as a tool for understanding, studying, and predicting human behavior. Thus, psychological theories are one tool we can use to explain how personality development may deviate off the path toward healthy development and instead steer toward unhealthy development or personality disorder.

Students often ask, "Why are there so many theories? Wouldn't just one theory suffice?" In order to respond to this legitimate concern, we find it useful to draw an analogy between the mind and a house: in order to build a house, an architect constructs a set of plans, and there are many different architectural styles, from modern to traditional, but each architectural plan is still a design for the essential framework of a house. The same is true of theories of personality. There are many different "styles" or ways to describe the mind's architecture, but the end result is the same: each of these different theories describe the framework of the mind, according to different "styles" (different branches of psychology or different schools of thought). Nonetheless, each design, regardless of its particular "style," is still describing the essential framework of the mind.

A discussion of the theories of personality can become quite difficult and confusing because we must necessarily dive into highly abstract concepts about the architecture of the human mind, and the structures which form the framework of that architecture. Despite these difficulties, we feel this discussion is worthwhile because these theories represent the foundation upon which the various principles of criminal profiling rest.

PERSONALITY THEORY AND TRAITS

"Personality" is a dynamic and organized set of characteristics possessed by a person that uniquely influences his or her cognitions, emotions, motivations, and behaviors in various situations. The word "personality" originates from the Latin *persona*, which means mask. In the theater of the ancient Latin-speaking world, the mask was not used as a plot device to *disguise* the identity of a character, but instead was a convention employed to represent or *typify* that character.

Personality also refers to the pattern of thoughts, feelings, social adjustments, and behaviors consistently exhibited over time that strongly influences one's expectations, self-perceptions, values, and attitudes. It also predicts human reactions to other people, problems, and stress. There is still no universal consensus on the definition of "personality" in psychology. Allport[f] (1937) described two major ways to study personality: the nomothetic and the idiographic. *Nomothetic psychology* seeks general laws that can be applied to many different people, such as the principle of self-actualization or the trait of extraversion. *Idiographic psychology* is an attempt to understand the unique aspects of a particular individual.

According to the *Diagnostic and Statistical Manual* of the American Psychiatric Association, personality traits are "enduring patterns of perceiving, relating to, and thinking about the environment and oneself that are exhibited in a wide range of social and personal contexts." Theorists generally assume that

1. traits are relatively stable over time;
2. traits differ among individuals;
3. traits influence behavior.

Personality traits are consistently used in order to help define people as a whole. Traits are relatively constant; they do not usually change. Traits are also bipolar; they vary along a continuum between one extreme and the other (eg, friendly vs unfriendly).

The most common models of traits incorporate three to five broad dimensions or factors. All trait theories incorporate at least two dimensions, extraversion, and neuroticism, which historically featured in Hippocrates' humoral theory[g]

Allport (1937) delineated different kinds of traits, which he also called dispositions. *Central traits* are basic to an individual's personality, while *secondary traits* are more peripheral. *Common traits* are those recognized within a culture, and thus may vary from culture to culture. *Cardinal traits* are those by which an individual may be strongly recognized.

---

[f] **Gordon Allport** was an American psychologist. Allport was one of the first psychologists to focus on the study of the personality, and is often referred to as one of the founding figures of personality psychology. He contributed to the formation of Values Scales and rejected both a psychoanalytic approach to personality, which he thought often went too deep, and a behavioral approach, which he thought often did not go deep enough. He emphasized the uniqueness of each individual, and the importance of the present context, as opposed to past history, for understanding the personality. His seminal book was *Personality: A Psychological Interpretation* (1937).

[g] **Humourism** is a now discredited (but historically important) theory of the makeup and workings of the human body, adopted by Ancient Greek and Roman physicians and philosophers, positing that an excess or deficiency of any of four distinct bodily fluids in a person directly influences their temperament and health. From Hippocrates onward, the humoral theory was adopted by Greek, Roman, and Islamic physicians, and became the most commonly held view of the human body among European physicians until the advent of modern medical research in the 19th century. The four humors of Hippocratic medicine are black bile, yellow bile, phlegm, and blood, and each corresponds to one of the traditional four temperaments: sanguine (pleasure-seeking and sociable), choleric (ambitious and leader-like), melancholic (analytical and thoughtful), and phlegmatic (relaxed and quiet).

Raymond Cattell's[h] research propagated a two-tiered personality structure with 16 "primary factors" (16 Personality Factors) and five "secondary factors." In Cattell's lengthy career, he had written 50 books, 500 journals, and 30 different types of standardized tests. For Cattell, personality itself was defined in terms of behavioral prediction. He defined personality as *that which permits a prediction of what a person will do in a given situation.*

Hans Eysenck[i] believed just three traits—extraversion, neuroticism, and psychoticism—were sufficient to describe human personality.

Lewis Goldberg[j] proposed a five-dimension personality model, nicknamed the "Big Five":

1. *Openness to Experience*: The tendency to be imaginative, independent, and interested in variety versus practical, conforming, and interested in routine.
2. *Conscientiousness*: The tendency to be organized, careful, and disciplined versus disorganized, careless, and impulsive.
3. *Extraversion*: The tendency to be sociable, fun-loving, and affectionate versus retiring, somber, and reserved.
4. *Agreeableness*: The tendency to be softhearted, trusting, and helpful versus ruthless, suspicious, and uncooperative.
5. *Neuroticism*: The tendency to be calm, secure, and self-satisfied versus anxious, insecure, and self-pitying

The Big Five contain important dimensions of personality; however, some personality researchers argue that this list of major traits is not exhaustive. Some support has been found for two additional factors: excellent/ordinary and evil/decent.

Trait models have been criticized as being purely descriptive and offering little explanation of the underlying causes of personality. Eysenck's theory, however, proposes biological mechanisms as driving traits and modern behavior genetics[k]

---

[h] **Raymond Cattell** was a British and American psychologist, known for his exploration of many areas in psychology which included the basic dimensions of personality and temperament, a range of cognitive abilities, the dynamic dimensions of motivation and emotion, the clinical dimensions of personality, patterns of group and social behavior, applications of personality research to psychotherapy and learning theory, predictors of creativity and achievement, and many scientific research methods for exploring and measuring these areas. Cattell was famously productive throughout his 92 years, authoring, and coauthoring over 50 books and 500 articles, and over 30 standardized tests. His theory of personality factors and the instrument used to measure them are known respectively as the 16 Personality Factor Model and the 16PF Questionnaire.

[i] **Hans Eysenck** was a German psychologist, who spent his professional career in Great Britain. He is best remembered for his work on intelligence and personality, though he worked in a wide range of areas. At the time of his death, Eysenck was the living psychologist most frequently cited in science journals.

[j] **Lewis R. Goldberg** is an American personality psychologist and a professor emeritus at the University of Oregon who is closely associated with the Big Five taxonomy of personality (he coined the term "Big Five").

[k] **Behavioral genetics** is the field of study that examines the role of genetics in animal (including human) behavior. Often associated with the "nature versus nurture" debate, behavioral genetics is highly interdisciplinary, involving contributions from biology, genetics, epigenetics, ethology, psychology, and statistics. Behavioral geneticists study the inheritance of behavioral traits. In humans, this information is often gathered through the use of the twin study or adoption study.

researchers have shown a clear genetic substrate to them. Another potential weakness of trait theories is that they may lead some people to accept oversimplified classifications—or worse, offer advice—based on a superficial analysis of personality. Finally, trait models often underestimate the effect of specific situations on people's behavior, for example, the influence and importance of context.

Many researchers and psychologists do not explicitly identify themselves with a certain perspective and instead take an eclectic approach. Research in this area is empirically driven (such as dimensional models), based on multivariate statistics (such as factor analysis) or emphasizes theory development (such as that of the psychodynamic theory). In psychological education and training, the study of the nature of personality and its psychological development is usually reviewed as a prerequisite to courses in abnormal psychology or clinical psychology and other applied behavioral sciences.

MAJOR THEORIES IN BEHAVIOR ETIOLOGY

Evolutionary theory

Charles Darwin is the founder of the theory of the evolution of the species. The evolutionary approach to personality psychology is based on this theory. This theory examines how individual personality differences are based on natural selection. Through natural selection, organisms change over time through adaptation and selection. Traits are developed and certain genes come into expression based on an organism's environment, and how these traits aid in an organism's survival and reproduction.

The theory of evolution has wide ranging implications on personality psychology. Personality viewed through the lens of evolutionary psychology places a great deal of emphasis on specific traits that are most likely to aid in survival and reproduction, such as conscientiousness, sociability, emotional stability, and dominance. The social aspects of personality can be seen through an evolutionary perspective. Specific character traits develop and are selected for because they play an important and complex role in the social hierarchy of organisms. Such characteristics of this social hierarchy include the sharing of important resources, family and mating interactions, and the harm or help organisms can bestow upon one another.

Psychodynamic theory

Psychoanalytic theories explain human behavior in terms of the interaction of various components of personality. Sigmund Freud was the founder of this school of thought. Freud drew on the physics of his day (thermodynamics) to coin the term psychodynamics. Based on the idea of converting heat into mechanical energy, he proposed psychic energy could be converted into behavior. Freud's theory places central importance on dynamic, unconscious psychological conflicts.

Freud divided human personality into three significant components: the id, ego, and superego. The id acts according to the *pleasure principle*, demanding immediate gratification of its needs regardless of external environment; the ego then must emerge in order to realistically meet the wishes and demands of the id in accordance with the outside world, adhering to the *reality principle*. Finally, the superego (conscience) inculcates moral judgment and societal rules upon the ego, thus forcing the demands of the id to be met not only realistically but morally. The superego is the last function of the personality to develop and is the embodiment of parental/social ideals established during childhood. According to Freud, personality is based on the dynamic interactions of these three components.

Behaviorist theory

Behaviorists explain personality in terms of the effects external stimuli have on behavior. The approaches used to analyze the behavioral aspect of personality are known as behavioral theories or learning–conditioning theories. These approaches were a radical shift away from Freudian philosophy. One of the major tenets of this concentration of personality psychology is a strong emphasis on scientific thinking and experimentation. This school of thought was developed by B. F. Skinner[l] who put forth a model which emphasized the mutual interaction of the person or "the organism" with its environment. According to this theory, people's behavior is formed by processes such as operant conditioning. Skinner put forward a "three-term contingency model" which helped promote analysis of behavior based on the "Stimulus–Response–Consequence Model" in which the critical question is "Under which circumstances or antecedent 'stimuli' does the organism engage in a particular behavior or 'response,' which in turn produces a particular 'consequence'?"

Social cognitive theory

In cognitive theory, behavior is explained as guided by cognitions (eg, expectations) about the world, especially those about other people. Cognitive theories of personality emphasize cognitive processes, such as thinking and judging. Albert Bandura[m], a social learning theorist suggested the forces of memory and emotions worked in conjunction with environmental influences.

---

[l] **Burrhus Skinner** was an American psychologist, behaviorist, author, inventor, and social philosopher. Skinner invented the operant conditioning chamber, also known as the Skinner Box. He was a firm believer of the idea that human free will was actually an illusion, and any human action was the result of the consequences of that same action. If the consequences were bad, there was a high chance that the action would not be repeated; however if the consequences were good, the actions that lead to it would be reinforced. He called this the principle of reinforcement.

[m] **Albert Bandura** is a Canadian psychologist who is the David Starr Jordan Professor Emeritus of Social Science in Psychology at Stanford University. For almost six decades, he has been responsible for contributions to many fields of psychology, including social cognitive theory, therapy, and personality psychology, and was also influential in the transition between behaviorism and cognitive psychology. He is known as the originator of social learning theory and the theory of self-efficacy, and is also responsible for the influential 1961 Bobo doll experiment.

Humanistic theory

Humanistic psychology emphasizes that people have free will and that this plays an active role in determining how they behave. Accordingly, humanistic psychology focuses on subjective experiences as opposed to forced, definitive factors that determine behavior.

Biopsychosocial theory

While we do not yet know the precise combination of factors that merge in some fashion to yield a (disordered) personality, we do know that both nature and nurture play an interactive role. While each theory differs in terms of the weight or importance it assigns to the biological, psychological, or social factors influencing personality development, they each acknowledge there is an important interrelationship between nature (biology and temperament) and nurture (the environment and life experiences) in the formation of personality. As such, all of these theories can be described as exemplars of the more generalized "Bio–Psycho–Social" model of human behavior, an integrative model which today is widely prevalent within social sciences.

Biology plays a very important role in the development of personality. The study of the biological level in personality psychology focuses primarily on identifying the role of genetic determinants, and how they mold individual personalities. Some of the earliest thinking about possible biological bases of personality grew out of the case of Phineas Gage[n].

GENETIC BASES OF PERSONALITY

Ever since the Human Genome Project[o] allowed for a much more in-depth understanding of genetics, there has been an ongoing controversy involving heritability, personality traits, and environmental versus genetic influence on personality.

The human genome is known to play a role in the development of personality. Previously, genetic personality studies focused on specific genes correlating to specific personality traits. Today's view of the gene-personality relationship focuses primarily on the activation and expression of genes related to personality. Genes provide numerous options for varying cells to be expressed; however, the environment determines which of these are activated. DNA-environment interactions are important in the development of personality because this relationship determines what part of the DNA code is actually made into proteins that will become part of an individual. It has been noted that while different choices are made available by the genome, in the end, the environment is the ultimate determinant of what becomes

[n] **Phineas P. Gage** was an American railroad construction foreman remembered for his improbable eleven-year survival following an accident in which a large iron rod was driven completely through his head. Much of his brain's left frontal lobe was destroyed, reportedly affecting his personality and behavior so profoundly.

[o] The **Human Genome Project** is an international scientific research project with a primary goal of determining the sequence of chemical base pairs which make up DNA, and of identifying and mapping the approximately 20,000–25,000 genes of the human genome from both a physical and functional standpoint.

activated. Small changes in DNA in individuals are what lead to the uniqueness of every person as well as differences in looks, abilities, brain functioning, and all the factors that culminate to develop a cohesive personality.

Cattell and Eysenck both proposed that genetics have a strong influence on personality. A large part of the evidence collected linking genetics and the environment to personality have come from twin studies. This "twin method" compares levels of similarity in personality using genetically identical twins. One of the first of these twin studies measured 800 pairs of twins, studied numerous personality traits, and determined that identical twins are most similar in their general abilities. Personality similarities were found to be less related for self-concepts, goals, and interests.

NEUROBIOLOGY

Rapid technological advancement, particularly within the field of neuroimaging, has allowed us to study the brain as never before. These new imaging technologies have enabled researchers to study brain regions and structures that are believed to influence our subjective interpretations of our environment; our emotions, and our ability to regulate our emotions.

According to LeDoux (2002), nature (genetic makeup) and nurture (life experiences) both influence the encoding of information at the synaptic level. Each person has a unique synaptic pattern, formed first by genetics and then heavily modified by life experiences. The cumulative state of the synapses and the information encoded into these connections is the key to understanding who we are. In other words, personality reflects specific patterns of interconnectivity that manifest over time between the neurons in each individual's brain.

The biopsychosocial model further takes into account cognitive factors such as perception, learning, and decision making which reflect processes unique to each individual in their neural routing as much as in their emotional and social contents. The information which weighs on these processes in a substantial fashion comes largely from personal development and history as well as social context. Psychosocial development is fundamental in this model as it links with genetic predispositions to create a person's character and behavioral patterns.

Most importantly, the biopsychosocial model posits that all human behavior is multifaceted and multicausal which is the same as to say that it results from a hugely complex interaction of biological predispositions, mediated by individual cognitive processes which are put into context by one's social environment (family history and social setting). The same goes for deviant or abnormal behavior.

This model further accounts for the difficulty in predicting human behavior: the way in which biological, psychological, and social ingredients combine to produce behavior is unique, highly volatile, and extremely sensitive. One abused child may grow up to be a compassionate, loving, caring parent, and citizen, while another child from a supportive home with a prosocial outlook may one day turn his rage on fellow coworkers under extreme pressure and in the grip of mental illness.

Even though our genetic predispositions are not life sentences, they do makes us more sensitive to emotional and social contexts which can precipitate a chain of interactive events leading to destructive and antisocial behavior.

Over the late part of the 20th century behavioral science researchers invested greatly in identifying and isolating indicators/predictors of antisocial behavior. The main conclusion being that one cannot define one type of faulty personality, corrupted cognitive processes, or damaging social settings, but rather that it is the combination of specific personality traits (mostly genetically disposed, such as low empathy, egocentricity, impulsiveness, aggressiveness, etc.) traumatic upbringing and unresolved emotional baggage and social settings ample with deviant opportunities (substance use, violence, promiscuity, etc.), which are more likely to produce abnormal behavior.

HUMAN MOTIVATION

Motivation is a psychological feature that arouses an organism to act toward a desired goal and elicits, controls, and sustains certain goal-directed behaviors. It can be considered a driving force; a psychological one that compels or reinforces an action toward a desired goal. For example, hunger is a motivation that elicits a desire to eat. Motivation is the purpose or psychological cause of an action.

Motivation has been shown to have roots in physiological, behavioral, cognitive, and social areas. Motivation may be rooted in a basic impulse to optimize well-being, minimize physical pain, and maximize pleasure. It can also originate from specific physical needs such as eating, sleeping or resting, and sex.

> *Motivation is the concept we use when we describe the forces acing on or within an organism to initiate and direct behaviour. We also use the concept of motivation to explain the differences in the intensity of behaviour.*
>
> **Petri (1981, p. 3)**

In criminal profiling while motivation in the larger, existential sense is not always important, we find that having an overall understanding of what propels humans to act be it in deviant ways or not is enriching in understating human psychology. Often students, and the public in general, are struck by the question "why would someone do something so awful or heinous or shocking or stupid? ". The basic answer really is "who knows?", but there are underlying processes in human motivation which can provide some insight when reflecting on the subject.

INTRINSIC AND EXTRINSIC MOTIVATION

Intrinsic motivation refers to motivation that is driven by an interest or enjoyment in the task itself, and exists within the individual rather than relying on external pressures or a desire for reward.

Extrinsic motivation refers to the performance of an activity in order to attain an outcome, whether or not that activity is also intrinsically motivated. Extrinsic motivation comes from outside of the individual. Common extrinsic motivations are rewards (for example, money or grades) for showing the desired behavior, and the threat of punishment following misbehavior. Competition is in an extrinsic motivator because it encourages the performer to win and to beat others, not simply to enjoy the intrinsic rewards of the activity. A cheering crowd and the desire to win a trophy are also extrinsic incentives.

THEORIES OF HUMAN MOTIVATION

In The Republic, Plato[p] advances a tripartite theory of the soul, which consists of three parts: reason, spirit, and appetite. All parts of the soul have desires; however, not all desires are the same. Desires take many different forms and have many different responses or results. Machiavellianism[q] argues that human beings are motivated to seek power and status above all. Modern research argues that people who are high in this trait do indeed seek power and money and are willing to use others as instruments toward that end.

A number of motivational theories emphasize the distinction between conscious and unconscious motivations. In evolutionary psychology[r], the "ultimate," unconscious motivation may be a cold evolutionary calculation; the conscious motivation could be more benign or even positive emotions.

The self-control aspect of motivation is increasingly considered to be a subset of emotional intelligence; it is suggested that although a person may be classed as highly

---

[p] **Plato** was a philosopher in Classical Greece. He was also a mathematician, student of Socrates, writer of philosophical dialogues, and founder of the Academy in Athens, the first institution of higher learning in the Western world. Along with his mentor, Socrates, and his student, Aristotle, Plato helped to lay the foundations of Western philosophy and science.

[q] **Niccolo dei Machiavelli** was an Italian historian, politician, diplomat, philosopher, humanist, and writer based in Florence during the Renaissance. He was for many years an official in the Florentine Republic, with responsibilities in diplomatic and military affairs. He was a founder of modern political science, and more specifically political ethics. He also wrote comedies, carnival songs, and poetry. His personal correspondence is renowned in the Italian language. He was Secretary to the Second Chancery of the Republic of Florence from 1498 to 1512, when the Medici were out of power. He wrote his masterpiece, *The Prince*, after the Medici had recovered power and he no longer held a position of responsibility in Florence. His moral and ethical beliefs led to the creation of the word Machiavellianism which has since been used to describe one of the three dark triad personalities in psychology.

[r] **Evolutionary psychology** is an approach in the social and natural sciences that examines psychological traits such as memory, perception, and language from a modern evolutionary perspective. It seeks to identify which human psychological traits are evolved adaptations—that is, the functional products of natural selection or sexual selection. Adaptationist thinking about physiological mechanisms, such as the heart, lungs, and immune system, is common in evolutionary biology. Some evolutionary psychologists apply the same thinking to psychology, arguing that the mind has a modular structure similar to that of the body, with different modular adaptations serving different functions. Evolutionary psychologists argue that much of human behavior is the output of psychological adaptations that evolved to solve recurrent problems in human ancestral environments Evolutionary psychologists hold that behaviors or traits that occur universally in all cultures are good candidates for evolutionary adaptations including the abilities to infer others' emotions, discern kin from nonkin, identify and prefer healthier mates, and cooperate with others. They report successful tests of theoretical predictions related to such topics as infanticide, intelligence, marriage patterns, promiscuity, perception of beauty, and parental investment.

intelligent (as measured by many traditional intelligence tests), they may remain unmotivated to pursue intellectual endeavors. Vroom's Expectancy Theory[s] provides an account of when people may decide to exert self-control in pursuit of a particular goal.

DRIVE THEORY

A drive or desire can be described as *a deficiency or need that activates behavior that is aimed at a goal or an incentive*. These drives are thought to originate within the individual and may not require external stimuli to encourage the behavior. Basic drives could be sparked by deficiencies such as hunger, which motivates a person to seek food whereas more subtle drives might be the desire for praise and approval, which motivates a person to behave in a manner pleasing to others. Another basic drive is the sexual drive which like food motivates us because it is essential to our survival. The desire for sex is wired deep into the brain of all human beings as glands secrete hormones that travel through the blood to the brain and stimulates the onset of sexual desire.

A reinforcer is any stimulus change following a response that increases the future frequency or magnitude of that response. Positive reinforcement is demonstrated by an increase in the future frequency or magnitude of a response due to in the past being followed contingently by a reinforcing stimulus. Negative reinforcement involves stimulus change consisting of the removal of an aversive stimulus following a response. Positive reinforcement involves a stimulus change consisting of the presentation or magnification of a positive stimulus following a response. From this perspective, motivation is mediated by environmental events, and the concept of distinguishing between intrinsic and extrinsic forces is irrelevant.

MASLOW'S HIERARCHY OF NEEDS THEORY

Abraham Maslow's[t] theory is one of the most widely discussed theories of motivation. Maslow developed the hierarchy of needs consisting of five hierarchic classes, according to which, people are motivated by unsatisfied needs. The needs, listed from basic (lowest–earliest) to most complex (highest–latest) are as follows: (1) physiology, (2) safety/security/shelter/health, (3) belongingness/love/friendship, (4) self-esteem/recognition/achievement, and (5) self-actualization.

Maslow's Hierarchy of Needs theory can be summarized as follows:

- Human beings have wants and desires, which influence their behavior. Only unsatisfied needs influence behavior, satisfied needs do not.
- Needs are arranged in order of importance to human life, from the basic to the complex.

---

[s] **Expectancy theory** is about the mental processes regarding choice or choosing. It explains the processes that an individual undergoes to make choices. In the study of organizational behavior, expectancy theory is a motivation theory first proposed by Victor Vroom.

[t] **Abraham Maslow** was an American psychologist who was best known for creating Maslow's hierarchy of needs, a theory of psychological health predicated on fulfilling innate human needs in priority, culminating in self-actualization. Maslow stressed the importance of focusing on the positive qualities in people, as opposed to treating them as a "bag of symptoms."

- The person advances to the next level of needs only after the lower level need is at least minimally satisfied.
- The further the progress up the hierarchy, the more individuality, humanness, and psychological health a person will show.

According to Petri "the study of motivation at the level of the individual involves research aimed at understanding motivational changes that occur to a person as a result of internal or external conditions." Turvey (2009) reminds us that one can study motivation nomothetically, by looking for similarities that form groups, or ideographically, to determine the motivation evident in a particular person or event. With this in view we explore two different motivational models for human criminal behavior.

THE BEHAVIORAL–MOTIVATIONAL TYPOLOGY MODEL

This model was first developed by Dr. Nicholas Groth[u] in 1950 and adapted by Turvey and Petherick (2010) provides an excellent working typology with examples of offender behavior. Essentially the shift in focus from classifying offenders to classifying crime scene behaviors, which the authors offer, changes the typology from a nomothetic offender labeling system to an idiographic tool for crime scene analysis. The authors further advise that this modified typology is "constructed as a guide to help investigators and criminal profilers classify behavior, in context, in relationship to the crime scene behavior evidenced and the offender need it serves." The five categories are (1) power reassurance/compensatory, (2) power assertive/entitlement, (3) anger retaliatory/anger or displaced, (4) sadistic/anger excitation, and (5) profit/material gain. These are explored according to method of approach, method of attack, verbal behavior, sexual behavior, physical behavior, MO behavior, and signature behavior.

MOTIVATIONAL MODEL FOR SEXUAL HOMICIDE

Burgess et al. (1986)[v] provided a motivational model with an interesting conceptual framework for understanding sexual homicide and which also reflects important contributing factors in forming and expressing deviant and antisocial behavior. The model primarily deals with psychosocial and cognitive factors, failing to address the influence of neurobiology or genetic factors that may be present under certain conditions. The five interacting components described are (1) the murderer's social environment, (2) child and adolescent formative events, (3) patterned responses to these events, (4) resultant actions toward others, and (5) the killer's reactions, via a mental "feedback filter," to his murderous acts.

---

[u] **Nicholas Groth** was an American clinical psychologist who worked with sexual offenders and their victims.

[v] **Ann Wolbert Burgess** is an internationally recognized pioneer in the assessment and treatment of victims of trauma and abuse. She has received numerous honors including the Sigma Theta Tau International Audrey Hepburn Award, the American Nurses' Association Hildegard Peplau Award, and the Sigma Theta Tau International Episteme Laureate Award. Her courtroom testimony has been described as "groundbreaking," and she has been called a "nursing pathfinder." This model can be found in *Sexual homicide: Patterns and motives*, by Robert K. Ressler, Ann W. Burgess, and John E. Douglas. Lexington, MA: Lexington Books, 1988.

THE BEHAVIORAL EVIDENCE ANALYSIS MODEL

AIMS

- Understand the aims and contexts of the BEA profiling model;
- Know the underlying principles;
- Learn the main components of the model;
- Understand the application of its main components.

The BEA model for criminal profiling favors the deductive method, in which the criminal profiler possesses an open mind; questions all assumptions, premises, and opinions put forth; and demands collaboration regardless of how distinguished the supplier of the input. The emphasis is on the profiler's objectivity, self-knowledge and self-awareness (to overcome transference distortions), critical thinking skills and an all-important ability to try and understand which needs are being satisfied by each behavior of the offender as well as the offender's patterns.

Turvey's model places great emphasis on all forms of forensic analysis (eg, wound analysis, blood stain pattern analysis, and bullet trajectory analysis), crime scene characteristics (including photos), victim and witness statements, and a thorough study of the characteristics of the victim. He uses the crime scene characteristics to differentiate between modus operandi (MO) and "signature behaviors" (ie, actions unique to the crime but not necessary to commit the crime), as well as to determining inferences about the offender's state of mind at the time of the crime, his/her planning, level of skill, victim selection, fantasy, motivation, and degree of risk taken.

In the BEA model, a criminal profiler has several roles, being a monitor, coordinator, interpreter, and advisor to the different branches of the investigatory hierarchy with particular emphasis placed on facts rather than theories.

In BEA the value of teamwork is crucial. Each team member must recognize the complementarity of all team members and be willing to share information. Furthermore, there are differences in skill levels among team members, despite the number of years of experience.

THE PRINCIPLES OF BEHAVIORAL EVIDENCE ANALYSIS[w]

Turvey and Petherick (2010) set down the basic principles of BEA by drawing from behavioral and biological sciences and identified them as:

1. **The Principle of Uniqueness:** Individuals develop uniquely over time, in response to biological, environmental, and subsequent psychological factors.
2. **The Principle of Separation:** Individuals have their own unique constellation of associations with respect to pleasure, pain, taste, and distaste independent of the profiler.
3. **The Principle of Behavioral Dynamics:** Offense-related behavior, including MO, is not static.

[w] For a complete description *vide* ***Criminal Profiling: an introduction to Behavioural evidence analysis*** (2009) p. 141.

4. **The Principle of Behavioral Motivation:** All behavior has underlying causes and origins (conscious or unconscious). Motivations are strongly influenced by emotions, mental defect and mental illness, and the use of drugs and alcohol.
5. **The Principle of Multidetermination:** Offense-related behavior is complex and multidetermined serving multiple aims and purposes.
6. **The Principle of Motivational Dynamics:** An individual offender is capable of multiple motives over the commission of multiple offenses or even during the commission of a single offense.
7. **The Principle of Behavioral Variance:** Different offenders can invoke the same or similar behavior/choice/action for completely different motives.
8. **The Principle of Unintended Consequences:** Not all the results of behavior are intended.
9. **The Principle of Memory Corruption:** This refers to the fact that witness statements are inherently unreliable for a variety of reasons.
10. **The Principle of Reliability:** The results of forensic examinations, including criminal profiling, are only as reliable as the underlying evidence and reasoning.

BEHAVIORAL EVIDENCE ANALYSIS AIMS AND CONTEXTS[x]

"BEA should be viewed as a not as a process after a fixed result but as an ongoing, dynamic, critical, analytical process that examines offender behaviour as it changes over time" (Turvey and Petherick, 2010). Therefore one of the main purposes of BEA is to assist an investigation, at any stage, to move from a broad, universal, set of suspect characteristics to a more discrete, focused, set of suspect characteristics. It is important to say that BEA cannot point specifically at one suspect or person, or separate one suspect from all others; what it can do is assist investigative efforts and educate the intervenients in forensic contexts like criminal proceedings, civil proceedings, and public hearings.

BEA has two separate yet equal contexts, which are determined according to goals and priorities rather than method:

1. **Investigative Phase:** Before a suspect has been arrested (or before a defendant is taken to court); involves behavioral evidence analysis of the patterns of unknown offenders for known crimes.
2. **Trial Phase:** While a suspect is being tried for a crime (or put on trial for damages); involves behavioral evidence analysis of known crimes for which there is a suspect or a defendant.

THE COMPONENTS OF BEHAVIORAL EVIDENCE ANALYSIS (TURVEY, 2009)

The BEA model involves the examination and interpretation of physical evidence, victimology and crime scene characteristics. The results of these individual

---

[x] For a complete description ***vide Criminal Profiling: an introduction to Behavioural Evidence Analysis*** (2009) p. 138–139.

examinations can be analyzed for behavioral patterns and clusters, which may indicate offender characteristics of investigative or forensic relevance. "A BEA-styled crime scene analysis or criminal profile will not render a conclusion unless the evidence exists to demand it (...) this methods requires more, more study, and more humility than the alternative methods of profiling" (Turvey and Petherick, 2010).

1. **Equivocal Forensic Analysis**: "Equivocal" refers to anything that can be interpreted in more than one way or when the interpretation is questioned. Equivocal forensic analysis refers to a review of all available physical and behavioral evidence, and thus questions all assumptions and conclusions.
2. **Victimology**: It is the process of investigating, establishing, and evaluating victim traits and history. It may lead to inferences about an offender's fantasy, motive, MO, knowledge, and skill. A fundamental part of victimology is risk assessment or *exposure assessment.*
3. **Crime Scene Analysis**[y]**:** It is the process of investigating, establishing, and evaluating behavioral evidence from a crime in order to catalog it (Baeza et al., 2000). Crime scene characteristics are interpreted from an examination of the established behavioral evidence and victimology. These characteristics may include, among many other things, method of approach, method of attack, method of controlling the victim, location, nature, type, and sequence of sexual acts, materials used, verbal statements, and precautionary acts taken by the offender.
4. **Deduction of Offender Characteristics:** The first three steps are for the most part based on the scientific tenets of crime scene reconstruction and established forensic sciences; however, while relaying on these inputs, the fourth step is more artful and therefore a matter of expertise rather than science. "Deducing offender characteristics is about asking the right questions of offense-related behavior. The first part of the question is defining the characteristic (eg, a sadistic motive). The second part is agreeing on what type of behavior evidences that characteristic (eg, evidence of offender sexual gratification from victim suffering" (Turvey, 2009).

OTHER IMPORTANT ANALYTICAL PARAMETERS IN CRIMINAL PROFILING

AIMS

- Understand that crime reconstruction is about forensic evidence as well as interpretation of this forensic evidence;
- Understand the importance of victimology in determining offender characteristics;
- Assess victim and offender exposure;

[y] As part of the teaching methodology, the author specifically refers to the Crime Scene Characteristics guide proposed by Turvey (2009, p. 202) and it is also used as the base for the crime scene analysis item of the group work project in part V.

- Know the importance of building a timeline of events leading up to the crime;
- Comprehend general guidelines for constructing a victimology assessment;
- Understand the difference between MO and signature behavior;
- Understand the importance of MO and signature in an investigation;
- Understand how MO and signature impact of case linkage analysis;
- Know the purpose of case linkage analysis.

CRIME RECONSTRUCTION

Crime reconstruction or crime scene reconstruction is the forensic science discipline in which one gains explicit knowledge of the series of events that surround the commission of a crime using deductive and inductive reasoning, physical evidence, scientific methods, and their interrelationships. It further entails evaluating the context of a scene.

Chisum and Turvey (2007, p. 155) explain that "crime reconstruction is the development of actions and circumstances based on the system of evidence discovered and examined in relation to a particular crime. In this philosophy, all elements of evidence that come to light in a given case are treated as interdependent; the significance of each piece, each action, and each event falls and rises on the backs of the others." The authors further explain that to perform crime reconstruction one need not "be an expert in all forensic disciplines" but "must become an expert in only one: *the interpretation of the evidence in context*." A profiler may not be the person who carries out laboratory analysis of evidence such as developing DNA profiles or performing firearms and toolmark analysis; however, the competent profiler must understand the meaning of each various piece of evidence, and how it fits within the overall context of the scene. In this way, the profiler is able to assemble the necessary puzzle pieces to make the picture visible.

FORENSIC VICTIMOLOGY

An important aspect of investigating a violent crime is an understanding of the victim and the relation that their lifestyle or personality characteristics may have contributed to the offender choosing them as a victim.

Victims are classified during an investigation in three general categories that describe the level of risk their lifestyle represents in relation to the violent crime that has been committed. The importance of understanding this in an investigation is directly related back to the level of risk that the offender has incurred during the commission of the crime. This information is important to the investigation to better understand the sophistication (exposure) or possible pathology of the offender.

High Risk/Exposure Victims—Victims in this group have a lifestyle that makes them a higher risk for being a victim of a violent crime. The most obvious high-risk victim is the prostitute. Prostitutes place themselves at risk every single time they go to work. Prostitutes are at high risk because they will get into a stranger's car, go to secluded areas with strangers, and for the most part attempt to conceal their actions for legal reasons. Offenders often rely on all these factors and specifically target prostitutes because it lowers their chances of becoming a suspect in the crime. Therefore, in this example, the prostitute is a high-risk victim creating a lower risk to the offender.

Moderate Risk/Exposure Victims—Victims that fall into this category are lower risk victims, but for some reason, were in a situation that placed them in a greater level of risk. A person that is stranded on a dark, secluded highway due to a flat tire, who accepts a ride from a stranger and is then victimized would be a good example of this type of victim-level risk.

Low Risk/Exposure Victims—The lifestyle of these individuals would normally not place them in any degree of risk for becoming a victim of a violent crime. These individuals stay out of trouble, do not have peers that are criminal, are aware of their surroundings, and attempt to take precautions to not become a victim. They lock the doors, do not use drugs, and do not go into areas that are dark and secluded. An offender who targets this kind of victim will probably incur great risk of detection and/or go to great length to avoid detection, both behaviors are informative.

After all the information has been gathered, a timeline of events leading up to the crime should be created in order to better understand how a specific individual became the victim of a violent crime. The author recommends to students Turvey and Petherick (2010, p. 388) general guidelines for constructing a victimology assessment.

MODUS OPERANDI

Generally, the Latin term MO means method of acting and represents the functional components which are necessary for an offender to be successful in committing a crime. It is a characteristic style of sorts. An offender's MO comprises choices and behaviors that are intended to assist in the completion of a crime (Turvey, 2009).

Historically, the MO has been used to link cases because offenders may use similar methods during the commission of their crimes. The MO may include factors such as a time of day or location an offender chooses to strike, the type of victim, points or techniques for gaining entry, as well as what tools were used for committing the crime.

The MO can change over time as offenders become more experienced or learn new techniques that will make them more successful or lower their chances of being identified. On the other hand, the MO is also sensitive to variables which are beyond the offender's control, and which are mostly environmental in nature. This means that the MO is a dynamic aspect of behavior and therefore may not always be reliable for case linkage.

SIGNATURE

Signature behaviors go beyond what is necessary to commit the crime and fulfill a psychological need of the offender. Unlike the MO, signature aspects are stable over time and can be witnessed at each crime scene throughout a series. Although there may be subtle differences from crime to crime, there will be an evident theme.

Signature behavior speaks of a psychological need of the offender, thus reflecting personal fantasies and fetishes. Signature aspects are symbolic and hold special significance to the offender, and may not be understood by anyone other than the offender.

Hazelwood and Warren (2003) have also incorporated a description of ritual into the discussion of MO and signature to indicate the fantasy and motivational factors that are at times an aspect of violent crimes. Ritual is indicated at crime scenes as behaviors that are psychologically based and fulfill a need of the offender, which is also not necessary for the successful commission of a crime. Ritual may be indicated at a crime scene with bindings on the victim, posing of victims, unique markings on victims, or any other behaviors that appear symbolic. Ritual and signature seem to interact and produce behaviors that demonstrate the basic needs of the offender and can provide investigators with an indication of the offender's motivation.

Also, because signature behavior is highly distinctive and goes beyond the basic actions necessary for the commission of a crime, it tends to be a stable aspect of offender behavior. In terms of case linkage, signature behavior can at times be a very strong indicator of commonality between offenses/offenders.

MO and signature are important concepts to consider when investigating a series of crimes. By analyzing behaviors at crime scenes investigators are able to perform linkage analysis and determine if they are looking for one or more offenders.

CASE LINKAGE ANALYSIS

Case linkage refers to the process of determining whether or not there are discrete connections between two or more previously unrelated cases through crime analysis. Applying this logic requires establishing and comparing (1) the physical evidence, (2) victimology, (3) crime scene characteristics, (4) MO, and (5) signature behaviors.

Case linkage has two purposes according to Hazelwood and Warren (2003):

1. Assisting law enforcement in determining how to apply their investigative resources;
2. Assisting the court in determining whether or not sufficient behavioral evidence is present to suggest a common scheme or plan in order to address forensic issues, such as whether other crimes may be tried together or whether other crimes may be brought in as evidence.

Turvey (2009, p. 354) advises that "the use of linkage analysis in a forensic context is problematic at best and can even be irresponsible." The author suggests that the results of case linkage efforts, may be expressed with the following language which can be useful to investigators and the court, yet not misleading with respect to certainty: (1) behavioral dissimilarity, (2) an investigative linkage, (3) behavioral commonality, and (4) a probative link.

APPLYING LEARNED CONCEPTS: GENERATING A PROFILE

AIMS

- Develop research and presentation skills;
- Learn how to identify relevant information in a case;
- Apply profiling methodologies to interpret evidence;
- Generate a psychosocial profile;
- Develop critical thinking;
- Develop awareness toward investigative methods and outcomes.

At the beginning of each semester, we assign group projects to be presented in class. We provide students with a list of known, and documented, offenders from which to choose their case subject. The aim is to familiarize students with basic concepts and dynamics associated with processing information uncovered during an investigation by applying profiling methodology and terminology to closed cases. The project comprises of four parts:

Part 1: Researching and collecting available information about the offender and his/her victim(s)

The topic list we provide our students with includes classic, diverse, and well-documented cases. It has been our experience that as students begin researching their subject, they bring examples and stories into class which generates interesting debates and helps actualize many theoretical concepts. The list includes, among others, George Metesky, "The Mad Bomber"; Arthur Shawcross; David Carpenter, "The Railside Killer"; John Duffy, "The Railway Rapist"; Robert Hansen; Ted Bundy; Paul Bernardo; and Karla Homolka, "Barbie & Ken"; Wayne Williams, "The Atlanta Child Murderer"; Jeffrey Dahmer; Fred and Rosemary West; Ayleen Wuornos; Ed Gein; Jack, the Ripper; Charles Manson; "The Zodiac Killer"; Richard Colvin Reid "The Shoe Bomber"; and Andrei Chikatilo.

Part 2: Organizing data according to the first four stages of nomothetic methodology

The idea is to generate a profile by following the first four stages of nomothetic methodologies using as reference the FBI's six stages of profiling. The **first stage** consists of collecting all information such as physical evidence, photos, testimonies from witnesses, and reports. In the **second stage**, students will take all the collected information and develop a report consisting of possible motives, degree of sophistication and of planning, and possible sequence of actions before, during, and after the offense. The **third stage** entails analyzing information of the actual crime, the behavior and actions of the offender, and his/her victim. In this stage, students try to answer questions such as "what lead to this outcome?" and "what were the motives for the specific cause of death?" The **fourth stage** is generating the profile of the wanted offender. Based on preexisting studies and classifications, the profile will comprise mostly of projections regarding physical attributes such as gender, race and age, and other characteristics such as behavioral patterns and psychological factors. Students are also encouraged to apply geographical analysis using the principles of Investigative Psychology and Geoprofiling.

Part 3: Organizing and analyzing data according to Behavioral Evidence Analysis methodology

Behavioral evidence analysis can be broken down into four steps. The first step is **Equivocal Forensic Analysis**, this step instructs students to analyze the evidence (both physical and behavioral) knowing that there might be more than one meaning underpinning each event. Students can then assess the information and conclude on the most pertinent and logical meanings which fall in line with the behavioral evidence.

The second step is about profiling the victim through the process called **Forensic Victimology**. Students become aware of the importance of profiling the victim as well as the offender; by profiling the victim, students attempt to develop an accurate outline of the victims' lives and actions, aiming at pinpointing where and how they became victims.

The third step, **Crime Scene Characteristics**, is about looking at the "distinguishing features of a crime scene as evidenced by an offender's behavioral decisions regarding the victim and the offense location, and their subsequent meaning to the offender" Turvey (2009). Students analyze information about the crime scene and look for any stand-out features that would be relevant to generating the profile and which could lead to creating a suspect pool, narrowing down a suspect pool or identifying the offender.

After collecting and analyzing information through previous steps, the fourth step, **Offender Characteristics**, helps to organize and develop all the possible and most likely offender personality and behavioral traits. A fundamental rule of this step is that if any new information surfaces or if any old information is found irrelevant, then the profile and its characteristics must be revised.

Part 4: Class presentation

At the end of the process, students present their findings in class. The overall goals are to compare and present findings by demonstrating how both nomothetic methodology and ideographic methodology are applied, and how they contribute to the criminal profiling process. This should result in two offender profiles which follow a predefined structure (see below), one completed by using nomothetic methodology and the other completed by using BEA methodology.

1. Analysis of the type/nature of criminal acts and comparison to personality types who have committed similar crimes
2. Crime scene analysis
3. Forensic reports analysis
4. Forensic victimology
5. Geographic analysis
6. Motivational analysis
7. Case linkage
8. Assembly of offender traits

This project represents a significant undertaking and requires invested supervision to be effective. We recommend that tutors be available to supervise groups' discoveries and reflections as they piece the presentation together. It has been our experience that, time wise, the structure which we propose for our overall teaching program works best if classes are broken down into two parts: theory and practice. Every class begins with theory and the second half of class is devoted to working on the group project. Also it is important that the project is carried out by groups larger than three and smaller than six, and that groups work together in the classroom space because this provides ample opportunities for debate and clarification that benefit all at once.

The class presentation itself is comprised of several items which are compulsory and must follow this order: (1) brief introduction of the presenting crime(s) (carefully omitting the identity of the offender[z]), (2) identifying research sources and data collecting procedures, (3) generating a nomothetic profile, (4) generating a BEA profile, (5) revealing the identity and true profile of the offender, (6) reflecting on the profiling outcomes attained through both methods, (7) identifying and outlining the shortcomings as well as the advantages of each methodology in the investigative process, (8) concluding remarks, and (9) references.

The group project represents 50% of the students' assessment; the other 50% derives from two theoretical tests held over the semester. It has been our experience that splitting our student assessment in this way is fairer and more inclusive, as students have an equal opportunity to explore theoretical knowledge as well as practical knowledge.

READING LIST

AIMS

- Providing a widespread view on the issues concerning methodology, the scope, and the limitations of profiling across cultures and criminal justice systems.

REFERENCES

Ainsworth, P.B., 2001. Offender Profiling and Crime Analysis. Willan Publishing, Devon.

Allport, G.W., 1937. Personality: a psychological interpretation. Holt, Rinehart, & Winston, New York.

Baeza, J., Chisum, W.J., Chamberlin, T.M., McGrath, M., Turvey, B., January 2000. Academy of behavioral profiling: criminal profiling guidelines. Journal of Behavioral Profiling 1 (1).

Burgess, A.W., Hartman, C.R., Ressler, R.K., Douglas, J.E., McCormack, A., 1986. Sexual homicide: a motivational model. J. Interpers. Violence 1 (3), 251–272.

Chisum, W.J., Turvey, B., 2007. Crime Reconstruction. Elsevier Science, Boston.

[z] The authors have found that omitting the name of the chosen offender from the class audience has two effects: (1) generates keen attention and curiosity and (2) ensures that the analytical exercise works (many of the subjects on the list are popular so students might have some knowledge about the cases and we have found that it usually is not helpful information).

Hazelwood, R., Warren, J., 2003. Linkage analysis: modus operandi, ritual and signature in serial sexual crime. Aggression and Violent Behaviour 8, 587–598.

Holmes, R.M., Holmes, S.T., 1996. Profiling Violent Crimes: An Investigative Tool, second ed. Sage, Thousand Oaks, CA.

LeDoux, J., 2002. Synaptic Self: How Our Brains Become Who We Are. Viking Press, New York.

Petri, H., 1981. Motivation: Theory and Research. Wadsworth Pub. Co, Belmont, CA.

Turvey, B.E., 2009. Criminal Profiling: An Introduction to Behavioral Evidence Analysis. Elsevier, Boston.

Turvey, B., Petherick, W., 2010. An Introduction to Forensic Criminology. In: Turvey, B., Petherick, W., Ferguson, C. (Eds.), Forensic Criminology. Elsevier Science, San Diego.

CHAPTER

Colombia: Criminal Profiling Applications

8

D.M. Cardona

Policía Nacional de los Colombianos, Directorate of Criminal Investigation and Interpol (DIJIN), Bogota, Colombia

CHAPTER OUTLINE

For over a century, criminal profiling as a concept has generated worldwide enthusiasm and curiosity in the minds of those concerned with both criminal investigation and the study of the criminal mind. Sometimes this has led to professional attention, publications, and eventually even research. But more often it has remained a curiosity with only a few claiming any real knowledge or expertise.

However, during the past 15 years, the area of criminal profiling has received more formal attention in the United States and in other nations as well. This attention has sparked the desire for professional development, to include the need for specialized practitioners with the capacity to meet the challenges presented by modern crime and criminals. Certainly the author has observed this trend among professionals and law enforcement agencies in China, Korea, Spain, Portugal, Germany, Mexico, and of course Colombia.

Given the professional interest in, and application of, criminal profiling techniques in this level, there must be a daily effort made by those concerned. There must be consolidation of the discipline as a legitimate auxiliary mechanism in the criminal justice system. This mandates that the methods used achieve a sufficient evidentiary burden to prove its science, and reliability, in the courts.

As described in this work, criminal profiling in Colombia has evolved to become a part of the framework within courtroom proceedings in criminal matters. It has been projected into this, our forensic realm, as a specialized technique that relies upon the approach developed and refined by the International Association of Forensic Criminologists (IAFC) since the late 1990s: behavioral evidence analysis (BEA). The BEA

Behavioral Evidence Analysis. http://dx.doi.org/10.1016/B978-0-12-800607-8.00008-2

approach to profiling has been adopted because it achieves more useful and insightful results than the others during the examination of even the most complex cases because it provides a unifying language and framework for investigators, psychologists, and criminologists and because it relies on the scientific method (Turvey, 2011).

This chapter will discuss, in brief, the evolution of criminal profiling in Colombia. In doing so, it will discuss its successful application to criminal investigations and courtroom proceedings. More than just a historical review, it is hoped that this will serve others as a part of a model for success when integrating criminal profiling into their own criminal justice systems.

THE BEHAVIORAL SCIENCES AND CRIMINAL PROFILING GROUP

In May 2011, the CICOP was created within the Directorate of Criminal Investigation and Interpol (DIJIN) of Colombia. These are both part of the National Police of Colombia. CICOP was initially composed of 14 officials, including lawyers, psychologists, criminologists, and investigators with experience in murder and sexual offenses. Three of its members had training as profilers from working as part of the Criminal Behavior Analysis Unit at the Attorney General's office, founded in 2006 as part of an interagency agreement that ended in 2011[a]. The goal of the CICOP unit was to help determine and understand the characteristics of the offenders by examining their crime-related behavior.

CICOP profilers began to support research and casework at a national level, primarily by assisting police investigators and criminal prosecutors working on murders. The reports produced by these profilers were the result of comprehensive research. As a result, they included the use of multiple theoretical, technical, and bibliographic foundations. As this might suggest, the broad approach utilized by CICOP profilers integrated the literature of multiple profiling methodologies. This was done to help reduce bias and logical fallacies in any conclusions being offered—to ensure a solid theoretical and science-based foundation.

The literature on criminal profiling is published mostly in English; however, this did not prevent the translation of relevant texts and journal publications. This remains an ongoing effort within CICOP. It enables group members to get the most current information with respect to profiling concepts, and also to understand how they might be applied to criminal investigations.

In consulting the criminal profiling literature, CICOP found the work of Dr. Brent Turvey and the IAFC. Subsequently, CICOP became familiar with the profiling method that they had developed: BEA. This method of case examination and criminal profiling fit the needs of CICOP analysts: (1) because of its emphasis on ideographic analysis, objectivity, and the scientific method; (2) because of its demonstrable international utility; and (3) because of its proven courtroom admissibility. These elements are essential to the efforts of any professional law enforcement agency in the course of seeking both truth and justice.

[a]The profilers from the Criminal Behavior Analysis Unit were initially trained in the criminal investigative analysis method.

THE BEHAVIORAL SCIENCES AND CRIMINAL PROFILING GROUP CERTIFICATION

In order to facilitate the training of CICOP analysts, DIJIN worked with Yefrin Garavito Navarro, the director of the unidad de investigacion criminal de la defensa (UID/ trans. "the Criminal Defense Investigation Unit") of Colombia. UID is a government contractor that sources and offers training to public and private organizations working in association with the criminal justice system. UID, with the cooperation of DIJIN, contacted Dr. Turvey in his capacity as a representative of the IAFC. Dr. Turvey agreed to visit Colombia with several goals in mind: (1) to introduce the BEA profiling method to Colombia; (2) to begin the training of investigators and other officials associated with CICOP; and (3) also to begin the process of certification by the IAFC's credentialing entity—the Academy of Behavioral Profiling.

UID is a government contractor that sources and offers training to public and private organizations working in association with the criminal justice system. DIJIN, in collaboration with UID, worked to bring Criminal Profiling Certification to Colombia via the IAFC. Profiling Certification Training was completed by DIJIN CICOP analysts in February of 2015.

In November 2013, Dr. Turvey came to Bogota and gave a diploma course in criminal profiling at the DIJIN facilities. This 40+ hour course was attended by members of CICOP, by officials of the National Institute of Legal Medicine and Forensic Sciences, and by officials from the School of Criminal Investigation of the National Police. The purpose was to educate attendees about criminal profiling as a formal discipline and to inform them regarding the progress of criminal profiling in other countries. Particular emphasis was placed on the acceptance and utility of various profiling methods in court, and the function of the criminal profiler as an expert witness.

Once this seed was planted, the dedicated use of BEA methodology within CICOP began and quickly expanded. CICOP analysts continued to consult with investigators and prosecutors nationwide on their cases, but with a more structured emphasis on behavioral details (eg, modus operandi, motive, and offender signature) and forensic relevance (eg, public safety issues, investigative suggestions, and suspect development). Ultimately, their work improved under the guidance of IAFC protocols, and CICOP gained greater internal support and national credibility among investigators. Police agencies nationwide began to make requests for support in their own research and casework, making CICOP a valuable resource within the Colombian Federal Police.

Consequently, it was decided that CICOP analysts should seek formal certification in criminal profiling from the IAFC, in order to formally solidify and demonstrate their expertise in BEA profiling methodology. In January 2015, Dr. Turvey returned to Bogota and taught an Advanced International Certificate Course on Criminal Profiling to the members of CICOP, and selected officials form other investigative units. The result of this 80+ hour course was the certification of 14 officials from DIJIN in *criminal profiling* by the IAFC's certification board, the Academy of Behavioral Profiling[b]. This was an historic and essential event for professionalized criminal profiling in Colombia.

Graduates of the IAFC Certification course held at the DIJIN facilities in Bogota, Colombia, January–February 2015, with their instructor, Dr. Brent Turvey.

[b]Other individuals from various agencies and organizations were certified as well, as the course was attended by approximately 30 students in all, from all over Colombia—including investigators from UID, the National Police Homicide Unit, and the United Nations.

BEHAVIORAL EVIDENCE ANALYSIS UTILITY

It has not been easy to convince investigators and prosecutors of the utility of criminal profiling. Its history is checkered with error and arrogance. However, important steps have been taken in an attempt to rescue the image of its practice. Certification, of course, was among the first steps. Casework, research, and publications are the next.

Revista de Criminalidad (trans. The Journal of Crime), is the official publication of The Colombian National Police.

PUBLICATIONS

There have been two publications in the *Revista de Criminalidad of the National Police*. The first is entitled *Criminological Profiling: A review of literature and its application in criminal investigation in Colombia* (Norza et al., 2013). The second is *Analysis of criminal behavior of serial rapists in cases in Bogotá DC (2008–2012)* (Meléndez et al., 2014). These works were an effort to update criminal justice professionals on the evolution of profiling techniques, as well as their scope, within DIJIN and CICOP. They were, essentially, an introduction to the concept of BEA. They provided a review of existing physical evidence types in criminal proceedings and explained the difference between the study of criminal behavior, criminal psychology, and the examination of criminal conduct. Time was also spent demystifying the exclusive use of psychology as the central axis of analysis in criminal profiling. This was done with an emphasis on establishing and examining behavior without departing from analytical logic and the scientific method.

CASEWORK

Criminal profiling (specifically BEA) has proved useful in Colombia in many criminal investigations. For purposes of this writing, the author will refer to a particular case, in which the BEA method and the results were successfully applied. Not just a benefit to the identification and apprehension of the suspect, the report in this case was submitted at trial and was ultimately admitted as evidence—which is in itself a significant accomplishment.

On September 27, 2013, the murder of two priests occurred in the municipality of Roldanillo in the Department of Valle del Cauca (Colombia). Details are provided in the following case summary:

> *On September 27, 2013, at 11:30pm hours, were found the bodies of two priests, on the second floor of the rectory at the Church of Roldanillo, Victim #1*[c]*, man in 26 years old was lying on the door of a room near his, face down with a white towel around his neck, wearing pajamas wearing no shoes; according to the autopsy report, the body showed his throat cut, twenty-three stab wounds focused in the neck, chest and back and some additional seven defensive wounds on his upper extremities; Victim #2, 69-year-old was on his back, lying on the floor, wearing a shirt, trousers and shoes, according to the autopsy report, the body had been disgorging, nineteen stab wounds to the chest, four in the head, five defensive injuries type in upper extremities; None of the bodies showed signs of torture, sexual violence, or the use of illegal drugs or psychoactive substances.*
>
> *A police officer reported the victim No. 1 called his cell at 10:17pm, to tell him he had heard strange noises on the first floor of the house and just then the call is interrupted, the officer Police immediately called police patrol was on duty in the area of the church, who came to the property, rang the bell and knocked at the door, but no one came out, nor heard anything into the rectory, they not suspected something bad*

[c] For this writing the victim's names will be omitted because criminal proceedings are still underway.

happened to the priests, more than forty minutes later they called a collaborator of the priests who entered the house, observed what happened and opened up the front door for police officers so they entered; was so the bodies of the victims were found on large bloodstains product of multiple wounds during the deadly attack.

Crime Lab technicians from the police, collected several blood stains imprinted on the walls of the house, and four knives on the roof of the house, no other evidence left by the aggressors during the crime was found.

In this case the evidence was scarce. Investigators and prosecutors could not determine a motive for the crime. Nor could they determine a viable suspect. Subsequently, they sought support from CICOP profilers.

After reviewing all the documents in the case, to include the reports from investigators and technicians, as well as photographs of the crime scene and the autopsy, a criminal profile was generated. BEA methodology was employed, and the following results were ultimately reported:

CHARACTERISTICS OF THE OFFENDER (CRIMINAL PROFILE)

Knowledge of the Scene

At least one of the criminals knew the scene before the murder, as it requires knowing the property to gain entry and make the routes described in this report. This is supported by the fact that the presbytery has several passages therein which communicate with each other, and the visibility of the first floor was minimal according to the documented interviews with the first people who entered the building and found the bodies of the priests in the room on the second floor. The level of planning associated with this crime suggests that it is unlikely that it was an accidental or opportunistic crime.

Contradictory Acts

As indicated in the pictures taken in the priest's room (victim #2), living room wall, and wall above the skylight, there were found stains consistent with handprints. There was also the presence of bloody shoeprints on the roof of the public bath for women. Consistent with bloodstains on walls of the first floor of the vehicle rearview mirror; leaving this evidence increased the likelihood that the offenders' handprints and footwear pattern evidence could be later identified.

Knowledge of the Victim

It is the opinion of analysts in this group that a prior relationship or knowledge between at least one perpetrator and the victim(s) was necessary for the commission of this crime. Additionally, the location of the property allowed criminals undertake surveillance activities or monitor any of the victims before the murder.

Knowledge of Methods and Materials

The analysts in this group believe that the offender had both the knowledge of the methods and materials that were used in the commission of this crime. Knowledge of materials is evidenced by the fact that criminals took kitchen knives and a towel from another room to control and attack the clerics and had the physical ability and the confidence to use them. Likewise, it follows that no special knowledge or skills to commit this crime (see section: Evidence of Criminal Skill of this report) were required. Knowledge of the methods is demonstrated by the fact that the offenders knew how to control and reduce the victim and accomplish the crime.

Evidence of Criminal Skill

The findings in the scene demonstrate the presence of bloodstains on walls, broken tiles, footprints on the roof of the public baths, and defensive wounds evidenced in the upper limbs of the victims. These allow a determination that the offender did not have sufficient skills to reduce the likelihood of fleeing the scene without leaving evidence—indicating a lack of skill with this kind of crime. However, some precaution was taken with other evidence, supported by the cleaning performed on the neck and face of the victim #1, the deposit of cookware in the water tank for laundry, and concealment of other items on the roof of the rectory. These were attempts to keep from being immediately identified, but only for a short period of time.

Physical Characteristics

Given that victim #1 and #2 had a size of 1.77 and 1.80 cm, the forum of analysts infer that criminals had a level of physical ability to master the victims' strength and skill in overcoming physical obstacles in the property. However, based on the evidence, other characteristics cannot be inferred, such as racial ancestry, mental state and condition, family history, and other demographic data.

Motivation

It is the opinion of the analysis group that there are behaviors in the scene that suggest an anger-retaliatory motive by the perpetrators of the crime. The basis of this consideration is the presence of multiple injuries on the bodies of priests, as revealed by the photographs of the autopsy that finally caused their death and not produced by individuals without any bond or any prior relationship with the victim. These victim injuries show high levels of strength and evidence overkill.

Eventually, investigators received information from a citizen who said he knew two people that had allegedly participated in the double murder of priests. They included a 15-year-old boy and a man that had been released from prison three months prior for murder. The convicted murderer also had a criminal record for theft. He had proximity to victim #1, and occasionally visited the rectory to ask for money. He also assisted the priest as an altar boy during the Sunday Mass that the priests held in the local jail.

The 15-year-old boy had a criminal record that included theft and drug use. More recently, he had been working on the street committing a variety of high-risk crimes. There was, in fact, an attempt to kill him for stealing a quantity of drugs from local area drug traffickers.

With additional evidence related to phone call records, witness statements, digital evidence, and the criminal profiling report, the prosecution built its theory of the case. This was based on the existence of a preexisting relationship between the suspects and the victims. They theorized that the two attackers, acting under the consumption of hallucinogens, entered the rectory in order to steal valuables and money. These were being kept to build a new church in the municipality.

Additionally, the 15 year old had visited the priests just before the murders. He had asked for money but was denied. He was quite angered by this refusal.

On June 26, 2015, the author of this chapter testified at the trial of these defendants in the city of Buga in the department of Valle del Cauca, as an expert witness for the State. The prosecution sustained the presentation of the criminal profiling report, based on the characteristics of the criminal profile, because it corresponded to those in the defendant. Also, the description section and scene analysis, detailing each of the evidence collected by investigators and technicians from the crime lab police, was quite useful. It provided an analysis of the scene dynamics with respect to the physical evidence left behind, how the offense occurred, and the importance of these elements in understanding and prosecuting the crime (Chisum and Turvey, 2011). It also, and perhaps most importantly, gave insight as to the offenders' motivations for the crime. This permitted a more in-depth understanding as to why the assailants attacked the priests, and why overkill was a feature.

This case represents the first time that a criminal profile report has been introduced in Colombian courts as evidence, as well as the first time that a criminal profiler has been allowed to give expert evidence at trial. This was possible because BEA affords a number of advantages to the forensic expert. First, it is a solid method based on comprehensive case analysis and the scientific method. Second, there is a solid basis in professional literature with a scientific foundation and unified terminology (Chisum and Turvey, 2011; Ferguson et al., 2010; Turvey, 2011, 2013). And third, the principles of this methodology have been clearly laid out in these works and subsequent court-related casework and testimony over the past 15 years. These elements help not only to satisfy the admissibility tests laid out by the courts, but they also prepare the forensic expert to respond to the challenges of attorneys seeking to keep their evidence out. BEA methodology prepares the analysts to be the most effective expert witness possible, and forces them to have their logic, their science, and their conclusions well prepared before they ever step into the courtroom, which smooths admissibility enormously.

CONCLUSION

The BEA profiling method has proven to be a great benefit to criminal investigations and criminal trials in Colombia. This author has seen it work effectively in both realms, and has seen his colleagues improve their abilities and their reasoning as a result of its use. Moreover, it has gained acceptance by the courts in Colombia because of its demonstrable scientific validity and utility. In the future, as this method of case investigation and organization is taught to other investigative units throughout the country, we hope to see it lead to an increase in effective interagency communication, just case resolution, and helpful crime-related research.

REFERENCES

Chisum, W.J., Turvey, B., 2011. Crime Reconstruction, second ed. Elsevier Science, San Diego.

Ferguson, C., Petherick, W., Turvey, B., 2010. Forensic Criminology. Elsevier Science, San Diego.

Meléndez, C.D., Millán, V.H.L., Pérez, A.A., 2014. Análisis sobre la conducta criminal de violadores seriales en casos ocurridos en Bogotá, D. C. (2008–2012). Revista Criminalidad 56 (1), 9–34.

Norza, C.E., Morales, Q.L.A., Merchán, R.L., Meléndez, C.D., 2013. Perfilación criminológica: Una revisión de la literatura y su aplicación en la investigación criminal en Colombia. Revista Criminalidad 55 (3), 309–336.

Turvey, B., 2011. Criminal Profiling: An Introduction to Behavioral Evidence Analysis, fourth ed. Elsevier Science, London.

Turvey, B., 2013. Forensic Victimology, second ed. Elsevier Science, San Diego.

PART

3

Investigative Protocols

CHAPTER

Threshold Assessments

9

W.S. Crowder
Kennesaw State University, Kennesaw, GA, United States

B.E. Turvey
Forensic Solutions LLC, Sitka, Alaska, United States;
Institute of Forensic Investigation and Criminal Profiling, Juarez, Mexico

CHAPTER OUTLINE

A threshold assessment (TA) is an investigative report that reviews the initial physical evidence of the behavior, forensic victimology, and crime scene characteristics for a particular case, or a series of related cases, in order to provide immediate direction. It is not informed by complete access to all crime scene documentation, victim information, or the full analysis and interpretation of physical evidence by the necessary forensic scientists.

Though it may contain preliminary inferences about the offender, a TA is not to be confused with, or presented as, a fully refined criminal profile.

Behavioral Evidence Analysis. http://dx.doi.org/10.1016/B978-0-12-800607-8.00009-4

PURPOSE

A TA is used when an investigation lacks focus, direction, or has been unattended for a period of time for any number of reasons. It makes assessments of what is currently understood to be a fact, while identifying the unknown and the uninvestigated. It can include suggestions regarding potential evidentiary connections and analysis, insight into interview strategy, and any investigatively relevant first impressions that the profiler has regarding investigative priority and direction.

It has the greatest value with respect to putting investigations back on track by organizing what is known and highlighting what is not with respect to an unsolved case or series of cases.

There are two main reasons for making a TA of a case, as opposed to simply waiting for more information and rendering only a full criminal profile.

First, as already discussed, it provides investigative direction. A TA compiles and presents information and suggestions in a way that is concise and effective. It serves the general profiling goal of keeping an investigation on track. It also directs investigators to gather the type of information that will assist in creating the full criminal profile, and that will provide additional grist for leads, theories, and opinions apart from the profiling effort. This is because the type of suggestions for information gathering in the TA (designed to inform a criminal profile) will help everyone involved in an investigation, not just the criminal profiler.

Second, and most often in the investigative phase, is the issue of public safety. In cases where danger is imminent, we may not be able to wait for a criminal profile. We may decide that it is in the best interest of the affected community to draw up some insights based on initial and consequently incomplete information.

Investigators may only have time to get a profiler's first-blush response from the available case materials in order to organize investigative efforts within a given time constraint.

GUIDELINES

A TA should include the following elements (See Baeza et al., 2000; and Turvey, 2011):

1. Overview of the established facts of the case relevant to crime-related behavior, as appropriate.
2. Overview of the established facts of the case relevant to victimology, as appropriate.
3. Overview of the established facts of the case relevant to crime scene characteristics, as appropriate, with supporting argumentation.

4. Initial hypothesis regarding potential motivational behaviors and aspects, as appropriate, with supporting argumentation.
5. Initial hypothesis regarding potential offender characteristics, as appropriate, with supporting argumentation.
6. Suggestions regarding further facts that need to be determined or established in order to address logical breaks in the sequence of events surrounding the crime, including suggestions regarding additional forensic analyses that may be performed on available physical evidence.
7. Suggestions regarding further victimological information gathering.
8. Investigatively relevant suggestions regarding potential strategies or avenues for suspect development.

A TA is meant to be an investigative compass, or a "to do" list, compiled in any phase of a case that outlines what is known and what needs to be investigated further. It provides initial observations, concerns, and priorities. It should be made up of investigatively relevant questions, investigatively relevant suggestions, and first impressions where appropriate.

Although it can have the same written structure as a criminal profile, a TA is rendered under different circumstances for different purposes. It should therefore not be presented as, or used for the same purpose as, a full criminal profile. It is important to keep the different circumstances and purposes of criminal profiles and TAs in mind when writing reports, or when reading any reports generated by another criminal profiler who may not know the difference.

SAMPLE REPORT

Over the past 18 years, both authors have made the preparation of TAs an integral part of their teaching rubric at the university level for both graduate and undergraduate criminal justice and criminology students. Collectively, we have assigned, evaluated, and graded more than 2000 such reports related to active homicide investigations. This is to say nothing of our own case examination experience involving this kind of assessment. With that combined experience, the authors can say with confidence that the TA serves as both a powerful learning tool and as a powerful tool for case investigation and resolution.

One of the authors (Crowder) has done this in collaboration with multiple local law enforcement agencies in the state of Georgia. The following report, prepared by one of his students at Kennesaw State University, serves as a good example of a TA report writing style. Some reports will have more detail, some will have less, and some may require clearly operationalized terms depending on the intended audience. However, this report has all of the basics written in a logical fashion.

THRESHOLD ASSESSMENT: DEBORA LYN HAYES, EQUIVOCAL DEATH

BY: VALERIE P. POOL
KENNESAW STATE UNIVERSITY

ABSTRACT

The following TA is a review of the initial investigation into the unsolved homicide of 24-year-old Debora Lyn Hayes. This assessment analyzes the original investigation of the crime, including the crime scene evidence, victimology, and interviews of potential suspects. It has been determined that the initial investigation and the ensuing effort to solve this crime were regrettably inadequate. The collection of physical evidence from the crime scene was not properly documented and has since been destroyed. The victimology of Hayes was insufficient, as were the investigations of possible suspects. This TA will attempt to assist the investigation of Hayes' death through a detailed analysis of the crime scene evidence, police and medical examiner reports, personal interviews with friends and family of the victim, and information collected on potential witnesses and suspects of the crime.

BACKGROUND

The body of Debora Lyn Hayes was discovered in the early morning of Thursday, May 30, 1985. Debora's severely decomposed body was found by her half-brother, Marshall B. According to investigative reports, Marshall B. had gone to Debora's mobile home to check on her after he was unable to reach her by telephone. When he knocked on her door and she did not answer, he entered through a bedroom window on the rear left side of her mobile home. According to statements, although he immediately smelled the odor of decomposition, he did not have a clear view of Debora's body. Marshall B. then tried to turn on a light switch and use the living room telephone to make a call, but after discovering that both were inoperable, he exited out the front door. He then went to Debora's neighbor, Thomas W., and requested that he call the Austell Police Department. Officer Raymond L. Roberts received the notification at 0039 h and was the first law enforcement official to arrive at the scene. After quickly examining the scene, officer Roberts requested the assistance of the Cobb County Police Department and the Cobb County coroner's office. The Cobb County Sheriff's office began to take crime scene pictures and the crime scene was turned over to Cobb County detectives Lt. Morris and Sgt. Seay.

Through subsequent investigative reports, interviews, and autopsy findings, it was determined that Debora passed away on Saturday, May 25, 1985, 5 days prior to being discovered. The cause of Debora's death was established as a homicide by strangulation. It was also suspected that Debora may have been raped, although the advanced state of decomposition hindered the medical examiner's ability to make that determination. A list of possible suspects were developed, and investigators focused on an unknown bearded man with whom she was last seen dancing at the Holiday Inn lounge the last time she was seen alive. As of this date, no person has been charged with the death of Debora Lyn Hayes.

CRIME SCENE CHARACTERISTICS

The crime scene in this case, Debora's home, was located in a mobile home park in the city of Austell, Georgia. Debora's nude body was discovered in a face-down position on her bedroom floor. Her legs were bent underneath her so that her knees were supporting the bottom half of her body. The upper portion of her body was resting on a mound of sheets, blankets, and a pillow that had been pulled from her bed nearby, and a single sheet was tied tightly around her neck. Deborah's bed had been stripped of all coverings but a sheet and a pillow, and there was a pair of jeans, a shirt, and a bra lying on the floor. An ironing board stood on the other side of the bed along the wall, and two boxes were stacked in the far corner. The rest of the room was fairly neat and organized. Knickknacks, picture frames, and magazines were placed neatly on the dressers and night stand.

On the whole, the remainder of the house appeared orderly and clean, aside from bottles of various soft drinks and alcohol, cigarettes and ashtrays, and used drinking glasses in the living room and kitchen area. Drinking glasses, cigarette lighters, ashtrays and their contents, beer cans, clothes, bedding, and items from Debora's trash were among the items sent to the state crime lab for saliva, latent print, trace content, and sample analyses. However, none of the items yielded any fingerprints other than the victim's, and unfortunately in 1985 DNA testing was just starting to emerge as a method of forensic profiling (Butler, 2005). In addition, all evidence related to Hayes' death was destroyed between 1989 and 1990, making future analysis of these items impossible.

Debora's car, a 1979 white Toyota Corolla, was parked directly in front of the main door to her mobile home. A napkin and a Marlboro cigarette pack were found in the front seat of her car, along with two empty drinking glasses in the back seat. These items were tagged as evidence and transported to the crime lab along with the items from inside Debora's home. A Budweiser beer can was in the grass outside of the trailer, but it is unclear as to how long it had been there and it was not included in the collection of evidence sent to the crime lab. The outdoor crime scene photographs were taken at night, so it is also difficult to find any tire tracks or footprints outside Debora's mobile home.

AUTOPSY FINDINGS

Joseph L. Burton, Cobb County Chief Medical Examiner, performed the autopsy on Debora Lyn Hayes. Although there was no rigor mortis present, decomposition had kept her body in the position in which she had died. Between May 25 and May 30, 1985, the temperature in Austell ranged from 55–86°F (Weather Time Machine, 2010).

This heat, combined with a lack of air flow throughout the mobile home, presumably accelerated the decomposition process of her body. The ligature used to strangle her, a yellow-striped bed sheet, had preserved only a small area around her neck from decomposing. Ecchymosis, more commonly known as bruising, was present in the midline of her neck below the thyroid cartilage, consistent with strangulation. No other injuries worth noting were present on the victim's body, although decomposition may have concealed other major bruises or lacerations.

Debora's liver was negative for barbiturates, sedatives, and tranquilizers, but trace amounts of cocaine and marijuana were present. In addition, her liver fluid tested positive for ethyl alcohol, otherwise known as grain alcohol. According to officer Roberts' initial incident report, he noticed a bottle of Golden Grain alcohol on her coffee table as he entered her home.

Debora was not menstruating at the time of her death, however, blood-tinged fluid was found in her upper vaginal vault. Although this may be a result of decomposition, it could also signal consensual sex or rape in the hours just prior to her death. Another finding worth mentioning was the pulmonary congestion present in her lungs. Pulmonary congestion occurs when there is an increase of extravascular fluid in the lungs, and could have been caused by the trauma of strangulation (Kolbenstvedt et al., 2010). However, pulmonary congestion can also be a result of certain types of medication. This topic of medication will be addressed further in the following sections of this TA.

VICTIMOLOGY

According the medical examiner's report, Debora Lyn Hayes was a 24-year-old Caucasian female, 64.5 inches tall, and weighed between 135 and 140 pounds. She was described by her friends and family as someone who "liked to go out and party." According to Debora's best friend, Nancy S., she was single but had a lot of past relationships. According to a transcribed interview of her brother Marshall B. and her sister Sandy H., Debora drank Budweiser beer, tequila liquor, and smoked either Virginia Slims or Marlboro Lights, all of which were found in and around the crime scene.

An interview was conducted with Wanda S., a friend of Debora's who had known her since the ninth grade. During questioning Wanda S. told Cobb County detective Barry Banks and Lt. Carlton Morris that Debora was depressed. In photographs of the crime scene, several prescription bottles were positioned on the top of her refrigerator, but none of the labels were clear enough to determine the medication inside. However, if Debora had mixed any of those medications with alcohol on the night of her death, she may have experienced adverse reactions, such as a loss of consciousness. As a result, this may have increased her vulnerability to attack on the night she died.

LIFESTYLE RISK

Debora had a fairly high lifestyle risk, meaning that her living situation and daily activities caused her to have an increased risk of harm (Turvey and Petherick, 2009).

One of the contributing factors to her high lifestyle risk was the fact that she lived alone. Another was the Austell party scene where she spent a lot of her weekends. Spending time in clubs and lounges, combined with her practice of imbibing copious amounts of alcohol increased the likelihood that she would come into contact with potentially dangerous individuals. In addition, as previously mentioned, her autopsy findings indicated cocaine and marijuana in her system. The "International Association of Marijuana Growers and Users" plaque on her bedroom wall was a likely indicator that she was more than an occasional drug user.

SITUATIONAL RISK

The last time that Debora was seen alive was at the Holiday Inn lounge on Saturday, May 25, 1985. This was also the date on which medical examiner Burton estimated her death. Based on Debora's whereabouts and activities on that date, her situational risk, or risk of harm at the time of the crime, was substantially high (Turvey and Petherick, 2009). Several witnesses stated that they saw Debora drinking that night. Her friend Wanda S., who drove her to Chasers and the Holiday Inn lounge that night, stated that Debora was unable to drive because she had been drinking vodka prior to leaving her home for the evening. Then, at both Chasers and the Holiday Inn, Debora was seen with various drinks. In addition, the empty bottles, cans, and glasses around Debora's home suggested that she may have been drinking either immediately before going out or upon her return home. As previously mentioned, her autopsy report stated that she had ethyl alcohol in her liver fluid and no residual food in her stomach. At approximately 135 pounds, even if Debora had consumed one alcoholic beverage per hour, her blood alcohol level would have been between 0.10 and 0.30 at the estimated time of her death (Drink Wheel, 2010). Based on witness statements and autopsy results, it is likely that Debora's blood alcohol level was closer to 0.30 on the night that she died. At this level, most people not only lose the ability to fend off an attack, but many lose consciousness altogether. According to Dr. Reed Ginn, pharmacist, ingesting certain types of medication with alcohol is likely to result in a severely altered state or complete loss of consciousness (personal communication, February 23, 2010).

OFFENDER CHARACTERISTICS

Modus operandi

The perpetrator in this homicide displayed varying degrees of offender risk, meaning that he only took particular precautions to avoid detection and was not careful in all aspects of his crime (Turvey, 2008). His modus operandi, meaning how he completed his crime, appeared to be fairly planned out. It is likely that he knew that Debora lived alone, therefore ensuring that they would not be interrupted during the commission of his crime. This lowered his risk of situational exposure. Additionally, there was nothing found at the crime scene to suggest that he brought any of his own equipment to the attack, indicating that he may have been aware of Debora's altered state of consciousness and did not believe that it would be difficult to overpower her.

Methods of approach and attack

There were no signs of forced entry or a struggle at the crime scene, suggesting that Debora either knew her attacker or he was able to gain access through an unlocked door or open window. Since there were multiple drinking glasses found in the living room and kitchen areas, it is possible that Debora may have been entertaining company. If so, this would have had to occur after she returned home from the Holiday Inn lounge, as she was reportedly alone all evening until Wanda S. picked her up from her mobile home.

Method of control/use of force

Since it is quite probable that Debora did not have the wherewithal to defend herself at the time of her death, the single sheet ligature would have been sufficient to cut off her breathing and suffocate her. Several things about the way in which her body was found indicate that Debora was not even conscious when she died. First, Debora's home was fairly neat and organized, and a bed stripped of its bedding did not fit in. It is unlikely that Debora would have taken all of her sheets and blankets off of her own bed just to position them under her on the floor. Rather, the offender may have done this so that her limp body could be posed in such a way as to facilitate a sexual act. Second, the ligature around Debora's neck was tied over her hair. The majority of females would be compelled to pull their hair away from their neck, meaning that Debora probably did not consent to the fastening of the sheet where it would inevitably tug at her hair. Additionally, the ligature knot was located behind the right posterior occipital area of her neck. This may suggest a right-handed offender who held on to the ends of the sheet in order to control the upper portion of her body during the sexual act.

Suspects

Shortly after Debora's death a small group of suspects emerged. However, the suspect pool was quite small, disorganized, and inconclusive. In addition, most of these suspects were never questioned by investigators. Follow-up actions were not performed on the existing suspects, and the list was never expanded to include other likely offenders.

One of the first suspects in the case was Steve S. For starters, he admitted to being at Chasers and possibly the Holiday Inn lounge the last night that Debora was seen alive. He also drove his father's baby blue Dodge truck, which matched the description of a vehicle that was seen parked outside of Debora's mobile home during the night hours in the two weeks prior to her death. He also drank Budweiser beer, which was the type of beer can found at the crime scene. Additionally, a mug shot of Steve S. was taken on May 14, 1985 after a DUI (Driving Under the Influence) arrest. In the picture he had shoulder-length brown hair and a mustache, and by the time of Debora's death could have easily grown a beard to match the description of the man seen dancing with her at the Holiday Inn lounge. Furthermore, Steve S. failed to appear for his first scheduled polygraph and was instead found hiding at the home of his friend Daniel P.'s. When he finally did take the polygraph, he showed signs of deception. Unfortunately, no further questioning of Steve S. appears to have taken place.

Daniel P. was another viable suspect in Debora's death. Not only did he drive a blue truck like Steve S., but he seemed to exhibit several suspicious behaviors while this case was being investigated. When two law enforcement officers came to Daniel P.'s looking for Steve S., Daniel P. told the officers that he had clipped a newspaper article of Debora's death to put in his scrapbook. He explained that he wanted a memory of the crime because it was the first time he had been accused of murder. However, it was this incident that raised a red flag and placed Daniel P. in the pool of suspects. This newspaper clipping could be classified as a trophy, which (according to Turvey, 2008) is a symbol of victory, achievement, or conquest, and can be related to force or victim subjugation. It also could have been a souvenir which serves to remind offenders of a pleasant experience. Daniel P. came up in another conversation with law enforcement when Francis K. told authorities that her friend's husband, Tom G., was friends with Daniel P. and had heard about the scrapbook. According to Francis K., Daniel P. had hinted to Tom G. that he was somehow involved in Debora's death, and kept mementos of various murders in the scrapbook. Unfortunately, the scrapbook was not collected and Daniel P. was not questioned regarding this incident. Another factor that leads Daniel P. to be a feasible suspect in Debora's murder is his criminal history. Since Debora's death, his charges have included dangerous drugs on November 11, 1987, battery on June 2, 1997, aggravated stalking on August 15, 1997, and criminal solicitation on January 28, 2000. The battery charge was a result of domestic violence, which can be "physical, psychological, or sexual violence that occurs within the bounds of an existing or emotional relationship" (Turvey and Petherick, 2009, p. 334). Aggravated stalking is another felonious crime that stands out in Daniel P.'s criminal record and together with battery, emphasizes the fact that he should not be excluded from the suspect pool even now.

Another suspect in Debora's death was Daniel S. Like Daniel P., he too had a criminal history in Georgia, although his began prior to Debora's death. On August 15, 1979, he was charged with burglary and a sexual offense. Then on March 19, 1984, he was charged with public indecency and a peeping tom crime. Items found inside his impounded vehicle included electrical tape, a knife, and drug paraphernalia. Given Daniel S.'s propensity for crime, especially sexual offenses, he should have been considered a major suspect and a serious investigation should have ensued.

There were many more suspects identified during the initial investigation into Debora's death. However, these suspects seemed to appear in the case files without explanation. Through a secondary investigation, efforts should be taken to determine why these individuals were named as suspects. This can be done through interviews of the suspects themselves or through interviews with Debora's friends and acquaintances.

Investigative suggestions

Since there is no possible benefit to focusing only on the investigation's shortcomings, this section will focus on what might be done to help close this case. The first suggestion in this endeavor would be to reexamine all of the identified suspects. With today's investigative tools such as LexisNexis, Accurint, and Clear, it is not a difficult task to track an individual down. In addition to locating each suspect, their criminal histories should be run in the National Crime Information Center (NCIC) database. The individuals who show a pattern of violent or sexual offenses will need to be scrutinized carefully and ultimately questioned by authorities. However, these are not the only subjects that deserve attention. If an individual was identified as a possible suspect in 1985, even if the reason is unknown, they need to be reexamined today.

In addition to locating and running criminal histories on the suspects, other aspects of their lives should be revisited as well. For example, Steve S. worked at an electrical company one month before Debora's death. Since Marshall B., Debora's brother, told police that neither her phone nor her lights worked the night he found her, perhaps Steve S.'s electrical experience should be considered. Steve's coworkers and supervisors should be questioned regarding his employment at the electrical company, specifically his general character and the extent of his electrical knowledge. Then, perhaps it would be possible to determine if there are any discrete connections between this case and other previously unrelated cases in the same general area and around the same general time period. This process is referred to as case linkage or linkage analysis and may be helpful in several aspects of this case (Turvey, 2008).

Daniel S. is another witness who needs to be located and investigated. Given his record of sexual offenses prior to Debora's death, it is possible that he continued this pattern throughout his life. It may even be predicted that his offenses have escalated over the years. Additionally, if he was keeping a scrapbook of his crimes as a souvenir, it is very likely that he still has this scrapbook. If significant case linkage can be completed that connects other crimes to this case, especially if Daniel S. has considerable history of violent or sexual crimes, it may be possible to obtain a search warrant for his residence to obtain the scrapbook. Then if the scrapbook is found, and contains information to other crimes he may have committed, case linkage will have already been accomplished by the suspect himself.

It is documented in the case file that Daniel P. worked at a cleaning service. That company needs to be visited and old coworkers and supervisors of Daniel P. need to be questioned. Helpful information regarding Daniel P.'s lifestyle and disposition around the time of Debora's death may emerge from looking into his past place of employment.

In addition to reexamining persons of interest from the original investigation, the suspect pool needs to be widened considerably. The new list of suspects should include Debora's brother Marshall B., and any violent sexual offenders who were living around the Austell area at the time of her death. In addition, investigators need to visit Debora's friends and acquaintances. For example, it is recommended that an investigator speak with Thelma from Clarkdale, who was identified as one of Debora's close friends by her sister Sandy H. Even if Thelma's last name or other personal information is not in the case file, it is documented that she lived between Clarkdale Generator and the old Clarkdale Filling Station. Cobb County tax records from

1985 may be able to ascertain more information about Thelma and how to reach her today. Cindy G., who went to South Cobb High School with Debora, should also be questioned. Debora's old roommates Robin and Tim should be tracked down as well, perhaps through interviews with her friends or old leasing records. Although a long shot, it may be possible to ask the local Army National Guard units for assistance in identifying a soldier named Robin who lived in Debora's mobile home in 1985. This would be helpful because Robin might know of someone Debora may have been dating when she died, since Robin had moved out just weeks before Debora's death.

Debora was employed by Momar Chemicals when she passed away. Since she performed administrative duties there, it would be reasonable to assume that she had a fairly regular daytime schedule. If this was the case, the question arises as to why no one came looking for her or filed a missing person report after she had not shown up for work in the week between her death and the discovery of her body. If someone called in to MoMar on her behalf or if someone at MoMar covered for her absence, those occurrences would certainly give investigators some possible new leads in the case. Regardless of the result, many personnel from MoMar still need to be questioned regarding this issue.

Another action that should be taken by investigators is to go back and question the two Fulton County Sheriff's officers who were working security at the Holiday Inn the night Debora was last seen. One officer was identified as Robert Voit and the other as David. Records should be easily obtained by requesting the assistance of Fulton County in this investigation. Although the case is now over two decades old, the two officers may still remember details about that night that may assist in solving this case.

The crime scene revealed several mysterious items that raised suspicion. This included the two separate kinds of cigarettes, the Pepsi bottle, and the California Cooler bottle. Since most people have a favorite brand of cigarette, Debora's brand should be identified. By ruling out her brand, the other can be attributed to the offender. This same principle applies to the Pepsi and California Cooler bottles. As indicated by various case file reports, Debora favored Coke products, beer, vodka, and tequila. This makes the presence of competing products somewhat suspicious and may be used as a tool to narrow the suspect pool.

Throughout this TA the offender was referred to as a single individual. However, this does not mean that the crime was committed by only one perpetrator. A major theme in this TA was that more interviews and investigations need to be performed on past suspects and acquaintances of Debora, and only then can more information be deduced regarding the person or persons responsible for Debora's death. Additionally, speculations were made as to the manner of death and offender characteristics. These remain inductive hypotheses and, like every new lead in this case, will need to be verified by utilizing the scientific method. Once all possible leads are investigated and each hypothesis is tested, certain hypotheses will inevitably be falsified. Consequently, the investigation should then be narrowed down to a manageable amount of leads, one of which can be followed straight to Debora's killer.

REFERENCES

Baeza, J., Chisum, W.J., Chamberlin, T.M., McGrath, M., Turvey, B., January 2000. Academy of Behavioral profiling: criminal profiling Guidelines. Journal of Behavioral Profiling 1 (1).

Butler, J.M., 2005. Forensic DNA Typing. Academic Press, Oxford, UK.

Drink Wheel, 2010. Intoximeters Inc. From http://www.intox.com/wheel/drinkwheelresults.asp. Retrieved (21.02.10.).

Kolbenstvedt, A., Skjennald, A., Higgins, C.B., 2010. Pulmonary Congestion/Pulmonary Edema. Medcyclopaedia. From http://www.medcyclopaedia.com/library/radiology/chapter18/4/9.aspx. Retrieved (21.02.10.).

Turvey, B., 2008. Criminal Profiling. Academic Press, Oxford, UK.

Turvey, B., 2011. Criminal Profiling: An Introduction to Behavioral Evidence Analysis, fourth ed. Elsevier Science, London.

Turvey, B., Petherick, W., 2009. Forensic Victimology. Academic Press, Oxford, UK.

Weather Time Machine, 2010. Farmer's Almanac. From: http://www.farmersalmanac.com/weather/time_machine/1985/. Retrieved (21.02.10.).

CHAPTER

Equivocal Death Analysis 10

B.E. Turvey
Forensic Solutions LLC, Sitka, Alaska, United States;
Institute of Forensic Investigation and Criminal Profiling, Juarez, Mexico

CHAPTER OUTLINE

The word *equivocal* refers to anything that can be interpreted in more than one way or to any existing interpretation that is uncertain. This definition, which comes from the dictionary and should require no lengthy explanation, can be applied to many forensic opinions and conclusions. In other words, there are quite a few forensic findings that should be labeled equivocal, even as they are being offered as evidence in court. Those offering them, however, routinely fail to be forthcoming about this important limitation—either out of bias or ignorance (see an exhaustive explanation in Edwards and Gotsonis, 2009).

As described in Turvey (2012), an *equivocal forensic analysis* refers to a review of case evidence that seeks to question and critically evaluate prior assumptions and conclusions. This evaluative assessment of case "facts" and evidence helps insulate the forensic analyst from investments in preexisting case theories. It is done when there is a doubt, or a significant question is raised, regarding the accuracy or reliability of prior findings, methods, and testimony.

An equivocal forensic analysis is a necessary and useful tool in both investigative and forensic contexts. It is particularly relevant in those cases where the facts can lend themselves to multiple conclusions. If the case at hand is referred to as *rape*, the forensic examiner critically reviews the evidence which is meant to establish the elements of rape, such as the crime scene evidence, the medical report, the sexual assault kit, and any victim statements; if the crime at hand is referred to as a *homicide*, the forensic examiner critically reviews the evidence which is meant to establish the elements of homicide, such as the crime scene, the crime scene documentation, the autopsy report, and the autopsy photos. When the evidence supports prior conclusions, the forensic examiner may move forward with additional assessments; whenever there is a doubt or a reversal in findings, it must be noted and case theories stemming from those conclusions must be amended.

Behavioral Evidence Analysis. http://dx.doi.org/10.1016/B978-0-12-800607-8.00010-0

Case involvements that require equivocal forensic examinations typical to the engagement of this author have included the following:

1. cases involving suspected false allegations of sexual assault;
2. cases involving in-custody deaths classified as suicide, when homicide is suspected (negligent or intentional);
3. cases of autoerotic death misclassified as suicide;
4. cases involving forensic examiners suspected of dry-labbing (falsifying) forensic tests or findings.

IN-CUSTODY DEATHS

When an inmate that is being held by the state dies, this is referred to as an *in-custody death*. This can happen in a jail, in a prison, during transport to either, or while being detained by the police on a sidewalk. In-custody means that an individual is under the control and authority of the state, deprived of the ability to care for themselves let alone simply walk away from the dangers that they can be confronted with. They may be confined in a cell or a vehicle, they may be restrained by handcuffs or shackles, or they may simply be under verbal direction and compelled not to move by the threat of force. Subsequently, there is a duty of care by the state—to ensure that no harm occurs to the person being held in their custody.

Therefore when someone under the state's control and protection dies, that death must be investigated. This holds true whether the death is a suicide, or whether it occurs by virtue of natural causes such as disease or old age. It does not matter if the suicide or natural causes are believed to be "obvious" findings. An investigation is mandatory. As provided in Tartaro (2005, p. 113)

> *Officers are responsible for not only keeping inmates safe from each other, but they are obligated to keep inmates safe from themselves (Collins, 1995; Hanser, 2002). Officers and civilian staff in prisons, jails and police lock-ups have to deal with the possibility that inmates under their supervision might attempt to take their own lives.*

Again, in-custody death investigations are a requirement upon the death of anyone in law enforcement custody.

In-custody deaths are typically massive and involve far-reaching interviews of prison staff, inmates, and reviews of collateral information such as the inmate's property, medical charts, and institutional paperwork. Investigators must determine whether the event was foreseeable and whether all staff members involved with the inmate's care were performing their work in accordance with the policy during the time frame in question.

GARY "DON" EDWARDS

Consider the death of Gary D. Edwards, from the author's case files.

According to the "Report of Autopsy" in this case, 25-year-old Mr. Edwards died as a result of hanging himself on October 31, 2006. This was assumed as a fact by the medical examiner (ME)'s office at the beginning of the autopsy, not investigated or established by a review of the evidence. The cause of death was subsequently listed as "hanging" and the manner of death was determined to be "suicide". His blood alcohol was found to be .11 percent. This was an "in-custody death," as Mr. Edwards died while being held by law enforcement at the city of Marlow (Oklahoma) facilities building.

On July 14, 2008, the estate of Gary D. Edwards filed a wrongful death suit against the city and the police department. That lawsuit was settled out of court. After questions arose regarding the discovery material that had been provided, the estate contacted this author to examine the evidence in the case.

Contextually, it is important to understand that the cause and manner of death determinations across the United States are made every day by nonmedical personnel (eg, elected coroners, sheriffs, and even morticians; see Edwards and Gotsonis, 2009). In other words, these determinations are not medical findings as no diagnosis or treatment regiment is involved, necessarily. Rather, they are forensic determinations meant to be based on: a full reconstruction of the events considering the totality of the physical evidence, including a forensic examination of the body; a scrupulous examination of the death scene and the surrounding environments; and a complete and thorough history of the decedent. It may be a surprise to most that this is almost never done, and many who are charged with death investigation work do not actually know how to do it.

Guidelines for competent death investigations can be found for free, online, and published by the National Institute of Justice (NIJ, 1999). That is to say these guidelines have been around for a long time and have been widely accessible. Additionally, the author believes that most forensic examiners would have a great deal of enthusiasm for these guidelines, if only they would simply bother to read them.

In any event, this case is generally representative of the nature and circumstances of other equivocal death examinations conducted by the author. There were a number of significant institutional contexts and findings in this case. They are detailed in the following report, which is preceded by the ME's findings and related traumagram.

Board of Medicolegal Investigations
Office of the Chief Medical Examiner
901 N. Stonewall
Oklahoma City, Oklahoma 73117
(405) 239-7141 Voice
(405) 239-2430 Fax

CERTIFICATION
I hereby certify that this document is a true and correct copy of the original document. Valid only when copy bears imprint of the office seal.
By________________
Date________________

REPORT OF AUTOPSY

Decedent	Age	Birth Date	Race	Sex	Autopsy No	Case No
GARY DON EDWARDS	**25**	**1/11/1981**	**WH**	**M**	**926-06**	**0602424**

Type of Death	Means	ID By	Authority for Autopsy
Violent, unusual or unnatural		**TOE TAG**	**CHAI S. CHOI, M.D.**

Present at Autopsy
MIKE GRIFFIN

PATHOLOGICAL DIAGNOSIS

I. Hanging:
  A. Ligature (ripped T-shirt) around the neck with fixed knot
  B. Ligature mark around the neck

II. Superficial cutaneous abrasions, left arm, forearm and left shin with small abrasions of the right finger and right leg and right temple

III. Acute pulmonary congestion with edema (combined weight 1080 gm) due to # I

Comment: This 25 year old white male was found dead by an officer in cell # 1 at the Marlow Police Department. The officer was placing another prisoner in cell # 2 when he found the decedent hanging from his torn shirt that was tied to the window grate. EMS was called and found the decedent dead. There was no foul play suspected. A complete autopsy showed a ligature around the neck tied with a fixed knot. There are minor superficial abrasions over the left side of the arm, forearm and leg, and small abrasions of the right fingers and right ankle. Postmortem toxicological studies showed no evidence of a drug overdose other than 0.11% w/v of ethyl alcohol in his heart blood, with 0.15% w/v of vitreous humor. It is felt that the cause of death is hanging. The manner of death is suicide.

CAUSE OF DEATH: HANGING

The facts stated herein are true and correct to the best of my knowledge and belief.

Chai S. Choi, M.D.		OCME Central Division	11/2/2006 9:30 AM.
CHAI S. CHOI, M.D.	Pathologist	Location of Autopsy	Date and Time of Autopsy

CME-2 Page 1

FULL BODY, MALE – ANTERIOR AND POSTERIOR VIEWS (VENTRAL AND DORSAL)

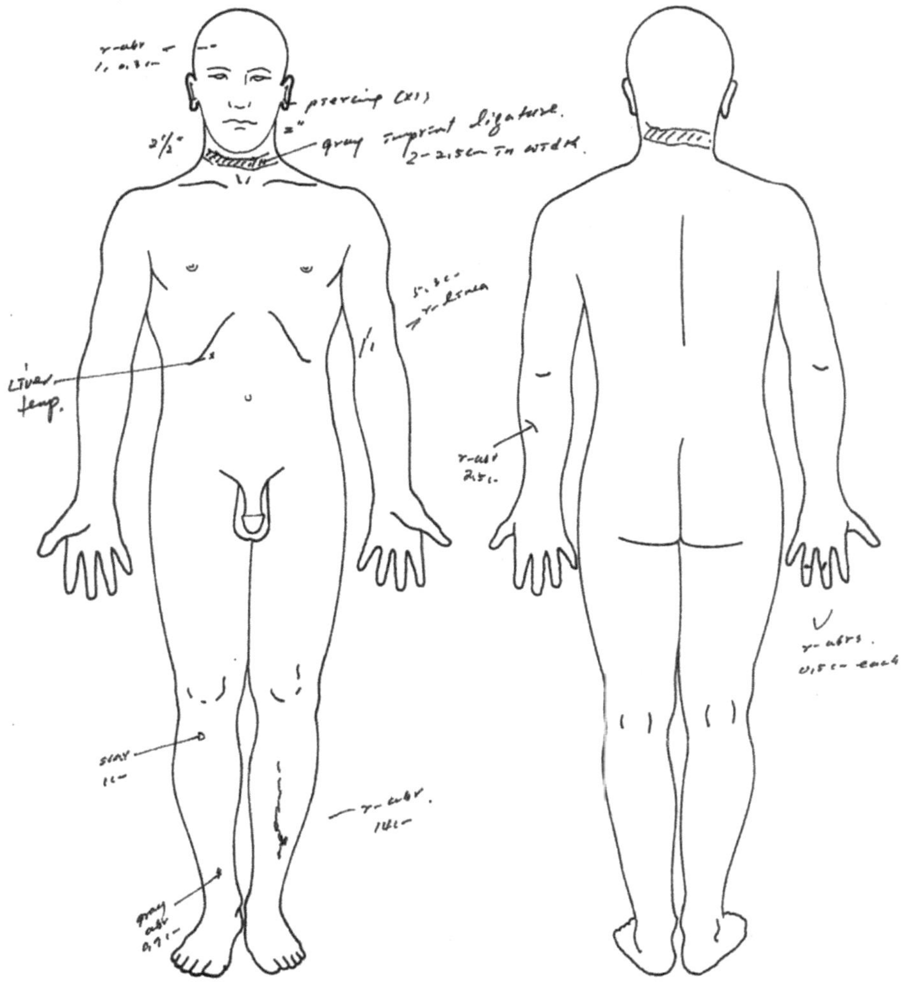

Name Gary Don Edwards Case No. 0602424

CME-1B6 (Series 1978) Date 11-2-06

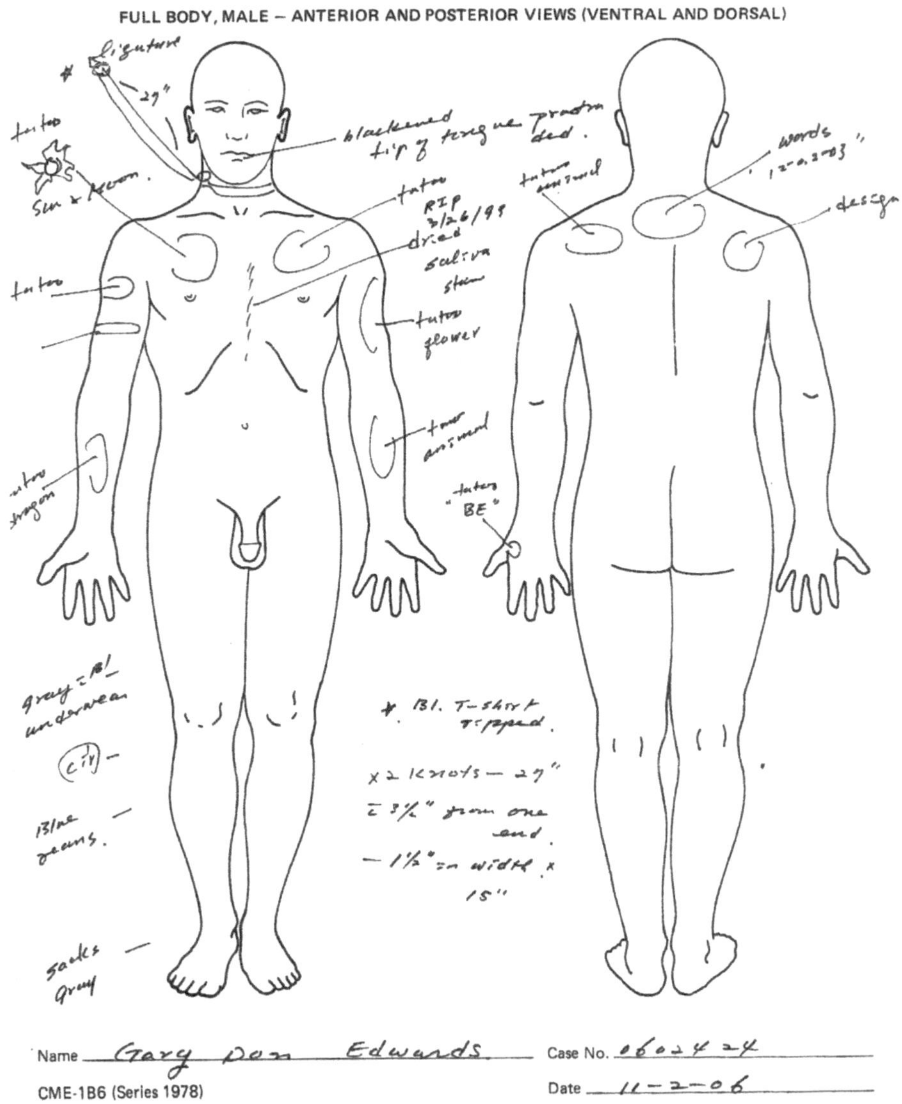
FULL BODY, MALE – ANTERIOR AND POSTERIOR VIEWS (VENTRAL AND DORSAL)
ligature
27"
blackened tip of tongue protruded.
tattoo
sun & moon.
tattoo
dried saliva stain
tattoo flower
tattoo dragon
tattoo "BE"
words
design
gray c̄ Bl underwear
Blue jeans.
socks gray
Bl. T-shirt ripped.
x 2 knots — 27"
— 1½" in width x 15"
Name Gary Don Edwards
Case No. 060424
CME-1B6 (Series 1978)
Date 11-2-06

FORENSIC EXAMINATION REPORT

Forensic Solutions, LLC
P.O. Box 2175, Sitka, Alaska 99835
(907) 747-5121

Equivocal Forensic Analysis

To: The Estate of Gary Don Edwards
c/o Toshia Williams
P.O. Box 328 Coal Hill
Arkansas 72832

Examiner: Brent E. Turvey, MS
Date: October 26, 2009
Case: In Custody Death
Decedent: Gary Don Edwards

PURPOSE

The purpose of this report is to provide an *equivocal forensic analysis* regarding the in-custody death of Gary Don Edwards. An *equivocal forensic analysis* refers to a review of the physical evidence in a given case, questioning all related assumptions and conclusions (Petherick and Turvey, 2009). It is generally conducted when there is a question or doubt regarding the nature and/or completeness of any aspect of the forensic or medicolegal investigation related to a particular case.

MATERIALS

The examiner was provided with, and relied upon, at least the following materials:

1. Marlow PD Booking "Sheet" re: Gary D. Edwards; 10/31/06;
2. Marlow PD Medical Questionnaire re: Gary D. Edwards; 10/31/06;
3. Marlow PD Medical Radio Log Record re: Gary D. Edwards; 10/31/06;
4. Scene photos of decedent's body in situ (labeled 6-21);
5. American Medical Response report prepared by Danny Reed; Ticket# 272256;
6. Marlow PD Jail Incident Report, unsigned, undated re: Gary D. Edwards; Re: 10/31/06;
7. Incident Reports by Marlow PD Officers re: Gary D. Edwards;
8. Marlow PD Internal Investigation Report of Chief Elvis Walker by Lt. Randy Johnson, unsigned;
9. "Report of Investigation" by DA Investigator Justin Scott; Case No. JRS: 103106S30; undated, unsigned.
10. Oklahoma State Department of Health, Jail Inspection "Report of Death Investigation" by Investigator Don Garrison; 11/1/06;
11. "Report of Autopsy" prepared by Chai S. Choi, MD, OCME, Oklahoma City, Oklahoma; 11/2/06;
12. City of Marlow's Response to Plaintiff's Interrogatories, *Estate of Gary Don Edwards et al. v. City of Marlow and the City of Marlow Police Department*; 01/07/09;
13. Photos of the decedent in his casket taken by family members prior to his internment;

14. Photo's of decedent's jeans taken by family subsequent to receipt from ME's Office;
15. Physical examination of decedent's jeans by the examiner, including photos taken with and without UV light.

RATIONALE

There are at least two issues of concern that strongly compel the need for an equivocal forensic analysis in this case. These relate to problems with the autopsy report, and recently discovered evidence related to the credibility of the primary investigating officer at the Marlow Police Department.

1. Autopsy Report

In this case, significant questions have arisen about the nature, quality, and accuracy of the non-medical conclusions found in the "Report of Autopsy" in this case, prepared by Chai S. Choi, MD, Office of the Chief Medical Examiner of the State of Oklahoma, Oklahoma City, Oklahoma.

The purpose of any autopsy report is to render an informed forensic opinion as to the *cause* and *manner* of death. It should be noted that an autopsy report does not necessarily involve the rendering of medical opinions (i.e. those related to diagnosis and treatment), unless the decedent succumbed to a particular disease that caused or contributed to their death. Specifically, opinions regarding wound patterns and a decedent's *manner* of death actually fall under the aegis of *crime reconstruction*, which is most appropriately performed by forensic scientists (see Chisum and Turvey, 2006; Turvey, 2008).

As explained in the recently published NAS Report regarding the current state of forensic science, the ME/ Coroner system in the United States is populated, for the most part, by elected coroners (many without a medical background) with insufficient forensic training and no accreditation or oversight (Edwards and Gotsonis, 2009; p.1-12):

> Most of the country is served by offices lacking accreditation. Similarly, requirements for training are not mandatory. About 36 percent of the population lives where minimal or no special training is required to conduct death investigations. Recently, an 18-year-old high school student was elected a deputy coroner in Indiana after completing a short training course.

In other words, in the United States it is common practice for those without a medical degree or forensic background to perform crime reconstructions and forensic autopsies, and render related opinions. In this case, the only written reconstruction of events comes from DA's Investigator Justin Scott, in his undated, unsigned "report of investigation" for Case No. JRS: 103106S30. This version of events, which essentially comes from the Officers on the scene and not the Investigator himself, appears to be accepted in the autopsy as an unquestioned fact.

It is significant to note that the Office of the Chief Medical Examiner of the State of Oklahoma recently lost its accreditation subsequent to an on-site audit by the National Association of Medical Examiners in April of 2009. The NAME Audit Report cited, among other ills, overworked staff operating with limited resources in too small a space. This audit came subsequent to an OSBI investigation into criminal charges related to the management of that office back in February of 2009. The OSBI investigation has resulted in a multi-county grand jury report which accuses that office of being a hostile, leaderless environment that is mismanaged, and allows for sexual harassment and the mishandling of evidence to be commonplace - rising to the level of criminal misconduct (Twelfth Multicounty Grand Jury, 2009).

However, this forensic examination report will not seek to question medical findings related to this case. Rather it will confine itself to a review of the physical evidence and forensic protocols as they relate to reconstructing the events surrounding the decedent's death.

2. Marlow Police Department investigation
Almost all of the contextual information, witness interviews, and physical evidence in this case come from or through the officers in the Marlow Police Department.

According to Bret Burns, District Attorney, his office recently determined that two Marlow Police Officers intentionally gave false testimony and offered "doctored" evidence logs as evidence in court regarding their arrest of a couple on charges relating to methamphetamine trafficking (Hopper, 2009). Those officers were Randy Johnson and Rodney Richards.

This is significant because Lt. Randy Johnson appears to have been second in command only to the chief on the evening of Gary Edward's death. He was also responsible for preparing Chief Walkers internal report regarding the matter.

It should be noted that this information came to light after this examiner completed his initial examination of the evidence in this case.

BACKGROUND
According to the "Report of Autopsy" in this case, 25-year-old Gary D. Edwards died as a result of hanging himself on Oct. 31, 2006. Again, this was assumed as fact at the beginning of the autopsy, not investigated or established by a review of the evidence. Cause of death was subsequently listed as "hanging"; manner of death was determined to be "suicide". His blood alcohol was found to be .11.

This was an "in-custody death", as Mr. Edwards died while being held at the City of Marlow Facilities Building. This building houses the police and fire departments, and two holding cells. The Marlow PD is not a registered jail; subjects may be held a maximum of 12 hours before they must be transported to a registered county jail (McPherson, 2008).

The Marlow police had been dispatched to Mr. Edward's home on a domestic disturbance call on Oct. 31, 2006 at 1813hrs. There had been a reported dispute between he and his wife. He left the residence before officers arrived.

After a brief search, the Marlow PD located him outside of a convenience store. Mr. Edwards was arrested at that location based on the officer's observation that he appeared to be intoxicated (the smell of alcohol, bloodshot and watery eyes, and apparent trouble keeping balance). Though he was able to give officers his correct name. He was taken into custody for public drunkenness and to permit "detoxification", according to police reports. The arresting officer was Tony Lynch of the Marlow PD.

Intake forms provide that Mr. Edwards was without injury and did not appear suicidal. Further, he was reported by Marlow PD Reserve Officer James Price to be cooperative during the booking process. Officer Price called Mr. Edwards' mother and explained he would be released in four hours, after his "detox". He allowed Mr. Edwards to speak with her as well.

Mr. Edwards was reportedly booked into Cell No. 1 by 1845hrs. Officer Price checked on Mr. Edwards at 1915hrs, and again at 1930hrs. Both times Mr. Edwards appeared to be fine. For approximately the next hour and thirty minutes, Mr. Edwards was reportedly not checked on again as all officers in the department was dispatched to another call.

Mr. Edwards was subsequently found deceased in his holding cell by Marlow PD Reserve Officer Orvil Robinson at 2104hrs. Officer Robinson was placing a female prisoner in holding cell No. 2 when he reportedly observed Mr. Edwards hanging in his cell and called for help.

Mr. Edwards was found in a seated position on the bench in his cell, with his shirt tied around his neck at one end, and around a window grate above at the other. His shirt had reportedly been torn into strips and tied lengthwise to reach from the window grate to his neck as he sat on the bench. A stray piece of his torn shirt was also discovered on the floor in the cell. He was also observed to be oozing fluid from his mouth. He was reportedly "cold to the touch" with visible signs of lividity in his arms and hands.

On July 14, 2008, the Estate of Gary Don Edwards filed a wrongful death suit against the city and the police department. That lawsuit was settled out of court. After questions arose regarding the discovery material that had been provided, the Estate contacted this examiner to review the case.

FINDINGS

1. **The various law enforcement investigations into the death of Mr. Edwards lack independence, relying on the same questionable source material.**

   This finding is based on at least the following:

   A standard investigation of an in-custody death involves an outside agency conducting interviews, gathering and examining evidence, and rendering an independent finding that is intended to be objective and impartial.

In this case, the officers at the Marlow Police Department all prepared written statements together prior to the arrival of any outside entity. Then, during the internal investigation, Lt. Randy Johnson conducted and reported on all of the officer interviews. His investigation assumed that the "incident" was a suicide; it concluded that there was no violation of statutes or policy, and no evidence of officer negligence.

The outside agencies involved did not appear to question the information they received in these statements or reports in any meaningful fashion. Rather, they appear to have been taken at face value and incorporated into subsequent reports. This includes the DA Investigator's report, the Autopsy report, and the Jail Inspection report. All demonstrate a pathological disinterest in performing an independent investigation into the events under review. So while there is the outward appearance of independent verification with respect to a determination of suicide, each outside entity appears to be relying on the same group of prepared officer statements and not the results of their own parallel investigation.

As further evidence of this, there is no record of any interview with the female prisoner being placed into her cell when Mr. Edwards' body was discovered – no by any agency. This is a major oversight.

Note: Officer D. Smith, Lt. R. Johnson, and DA Investigator Justin Scott reported taking death scene and holding cell photos in this case. In their interrogatories, the city reported to have turned over all photos. However, this examiner has received only 15 photographs labeled 6-21. 1-5 appears to be missing from this series, at the very least. This also indicates that at two sets of death scene photos were not provided in discovery – as each photographer would have their own numerical series.

Moreover, the cell of the death scene had a metal grate over it with two pipes alongside running into the ceiling (photo 18). However, photos 19-21 show a window without a grate in daylight. Both circumstances are inconsistent with the death scene and the times that the above individuals reported taking photos. This would indicate that these photos are actually unrelated to the case.

Note: None of the evidence collected in this case by the Police was submitted for testing or examination of any kind. At the very least, the clothing should have been examined for injury and biological fluid to support or refute the finding of suicide. Moreover, the ligature could have been examined to determine whether or not it could actually cause ligature strangulation without breaking under the weight of the decedent. Additionally the shirt fragment on the floor was not photographed or examined.

2. The Medicolegal death investigation in this case was inadequate.

This finding is based on at least the following:

a. According to the decedent's family, they were advised by a representative of the ME's office that the ME does not take autopsy photos in these kinds of cases, as that is unnecessary. No autopsy photos were provided in discovery to the family as part of their lawsuit. The failure to take photos during autopsy is a substandard forensic practice, as it fails to provide adequate documentation of areas with and without injury. This practice telegraphs that the finding of suicide was assumed rather than investigated and established by the ME. Moreover, it prevents independent verification of findings. Given that this was an in-custody death and litigation would be an ever-present concern for the experienced forensic examiner, the apparent failure to document this examination with photographs is a red flag that requires investigation.

b. The decedent was booked into the jail without physical injury. However, at the time of autopsy there is reported evidence of injury to the decedent unrelated to the ligature. These are mentioned on p.2 at the end of the paragraph, and drawn on the trauma-gram of the decedent's body. They include a vertical linear abrasion on the left shin, linear abrasions on the left arm, a linear abrasion on the left forearm, small abrasions on two of the right fingers, and an abrasion on the right temple. The failure to explain these injuries in the context of this death is not just a substandard forensic practice, it is an omission that should have been a red flag for further medicolegal investigation into the altercation that caused them after he was booked into custody.

c. The decedent was booked into the jail without physical injury. However, at the time of his funeral viewing there is clear evidence of significant injury to the back of the decedent's left hand. This injury was not mentioned in the autopsy, which itself is problematic. Again, and in combination with the previous finding, this is a red flag for further medicolegal investigation into the altercation that caused all of these injuries after the decedent was booked into custody.

d. According to officers at the scene, and medical personnel, the decedent's body was cool to the touch an hour and a half after the last time he was observed alive. A dead body loses, on average, about 1.5 degrees Fahrenheit per hour. Under the circumstances, the body should not have lost enough temperature to be "cool the touch". Moreover, in the trauma-gram section of the autopsy report there is the phrase "liver temp." written with a line drawn towards the body in the general area of the liver. This suggests that the body temperature may have been taken, but it does not appear to have been recorded in the notes or report. These facts in concert are red flag requiring further investigation.

e. As explained in Turvey (1996):

> Hanging cases can often be quickly distinguished because they are marked by a classic "V" shaped pattern on the victim's neck associated with the knot in the ligature. In cases involving a suspended hanging, the "V" will point away from gravity, and be much higher on the neck (Knight et al. [7]). In cases where the victim has been "hog tied" by an assailant, the "V" will point towards gravity...

In the scene photos, the ligature and body appear situated such that a classic interrupted v-pattern should result in the neck with no ligature furrow at the back. The knot in situ does not appear to have tight contact (if any) with the back of the decedent's neck. However, this is inconsistent with the autopsy report, which describes a "back of the neck imprint". The trauma-gram section further provides a drawing of the ligature pattern straight across the back of the neck, without interruption, more consistent with a homicidal strangulation (see also Dolinak, Matshes, and Lew, 2005).

f. According to the decedent's family, they were advised by a representative of the ME's office that the decedent's t-shirt (the ligature) has been lost or discarded. The actual disposition, they have been told, is unknown. Losing evidence, or being unaware of its actual disposition, is substandard forensic practice.

3. The Decedent's Jeans are Consistent with Having Been Washed.

This finding is based on at least the following:

a. According to the decedent's family, they were advised by a representative of the ME's office that the decedent's jeans were being returned unwashed, in the state they were found on the body.

b. This examiner is experience with the examination of jean material collected from those who have suffered violent injury. Upon close examination of the decedent's jeans, this examiner believes that they have been washed, as the material is thicker and the weave of the fabric is tight. This is in contrast to worn material where the fabric is looser and stretched by use and body movement. It is also remarkably clean of any dirt or debris.

c. Upon close examination of the decedent's jeans, this examiner found unexplained stains over the left front pocket that could be blood. There is no mention of observing blood on the jeans in any of the reports in this case.

RECOMMENDATIONS

Based on these findings, this examiner strongly recommends the following:

1. This report and related documentation should be given to OSBI for further investigation.

2. The Estate of Mr. Edwards should request of OSBI that his body be disinterred for a second, independent autopsy. Should they be unwilling to meet this request, the Estate should seek out their own independent forensic pathologist to perform a second autopsy on their behalf.

3. The Estate of Mr. Edwards should make a written request for all photos in this case, death scene and autopsy alike, to the District Attorney's office, citing this report.

4. The Estate of Mr. Edwards should make a written request for all photos and evidence in the custody of the ME's office - including the missing shirt.

5. The decedent's jeans should be testing for blood in the area of the left front pocket.

Brent E. Turvey, MS (Forensic Science)

Turvey/ EDA - G.D. Edwards; 9

REFERENCES

Chisum, W. J. and Turvey, B. (2006) *Crime Reconstruction*: Elsevier Science.

Dolinak, D., Matshes, E., and Lew, E. (2005) *Forensic Pathology: Principles and Practice,* Boston: Academic Press.

Edwards, H., & Gotsonis, C. (2009) *Strengthening Forensic Science in the United States: A Path Forward*, Washington, D.C.: National Academies Press.

Hopper, T. (2009) "District Attorney Burns upset with Marlow police department testimony," *The Duncan Banner*, October 17.

Knight, B. and Simpson, K. (1985) *Forensic Medicine, 9th Ed.*, London, UK: Edward Arnold Publishers, Ltd.

McPherson, J. (2008) "Camera system keeps holding cells in plain sight," *The Marlow Review*, August 28.

Petherick, W. and Turvey, B. (2009) *Forensic Criminology*, Sand Diego: Elsevier Science.

Turvey, B., "A Guide To The Physical Analysis Of Ligature Patterns In Homicide Investigations," *Knowledge Solutions Library*, Electronic Publication, URL: http://www.corpus-delicti.com/ligature.html, Winter, 1996.

Twelfth Multicounty Grand Jury, State of Oklahoma, Case No. SCAD-2009-18, District Court No. CJ-2009-1925 July 20, 2009.

Turvey, B. (2008) *Criminal Profiling: An Introduction to Behavioral Evidence Analysis, 3rd Ed.*, Sand Diego: Elsevier Science.

REFERENCES

Edwards, H., Gotsonis, C., 2009. Strengthening Forensic Science in the United States: A Path Forward. National Academies Press, Washington, DC.

National Institute of Justice (NIJ), 1999. Death Investigation: A Guide for the Scene Investigator. 10 Research Report NCJ 167568, Washington, DC.

Tartaro, C., 2005. Section 1983 liability and custodial suicide: a look at what plaintiffs face in court. Californian Journal of Health Promotion 3 (2), 113–124.

Turvey, B., 2012. Criminal Profiling: An Introduction to Behavioral Evidence Analysis, fourth ed. Academic Press, San Diego.

CHAPTER

Investigating Staged Crime Scenes

11

B.E. Turvey

Forensic Solutions LLC, Sitka, Alaska, United States;
Institute of Forensic Investigation and Criminal Profiling, Juarez, Mexico

CHAPTER OUTLINE

This case involves the 1998 double murder of Gaetano and Maria Russo in their home. Both victims were brutally beaten to death. Gaetano was found in the kitchen, and Maria was found outside next to the back steps.

In 2001, the author was contacted by a then Sgt. Graham Ross of the Victoria Police in Melbourne, Australia, to assist with the case. After examining the case materials, a profile was rendered which determined, in part, that the scene had been staged. Subsequently, the victim's son, Joseph (aka Giuseppe Russo) was arrested, tried, and convicted of their murder. He appealed, the case was overturned, and in 2005 he was tried and convicted for a second time. Ultimately, he was sentenced to 28 years.

Behavioral Evidence Analysis. http://dx.doi.org/10.1016/B978-0-12-800607-8.00011-2

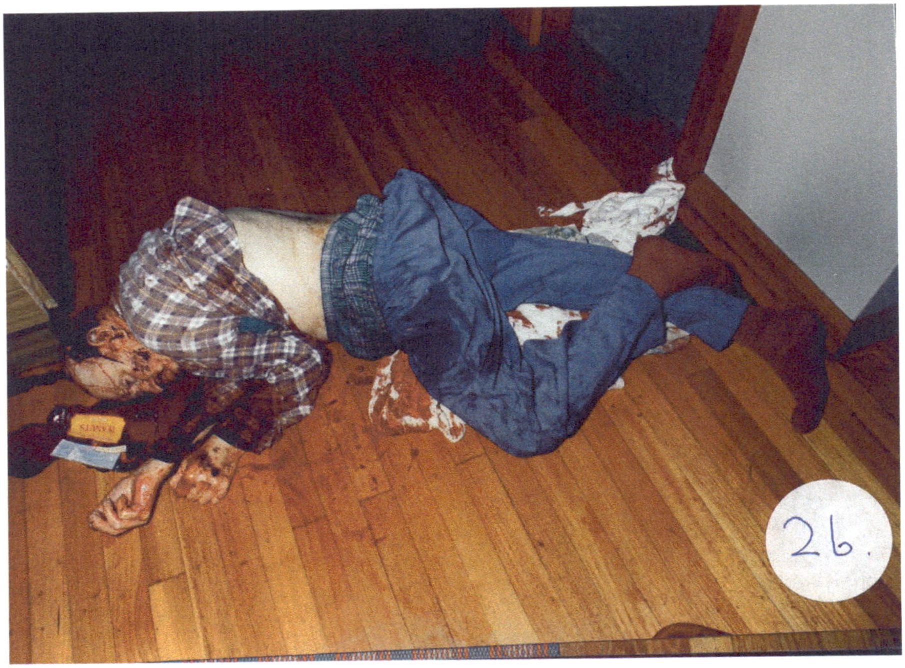

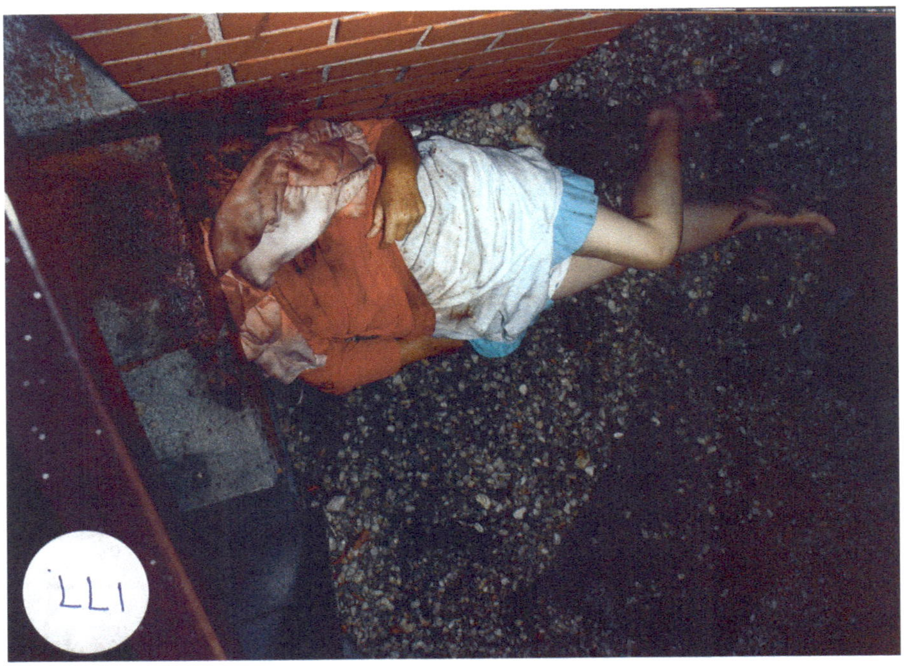

Gaetano Russo was found in the kitchen. He had been beaten to death, suffering multiple blunt force traumas to the head. Maria Russo was found outside their home next to the back steps. She suffered multiple blunt force traumas as well. Her face had been pounded into the cement repeatedly and then covered up.

In 2003, a jury found Russo, 39, guilty of murdering his 71-year-old father, Gaetano, and his mother, Maria, 70.

The facts of the case are taken from the original trial court ruling; Queen v. Russo (2003)[a]:

1. Your parents separately immigrated to Australia from Italy and married here in 1963. You were their only child and the sole beneficiary of their estates which was subsequently valued in excess of $200,000. They spoke little English and had few friends that visited them.
2. Your parents had been very generous in providing you with financial assistance. A unit at 55 Monash Street, Sunshine, was purchased for you and your wife to live in and when it was sold you received of the proceeds of sale. Subsequently, a property at Alma Avenue, Laverton was purchased by your parents, the Title being registered in the name of your father and yourself. They purchased a car for you and provided you with other financial assistance.
3. At the time that your parents were murdered you were separated from your wife and your two children and you were living with your girlfriend, Jenny Rinnan in her home at Heidelberg. You had been retrenched from the Victorian Railways in 1993 and since then had not been in gainful employ. You were in receipt of Unemployment Benefits. No evidence was placed before the jury as

[a]Queen v. Giuseppe Russo, [2003] VSC 164, Supreme Court of Victoria Melbourne, Criminal Division, No. 1452 of 2001.

to your life style or as to how you supported yourself. Some evidence which threw light on such matters was excluded by agreement between the Crown and your legal representatives in the course of the previous trial in which the jury was discharged prior to the completion of final addresses by counsel.

4. Your father had been ill for some time. He underwent surgery for bowel cancer and following such surgery used a colostomy bag. He was, it appears on the evidence, cancer free at the time of his death although he was in fairly frail health and needed walking sticks. You were a regular visitor at your parents' home assisting in changing your father's stoma every four or five days. You continued to irregularly stay overnight in your bedroom at your parents' home.
5. For some time prior to their death you had found it a burden to look after your parents. Prior to their deaths, you had spoken about them in an unkindly and resentful manner. On one occasion you had referred to your father as a silly old bastard who would be better off dead. A number of your former friends testified that you were tired of looking after your parents and that you were angry and frustrated that they did not give you more financial support. Approximately two weeks before their deaths, you revealed that you were in urgent need of a substantial amount of money and expressed frustration that your parents were not prepared to provide you with financial assistance. You said you would bash them. At that time you had virtually no money.
6. On 18 April 1998, you travelled with your wife to your parents-in-laws' home near Ararat to collect your children, returning to Melbourne in the mid-afternoon. After leaving them, you went to your parents' home and were observed walking toward the front door by a friend at about 5.00 pm. Shortly thereafter, you were heard by a neighbour having an argument with your parents in the back yard. Some time later you viciously assaulted your father in the lounge room of the house, [sic] using his walking sticks to inflict a large number of wounds to his head. At some stage you also assaulted your mother, first with the walking stick and then by bashing her head against the rear concrete steps on numerous occasions, causing multiple wounds and fractures to the facial bones. After she was dead you covered her face. You were aware that your parents kept a small portable safe on the top shelf of the kitchen pantry, the shelf being some 9 feet from the ground. You took the money from the safe and returned the safe to its position on the top shelf of the pantry. You disturbed the contents of your parents, and a third bedroom, in an attempt to make it appear as though there had been a burglary. There were numerous obvious places in these bedrooms and other parts of the house where your parents kept cash and other valuables, but you did not take these items. You left your bedroom undisturbed. There was evidence to suggest that you used the bathroom before leaving your parents' premises. Later that evening you were seen at the Crown Casino.
7. On Sunday, 19 April 1998, you looked after your son Guy. You left him with your wife in the early evening, informing your wife that you intended to go to your parents' home as you had not been able to raise them by telephone when

you had called them a number of times during the course of the day. You said that you were not intending to go inside but just to check to see that they were alright. You returned to your parents' home and went through the motions of discovering your parents' death. The police attended your parents' home at about 8.00 pm and thereafter you provided investigators with information about your movements on Saturday and Sunday. You had numerous conversations with police on that evening, and during the ensuing weeks and months. You told lies to the police which the jury were satisfied demonstrated a consciousness of guilt of your crime. You told numerous other lies which led to the jury's conclusion that much of your account to the police of your conduct on Saturday, 18 April 1998 was untruthful.

8. The jury, by its verdict, must have been satisfied about most, if not all of these facts. During the plea no other conclusions of fact were suggested as open, consistent with the jury's verdict. These were facts which were "logically crucial" to the prosecution case or facts which must by implication have been accepted by the jury. I do not regard it as necessary or appropriate to make any findings of fact beyond those to which I have referred.

Personal Circumstances

9. You are 39 years of age having been born on 1 December 1963 in Melbourne. In an understandably brief plea made on your behalf, I was told you attended Altona Gate Primary School and Altona North High School leaving school in Year 10 in 1979. You became an apprentice fitter and turner, completing your four year apprenticeship at Colonial Sugar Refineries. From 1984 you were self-employed, utilising your skills as a fitter and turner together with some mechanical knowledge to carry out mechanical repairs from the garage of your parents' home. You conducted this business until about 1989 when you became a guard on the Victorian Railways. You were retrenched from this position following government re-arrangement of the Railways in 1993 and since that time you have been unemployed. Following your retrenchment you became more involved in the welfare of your parents, particularly your father, who as a result of his serious illness required ongoing care and attention and assistance in travelling to and from medical and like appointments.

10. In 1988 you married Michelle Russo. You have two children from that marriage, Guy aged 12 and Gemma aged 9. Apart from your parents, your only close relative residing in Australia was your father's sister who married here, had a daughter who in turn has married and has two children of her own. I am informed by your counsel that this part of the family has remained supportive since the deaths of your parents.

11. You were charged with the murder of your parents on 3 May 2001 and you were on bail from 22 May 2001 until you were remanded in custody following the jury's verdict on 20 March 2003. Although it appears that your relationship with Jenny Rinnan continued after the death of your parents and you continued to reside with her in Heidelberg, no reference was made to any aspect of your personal life during the course of your plea. No evidence or information emerged during the course of the trial or on your plea which gave the Court any insight as to your life style since you separated from your wife some six years ago.

12. You have been receiving medication to address an anxiety state over the last year. You are currently receiving an anxiety suppressor, Ducene, and have required medication as a result of the stress and anxiety associated with your prosecution.
13. I take into account in your favour that you are a devoted father to your two children Guy and Gemma and that you have no prior convictions and no history of violence. Although you have not been in gainful employment since 1993 you were for some time a loyal son who provided support to his father after he underwent his surgery. These factors enhance your prospects of rehabilitation.

Nature and Gravity of the Offense

14. You have been found guilty of a most brutal and sustained attack upon both of your parents. Your father was struck at least 18 times and in circumstances where initially, despite his infirmity, he attempted to defend himself. Your mother's face was battered beyond recognition. I have already referred to the evidence of your motive for killing your parents. Despite the evidence of your pressing financial needs and your increasing resentment of your parents, the Crown do not challenge the submission made on your behalf that the facts do not support the conclusion that your conduct was premeditated. I propose to sentence you on the basis that your acts were spontaneous and followed an argument with your parents in which you lost control, brutally assaulted each of them and took the money from the safe. You returned the safe to its position on the top shelf of the pantry resolving to make it appear as a crime committed during an attempted burglary of the house by a stranger.
15. In assessing the appropriate penalty for your offences I take into account the fact that your parents were elderly and vulnerable. The manner in which you killed your parents has all of the hallmarks of anger and fury. It is implicit in the jury's verdict that you were, whether by great care or good fortune, able to conceal your involvement in these crimes. You concealed or disposed of the clothing which you wore at the time that you murdered your parents. You repeatedly lied to investigators about your movements and over the ensuing months gave detailed false explanations as to your conduct.
16. The video interviews did not demonstrate that you were suffering from any apparent psychological or psychiatric disturbance. Rather, the evidence suggests you proceeded under the misguided belief that your parents, who had been exceedingly generous to you, had some continuing obligation to meet your financial demands. The circumstances which led to your pressing financial need remains unknown. Most of your personal circumstances for some years prior to your conviction remain a mystery.
17. In determining the appropriate sentence I have considered the provisions of the Sentencing Act 1991 and the more important recent authorities dealing with multiple killings referred to in Camilleri v R (2001) 119 A Crim R 106 @ 139.
18. This is the second occasion within a relatively short time that this Court has found it necessary to sentence a son for the murder of a parent. Though it

can still be said that it is a rarity for a son to kill a parent, one of the purposes of the sentence which I must pronounce is to dissuade persons from taking human life whatever their relationship with the victim. This Court has an obligation to protect the sanctity of human life. The sentence which I must impose must reflect this Court's denunciation of your brutal conduct. It must deter others who are minded to resort to such violence as a solution to their problems.

19. Mr Russo, I have concluded that the appropriate sentences are as follows: on Count 1, the murder of your father, Gaetano Russo you are sentenced to be imprisoned for 18 years. On Count 2, the murder of your mother, Maria Russo, you are also sentenced to be imprisoned for 18 years. I order that ten years of Count 2 be served cumulatively with Count 1 resulting in a total effective sentence of 28 years. I fix a minimum of 23 years before you become eligible for parole. Pursuant to s 18 of the Sentencing Act 1991, I declare that the time that you have spent in custody in relation to these proceedings is 84 days (inclusive of today's date) and I direct that it be reckoned as a period of imprisonment already served under the sentence imposed.

The following profile was attached to the brief of evidence provided by police investigators who gave evidence in this case at both trials.

CRIMINAL PROFILE

Homicides of Maria & Gaetano Russo

Bodies found: Sunday, April 19, 1998, at approximately 7:35 pm by Joseph Russo (Vs-son)
Investigating Agency: Victoria Police, Crime Department, Homicide Squad, Melbourne

Report by:

Brent E. Turvey, MS Forensic Science
Forensic Scientist & Criminal Profiler
Knowledge Solutions, LLC
1961 Main Street, PMB 221
Watsonville, CA 95076
bturvey@corpus-delicti.com

For:

Victoria Police
C.I.B., Homicide Squad
St. Kilda Road
Melbourne, Victoria 3004
Australia

Contact: Det. Graham Ross at 011 61 3 9865 2382

After reviewing the case materials detailed below, a determination was made by this examiner that sufficient investigation and forensic analysis have been performed in this case to warrant the rendering of a *Criminal profile*.

A *Criminal profile* is a report that reviews and describes the investigatively relevant and/or probative characteristics of the offender responsible for a particular crime or a series of related crimes, based upon a thorough *crime analysis*. It should include crime analysis and victimological information as a foundation, as well as logical, evidence-based arguments for each offender characteristic elicited from that foundation (Baeza et al., 2000).

Crime analysis is the process of examining and evaluating the evidence from a crime, as well as the results of any tests or examinations, in order to form an opinion regarding the behavioral evidence for a particular crime or a series of related crimes (Baeza et al., 2000). It involves the employment of scientific principles and knowledge, including Locard's exchange principle, critical thinking, analytical logic, and evidence dynamics.

Locard's exchange principle, a cornerstone of the forensic sciences, states that when an offender comes in contact with a location or another person an exchange of evidence occurs (Saferstein, 1998). As a result of this exchange, the offender, both, leaves something of themselves behind and takes something of that person or place away with them when they leave.

Critical thinking may be described as the process of actively and skillfully conceptualizing, applying, analyzing, synthesizing, and/or evaluating information gathered from, or generated by, observation, experience, reflection, reasoning, or communication, as a guide to belief and action (Turvey, 1999). In terms of forensic analysis, it involves the evaluation of the real merits and limitations of physical evidence, and the results of subsequent tests performed on that evidence, as opposed to taking a position because it is agreeable to one's personal beliefs on an issue.

Analytical logic involves the ability to study a crime scene, and any subsequent documentation, and arrive at logical, well-reasoned conclusions. This ideally involves the formation of hypotheses that can be tested against the established facts of the case. The end result of this process is that conclusions may be drawn from, that follow naturally from the evidence that is present. Such conclusions may be referred to as deductions (Thornton, 1997).

Evidence dynamics refers to any influence that changes, relocates, obscures, or obliterates physical evidence, regardless of intent. It can occur during the interval that begins as the evidence is being transferred and ends when the case is ultimately adjudicated (Chisum and Turvey, 2000).

EXAMINATIONS PERFORMED

The examiner made this *criminal profile* of the above case based upon, but not limited to, a careful examination of the following case evidence:

- Victoria Police Department crime scene and investigative results;
- Victoria Police Department crime scene diagram;

- Various autopsy and crime scene photos;
- Victoria Police crime scene diagrams;
- Autopsy protocols and related statements;
- Various crime lab results;
- Various witness and suspect interviews;
- Various telephone records and telephone transcripts;
- Various financial records.

While this examiner has not visited the crime scene, extensive documentation of the crime scene was provided and determined to be more than sufficient basis for the opinions presented in this report.

BACKGROUND

According to documents in the Victoria Police Homicide Squad *Brief of Evidence, Appendix H*, the bodies of both victims were found at their home, 348 Blackshaws Road, Altona North, at approximately 7:35 pm on Sunday, April 19, 1998, by their then 34-year-old son, Joseph Russo. Joseph Russo states that after unsuccessful attempts to phone his parents during the afternoon, he went for a visit and discovered the body of Gaetano Russo, fully clothed, in the kitchen. He states that he then phoned his estranged wife, Michelle to arrange for an ambulance. He further states that he went on to search the house, and find the body of his mother, Maria Russo, against the back steps of the couple's home, with a pair of sweat-type pants placed over her face. Joseph Russo is adamant that he did not disturb either body.

Gaetano Russo had been struck in the head, face, and ribs with blunt force weapons that included one or more of his own walking sticks. Cause of death was multiple severe blunt force traumas to the head. Maria Russo was also found to have died of multiple severe blunt force traumas to the head. As evident in the crime scene photos and video, her head and face were pounded repeatedly into the East side concrete steps outside, and leading up to, the self-contained flat on the north end of the house.

VICTIMOLOGY

Victimology is a thorough study of all available victim information. This often includes items such as sex, age, height, weight, family, friends, acquaintances, education, employment, residence, and neighborhood. This also includes background information on the history and lifestyle of the victim such as overall personal habits, hobbies, criminal history, and medical histories. Establishing victimology is a necessary part of determining the context of some crimes (Baeza et al., 2000). Furthermore, it is generally accepted that the decedent's social-, medical-, and mental-health history can provide insight into the behavior/state of mind of an individual, focus further investigation, and produce clues that will aid in establishing the cause, manner, and circumstances of a death (NMRP, 1999).

Name: Maria Russo
Race: Caucasian
Sex: Female
DOB: July 6, 1927 (Militello, Italy)
Age: 70

Name: Gaetano Russo
Race: Caucasian
Sex: Male
DOB: November 16, 1926 (Buccheri, Italy)
Age: 71
Residence location: 348 Blackshaws Road, Altona North, Victoria

Residence type: As evident in the crime scene photos, the crime scene video, and the crime scene sketch, the decedents' home is a one story brick, three bedroom, single family dwelling. There is a garage on the west side, a long patio on the east side, and a self-contained flat on the north end that sits on the corner of a grassy backyard. The residence is surrounded by timber and brick fences.

Relationship Status: Maria and Gaetano Russo have been married and living together since April 20, 1963. On April 20, 1998 Maria and Gaetano Russo would have celebrated their 35th wedding anniversary.

Family history: According to the Victoria Police Homicide Squad *Brief of Evidence*, Maria and Gaetano Russo have only one child, Joseph (Guiseppe) Russo, who was born in Melbourne on December 1, 1963. At the time of the murders, Joseph Russo was living with his girlfriend of approximately 4 years, Jenny Rinon, at F3/75 Yarra St., Heidelberg. He met Jenny Rinon at the Harem brothel in South Melbourne.

Joseph Russo had been separated from his wife, Michelle Russo, for approximately 1 year. Joseph and Michelle's two children, Guy (7) and Gemma (4), lived with their mother.

According to the Victoria Police Homicide Squad *Brief of Evidence*, Maria and Gaetano Russo were not aware that their son was separated from his wife Michelle, and none of them were aware that he was living with his girlfriend, Jenny Rinon. Maria and Gaetano Russo were under the impression that Joseph and Michelle were still living together, and Michelle Russo was apparently of the understanding that Joseph had moved in with his parents or stayed with friends. Michelle Russo was not aware of Joseph's girlfriend, Jenny Rinon, until after the investigation in the murders began.

According to the Victoria Police Homicide Squad *Brief of Evidence,* Joseph Russo had been unemployed for the past 5 years, having worked previously for the railways as a railway guard for approximately 6 years. He has been receiving unemployment benefits since that time and admits to a history of gambling.

Work history: According to the Victoria Police Homicide Squad *Brief of Evidence*, Maria and Gaetano Russo were both pensioners at the time of their death. Gaetano had previously worked as a file acider at the Wiltshire File Company in Tottenham, from August 1967 to November 1987.

Criminal history: According to the Victoria Police Homicide Squad *Brief of Evidence*, neither victim has any criminal history or known dealings with the police while living in Australia.

Medical and mental health history: Gaetano Russo was suffering from cancer, used walking canes to assist his mobility, and had a colostomy bag which Joseph Russo changed regularly (every 3–4 days). According to Joseph Russo, it needed to be changed on Saturday, April 18, 1998. According to the Victoria Police Homicide Squad *Brief of Evidence*, the bag was flat and empty at the time of his murder. It should also be noted that some of the materials for maintaining the colostomy bag, as well as a pair of eye-glasses, were still on the table outside. This may suggest that the homicides occurred within a short time after the most recent maintenance to the bag.

Toxicology reports indicate benzodiazepines, diazepam, and nordiazepam in Gaetano Russo's system, and no drugs in Maria Russo's system.

Victim lifestyle risk: This term refers to the overall risk of becoming a victim that is inherent in an individual's lifestyle (Turvey, 1999). Due to their age, their health status, their dependence on others for some care and maintenance, these victims would have a low to medium lifestyle risk. This means that in some circumstances, especially those outside their home, they could be exposed to the possibility of violence, harm, or loss. This exposure would be spotty at best.

Victim incident risk: This term refers to the risk of becoming a victim that is present at the moment, when an individual is initially acquired by an offender (Turvey, 1999). As the victims were attacked in their home during waking hours, indicated by their manner of dress, and as the incidence of home invasion type–stranger burglaries in their area is extremely low, this would indicate a decreased incident risk of becoming the victim of such a crime.

SCENE CHARACTERISTICS

Location and scene types: The known death scene in this case is 348 Blackshaws Road, Altona North, the decedents' residence. It is an indoor and outdoor scene as described.

Point of contact: This is defined as the location where an offender first approaches or acquires a victim (Turvey, 1999). The available evidence strongly suggests that the offender was in the home and attacked while the victims were in the process of eating a snack or a meal. As described in the *Examination and Analysis of Crime Scene* section of the Victoria Police Homicide Squad *Brief of Evidence*, Gaetano Russo was attacked quite suddenly within his home, and his manner of dress indicates that he was not dressed for bed. Bloodstain patterns on the ceiling above, and on the wall near the armchair in the lounge strongly suggest that the initial attack against him began while he was seated in that chair.

The evidence allows that Maria Russo could have been initially approached by the offender either inside or outside the home. Ultimately, however, the offender made the first physical contact with her outside, most likely where her body was found, given the absence of evidence of an attack on her elsewhere in the residence.

Use of weapons: As evidenced by the distinctive nature of the victims' injuries, the wooden splinters found at the scene in association with their bodies, and the broken, bloody canes found throughout the scene, it is most likely that the victims were beaten with one or more of these wooden canes. There is no evidence that a firearm or sharp force object such as a knife was used in the commission of this crime.

Method of approach: This term refers to the offender's strategy for getting close to a victim (Turvey, 1999). In this case, the offender was able to approach both victims in their home while they were engaged in regular daily activity. This suggests that either the offender had gained their trust via an elaborate and prolonged con requiring extensive preplanning, or that the offender had a prior relationship with the victims which allowed them access to the victims' home. See the *Knowledge of victims* and *Trust of victims* sections of this report.

Method of attack: This term refers to the offender's mechanism for initially overpowering a victim once they have made their approach. It is appropriate to describe a method of attack in terms of the weapon and the nature of the force involved (Turvey, 1999). Evident in the crime scene photos and video, the offender used the immediate application of lethal levels of punishment-oriented force to overpower both victims. There is evidence in the form of wound patterns and bloodstain patterns that Gaetano Russo was attacked by the application of punishment-oriented and lethal force with one or more wooden canes. There is evidence in the form of wound patterns and bloodstain patterns that Maria Russo was attacked by the application of punishment-oriented and lethal force, as she was both beaten with and manually driven, head first, into concrete stairs from multiple angles.

Methods of control: This term refers to the means used by an offender to manipulate, regulate, restrain, and subdue victim behavior of any kind throughout the duration of an offense (Turvey, 1999). As suggested by previous sections, the offender did not evidence a great deal of interest in victim control, rather the offender ultimately physically punished both victims, as evidenced by the overkill in the crimes. See the *Anger motivation* section of this report.

Use of force: This refers to the amount of force used by the offender during an attack (Turvey, 1999). The amount of force used against both victims may be characterized as both punishment-oriented and lethal (Turvey, 1999). That is to say, it involved much more force than was necessary to achieve mere victim compliance, delivered repeatedly to a potentially lethal area of the body (neck, face, and head). Furthermore, the amount of force was not correctional, sexual, or merely control oriented. This is owing to the severity of the blows, their repetition, and the general physical infirmity of the victims, which decreased their ability to resist and protect themselves.

Victim resistance: This refers to the amount and type of opposition or noncompliance offered by the victim during an attack (Turvey, 1999). There is some evidence of limited victim resistance and defensive injuries to their hands. However, given the infirmity of the victims and the amount of force used against them, it is the opinion of this examiner that meaningful victim resistance could not have lasted more than a few moments.

Items taken: The only known items taken would have been the contents of the portable safe found in the pantry. However, as no firm documentation of the safe's contents exists, it is not possible to provide a reliable comment. It is important to note that this does seem to be the only other element of the crime of interest to the offender (see the *Evidence of Staging* section), aside from delivering punishment to the Russos. As such, the offender most likely expected something of value to have been in it, and subsequently had foreknowledge of both the safe and the item.

Sexual acts: This examiner did not find mention or evidence of sexual acts in this case.

Verbal behavior: Unknown.

Evidence of planning and precautionary acts: Precautionary acts are offender choices made before, during, or after an offense that are consciously intended to confuse, hamper, or defeat investigative or forensic efforts for the purposes of concealing their identity, their connection to the crime, or the crime itself (Turvey, 1999). Their existence may be used to suggest planning during various phases of a crime.

The weapons used in the commission of this crime were available material (brute strength, wooden canes, and the cement stairs). The nature of the force used, in combination with this fact and the victimology, suggest that the homicides were unplanned (see the *Anger motivation* section of this report for further discussion).

Though there is evidence of staging, these attempts lack sophistication and forensic knowledge. That is to say, the offender did make certain attempts to stage the scene, yet failed to sufficiently clean up or remove evidence of the actual events involved in the commission of the crime and in the staging. See the following sections for a more complete discussion.

Evidence of Staging: The simulated or staged crime scene is that in which evidence has been purposefully altered by the offender to mislead authorities and/or redirect the investigation. It is best identified by examining the inconsistencies, contradictions, and logical breaks in the physical/behavioral evidence found at the scene (Turvey, 2000). It is the opinion of this examiner that there is some evidence of offender attempts to stage the crime scene in this case to appear as a stranger burglary to investigators. The basis for my opinion on this issue resides in the consideration of the following:

1. A large glass table top was removed from its metal base and carefully placed on the floor, undamaged. This was done after the attack, as indicated by the fact that it covered areas of bloodstain pattern. This suggests that the offender took great care not to break this clearly expensive item, which would be paradoxical behavior for a stranger burglar.
2. Valuables remain evident in the scene (large amounts of cash, jewelry, watches, TV, etc.), contrary to a profit motivation.
3. The drawers in one of the rooms appeared rummaged through and placed carefully on the bed. Drawers in another room were pulled out yet not removed and only superficially "gone through." This appears to have been done by

the offender to give the illusion of a search for valuables. Given item #2, this rummaging was unrelated to a burglary, and was likely an attempt to create the illusion that a burglar was responsible.

The offender did move Gaetano Russo's body into the kitchen near the island counter area, dragging him from the lounge, as evidenced by bloody drag patterns on the kitchen floor and the state of the victim's clothing. It appears that the offender then placed a clean and unbroken wooden cane on the kitchen floor nearby. However, this examiner does not see this act as a part of a staging attempt by the offender. By itself, this act does not accomplish a redirection of the crime toward or away from any potential suspect group, given the absence of attempts to conceal or clean up clear evidence of dragging and victim relocation within the scene.

Rather, the blood smear evidence found on the inside and outside the portable safe, and the bloody fingerprint of Gaetano Russo found on the inside of the empty fan box used to conceal the portable safe, suggests to this examiner the following: It is possible, and even likely, that these were the result of the offender forcing a beaten and injured Gaetano Russo to locate and/or open the portable safe, which required a key. This could have been accomplished after the offender initially overpowered Gaetano Russo with a few blows, left him bleeding in the lounge, and then proceeded to attack a fleeing Maria Russo outside on the cement stairs.

It is important to note that some staging efforts remain, however, unskillful. The most plausible reason for staging a crime scene to appear as though a stranger burglar is responsible, is to conceal a preexisting relationship of some kind between the victims and the offender. That is to say, a stranger would not stage a crime scene to make it appear as though a stranger was responsible. Rather, they would wish to divert attention to a family member or away from the crime entirely (make a homicide appear as a suicide, for example).

OFFENDER CHARACTERISTICS

Anger motivation

It is the opinion of this examiner that there is overwhelming evidence of an anger motivation associated with the attacks on both victims. The basis for my opinion on this issue resides in the consideration of the following:

1. There is evidence of overkill in the injuries to both victims. In other words, both attacks involved the use of force well beyond that necessary to simply kill, suggesting intense rage on the part of the offender. This includes, as evident in the autopsy and crime scene photos: (1) the multiple and severe blunt force traumas to the heads and faces of both victims, and (2) the evidence of sustained rage across both homicides. In particular, Maria Russo was beaten with a blunt object consistent with one of the wooden canes found at the scene, as evidenced by the distinctive lacerations to her head. She also suffered an attack to her neck which resulted in a broken hyoid bone. She was finally rammed headlong and down against the edge of the cement stairs previously mentioned.

2. As already discussed, there is a lack of planning evident in the commission of the homicides, suggesting spontaneity.
3. There is an absence of sexual activity that would indicate a sexual motivation.
4. There is an absence of direct evidence of profit motivation, as items of value (large amounts of cash, jewelry, TV, etc.) were left behind at the scene. There is evidence that the offender forced Gaetano Russo to open the portable safe, but its specific contents are unknown. In fact, it could have been empty. Regardless, this came after the initial beating to Gaetano Russo and most likely after the severe attack on and subsequent death of Mario Russo.

Trust of victims

It is the opinion of this examiner that the offender had the trust of both of the victims. The basis for my opinion on this issue resides in the consideration of the following:

1. The victims had motion sensors installed in their home.
2. The front door had a security chain, peephole, and two door locks, including a deadbolt.
3. The outer wire mesh security door had a key lock.
4. There is no evidence of forced entry.
5. The attack took place inside the victims' home.
6. The victims were eating and/or involved in food preparation and other daily activities, as indicated by the presence of prepared/uneaten food at the time of the attack.

In concert, these strongly suggest that not only did the offender know the victims, but he was allowed entry into their home, and the victims went on about their regular routine with the offender present.

Knowledge of scene

In addition to the discussed indications of knowledge relating to the victims, and subsequently their home, it is the opinion of this examiner that the offender had intimate knowledge of the scene prior to the homicides. This is demonstrated by the fact that the offender knew precisely where the portable safe was hidden (in a ceiling fan box on the top shelf of the pantry in the kitchen), and/or that it existed at all. The evidence strongly suggests that the offender forced an injured Gaetano Russo to open this portable safe, as evidenced by the blood smears inside and outside, and the bloody fingerprint on the box, while ignoring items of clear value in the residence.

Evidence of remorse

Maria Russo's body was found with a pair of pants placed over her face, which had been disfigured from repeated pounding into the concrete steps as previously mentioned. It is the opinion of this examiner that the offender concealed this victim's face with the pants, which were determined to be available at the scene with other laundry hanging outside the residence, out of remorse over the consequences of the violence inflicted upon her. Put another way, the offender could not emotionally bear to look at the victim's bloody, disfigured face.

The basis for my opinion on this issue resides in the consideration of the following:

1. This act was not committed in concert with sexual activity, reducing the possibility that it was meant to facilitate fantasy behavior.
2. This act was committed after death, eliminating the possibility that it was meant to serve as a precautionary act (conceal the identity of the offender from the victim).
3. This response from the offender is consistent with a reaction that an offender could have if the homicide was committed out of anger which dissipated with the conclusion of the violence, as is indicated by the evidence in this case.
4. This response from the offender is consistent with a reaction that an offender could have with a victim who is known to them, as is indicated by the evidence in this case.

INVESTIGATIVE SUGGESTIONS

The following is a list of suggestions for further investigating and establishing the facts of this case:

1. All food evidence found in the kitchen should be submitted to the crime lab for STR DNA analysis. This requires only a single epithelial cell, and many such cells are left behind by human saliva on food, cups, and silverware during a meal.
2. Vacuum metal deposition and alternative (ie, laser, etc.) light source examination should be made of the fan box, the interior of the portable safe, and the pants found covering Maria Russo's face.
3. The pants found covering Maria Russo's face should be submitted to a crime lab with extensive experience in recognizing, documenting, and collecting bloody fingerprints on the clothing.
4. A thorough interview with Jenny Rinon should be conducted, wherein she is confronted with the full scope of the inconsistencies of the case and the physical evidence. This should be done prior to any contact with her then boyfriend, Joseph Russo.
5. A thorough interview with Joseph Russo should be conducted, wherein he is confronted with the full scope of the inconsistencies of the case and the physical evidence. During the interview, he should be shown the crime scene photographs and autopsy photographs of his mother, and subsequently given the opportunity to change the content of his previous statements.

I swear and affirm to the best of my knowledge that the above statements are true under penalty of perjury.

Brent E. Turvey, MS
Forensic Scientist

REFERENCES

Baeza, J., Chisum, W.J., Chamberlin, T.M., McGrath, M., Turvey, B., January 2000. Academy of behavioral profiling: criminal profiling guidelines. Journal of Behavioral Profiling 1 (1).

Chisum, W.J., Turvey, B., 2000. Evidence dynamics: Locard's exchange principle & crime reconstruction. Journal of Behavioral Profiling 1 (1).

National Medicolegal Review Panel (NMRP), 1999. Death Investigation: A Guide for the Scene Investigator. National Institute of Justice.

Saferstein, R., 1998. Criminalistics: An Introduction to Forensic Science, sixth ed. Prentice Hall.

Thornton, J.I., 1997. The general assumptions and rationale of forensic identification. In: Faigman, D.L., Kaye, D.H., Saks, M.J., Sanders, J. (Eds.), Modern Scientific Evidence: The Law and Science of Expert Testimony, vol. 2. West Publishing Company.

Turvey, B., 1999. Criminal Profiling: An Introduction to Behavioral Evidence Analysis. Academic Press.

Turvey, B., 2000. Staged crime scenes: a preliminary study of 25 cases. Journal of Behavioral Profiling 1 (3).

CHAPTER

Investigating Fetish Burglaries

12

B.E. Turvey

Forensic Solutions LLC, Sitka, Alaska, United States;
Institute of Forensic Investigation and Criminal Profiling, Juarez, Mexico

A **sexual fetish** is the attribution of erotic or sexual significance to a nonsexual inanimate object or nonsexual body part. As explained in Lowenstein (2002, p. 136), "among the objects frequently sought as fetishistic are shoes, bras, and panties, etc. Sometimes in a search for fetishist objects housebreaking occurs as the individual searches for women's used bras or panties." When burglary is committed in whole or in part to gather these kinds of items for sexual purposes, it may be properly referred to as a **fetish burglary**. Gebhard et al. (1965, p. 413), however, refer more generically as "fetish theft."

Consider the case of Tyrel Pitka, as reported in Morris (2006):

> *A man accused of burglarizing at least 27 houses in the Valley and committing strange, solitary sex acts inside was sentenced Tuesday to seven years in prison.*
>
> *Tyrel Pitka, 20, was charged with two counts of first-degree burglary and one count of second-degree burglary. Superior Court Judge Larry Weeks sentenced Pitka to 12 years, then suspended five years of the sentence. He also placed Pitka on five years probation and ordered him to receive sex-offender treatment.*
>
> *According to court testimony and documents, Pitka admitted to burglarizing at least 27 homes. Investigators said they linked Pitka to several other burglaries, but he wasn't charged with those crimes. According to investigators, Pitka started hitting homes in Mendenhall Valley on Nov. 22, 2005, working from trails that crisscross the Loop Road area and scouting for houses where the occupants were gone. From December to January of the same year, Pitka went to Sitka.*
>
> *Officials said Pitka committed three burglaries in Sitka. In February when Pitka returned to Juneau, he started burglarizing houses again, until his arrest on April 7. According to court records Pitka committed one burglary in Angoon.*
>
> *Juneau District Attorney Doug Gardner said in court that Pitka used money from the robberies to buy drugs and alcohol. The crimes also had strong sexual overtones.*
>
> *In a sentencing memorandum, Gardner said Pitka "searched the residences in many of the cases for pornography, sex toys, or other personal and intimate*

Behavioral Evidence Analysis. http://dx.doi.org/10.1016/B978-0-12-800607-8.00012-4

photographs…In addition, the defendant made a video tape of himself masturbating, using a victim's video camera, and masturbated while in at least two of the locations…leaving semen in two stuffed toy animals."

In court, Gardner said that Pitka also used his victims' computers to look at pornography. In one of Pitka's filming sessions, he recorded over a video of a woman giving birth to her son. In another incident, Pitka returned a sex toy to the house of its owner with a vulgar, suggestive note attached to it.

By 2011, Mr. Pitka had been released from custody and rearrested for criminal trespassing and providing false information to the police.

Consider also the case of the bra bandit of Yulin, city in southeast China. He was identified and arrested when the ceiling of his apartment collapsed under the weight of all the underwear and bras that he had stolen over the years (pictured).

As reported in (2014): The bra bandit, named only as Tan, had hidden more than 2000 pairs of pilfered pants and brassieres in the cavity above his bedroom in the Guangxi Zhuang Autonomous Region's second-largest metropolis.

The police report that Mr. Tan broke into his victims' homes while they were at work, and stole the undergarments from their closets and clothing drawers.

It is noteworthy that the fetish burglar generally shows a preference for used objects and garments. That is to say, they cannot simply buy perfumes, clothing, or other items at the store to satisfy their desires in private. The items must have been owned previously, touched, or otherwise possessed by someone (often a specific person) so that there is a greater meaning in the acquisition. However, the items taken need not be soiled or freshly used (Gebhard et al., 1965). Many fetish thieves take clothes, for example, directly off clotheslines or out of publicly accessible dryers in apartment buildings and college or university dormitories.

Although the true prevalence of fetish burglary is unknown, as law enforcement does not keep such statistics, fetishism itself "tends to begin during adolescence or even before. It persists for most of the individual's life. Frequently such individuals are shy and socially withdrawn. They may well be ashamed of their dependence on their particular fetish, and hence attempt to keep their fetish secret," (Lowenstien, 2002, p. 136). As with bestiality, the recent window offered into human sexual behavior and preferences by the Internet moves fetishism in all its forms into an era of more accurate research and understanding.

The sex crime investigator must pay close attention to instances of fetish burglary, as these can be associated with, or evolve into, sexual assault–related behavior. The author is aware of many cases where fetish burglary is a feature of victim surveillance by an experienced serial rapist. Similarly, burglary can provide the opportunity for rape under certain circumstances, especially when associated with offender behavior and motives that are already sexually oriented. Therefore, each case of fetish burglary must be investigated as though it is a part of a larger series, no matter how trivial the intrusion and theft seem. Doing so can help to reveal a serial pattern or even prevent one from emerging.

In fact, according to Brankley et al. (2014, p. 115):

> *…studies reveal an escalation in sexual offender behaviour from non-contact to contact offending, with an ever-increasing likelihood of sexual violence and homicide. In particular, researchers have found that sexual offenders often have a history of committing burglaries prior to contact offences. Accordingly, researchers have suggested that burglaries may be associated with an increased likelihood of future sexual offending, particularly when they have a sexual element to them. However, to date, there has been little quantitative research focusing on the mechanisms of escalation in sexual offences.*

Consider the following case report prepared by this author at the request of law enforcement in relation to a series of unsolved fetish burglaries in Pennsylvania:

SUBJECT: UNSOLVED FETISH BURGLARIES, 2002–03; (REDACTED) APARTMENTS

At the request of (**redacted**), this examiner reviewed investigative reports and witness accounts from the above-mentioned cases. There were several cases reported in 2002, and 11 more cases have been reported since the January of 2003. This examiner has neither visited the crime scene nor has he examined crime scene photographs.

Continued

SUBJECT: UNSOLVED FETISH BURGLARIES, 2002–03; (REDACTED) APARTMENTS—cont'd

Because of the nature of this case, it would not be prudent or fruitful for this examiner to prepare a full criminal profile. However, there are a number of pointed investigative suggestions that can be offered in the form of a limited threshold assessment.

Conclusions

After a careful review of the available case material, the following are my conclusions and their basis.

Conclusion #1

Case linkage is the general process of demonstrating discrete connections between two or more previously unrelated cases. An *investigative link* is a connection between one or more solved or unsolved cases that serves to inform the allocation of resources toward the investigation of facts (ie, in terms of behavior, general, or opportunistic circumstances of the offense; general similarities in modus operandi and offense signature).

It is this examiner's conclusion that there is an investigative link between the cases provided. This is based on the following facts:

1. The majority of the crimes involves a female tenant from the (**redacted**) apartments.
2. The majority of the crimes involves a female tenant from the (**redacted**) apartments who lives alone.
3. The majority of the crimes involves a female tenant from the (**redacted**) apartments who was not home, or believed not to be home, at the time of the burglary.
4. Each of the crimes involves a generally similar method of entering and exiting the apartments (lack of forced entry, potential use of master key to gain entry and secure the apartment while inside; entry and exit through a bedroom window; entry and exit through a front door).
5. Each of the previous year's crimes involves the theft of a victim's personal undergarments (underwear and/or bras).
6. At least a few of the current year's crimes involve the theft of a victim's personal undergarments (underwear and/or bras).
7. None of the crimes involves the theft of valuables (except victim #9; two checkbooks were reportedly stolen).
8. The deadbolt was activated by the offender from inside the apartment on three occasions at the same residence (3—requires a key).
9. The deadbolt was activated by the offender from outside the apartment on at least one occasion (11).
10. There is a distinctive offense signature behavior which more strongly connects several of the cases in a thematic way. This behavior is intended to exercise sexual and personal control over the victim and their home, and induce embarrassment or humiliation. It includes, but is not limited to:
    - theft of undergarments;
    - urinating in the toilet (1) and not flushing (2);
    - calling adult telephone numbers (3);
    - watching TV (3);
    - using the kitchen (2, 3);
    - walking around the apartment, leaving behind grease stained boot-marks (4, 7, 8).

Conclusion #2:

It is this examiner's conclusion that the suspect pool is confined to those individuals who have extensive knowledge of the property, the apartments, and access to either a master key, or key to victim #3's residence. This is based on the following facts:

1. Victim selection is not random and requires specific knowledge of the complexes and residents.
2. Offense times may reflect knowledge of victim schedules or victim vehicles (to observe when they are not in the parking lot).

SUBJECT: UNSOLVED FETISH BURGLARIES, 2002–03; (REDACTED) APARTMENTS—cont'd

3. Deadbolt unlocked from inside on three occasions at same residence (3—requires a key).
4. Locked sliding glass door left ajar at scene with no forced entry; may indicate the use of a key to gain entry (6, 9).
5. The offenses are of a personal nature rather than of a profit-motivated nature, suggesting prior contact, or even a prior/current relationship, between the victims and the offender.

Investigative Suggestions

1. In one of the 2002 cases (**redacted**), cigarette butts were apparently collected from outside her bedroom window. These should be examined first for STR DNA, and then for latent prints. Comparison of biological samples should be obtained surreptitiously from all maintenance personnel. This examiner has had great success in obtaining publicly discarded cigarette butts from suspects and using them as known standards for comparison.
2. The existence of the cigarette butts with potential DNA evidence may be used effectively during an interview with a suspect.
3. MUDs and LUDs records (reference to incoming and outgoing local and long-distance calls) should be obtained for all the victims to determine the origin of harassing phone calls.
4. If possible, a careful examination of the grease stains should be performed with an eye toward identification, and the area searched for places where such material could have transferred on to the offender's footwear.
5. Investigators should conduct a door to door walk of the (**redacted**) apartments and speak with each female tenant. The purpose of this should be to impart upon them security concerns, as well as the need for reporting any future burglaries immediately in order to preserve valuable physical evidence. They should be encouraged to contact the police department before touching or moving anything in their homes if they feel they have been burglarized.
6. A careful protocol for processing future scenes should be developed to include the search for footwear impressions and cigarette butts, both inside and outside the residence, fingerprinting the points of entry and exit (and other areas of activity such as drawers), and searching for/collecting all potential biological transfer (urine, semen, etc.) from areas of activity and potential activity. This should also include photo-documentation. Everything that the offender handled should be examined for prints.
7. If possible, phone records for suspect residences should be examined to determine if they have called adult phone numbers matching those from victim #3.
8. A list of currently employed maintenance personnel should be obtained from (**redacted**) apartments.
9. The criminal histories of currently employed maintenance personnel should be obtained.
10. Maintenance employee work sheets (hours, days, and times on duty) for the current and previous year should be obtained from (**redacted**) apartments.
11. Maintenance service records and requests for the current year should be obtained from (**redacted**) apartments.
12. A list of individuals who have master keys should be obtained from (**redacted**) apartments.
13. This report should not be released to public, as it contains no information that could lead to tips of value from the public. The suspect pool is sufficiently narrow.

Subsequent to this report, law enforcement investigators identified a suspect associated with property management, resulting in an arrest-successful prosecution using DNA evidence.

REFERENCES

Brankley, Goodwill, Reale, 2014. Escalation from fetish burglaries to sexual violence: a retrospective case study of former col., D. Russell Williams. Journal of Investigative Psychology and Offender Profiling 11 (2), 115–135.

Gebhard, P., Gagnon, J., Pomeroy, W., Christenson, C., 1965. Sex Offenders: An Analysis of Types. Harper & Row Publishers, New York.

Lowenstein, L.F., Summer 2002. Fetishes and their associated behavior. Sexuality and Disability 20 (2).

Morris, W., 2006. Sex burglar gets 7 years. Juneau Empire. Available from: www.juneauempire.com/stories/110106/loc_20061101015.shtml accessed on 01.11.08.).

PART

Forensic Protocols

4

CHAPTER

Applied Crime Scene Analysis

13

B.E. Turvey

Forensic Solutions LLC, Sitka, Alaska, United States;
Institute of Forensic Investigation and Criminal Profiling, Juarez, Mexico

CHAPTER OUTLINE

As detailed thoroughly in Turvey (2011), *Crime scene analysis* (CSA) (aka crime analysis) refers to the analytical process of interpreting the specific features of a crime in the context of all evidence from related crime scenes. Potential crime scene characteristics that must be established or at least considered include, among many others, victim selection/targeting, method of approach, method of attack, method of control, location type, nature and sequence of sexual acts, materials used, evidence of skill or planning, any verbal activity, precautionary acts, contradictory acts, modus operandi (MO), signature behavior, and the amount of time spent in the commission of the crime.

Crime scene characteristics are interpreted subsequent to and in consideration of an integrated examination of the physical evidence and victimology. If the crime has not been properly reconstructed, a CSA is not possible. In the same fashion, if the victimology has not been conducted, a CSA will have several major holes in it. In other words, if an examiner does not have a solid reconstruction to work with, or comprehensive victim background information, then they cannot make interpretations. This has not stopped many from doing it anyway. That is when professionals need to step in and make a clear record regarding what can and cannot be said based on the available evidence.

Behavioral Evidence Analysis. http://dx.doi.org/10.1016/B978-0-12-800607-8.00013-6

THE LIMITS OF THE EVIDENCE

Because they depend on evidence, and complete evidence is not always available, not all crime scene characteristics may be established in every case. This can limit any subsequent findings, and in some cases may even prevent meaningful profiling efforts. When limits are present due to a lack of available evidence, their existence becomes a significant forensic finding that must be explained in the report. In doing so the examiner makes it evident that not only are they barred from making a finding on a particular issue, but so is everyone else.

Consequently, the results of CSA may be used at the outset to determine the limits of the available evidence and the need for additional investigative and forensic efforts, perhaps even in the context of a threshold assessment. When sufficient behavioral evidence is available, the same results may also be used to infer offender MO and signature behaviors, evidence of crime scene staging, crime scene motive, and offender characteristics, or to assist with linkage analysis efforts.

CRIME SCENE ANALYSIS GOALS

The CSA process is intended to provide a language for categorizing, explaining, and comparing victim and offender behavior. Ultimately, it is an interpretive stage of crime scene investigation as it is defined by DeForest (2005), subsequent to crime scene processing and reconstruction efforts. The relationship between physical evidence and CSA may be expressed in the following manner: crime scene processing efforts provide a foundation of physical evidence unique to each case; the narrow bandwidth of physical evidence that is collected is then examined (partially) and interpreted through laboratory analysis and crime reconstruction efforts—this provides raw behavioral evidence; the behavioral evidence is examined and classified by the forensic examiner to establish evidence of motive, staging, offender MO, and signature behaviors. This information can be used to suggest further evidence or information that must be developed (and how) in order to have the most complete understanding of the crime, and what is known can be compared to other cases for linkage purposes.

CASE REPORTS

Consider the following case reports prepared in two separate consultations: the sexual homicide of a child, Cannie Bullock, and a suspected serial case involving the murders of three separate prostitutes. This author examined case material and testified as a forensic expert on behalf of the defense in both cases. Contrary to popular belief, such testimony is not generally offered to address the issue of guilt. That is an issue for the jury. Rather, it is provided to suggest the limits of the evidence to the court, and then to the jury if necessary.

The question addressed in such reports is generally not who committed the crimes, but rather how they were committed, why, and under what precise circumstances. The CSA report has great value in this regard, and can organize the thoughts and impressions of litigators tremendously, to say nothing enduring more informed court proceedings. Unfortunately there are many "experts" that misunderstand their role in the criminal justice process. They will identify themselves immediately by violating the ultimate issue (eg, using their findings to improperly establish or suggest the guilt of a specific individual), by misusing or misunderstanding basic terminology, by not understanding the value of basic CSA considerations such as victimology, or by cherry-picking evidence to support specific predetermined findings.

It is important to understand that while these reports provide an important instructional guide, they are a guide only. The characteristics suggested are a starting point, not a conclusive end. Not all characteristics will be relevant in every case (though most will), and new cases will bring to light the need for the consideration of characteristics not imagined in these pages. Examiners are therefore admonished to understand that these are guidelines, and they are not to be used pedantically. This would be a mistake, limiting their thinking and their understanding.

Turvey / Page 1

Brent E. Turvey, MS
Forensic Solutions, LLC
P.O. Box 2175
Sitka, Alaska 99835
(907) 747-5121

November 28, 2006

Mitchell Hauptman, Attorney at Law
333 Armstrong Street
Lakeport, California 95453
Bus:(707) 263-3707

Re: *California v. Joseph S. Cordova*, Contra Costa County

Joseph S. Cordova is accused of the sexual murder of 8-year-old Cannie M. Bullock, whose nude body was discovered in her backyard, covered with a blanket, on Saturday, August 25, 1979 during the early morning hours. Mr. Cordova was identified as a suspect in her murder after a "cold hit" in 2002 matched his DNA to sperm found in the victim's vagina.

Mr. Mitchell Hauptman, an attorney representing Mr. Cordova, asked this examiner, Brent E. Turvey, MS of Forensic Solutions LLC of Sitka, Alaska, to perform a crime analysis of the above mentioned case. A crime analysis examines and interprets the behavioral evidence in a particular crime. Crime analysis requires examination and analysis of the forensic evidence, victimology and crime scene characteristics in a particular case or series of cases (Turvey, 2002).

In order to complete the assigned task, this examiner was provided with at least the following case material relating to the following cases:

1. A CD-Rom containing police reports, interviews, and notes; crime scene reports; scene diagrams; autopsy reports; medical reports; evidence reports; evidence logs; forensic reports; scene photos; autopsy photos; arrest reports; court documents; and various court transcripts relating to the above cases - as well as the murder of Cannie Bullock.

This examiner has read and/ or examined all of material provided on this CD-Rom.

Crime Analysis

Background / Timeline

The following background and timeline information is rendered from police reports, including the statements of Linda Bullock (29 y.o.) (the victim's mother), Debra Fisher (19 y.o.), and Mary Magdeline Sequeira (31 y.o.). It should be noted that during this

Turvey / Page 2

period of time, Linda Bullock has admitted to frequently abusing both alcohol and methamphetamine. She also stated to police that she and Cannie (8 y.o.) had lived at 2628 ½ Dover Ave for approximately 3 months prior to Cannie's murder. She explained to police they moved there from Richmond where she had lived with her ex-boyfriend, Larry Buholzer, a member of a biker gang. They had recently broken up. While living with Buholzer, she admitted to frequently having different male visitors over to have sex and do drugs in her bedroom. Police directly asked her whether she had prostituted herself or her daughter Cannie for drugs or money, though Linda Bullock denied doing either (this issue is revisited in the *victimology* section of this report).

1. 8/24/79 just prior to 2300hrs – According to Debra Fisher, Cannie Bullock got in the shower and then Linda Bullock, who also wanted to take a shower, kicked her out. Cannie got out and dressed in her white bathrobe. According to Debra Fisher, who lived with Linda and Cannie at the time, it is unlikely that Cannie was wearing anything beneath the bathrobe.

2. 8/24/79, between 2300 and 2330hrs – Linda Bullock and Debra Fisher left the Bullock residence, 2628 ½ Dover Ave, San Pablo, for Oscar's Bar in Richmond, to play pool. Cannie was left home alone with instructions not to open the door for strangers. Linda Bullock claimed to have the only key to the residence, and locked Cannie inside as she left. She also made certain to latch the front gate on her way out. Starting out on foot, Linda and Debra ultimately hitched a ride to Oscar's with a man they knew named Bobby. It should be noted that the precise nature of the relationship between Bullock and Fisher (friends, lovers, etc…) has not been made clear. This issue should be investigated further.

3. 8/25/79, 0200hrs – Debra Fisher and Mary Magdeline Sequeira (a bartender at Oscars, aka "Bobby") left Oscars Bar for Cleo's Corner to play pool. Linda Bullock stayed at Oscar's Bar to play pool with a man named Dennis (also a bartender at Oscar's).

4. Between 2330 and 0300 -While at Oscar's Bar, Linda Bullock got into a fight with "Pam" over a previous altercation that had occurred at a house party at Bullock's residence. That evening, Linda Bullock threw a drink in Pam's face, while Pam threw a cigarette in Linda Bullock's face.

5. 8/25/79, between 0245 and 0300hrs – Linda Bullock got a ride home with Dennis the bartender. She explained to police that she was afraid of retaliation by Pam, and Dennis was escorting her. Dennis entered the house with her. Linda found the front gate unlatched, the front door ajar, the porch light off and non-functioning, and Cannie missing. She searched the residence and found the sofa bed where Cannie sleeps in disarray, and Cannie's bathrobe at the foot of the sofa bed with red stains on it. She subsequently asked Dennis to leave.

6. 8/25/79, 0245hrs to 0330hrs – Linda Bullock searched for Cannie, during which she found the gate ajar in the backyard. However, she did not report seeing the blanket or finding the body in the backyard.

7. 8/25/79, 0300hrs – Debra Fisher and Mary Magdeline Sequeira left Cleo's Corner for Linda Bullock's residence, where Fisher planned to spend the night. They found Linda Bullock yelling for Cannie and further assisted with the search. Mary Sequeira observed torn bedding on the sofa, and Cannie's bathrobe stuffed between the mattress and the sofa bed. They still do not seeing the blanket or finding the body in the backyard.

8. Note: CSI Bentley found the victims robe on the floor near the doorway to the kitchen area where he understands Linda Bullock dropped it. He takes time in his report to explain that persons entering the residence would likely have stepped on the robe. This issue is revisited in the *investigative suggestions* section of this report.

9. 8/25/79, after 0300hrs – Linda Bullock reportedly contacted her landlady, Rose Azevedo, at 2628 Dover (the house in front of hers). In the past, Azevedo has taken Cannie into her home when her mother has been out late. There is some hostility between them. On this occasion, Azevedo reportedly refused to let Linda Bullock into her home to search for Cannie, or to use the phone to call authorities. Linda Bullock does not have a phone

10. 8/25/79, prior to 0330hrs – Cannie Bullock is reported missing to San Pablo Police Department by Debra Fisher, who uses Linda Bullock's name. Debra Fisher reportedly got Azevedo to agree to let her use the phone. At this point, no one has reported seeing the blanket or finding the body in the backyard.

11. 8/25/79, prior to 0330hrs – Lt. Burke and Officer Vaughan searched the interior and exterior of Bullock's residence at 2628 ½ Dover, finding Cannie's body in the backyard.

12. 8/25/79, approx. 0451hrs – Police inform Linda Bullock that her daughter Cannie is dead. She subsequently becomes hysterical, sits on the floor, starts crying, and then passes out. Police are unable to get any further information from her at this point.

13. 8/27/79, approx. 1400hrs – During a police initiated interview at her home in Pinole, Debra Fisher presents Det. Bennet with a Sear's sewing machine catalog and a small charm resembling the zodiac sign of Sagittarius (the Archer). Fisher explained that she and Linda Bullock had found these items on the coffee table of Bullock's living room. She explained that they did not know where they came from, and that neither owned a sewing machine.

Victimology

Victimology is the study of available victim information for the purposes of assessing their risk of becoming the victim of a particular type of crime. There are two kinds of victim risk to assess: *lifestyle risk* and *incident risk. Lifestyle risk* is a term that refers to the overall risk present by virtue of an individual's personality, and their personal, professional, and social environments. I*ncident risk* is a more specific term that refers to the risk present at the moment an offender initially acquires a victim, by virtue of the victim's state of mind, and the hazards of the immediate environment (Burgess & Hazelwood, 1995; Turvey, 2002).

Each type of victim risk may be generally characterized in one of three ways: low, medium, or high. The term *low-risk victim* refers to an individual who's personal, professional, and social live do not normally expose them to a possibility of suffering harm or loss. The term *medium-risk victim* refers to an individual whose personal, professional, and social lives can expose them to a possibility of suffering harm or loss. The term *high-risk victim* refers to an individual whose personal, professional, and social lives continuously expose them to the danger of suffering harm or loss (Burgess & Hazelwood, 1995; Turvey, 2002).

In this case, we have a victim (Cannie Bullock) with a high lifestyle risk, and a high incident risk. Cannie Bullock would be classified as having a **high lifestyle risk** because of at least the following lifestyle influences:

1. Cannie Bullock was an 8-year-old child that spent much of her time without monitoring or parental supervision.

2. Cannie Bullock and her mother lived in a home in a secluded area behind their landlady's house where it is extremely difficult to observe activity from the street.

3. Cannie Bullock's only true caregiver (her mother, Linda Bullock) abused both alcohol and methamphetamine prior to and up until the time of her death.

4. Cannie Bullock was left without care or supervision until the early hours of the morning on a regular basis.

5. Cannie Bullock's mother was known to have an angry temper.

6. Cannie Bullock's mother was known to frequently have different male visitors in their home to have sex and consume drugs.

7. Cannie Bullock's mother had just recently ended a long-term relationship with a male in a biker gang.

Note: It is unknown whether or not Cannie Bullock suffered from chronic physical or sexual abuse prior to her death. These issues were not addresses sufficiently at autopsy. It is strongly recommended that an investigation be conducted into whether or not Child

Protective Services, or some similar child welfare organization, had a file on Cannie Bullock, or this home. In cases such as this, it is common for investigators to fail with respect to investigating or establishing these circumstances, for fear of alienating a parent as a witness.

Cannie Bullock would be classified as having a **high incident risk** because of at least the following circumstances present on the evening of her death:

1. Cannie Bullock's home is a nexus for high-risk activity (drug abuse, alcohol abuse, partying, sexual activity with an increasing number of different men, etc…). Simply being at that specific location increased her risk of harm.

2. Cannie Bullock had been left at home alone.

3. Cannie Bullock was an 8-year-old child; she would be less able to physically defend herself from any form of danger that presented itself that evening.

4. Cannie Bullock had been left at home after 11pm on a Friday night. Because of the time of day, the darkness, and the fact that it was the beginning of the weekend in conjunction with the activities regularly associated with the home, Cannie was essentially left alone to confront anyone who came looking for any of the above mentioned high risk activities.

5. Cannie Bullock's mother had gone to the bar that night to drink, leaving Cannie at home alone.

6. Cannie Bullock's mother had gotten into a fight that night before coming home.

It should be noted that the police specifically asked Linda Bullock whether she had prostituted herself or her daughter Cannie for drugs or money. This means they had specific reasons to suspect that this activity was going on, as these are not questions to be asked lightly. Indications of both exist in the material provided to this examiner, though there is no definitive evidence. If either circumstance were the case, the very highest level of lifestyle and incident risks would be in play.

Given the lifestyle and incident risk in this case, this examiner concludes that the number of potential suspects for the homicide in this case is quite high. At the same time, this victimology also strongly suggests that Cannie Bullock would not have opened the door for a complete stranger.

Crime Scene Characteristics

Due to the nature of the physical evidence in this case, some crime scene characteristics may not be reliably established.

Location & Scene Types
The victim was attacked in her bed, and her body was disposed of outside in the backyard. This was an indoor primary scene, with an outdoor disposal site.

Point of Entry/ Point of Exit
The backdoor to the backyard (in the back bedroom) is locked from the inside, and is blocked on the inside by a box, furniture, and most importantly the bed itself. These appear undisturbed in the photograph, making the use of this door essentially impossible without leaving evidence of disturbance. Access through the window in the same room, which leads into the back yard, is possible. However, one would have to cross the bed going in or out, as it is directly beneath the window. The bed is not perfectly made, but shows no signs of anyone stepping on it as would be expected. This makes the use of this window extremely unlikely.

As a consequence of this evidence, the most likely point of entry, exit and body removal is the front door. The front door shows no evidence of forced entry related to this incident. This would strongly suggest that Cannie Bullock opened the door for the person who killed her.

Methods of Attack/ Methods of Control
The cause of death was determined to be strangulation. It is not known whether this was manual, but there is no evidence that a ligature was used. There is further no evidence that non-lethal controlling bindings or ligatures were used. And there is further no evidence that a weapon of any kind was used during any portion of the attack.

Use of Force
The use of force in this case is uncertain. Certainly the level of force used was lethal, but the autopsy findings, as well as photos taken at the scene and at the time of autopsy, are of insufficient quality to distinguish between injuries received prior to the date of the homicide, injuries received during the attack which lead to the victim's death, fingerprint powder on the body, and the tremendous amount of insect activity (namely ants) which causes and simulates certain kinds of injury.

Sexual Acts
The victim in this case suffered at least one violent sexual penetration, resulting in a single tear of the fourchette and introitus of the vagina, 2cm in length. There is no evidence of oral or anal penetration.

Precautionary Acts
Precautionary acts are intended to consciously confuse, hamper, or defeat investigative or forensic efforts for the purposes of concealing the offender's identity, their connection to the crime, or the crime itself.

The victim's nude body was removed from her sofa bed to the backyard, just inside the left of the back gate. She was subsequently covered by a flower-patterned blanket from her bed. Additionally, a polka-dot bed sheet was found in-between the back door and the victim's covered body. It is possible that she was removed from her sofa bed to the outside of the house, and the bed sheet put in place, to leave the impression that someone carried her out the back door. In doing so, the bed sheet, the body, and the blanket would be meant to appear to have been dropped along the way. Certainly this did not occur, but it is possible that investigators were meant to think so, in an effort to direct investigative efforts away from the home. This would be consistent with an effort to stage the crime scene as a stranger attack.

It should be noted at this point that it is implausible for someone to have inspected the gate to the back yard in a search for the victim without seeing the white, flower patterned bed sheet that covered the body. It was big, obvious, right insight the gate, and completely out of place. Anyone searching for the body would have discovered this blanket.

Contradictory Acts

The removal of the victim's body to the backyard might initially throw investigators off, but there was no attempt to conceal or destroy evidence of the attack in the home, such as the blood in the sofa bed area, and on the victim's bathrobe. Moreover, there is no other place to take the victim's body except out the front door and onto the main street, past the landlady's house. This would have increased the risk of being caught in the act. The existence of this evidence, and the evidence demonstrating that the backdoor and window could not have been used, contradicts the precautionary value of removing the body and trailing the bed sheet from the back door. It could not serve the function of actually removing the body away from the scene, and it could not have complete value without cleaning up the blood evidence inside. This strongly suggests that the offender did not commit these acts solely for precautionary reasons, that these acts were interrupted or incomplete, that they were suffering from defects of reasoning (drug use, mental illness, etc..), or perhaps all of the above.

Evidence of Concern and Remorse

Remorse is evidenced in a crime by actions that suggest deep and painful regret. The removal of the victim, and the covering of her naked body, is most consistent with an act of concern and remorse. The offender could not bear to witness what they had done, so they took the time to move her body outside. The offender further could not bear the victim outside uncovered, so they took the time to put one of her blankets over her – almost to the point of attempting to undo the crime.

Items Taken/ Items Left Behind

There is no evidence to suggest that any valuables (cash, jewelry, drugs, etc…) were taken from the scene. There are multiple purses and containers in the scene photos, all of which are undisturbed. The drawers in most of the rooms are open, with clothes hanging out, but this was reported to be the normal state of affairs in this home. However, there is no indication that police made an effort to determine what if any items of value were in the home (cash, drugs, etc…).

Two days after the homicide, Debra Fisher presented Det. Bennet with a Sear's sewing machine catalog and a small charm resembling the zodiac sign of Sagittarius (the Archer). Fisher explained that she and Linda Bullock had found these items on the coffee table of Bullock's living room. She explained that they did not know where they came from, and that neither owned a sewing machine. The inference may be that these came from the offender, though the absence of evidence supporting this makes it difficult to determine.

It should be noted that crime scene photos of the coffee table and the kitchen table do not show either of these items being present. Furthermore, this examiner is not aware of any photos of these items at the scene at all.

Investigative Shortcomings & Suggestions

William Flores

From 1979 to 2002, police investigative efforts in this case focused almost entirely on a suspect who lived only a few doors down named William Flores. Flores was considered a strong suspect in the death of Cannie Bullock for a variety of circumstantial reasons. So much so, that Det. Mark Harrison of the San Pablo Police Department wrote a psychological profile on April 11, 1996, implicating William Flores in order to facilitate the exhumation of his body for DNA testing, 13 years after Flores committed suicide by self-immolation and stabbing. Moreover, according to Det. Harrison, his mother, Mary Flores, and his sister, Linda Smith, felt that William Flores was responsible for the death of Cannie Bullock. Linda Smith stated that not only had William Flores attempted to sexually assault her in the past, but that on the night of Cannie Bullock's murder William came home with his shirt covered in blood – and that his mother burned the shirt.

Based on this and other information regarding the background and propensities of William Flores, Commander Joseph Aita of the San Pablo Police Department wrote a memo on April 16th, 2002 to the Chief of Police agreeing with Det. Harrison that Flores was "a likely suspect in the Bullock homicide." He further approved the disinterment of William Flores' remains for DNA testing.

DNA testing ultimately excluded William Flores with respect to the rape, but not necessarily the homicide. There is no direct evidence that the same person must have committed the rape and the homicide of Cannie Bullock. Given the lifestyle and incident risk in this case, it would be inappropriate to make this assumption.

Other Suspects

There are a number of investigative shortcomings in this case. Addressing these issues would help expand or narrow the suspect pool with respect to the murder of Cannie Bullock considerably. In any case where the homicide and the rape have not been sufficiently connected, this is incumbent upon investigators.

Prior to the development of Joseph Cordova as a suspect in 2002, all investigative efforts seemed to focus on proving the guilt of William Flores. Few other investigative avenues were seriously considered. This has left the investigation with a number of investigative holes and without serious attention to developing alternate suspects. Some of these issues have been touched on previously in this report, but they bear repeating.

1. The providence of the Sear's Sewing manual that may have belonged to William Flores, and how it came to the police through the crime scene and Debra Fisher, has not been reliably investigated or established. This would seem to be a fairly important piece of evidence.

2. Subsequent to the 2002 "cold hit" on Joseph Cordova for the rape of Cannie Bullock, investigative efforts with respect to further suspect development in the homicide ceased. As already stated, this assumes that the person responsible for the rape is also responsible for the homicide. This assumption is inappropriate in this case as there is no physical to support it. The possibility that two people were involved, either together or separately, is plausible with this victimology, and has not been investigated.

3. The conduct and statements of Linda Bullock with respect to this crime combine to suggest her potential knowledge of suspects or potential involvement. (i.e. she never found the blanket despite searching; she asked Dennis, her alleged protector, to leave, when evidence of violence was discovered at her home; she told Debra Fisher she knew who killed Cannie; she has refused to participate in the investigation of the crime and the subsequent prosecution of Joseph Cordova; etc…). She was not, however, adequately investigated on any of these issues. At a bare minimum, her precise activities that evening should have been investigated, her clothes taken as evidence, and everyone in her life should have been scrupulously interviewed. To say nothing of establishing all of those who regularly visited her home, and where/ how she obtained her drugs. As it stands, a decent criminal history was not even established.

4. Larry Buholzer, Linda Bullock's ex-boyfriend, was implicated several times by witnesses as a possible suspect with a revenge motive. This examiner has no evidence that Mr. Buholzer was interviewed and his whereabouts accounted for on the night of the murder. This to account for the nature of his relationship with Linda Bullock, and why it ended. Moreover, his criminal history should have been established.

5. Cannie Bullock's sexual history was not established by either the police investigation or the forensic examination of her body. Given the victimology in this case, this should have been done.

6. Cannie Bullock's history of physical abuse and/ or neglect was not established by either the police investigation or the forensic examination of her body. Given the victimology in this case, this should have been done.

7. Cannie Bullock's robe was not properly examined for trace evidence; rather it was assumed to have no value because of where it was found and who may have touched it. A list of people who may have had legitimate contact with the robe can be made, and any foreign material identified and use for the development of suspects. Additionally, an effort should have been made to determine precisely how and where the blood transferred onto the bathrobe, and whether it was worn after the rape.

8. Debra Fisher, who was living with Linda Bullock at the time of the murder, was not interviewed regarding the precise nature of her relationship with Linda Bullock (friends, lovers, etc…), or the reason she left Oscar's Bar with another woman (Mary Sequeira) that night. Nor is it clear whether they left before of after the fight between Linda Bullock and "Pam". In her interviews, she seemed to know quite a bit about the abuse suffered by Cannie Bullock at the hands of her mother, but she was not asked to elaborate or explain. Moreover, her criminal history should have been established.

9. Mary Sequeira was not interviewed regarding the nature of her relationship with Debra Fisher, why left Oscar's Bar together for Cleo's Corner, what they did at Cleo's Corner, and whether there were any witnesses.

10. Oscar's Bar was not canvassed for witnesses who may have observed the activities of Linda Bullock, "Pam", Debra Fisher or Mary Sequeira that night.

11. Cleo's Corner was not canvassed for witnesses who may have observed the activities of Debra Fisher or Mary Sequeira that night.

12. "Pam", from Oscar's Bar, was not actually identified or interviewed regarding the reason for her argument with Linda Bullock.

13. "Dennis", the man who gave Linda Bullock a ride home from Oscar's Bar, was not interviewed about either Linda Bullock's arguments and conduct or his observations at the crime scene that evening. Nor was it established why he left at Linda's direction.

Although the DNA evidence in this case with respect to the rape of Cannie Bullock suggests that Joseph Cordova is the only suspect for her murder, it bears repeating that this assumption is not appropriate given the victimology (the sheer volume of circumstances and suspects), and the investigative failures outlined in this report.

____

Brent E. Turvey, MS – Forensic Science

REFERENCES

Burgess, A., Hazelwood, R. (Eds.) (1995) *Practical Aspects of Rape Investigation, 2nd Ed.*, Boca Raton: CRC Press.

Turvey, B. (2002) *Criminal Profiling: An Introduction to Behavioral Evidence Analysis, 2nd Ed.*, San Diego: Elsevier Science.

Linkage Analysis Report

Forensic Examiner
Brent E. Turvey, MS – Forensic Science
Forensic Solutions, LLC
Sitka, Alaska
www.forensic-science.com
bturvey@forensic-science.com

Date of Report
August 4, 2011

Report for
Janet A. Gandolfo, Esq.
174 Webber Avenue
Sleepy Hollow, New York 10591
(914) 332-0505

In Re: *New York v. Francisco Acevedo*

Purpose

The purpose of this forensic report is to answer the following questions, at the request of the Attorney Janet A. Gandolfo:

1. What are the nature, scope and limits of Linkage Analysis?

2. Do the murders of Maria Ramos (1989), Tawanda Hodges (1991), and Kimberly Moore (1996) share a common scheme, or pattern, of behavioral factors distinctive enough to suggest whether multiple offenders may have been responsible.

Linkage Analysis

Linkage analysis refers to the process of determining whether or not there are discrete connections, or behavioral commonalities, between two or more previously unrelated cases through *Crime Analysis* (aka, *Crime Scene Analysis*) (Petherick and Turvey, 2010). As explained in Turvey (2011), it is most often employed to serve one of two purposes: (1) to assist law enforcement with the application of its resources by helping to direct investigative efforts; and (2) to assist the court in determining whether or not there is sufficient behavioral evidence to suggest a common scheme or plan in order to address forensic issues, such as whether similar crimes may be tried together or whether other crimes may be brought in as evidence (Hazelwood and Warren, 2003).

As will be discussed, it is understood that there are very different thresholds of evidence for *investigative* and *forensic* conclusions.

Crime Scene Analysis

Crime Scene Analysis is the process of establishing and interpreting the specific features and characteristics of a particular crime and related crime scenes. It involves the examination of physical evidence (crime reconstruction), victimology, crime scene characteristics, modus operandi, motive, and signature behaviors. As a direct result of this analysis, the examiner categorizes victim and offender behavior for eventual comparison to other cases suspected of being related (Turvey, 2011).

Modus Operandi

Modus operandi (MO) is a Latin term that means *method of operating*. It refers to the manner in which a crime has been committed. A criminal's modus operandi is comprised of choices and behaviors that are intended to assist in the completion of a crime (Turvey, 2011). *Black's Law Dictionary* (Black, 1990, p. 1004) translates the phrase *modus operandi* as "method of operation or doing things," and states that it is "used by police and criminal investigators to describe the particular method of a criminal's activity."

As explained in Gross (1924), some repeat offenders (such as sex offenders and thieves) may develop a characteristic style, or MO, which they rarely depart from. Atcherley (1913) refers to this as an offender's "trademark". However the development of an MO with a trademark is by no means assured. Weston and Wells (1974, p. 110) state more accurately that not all criminals have a particular MO, but some can develop and maintain similar enough methods to justify linking cases *investigatively*.

MO is adaptive, changing sharply based on the flexible state of the offender (e.g. mood, substance abuse, mental illness), the victim (e.g. mood, substance abuse, fear response), and the crime scene (e.g. day/night, weather, witnesses). Therefore, while investigatively helpful, is not considered a sufficiently reliable mechanism for linking or unlinking cases in a forensic (aka legal) context.

Offender Signature

An offender's *signature* is a pattern evidenced by an accumulation of signature behaviors. *Signature behaviors* are individual acts committed by an offender that are not necessary to commit the crime but that suggest the psychological or emotional needs of that offender (Turvey, 2008). While every offender engages in signature behaviors, not all signature behaviors will add up to a unique offender signature. That is to say, it is the case that different offenders can evidence the same set of signature behaviors.

Unlike MO, signature can be more stable over the lifetime of an offender, as it is reflective of more enduring psychological motives and themes. This is particularly the case in sexual offenses, where the offender may have a specific pattern of behaviors and associated feelings, or even a specific fantasy, that they are trying to live out through the offense (Money, 1988). In such instances, this can make signature a more reliable case linkage tool.

Rationale

This report will objectively examine each homicide of concern by means of crime analysis. Then, it will compare the distinguishing behavioral factors (MO, signature and victimology related behaviors) of each case to determine whether discrete connections exist. This will include negative documentation as dictated by the positive findings in each case.

Case linkage analysis involves the employment of scientific principles and knowledge, including ***Locard's exchange principal***, *critical thinking*, *analytical logic*, and *evidence dynamics* (Turvey, 2011).

Limitations

This examiner admonishes readers of this linkage analysis report to understand the following limitations:

1. *Garbage in, garbage out*
   The accuracy of the findings provided in this report is dependent on the accuracy of the findings in the materials examined. While best efforts have been made to assess to the quality of materials examined, and that quality appears sufficient, it is not possible for this examiner to vouch for the accuracy of every investigative and forensic report provided. Therefore, should any major inaccuracies be identified in the materials provided, the findings in this case linkage analysis must be re-evaluated.

2. *Additional and newly discovered evidence or findings*
   Should any additional or new evidence or findings be provided to this examiner subsequent to this report, the findings in this case linkage analysis must be re-evaluated.

3. *Investigative and Forensic thresholds are different*
   As discussed in Turvey (2011), investigative and forensic analyses are different. An investigative analysis is done during the investigation, while facts are still being established and before a complete picture of the case is understood. It is conducted to move the case forward and lead investigators towards additional evidence. It is also subject to rapid change as new evidence and information are constantly being gathered. Investigative tools and their results are not necessarily designed or even intended for courtroom use and, therefore, must be offered and regarded with humility.

   A forensic analysis is conducted in accordance with legal guidelines in order to achieve admissibility in court. It is based on the facts and evidence that are brought forth to make a legal finding, and therefore less subordinate rapid changes of fact and evidence. Because a forensic analysis is meant to be court worthy and have impact on court rulings, a higher standard competency must be evident in examiner education and training, as well as in their findings. In other words, forensic examinations are no place for assumptions or unsupported, inexpert supposition presented with inappropriate levels of certainty and without the appropriate scientific humility.

Materials Examined

This examiner rendered the crime analysis and linkage analysis findings in this report based on a careful examination of case material requested from and provided by Ms. Gandolfo from March 18 – May 7, 2011. That case evidence included, but was not limited to, the following:

1. Original and supplemental police investigative reports and notes re: the murders of Maria Ramos (1989), Tawanda Hodges (1991), and Kimberly Moore (1996);
2. Crime scene photos and sketches re: the murders of Maria Ramos (1989), Tawanda Hodges (1991), and Kimberly Moore (1996);

3. Autopsy reports and photos re: the murders of Maria Ramos (1989), Tawanda Hodges (1991), and Kimberly Moore (1996);
4. Crime scene video re: the murder of Kimberly Moore (1996);
5. Evidence examination reports re: the murders of Maria Ramos (1989), Tawanda Hodges (1991), and Kimberly Moore (1996);
6. NYPD arrest records of Maria Ramos (1989), Tawanda Hodges (1991), and Kimberly Moore (1996);
7. FBI linkage analysis report re: the murders of Maria Ramos (1989), Tawanda Hodges (1991), and Kimberly Moore (1996);
8. FBI criminal investigative analysis report and related documentation re: the murders of Maria Ramos (1989), Tawanda Hodges (1991), and Kimberly Moore (1996);

The total volume of material examined exceeds 3000 pages.

Conclusion: While there is an investigative link between these cases, there is also significant behavioral dissimilarity. Consequently, these crimes do not share a common scheme, or pattern, of behavioral factors distinctive enough to suggest that a single offender must be responsible. Rather, the evident behavioral factors suggest the possibility of multiple offenders.

FINDINGS

1) MARIA L. RAMOS (1989)

Victim last seen:
Last seen by Migdalia Nunez on Friday, February 3, 1989 at approx. 10pm, entering a burgundy Thunderbird owned by Willie Rodriguez in front of the Olympic Restaurant on Jerome Avenue.

Body found:
Reported February 5, 1989 at 0852hrs; found at 78 Fernbrook St., Yonkers, nude on the sidewalk across the street from the Westchester Co. Waste Treatment Plant.

1.1) Victimology

Race: Hispanic
Sex: Female
D.O.B: February 5, 1962
Age: 26
Height: 5'4"
Weight: 117lbs
Hair Color: Black
Home Residence: 228 West Tremont Ave, #9A, Bronx, NY

A. Residence type and description
At the time of the homicide, Maria Ramos' last known address was 228 West Tremont Ave, #9A, Bronx, NY.

B. Employment history
Maria Ramos earned money as a prostitute and thief.

C. Social history

Born in Puerto Rico, Maria Ramos was known by other prostitutes, and was reported to be best friends with a prostitute named Migdalia Nunez (they often worked together). She was also reported to be regularly seeing a steady "john": a married Dominican man named Willie Rodriguez (aka Raul), in his 50s, for the past 3-4 months. Normally picked up by Raul on Friday afternoons and dropped off Sunday afternoons or evenings via private care service; spent time with him at an apartment in Yonkers and always came back with a few hundred dollars.

D. Criminal history

Maria Ramos had a history of arrests for prostitution in multiple precincts, for grand larceny, and was reported by other prostitutes to regularly rip-off her "johns".

E. Drug and alcohol use

Maria Ramos was an I.V. drug user as indicated by track marks on her arms, and was reported to abuse cocaine and heroine.

F. Medical and mental health history

Maria Ramos was suspected of having AIDs and suffered from heroine addiction.

1.2) Victim Exposure

Victim exposure is the amount of contact or vulnerability to harmful elements experienced by the victim. It is a function of both lifestyle and situational exposure.

A. Lifestyle exposure

A victim's *lifestyle exposure* is related to the *frequency* of potentially harmful elements experienced by the victim and resulting from the victim's usual environment and personal traits, as well as past choices (Turvey, 2011).

Mario Ramos was an *extreme-exposure victim* (exposed to the possibility of suffering harm or loss every day (7 days a week*)*. This is supported by the fact that she was a prostitute working the streets, was regularly seeing a married man, was regularly engaged in criminal enterprise including theft, and was also a drug addict.

B. Situational exposure

A victim's *situational* or *incident exposure* refers to the amount of actual exposure or vulnerability to harm resulting from the environment and the victim's personal traits *at the time of victimization.* This is distinct from lifestyle exposure, which again refers to harmful elements that exist, generally, in a victim's everyday life (Turvey, 2011).

Mario Ramos was a *high situational exposure* victim, in that she was exposed to harm or loss immediately prior to victimization. This is supported by the fact that she was a prostitute, a drug addict, and that she was last seen in a vehicle with one of her regular "johns".

The victim exposure in this case dramatically increases the possibility of suffering violence, sexual violence, and homicide. It also dramatically increases the suspect pool as opposed to narrowing it.

1.3) Crime Scene Characteristics

A. Location type
The naked body of Maria Ramos was found lying face up at an outdoor location on concrete.

B. Location of the scene
The naked body of Maria Ramos was found in an industrial area on the sidewalk, across the street from the Westchester Co. Waste Treatment Plant. It was snowing when the body was found; there was some snow on the body; there was no snow underneath the body; and there were areas of dryness beneath the body.

C. Crime scene type
The crime scene where the naked body of Maria Ramos was found was a *disposal site* only. The primary scene (the location where the offender engaged in the majority of his or her principal offense behavior) has not been located and is therefore unknown. Additionally, it is unknown how the offender transported the victim from the primary to the secondary scene.

D. Victim location
This term refers to the characteristics of the victim's location prior to the point of contact. This location is unknown.

E. Victim selection
This term refers to the process by which an offender intentionally chooses or targets a victim (Turvey, 2011). In this case, it is possible that Maria Ramos was targeted by a stranger, by virtue of her occupation; or by virtue of a pre-existing personal relationship, by virtue of the company she kept, the drugs she used, and her ongoing criminal activities. Consequently, the nature of victim selection in this case is unknown.

F. Point of contact
This term refers to the precise location where the offender first approached or acquired the victim (Turvey, 2011). This location is unknown.

G. Method of approach
This term refers to the offender's strategy for getting close to a victim (Turvey, 2011). This includes things like a surprise attack, a con or ruse, or the existence of a pre-existing trust. The method of approach is unknown.

H. Use of weapons
The physical evidence provides that least the following weapons were used in the commission of this crime:

1. A sharp force instrument (likely a knife);
2. A neck compression mechanism (e.g., manual or ligature strangulation)

I. Use of force

This term refers to the amount of force used by the offender during an attack (Turvey, 2011).

There is evidence of *control-oriented force* (physically aggressive behavior that is intended to restrict victim movements) in the form of ligatures to the wrist and neck compression. No blunt force trauma or injury to the face is noted.

There is evidence of *lethal force* (physically aggressive behavior that is sufficient to kill) in the form of sharp force stab wounds to the victim's chest.

J. Method of attack

This term refers to the offender's mechanism for initially overpowering a victim after making the approach. It is appropriate to describe a method of attack in terms of the weapon and the nature of the force involved (Turvey, 2011).

Mario Ramos was apparently attacked when naked, prior to her hands being bound (evidenced by blood on her hands and defensive cuts and bruising on her arms). She was also standing at the time, as evidence by the blood on the bottom of her feet. It is unknown if the offender forced the victim to become naked, or whether she was already naked as the result of a consensual encounter.

There is no evidence of a *blitz* attack (immediate, overpowering force such as a blow to the head).

K. Methods of control

This term refers to the means an offender uses to manipulate, regulate, restrain, and subdue victim behavior of any kind throughout the offense (Turvey, 2011). The physical evidence provides that least the following methods of control were used in the commission of this crime:

1. Victim's hands were bound behind her back with black pantyhose.
2. Non-lethal neck compression indicates control of victim's airway.
3. A bloody seatbelt was found beneath the victim's head and may have been used in the commission of the crime as a ligature or restraint.

L. Method of Killing

While there is some evidence of neck compression, this was apparently insufficient to cause death. Method of killing was a stab wound to the aorta (the largest artery in the human body, originating from the left ventricle of the heart).

M. Evidence of multiple offenders

There is no evidence in this case to suggest that multiple offenders were involved in the commission of this crime.

N. Victim resistance

This term refers to the amount and type of opposition or noncompliance offered by the victim during an attack (Turvey, 2011). Mario Ramos put up both physical and likely verbal resistance, as evidenced by the defensive injuries and the methods of control eventually employed by the offender.

O. Items missing

Mario Ramos was found wearing an earring and four rings on her fingers. She was not found with shoes, socks, underwear, a bra, wallet/ purse/ handbag, or personal identification. An olive colored dress was recovered approximately 50ft. away from her body. However, it is unknown what she was wearing when last seen.

As a consequence, a reliable list of items missing from the victim has not been established.

P. Sexual acts

A *sexual act* is any offender behavior involving sexual organs, sexual apparatus, or sexualized objects (Turvey, 2011). The physical evidence in this case (e.g., DNA) does not confirm sexual activity in direct association with the death of the victim. Such an assumption would in fact be a *fallacy of logic* that is referred to as "Cum hoc, ergo propter hoc," or "with this, therefore because of this" (Chisum and Turvey, 2011; p. 622). This occurs when one jumps to a conclusion about causation based on a correlation between two events, or types of event, that occur simultaneously. In other words: just because two things are found together at a crime scene does not mean that they must be the result of the same actions and events, or that they must have occurred at the same time. This is especially true of evidence of sexual activity found in association with sex workers, such as prostitutes. Any evidence of sexual activity found (e.g., DNA) must therefore be independently linked in some fashion to the homicide via a proper reconstruction of the crime, and not assumed; the mere presence of such evidence is not sufficient basis in this context. The sexual acts in this case, as directly related to the homicide, are therefore unknown.

Q. Time

The length of time the offender spent with the victim is unknown.

R. Evidence of planning

The extent of offender *planning* may be determined by assessing whether or not the offender possessed the means for the commission of the crime upon arrival (Turvey, 2011). In this case, there is evidence to indicate that the disposal of the body was planned, but not the homicide.

It is unknown if Mario Ramos was targeted or opportunistic. Either may be the case, given the victimology.

The homicide was committed with available materials (e.g., victim clothing). If the knife used were indeed a kitchen knife as police first speculated, then this would be opportunistic as opposed to planned.

The homicide was also committed at a location that the offender did not wish to be associated with. This necessitated moving the body after the homicide.

S. Opportunistic elements

Opportunistic elements refer to any unplanned elements that the offender seized on for inclusion in an offense (Turvey, 2011). It is the opinion of the examiner that the following opportunistic elements are evident:

1. **Use of the victim's pantyhose as a wrist ligature/ restraint.**

It is unknown if Mario Ramos was targeted or opportunistic. Either may be the case, given the victimology.

T. Precautionary acts

Precautionary acts refer to behaviors that an offender commits before, during, or after an offense that are consciously intended to confuse, hamper, or defeat investigative or forensic efforts for the purpose of concealing the offender's identity, connection to the crime, or the crime itself (Turvey, 2011). It is the opinion of the examiner that the following precautionary acts are evident:

1. Withholding/ disposing of victim clothing (e.g., shoes, socks, underwear, a bra, wallet/purse/handbag, and personal identification).
2. Transportation of the victim from the primary scene to a disposal site.
3. Disposing of the knife.

If the victim were targeted because she was a prostitute and less likely to be missed, this would also be a precautionary act. However, this may not be a stranger crime given the victimology.

U. Posing

The body of Mario Ramos appears intentionally posed, nude, in a public location where it was certain to be found. This is often done to humiliate the victim sexually, suggesting the origin of the offender's anger.

V. Motivation

Motive is comprised of the emotional, psychological, and material needs that impel and are satisfied by behavior (Turvey, 2011). The motive in this case is most consistent with *anger*. This is evidenced by the posing/ display of the victim's nude body in a public place, and the evidence of an altercation while the victim was nude that resulted in victim defensive injuries, victim restraint, and then lethal force.

1.4) Distinguishing Behavioral Factors

Distinguishing behavioral factors are elements of a crime that may be useful to determine whether a behavioral linkage is present across multiple cases, including offender modus operandi, motive, signature and relevant victimology. They are comprised of M.O. and signature behaviors that reduce the suspect pool.

Modus operandi is a term that refers to the offender's method of operating. M.O. behaviors are those that are intended to assist the criminal in the completion of the crime and are functional in nature (Turvey, 2011). All of the known behaviors in this case are M.O. related save one.

A *signature behavior* is an act committed by an offender that is not necessary to commit the crime but suggests the psychological or emotional needs of that offender (Turvey, 2011). The known signature behaviors in this case include:

1. Posing the victim's body nude, outdoors, in a location where it would be found – evidencing sexually oriented anger.
2. Use of pantyhose (an intimate item of clothing) as a wrist restraint.

This signature behavior is not distinctive, however it is not present in the homicides of Tawanda Hodges or Kimberly Moore.

2) TAWANDA HODGES (1991)

Victim last seen:
Last seen by mother, Devon Hodges, on Tuesday, March 26, 1991 at 7pm at her apartment. Left on a "date". Called ½ hr later looking for her keys. Never seen or heard from again.

Body found:
Reported March 28, 1991 at 1103hrs; found at the Dead End of 1 Federal St., Yonkers, nude except for 2 layers of socks (gray and red) on a pile of gravel in an enclosed area.

2.1) Victimology

Race: Black
Sex: Female
D.O.B: February 18, 1963
Age: 28
Height: 5'2"
Weight: 126lbs
Hair Color: Black
Home Residence: 2690 Valentine Ave., Apt. 2A, Bronx, NY

A. Residence type and description
At the time of the homicide, Tawanda Hodges' last known address was 2690 Valentine Ave., Apt. 2A, Bronx, NY.

B. Employment history
Tawanda Hodges earned money as a prostitute and thief (stealing from cabbies and "johns").

C. Social history
Tawanda Hodges lived with her mother, Devon Hodges, and her two daughters (LaTiesha Hodges, B/F/5; Tara Lothian, B/F/4). Her son (Lameek Hodges, B/M/9) lives with her great-grandmother Lucille Hunter at 420 W. 130 St., Apt. 17. Dating a man named Rodney Rodgers for 2-3 years, with whom she had been arrested for armed robbery of a cab driver. Ron was incarcerated at Riker's Island at the time of her murder.

Previously, Tawanda Hodges had lived with Clive Lothian for about four years. He is the father of her children LaTiesha and Tara. At the time, he was a cab driver. Tawanda Hodges was engaged in drug use and prostitution while they were together. He reported last seeing Tawanda Hodges one month prior to her murder.

D. Criminal history

Tawanda Hodges had a history of arrest for robbery. She was also engaged in prostitution, crack cocaine use, and had a history robbing her "johns".

E. Drug and alcohol use

Tawanda Hodges had a long history of crack cocaine abuse, and was found to have cocaine in her system at the time of her death.

F. Medical and mental health history

Unknown.

2.2) Victim Exposure

Victim exposure is the amount of contact or vulnerability to harmful elements experienced by the victim. It is a function of both lifestyle and situational exposure.

A. Lifestyle exposure

A victim's *lifestyle exposure* is related to the *frequency* of potentially harmful elements experienced by the victim and resulting from the victim's usual environment and personal traits, as well as past choices (Turvey, 2011).

Tawanda Hodges was an *extreme-exposure victim* (exposed to the possibility of suffering harm or loss every day (7 days a week*)*. This is supported by the fact that she was a prostitute, was regularly engaged in criminal enterprise including theft, and was also a drug addict.

B. Situational exposure

A victim's *situational* or *incident exposure* refers to the amount of actual exposure or vulnerability to harm resulting from the environment and the victim's personal traits *at the time of victimization.* This is distinct from lifestyle exposure, which again refers to harmful elements that exist, generally, in a victim's everyday life (Turvey, 2011).

Tawanda Hodges was a *high situational exposure* victim, in that she was exposed to harm or loss immediately prior to victimization. This is supported by the fact that she was a prostitute, a drug addict, and that she was last known to be going out to meet one of her "johns".

The victim exposure in this case dramatically increases the possibility of suffering violence, sexual violence, and homicide. It also dramatically increases the suspect pool as opposed to narrowing it.

2.3) Crime Scene Characteristics

A. Location type

The mostly naked body of Tawanda Hodges was found lying face up at an outdoor location on a pile of dirt, gravel and industrial debris.

B. Location of the scene

The mostly naked body of Tawanda Hodges was found in an industrial area on top of a pile of gravel, dirt, and industrial debris in the corner of lot open to the elements but surrounded on three sides by concrete retaining walls. This lot was large enough for a vehicle to have driven in to it. The open side and center area of the lot were generally clear of debris.

C. Crime scene type

The crime scene where the mostly naked body of Tawanda Hodges was found was a *primary scene* and *disposal site*. The primary scene appears to be located in the center of the lot where there is evidence of vehicle tire marks and an altercation on the ground. Drag marks from that central area indicate that she was dragged and disposed of where found subsequent to an altercation. Some of the altercation may have taken place in the vehicle.

D. Victim location

This term refers to the characteristics of the victim's location prior to the point of contact. This location is unknown.

E. Victim selection

This term refers to the process by which an offender intentionally chooses or targets a victim (Turvey, 2011). In this case, it is possible that Tawanda Hodges was targeted by a stranger, by virtue of her occupation; or by virtue of a pre-existing personal relationship, by virtue of the company she kept, the drugs she used, and her ongoing criminal activities. Consequently, the nature of victim selection in this case is unknown.

F. Point of contact

This term refers to the precise location where the offender first approached or acquired the victim (Turvey, 2011). This location is unknown.

G. Method of approach

This term refers to the offender's strategy for getting close to a victim (Turvey, 2011). This includes things like a surprise attack, a con or ruse, or the existence of a pre-existing trust. The method of approach is unknown.

H. Use of weapons

The physical evidence provides that least the following weapons were used in the commission of this crime:

1. Blunt force object (as evidenced by blunt force trauma suffered by the victim); possibly fists.
2. Thin linear abrasions to neck (1/8" equidistant): suggest material pattern compression (e.g. clothing or cloth item used as ligature)
3. Focal contusions to neck: suggest manual strangulation

I. Use of force

This term refers to the amount of force used by the offender during an attack (Turvey, 2011).

There is evidence of *brutal force* (physically aggressive behavior involving one or more injuries that result in tremendous damage, often to the point of death) in the form of repeated bone-crushing blunt force trauma to the face, head, and neck. Brutal force does not always result in death, nor is it necessarily intended to kill. It is generally employed in the service of anger

There is evidence of *lethal force* (physically aggressive behavior that is sufficient to kill) in the form of manual and ligature strangulation to the victim's neck and blunt force trauma to the victim's head.

No injuries were inflicted to the victim's chest in this case.

J. Method of attack

This term refers to the offender's mechanism for initially overpowering a victim after making the approach. It is appropriate to describe a method of attack in terms of the weapon and the nature of the force involved (Turvey, 2011).

Tawanda Hodges was apparently attacked in a blitz (repeated blows to the head and face), and then strangled prior to being bound (resulting in two self-inflicted linear abrasions in the neck and broken nail during the struggle). At some point afterwards she was disrobed, bound, and strangled again, this time to the point of death.

K. Methods of control

This term refers to the means an offender uses to manipulate, regulate, restrain, and subdue victim behavior of any kind throughout the offense (Turvey, 2011). The physical evidence provides that least the following methods of control were used in the commission of this crime:

1. Tawanda Hodges' hands were bound behind her back with her own black underwear and bra tied together with a series of knots.
2. Manual or ligature strangulation prior to death.
3. Physical violence

L. Method of Killing

Method of killing was manual or ligature strangulation, in concert with blunt force trauma to the head.

M. Evidence of multiple offenders

There is no evidence in this case to suggest that multiple offenders were involved in the commission of this crime.

N. Victim resistance

This term refers to the amount and type of opposition or noncompliance offered by the victim during an attack (Turvey, 2011). Tawanda Hodges put up both physical and likely verbal resistance, as evidenced by the defensive injuries and the methods of control employed by the offender.

O. Items missing

Tawanda Hodges was last seen wearing a black bra, black underwear, black silk blouse, blue dungarees, black suede shoes, knee high stockings, a rust colored suede jacket, yellow metal round wristwatch, a pair of large round earrings, three or four yellow metal bracelets on both wrists, a yellow metal necklace with a charm, and two yellow metal rings on the fingers of both hands. She was also carrying a black leather "Core Sports" book bag with a shoulder strap containing clothing. She forgot her keys at home.

Tawanda Hodges was found naked except for two layers of socks on each foot: one gray and one red each. Recovered from the scene was a brown jacket; a red and white shirt with white undershirt; one metal yellow earring; and the bra and underwear from around her wrists. The other items of clothing and jewelry, including in book bag, were removed prior to the attack (given the absence of associated injury during the altercation) and kept/ discarded by the offender. These were items of evidence and possibly items of value.

P. Sexual acts

A *sexual act* is any offender behavior involving sexual organs, sexual apparatus, or sexualized objects (Turvey, 2011). There is no direct evidence of sexual activity with the victim in direct association with the homicide. See prior discussion re: *cum hoc ergo propter hoc* reasoning in Section 1.3 P of this report.

Q. Time

The length of time the offender spent with the victim is <u>unknown</u>.

R. Evidence of planning

The extent of offender *planning* may be determined by assessing whether or not the offender possessed the means for the commission of the crime upon arrival (Turvey, 2011). In this case, there is evidence to suggest that both the homicide and the disposal of the body were planned. The victim appears to have been driven to the location alive, beaten and strangled to death at that location with available material, and then disposed. The purpose of selecting this remote and secluded location would be because of the absence of any connection to the offender, and the absence of any immediate witnesses.

S. Opportunistic elements

Opportunistic elements refer to any unplanned elements that the offender seized on for inclusion in an offense (Turvey, 2011). It is the opinion of the examiner that the following opportunistic elements are evident:

1. Use of the victim's underwear and bra as a ligature/ restraint.

It is <u>unknown</u> if the victim was targeted or opportunistic. Either may be the case, given the victimology.

T. Precautionary acts

Precautionary acts refer to behaviors that an offender commits before, during, or after an offense that are consciously intended to confuse, hamper, or defeat investigative or forensic efforts for the purpose of concealing the offender's identity, connection to the crime, or the crime itself (Turvey, 2011). It is the opinion of the examiner that the following precautionary acts are evident:

1. Transportation of the victim to a secluded location, without witnesses, prior to killing her.
2. Withholding/ disposing of victim clothing and personal items. Some of these may have received transfer evidence linking back to the offender.
3. Dragging her body to the secluded area of the lot, to delay its discovery.

If the victim were targeted because she was a prostitute and less likely to be missed, this would also be a precautionary act. However, this may not be a stranger crime given the victimology.

U. Posing

The body of Tawanda Hodges does not appear intentionally posed at the crime scene. Rather, it was dragged to the secluded area of an industrial debris pile, evidencing the offender's regard for her. Her body was not meant to be immediately found.

V. Motivation

Motive is comprised of the emotional, psychological, and material needs that impel and are satisfied by behavior (Turvey, 2011). The motive in this case is most consistent with *anger*. This is evidence by the disposal of the victim's mostly nude body in a trash heap, the evidence of an altercation in victim defensive injuries, victim restraint, and then brutal and lethal force. It is also possible that the offender was motivated in some part by profit, as her jewelry was not found. This depends on the value and uniqueness, which are unknown.

2.4) Distinguishing Behavioral Factors

Distinguishing behavioral factors are elements of a crime that may be useful to determine whether a behavioral linkage is present across multiple cases, including offender modus operandi, motive, signature and relevant victimology. They are comprised of M.O. and signature behaviors that reduce the suspect pool.

Modus operandi is a term that refers to the offender's method of operating. M.O. behaviors are those that are intended to assist the criminal in the completion of the crime and are functional in nature (Turvey, 2011).

A *signature behavior* is an act committed by an offender that is not necessary to commit the crime but suggests the psychological or emotional needs of that offender (Turvey, 2011). The known signature behaviors in this case include:

1. Brutal force;
2. Disposal of the victim, mostly naked, on a pile of industrial debris (trash);
3. Combining victim's bra and underwear to make a wrist restraint;
4. Possibly keeping personal items of non-evidentiary value as trophies or for profit (jewelry).

This signature behavior is not distinctive. However, combining a victim's bra and underwear to make a wrist restraint is uncommon and possibly even rare. In any case, these signature behaviors are not present in the homicides of Maria Ramos or Kimberly Moore.

3) KIMBERLY MOORE (1996)

Victim last seen:
Last seen on May 24, 1996 by the Trade Winds Motel manager (Carlos Gonzalez) at approx. 2:30pm, entering room #45 with an unknown white male.

Body found:
Found by Trade Winds Motel housekeeper (Katrina Fadda) and on May 24, 1996 at approx. 6:45pm in Trade Winds Motel, room #45, Yonkers, NY.

3.1) Victimology

Race: Black
Sex: Female
D.O.B: unknown
Age: 30
Height: 5'5"
Weight: 110lbs
Hair Color: Black
Home Residence: 13 Beach St., Mt. Vernon, NY

A. Residence type and description
At the time of the homicide, Kimberly Moore's last known residence was 13 Beach St., Mt. Vernon, NY. No further information was provided.

B. Employment history
Kimberly Moore earned money as a prostitute.

C. Social history
On the morning of the day of her murder, Kimberly Moore had an argument with her boyfriend/ pimp. She left him in the Bronx and was working the street on Yonkers Ave. in front of the Trade Winds Motel late that morning and throughout the afternoon. No further information was provided.

D. Criminal history
Kimberly Moore had a history of prostitution and drug addiction. Her criminal history was not provided to this examiner and is therefore <u>unknown</u>.

E. Drug and alcohol use
Kimberly Moore was found in a Motel room with empty alcohol bottles and drug paraphernalia. She was also known to be a crack cocaine addict. Cocaine was found to be in her system at the time of her death, but not alcohol.

F. Medical and mental health history

Drug addict; otherwise unknown.

3.2) Victim Exposure

Victim exposure is the amount of contact or vulnerability to harmful elements experienced by the victim. It is a function of both lifestyle and situational exposure.

A. Lifestyle exposure

A victim's *lifestyle exposure* is related to the *frequency* of potentially harmful elements experienced by the victim and resulting from the victim's usual environment and personal traits, as well as past choices (Turvey, 2011).

Kimberly Moore was an *extreme-exposure victim* (exposed to the possibility of suffering harm or loss every day (7 days a week). This is supported by the fact that she was a prostitute working the streets and was also a drug addict.

B. Situational exposure

A victim's *situational* or *incident exposure* refers to the amount of actual exposure or vulnerability to harm resulting from the environment and the victim's personal traits *at the time of victimization.* This is distinct from lifestyle exposure, which again refers to harmful elements that exist, generally, in a victim's everyday life (Turvey, 2011).

Kimberly Moore was a *high situational exposure* victim, in that she was exposed to harm or loss immediately prior to victimization. This is supported by the fact that she was a prostitute, a drug addict, and that she was last known to be entering her motel room with one of her "johns".

The victim exposure in this case dramatically increases the possibility of suffering violence, sexual violence, and homicide. It also dramatically increases the suspect pool as opposed to narrowing it.

3.3) Crime Scene Characteristics

A. Location type

The half naked body of Kimberly Moore was found at an indoor location, lying face up on a bed in room #45 of the Trade Winds Motel.

B. Location of the scene

The body of Kimberly Moore was found lying face (half naked from the waist down) up on a bed in room #45 of the Trade Winds Motel. Her shirt and bra were pulled up to expose her breasts and abdomen. Her hands were bound behind her back with the telephone cord taken from the room. Her black underwear where fashioned in a tightened slipknot around her neck. Other items of clothing were found in the room. Her body had been pulled down away from the pillow at the head of the bed, such that one of her legs dangled over the end. She was found by the housekeeper and another prostitute at the scene.

C. Crime scene type

The crime scene where the half naked body of Kimberly Moore was found was a *primary scene* and *disposal site*. The evidence suggests that she entered this room alive, was killed, and then left there by the offender.

D. Victim location

This term refers to the characteristics of the victim's location prior to the point of contact. The evidence suggests that Kimberly Moore originally met the offender somewhere outside of her room at the Trade Winds Motel, where she was strolling for "johns".

E. Victim selection

This term refers to the process by which an offender intentionally chooses or targets a victim (Turvey, 2011). In this case, it is most reasonable to infer that a stranger targeted Kimberly Moore for attack, by virtue of her occupation.

F. Point of contact

This term refers to the precise location where the offender first approached or acquired the victim (Turvey, 2011). The evidence suggests that Kimberly Moore originally met the offender somewhere outside of her room at the Trade Winds Motel and entered with him of her own free will.

G. Method of approach

This term refers to the offender's strategy for getting close to a victim (Turvey, 2011). This includes things like a surprise attack, a con or ruse, or the existence of a pre-existing trust. The method of approach in this case appear to be a con or a ruse, where the offender acted as a "john" in order to get Kimberly Moore alone in the motel room away from direct witnesses.

H. Use of weapons

The physical evidence provides that least the following weapons were used in the commission of this crime:

1. Possibly a sharp force instrument (e.g., a knife);
2. Possibly a blunt force object (e.g. telephone);
3. A ligature (Kimberly Moore's black underwear fashioned into a slip-knot).

See "Use of Force" section below.

I. Use of force

This term refers to the amount of force used by the offender during an attack (Turvey, 2011).

There is no evidence of *brutal force* in this case.

There is evidence of *lethal force* (physically aggressive behavior that is sufficient to kill) in the form of ligature strangulation to Kimberly Moore's neck and possibly blunt force trauma to the victim's head.

No injuries were inflicted to Kimberly Moore's chest in this case.

It should be noted that the cause of death in this case is provided as "asphyxia due to strangulation; sharp and blunt force injuries of the head and extremities". While it is clear that ligature asphyxia is the cause of death, it is less clear what role sharp and blunt force played.

Blunt force is mentioned in terms of abrasions on the victim's extremities and head. The autopsy report states, "Over the distal end of the right eyebrow is a parallel wide abraded 1 ¼ inch laceration. Above the distal end of eyebrow is a V-shaped laceration." There are NO GOOD PHOTOS of the right side of the victim's face. "Medical Examiner Images 091.jpg" is a straight photo of the face, showing now injury to the right side. "Medical Examiner Images 077.jpg" is picture of the victim at the scene showing the right side of her face. No injury is evident on the right side of her face in this photograph. However, there is an inverted photo (evident from the inverted ME ruler) of the left side that could be confused for the right ("Medical Examiner Images 082.jpg").

Also, police initially stated in their reports that Kimberly Moore had been struck with the phone in the head, but the phone was not photo documented sufficiently for examination. Furthermore, the death investigation report refers to the injury next to the left eyebrow as a laceration and not a stab. Firm conclusions regarding blunt force in this case are therefore not possible.

Sharp force is mentioned with respect to the injury near the victim's left eyebrow. Upon close inspection of the injury photos, this injury does not appear to be from sharp force, but rather a laceration from blunt force trauma. Also it is reported to be ½" deep and ¾" wide. This would make it a cut, not a stab. This issue must be re-examined by a forensic pathologist before firm conclusions may be made about the use of a sharp force object on this victim.

Sharp force is mentioned with respect to 2 superficial incise wounds behind the victim's left ear. There are no photos of this injury provided to this examiner, and no documentation that they exist. This issue must be re-examined by a forensic pathologist before firm conclusions may be made about the use of a sharp force object on this victim.

J. Method of attack

This term refers to the offender's mechanism for initially overpowering a victim after making the approach. It is appropriate to describe a method of attack in terms of the weapon and the nature of the force involved (Turvey, 2011).

Kimberly Moore was possibly attacked in a *blitz* (an overpowering blow to the head), and then certainly bound behind the back with a ligature set in place around her neck.

K. Methods of control

This term refers to the means an offender uses to manipulate, regulate, restrain, and subdue victim behavior of any kind throughout the offense (Turvey, 2011). The physical evidence provides that least the following methods of control were used in the commission of this crime:

1. Blitz attack to overpower victim;
2. Victim's underwear around the neck in a slipknot to control airway.

L. Method of Killing

Method of killing was ligature strangulation, possibly in concert with blunt force trauma to the head.

M. Evidence of multiple offenders

There is no evidence in this case to suggest that multiple offenders were involved in the commission of this crime.

N. Victim resistance

This term refers to the amount and type of opposition or noncompliance offered by the victim during an attack (Turvey, 2011). There is no evidence that Kimberly Moore physically resisted during the commission of this crime.

O. Items missing

There is no evidence that any items belonging to Kimberly Moore are missing. She was found with all known clothing and jewelry at the scene.

P. Sexual acts

A *sexual act* is any offender behavior involving sexual organs, sexual apparatus, or sexualized objects (Turvey, 2011).

There is evidence that the offender engaged in sexual activity with the Kimberly Moore, given the removal of the bottom half of her clothing, the fact that she was laying on a bed, and the fact that her breasts were exposed. There is also evidence of vaginal and anal sexual activity in this case (semen and sperm). However, given the fact that Kimberly Moore was a prostitute and had multiple male sex partners on this day prior to her death, it is not possible to connect this vaginal and anal evidence exclusively with the events surrounding her death. See prior discussion re: *cum hoc ergo propter hoc* reasoning in Section 1.3 P of this report.

Q. Time

The length of time the offender spent with Kimberly Moore is unknown, but it must have been less than three hours.

R. Evidence of planning

The extent of offender *planning* may be determined by assessing whether or not the offender possessed the means for the commission of the crime upon arrival (Turvey, 2011). In this case, there is evidence that a sexual fantasy was planned, but not necessarily Kimberly Moore's death. The slipknot must have been thought out prior, as well as the kind of victim to attack. However, the victim's death may have been unintended, as there is an absence of violent injury to the neck. This appears to have been a slow strangulation process and not one that involved broken bones, contusions, fighting, or other injury associated with victim resistance to forced strangulation. Unintended death resulting from forced sexual assault involving neck ligatures is a possibility.

S. Opportunistic elements

Opportunistic elements refer to any unplanned elements that the offender seized on for inclusion in an offense (Turvey, 2011). It is the opinion of the examiner that the following opportunistic elements are evident:

1. Use of victim's underwear as neck ligature.
2. Use of telephone cord from room as wrist ligature.

T. Precautionary acts

Precautionary acts refer to behaviors that an offender commits before, during, or after an offense that are consciously intended to confuse, hamper, or defeat investigative or forensic efforts for the purpose of concealing the offender's identity, connection to the crime, or the crime itself (Turvey, 2011). It is the opinion of the examiner that the following precautionary acts are evident:

1. Victim selection.
2. Use of available materials

Evidence destruction is also mentioned in the police reports, but it unclear what is meant by this.

U. Posing

The body of Kimberly Moore does not appear intentionally posed at the crime scene.

V. Motivation

Motive is comprised of the emotional, psychological, and material needs that impel and are satisfied by behavior (Turvey, 2011). The motive in this case is most consistent with *sexual gratification from victim dominance and possible suffering (i.e., assertive and possibly sadistic motive).* The offender's basic fantasy involved overpowering a victim and engaging a slipknot from the victim's underwear to control her airway, maintain dominance, and achieve compliance. This fantasy may have involved non-lethal cutting of the victim for sexual gratification, but this cannot be confirmed. This fantasy may have also involved vaginal or anal sexual penetration, but this cannot be confirmed.

3.4) Distinguishing Behavioral Factors

Distinguishing behavioral factors are elements of a crime that may be useful to determine whether a behavioral linkage is present across multiple cases, including offender modus operandi, motive, signature and relevant victimology. They are comprised of M.O. and signature behaviors that reduce the suspect pool.

Modus operandi is a term that refers to the offender's method of operating. M.O. behaviors are those that are intended to assist the criminal in the completion of the crime and are functional in nature (Turvey, 2011).

A *signature behavior* is an act committed by an offender that is not necessary to commit the crime but suggests the psychological or emotional needs of that offender (Turvey, 2011). The known signature behaviors in this case include:

1. Use of the victim's black underwear as a slipknot around her neck to control her airway.

2. The ligature was left in place around the victim's neck.
3. Exposure of, and apparent sexual activity involving, the victim's breasts.
4. Covering the victim's body with the blanket before leaving.

This signature behavior is not distinctive. However, use of a victim's black underwear as a slipknot around her neck to control her airway is uncommon and possibly even rare. In any case, these signature behaviors are not present in the homicides of Maria Ramos or Tawanda Hodges.

4) Linkage Analysis

It should be noted that this report acknowledges the DNA link between these cases that has been associated with the defendant. However, the purpose of this report is to assess behavioral linkage outside the issue of DNA. This is *first* done for reasons of reliability and circumstance: the victims in this case were prostitutes working in the same areas and would likely have encountered the same potential clientele. This increased the corresponding likelihood of finding DNA from the same individual associated with sexual activity related to each of the victims. Consequently, and given the length of time that semen and sperm can survive under such circumstances (48 hours or more under the right circumstances), a direct link between the transfer of the defendant's DNA material in each homicide is needed to create a definitive causal link. Currently, the conditions of transfer and the associated time interval have not been reliably established for any of the DNA material in this case. *Secondly*, each legal jurisdiction applies its own standard when determining the admissibility of similar fact evidence. Often this sets aside the issue of DNA and other physical evidence, and deals only with issues of theme, M.O. and behavioral distinctiveness. Consequently, the DNA evidence in this case is its own separate issue, with its own legal ramifications and inherent forensic limitations.

With respect to the behavioral evidence in this case: While there may be general or thematic similarities between some cases, it is the nature of the dissimilarities that are of greater weight and importance to rendering final linkage analysis conclusions. Linkage analysis efforts that fail to account for dissimilarity, focusing on similarities, should be considered inadequate at best, if not biased.

To express linkage analysis findings in a manner that is useful to investigators and the court but does not mislead with respect to certainty, carefully defined confidence statements must be employed. The results of case linkage efforts, or linkage analysis, may be expressed with the following language:

1. Behavioral dissimilarity
2. Investigative linkage
3. Behavioral commonality
4. Probative link

Behavioral dissimilarity means just that: behavioral factors have been compared and they are dissimilar. For example, two homicide cases are presented. One involves use of a handgun with a single high caliber shot to the victim's head. The other involves manual strangulation and asphyxiation. Even if all other behavioral factors in the two cases were the same, this would be evidence of a behavioral dissimilarity with respect to the type of weapon used and the method of killing. It would also mean that they could not be linked together in their commission using behavior. This does not mean the same offender couldn't be responsible. It simply means that they cannot be linked via behavioral factors.

An *investigative link* is a general class connection of *common behavioral factors* between one or more cases that serves to inform the allocation of investigative resources (i.e., in terms of behavior, general or opportunistic circumstances of the offense; general similarities in *modus operandi*; same general motive; and similar signature aspects evidenced by signature behaviors that are perhaps dissimilar). Such a link, as the name suggests, requires further investigation. It is not conclusive. An example of an investigative link would be finding two women murdered in their homes, in generally the same fashion, in the same community, over the course of a year. The general description is of interest and resources should be applied to investigate further possible connections such as may be found in victimology, MO, signature behavior, and the physical evidence. During any one of these examinations, a more certain linkage may be established or refuted. If more information is not available, it must be remembered that an investigative linkage is not sufficient to suggest a *behavioral commonality* let alone a *probative link*.

A *behavioral commonality* is present when behavioral factors have been compared and they are similar, perhaps with similar contexts and origins, but not necessarily unique. For example, two convenience robberies occur in broad daylight. Both involve a .357-magnum handgun. Both involve an offender wearing a mask. This would evidence a behavioral commonality with respect to time of day, precautionary acts, location type, use of weapon, and even motive. However, this particular fact pattern is not uncommon, rare, or unique, especially in large urban areas.

A *probative link* is evidenced by either a unique behavioral factor, or cluster of uncommon and/or rare behavioral factors, that is shared across two or more cases, with limited behavioral dissimilarity. It is a connection that is sufficiently unique to support the inference that the same person is likely responsible. Physical evidence, such as DNA or fingerprints, may also provide a probative link – and must therefore not be ignored unless intentionally set aside for court purposes.

Conclusion: While there is an investigative behavioral link between these cases, there is also significant behavioral dissimilarity. Consequently, these crimes do not share a common scheme, or pattern, of behavioral factors distinctive enough to suggest that a single offender must be responsible. Separately, with respect to the DNA evidence in these cases, this behavioral finding gives further weight to the notion that this may be an adventitious match rather than a causal one. This should have resulted in further investigation and attempts at reconstruction.

4.1. Similarities

All three victims share general traits and circumstances that, investigatively, should cause law enforcement to at least consider whether the crimes might be related. These include primarily the following:

1. The victims in the case are very similar, in that all three share common traits such as working as age group (26-30), being prostitutes, being drug addicts, and being of the same exposure (extreme lifestyle; high incident). However these similarities actually broaden the suspect pool rather than narrowing it, as such victims are frequently chosen by a variety of stranger and non-stranger offenders for retaliation, violence and sexual violence.

2. The victims were all last seen engaged in prostitution related activities. Either headed that direction (Hodges), or with a "john" (Ramos and Moore).

3. All three victims were found in some state of undress.

4. All three victims suffered from neck compression of some kind.

5. All three victims were found bound with their hands behind their back.

6. The victims were all found dead in Yonkers.

However, the investigative link between these cases is superficial only, which is revealed after a careful examination of both M.O. and Signature behaviors.

4.2. Dissimilarities

There are significant behavioral dissimilarities across these cases. These include primarily the following:

1. There are a number of unknown behavioral factors across these cases that prevent the level of comparison required for a probative link. However, the existing behavioral factors are sufficient to establish significant behavioral dissimilarities.

2. None of these cases share any of the signature behaviors identified.

3. The motives in each case are very different:
   a. Ramos: sexually oriented anger with a desire to humiliate
   b. Hodges: anger, with either a profit component or desire to take trophies
   c. Moore: sexual gratification from victim dominance and possible suffering (i.e., assertive and possibly sadistic motive)

4. One of the victims (Hodges) was beaten about the face with brutal, bone crushing force; the other two (Ramos and Moore) were not. (Note: Hodges may have been struck in the face with a single blow, however her injuries are unclear given the inconsistencies between the autopsy report, the death investigation report, and the photographs).

5. One of the victims was stabbed multiple times in the chest (Ramos); the others (Hodges and Moore) were not.

6. One of the victims was sexually assaulted in some fashion prior to death (Moore); although the others (Ramos and Hodges) show evidence of sexual activity, there is no direct physical evidence of sexual assault. See prior discussion re: *cum hoc ergo propter hoc* reasoning in Section 1.3 P of this report.

7. Each of the victims was bound quite differently, upon close examination. This involved different material on different locations with different meaning:

   a. Ramos: Bound, hands behind her back, with her own pantyhose (intimate item).

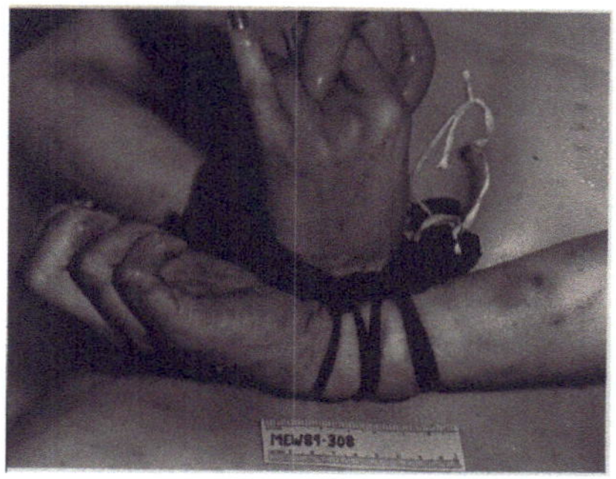

b. Hodges: Bound, hands behind her back, using her own bra and underwear interlaced (complex knot; intimate item; granny style knot).

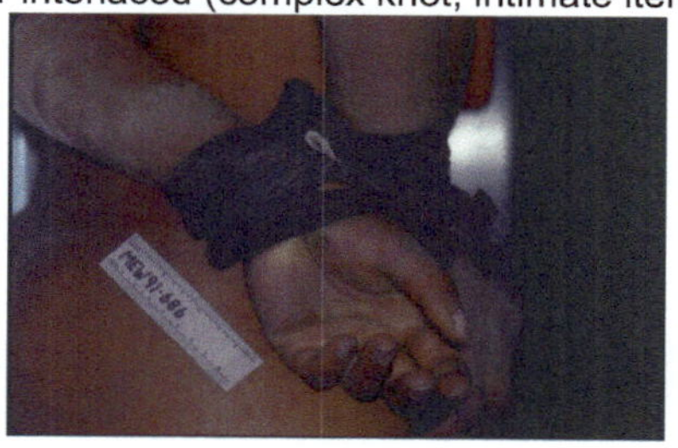

c. Moore: Bound, hands behind her back, with telephone cord (avalaible material; multiple wraps over wristwatch).

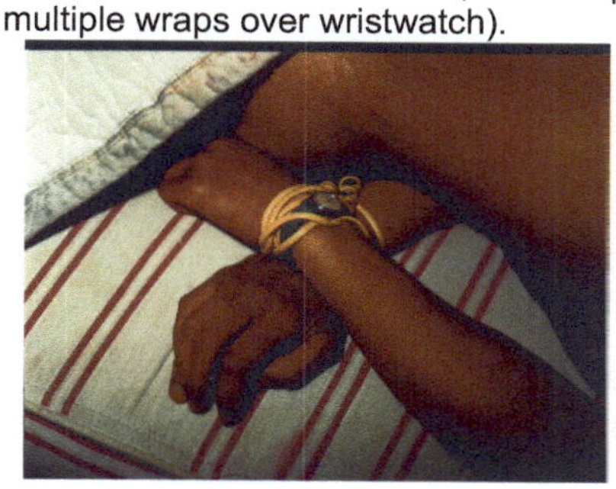

8. One of the victims was found with an intimate ligature left in place around her neck (Moore); the other two were found with nothing around their necks (Ramos and Hodges).

9. One of the victims was killed using a slipknot made from her underwear (Moore; picture below). There is no evidence that a slipknot was used in any of the other crimes.

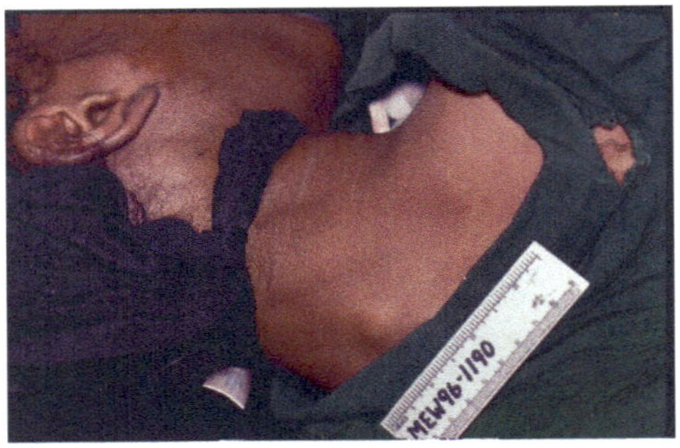

10. One of the victims was killed by a sharp force stab wound to the chest (Ramos); the others (Hodges and Moore) dies from asphyxiation.

11. One of the victims was found without her jewelry (Hodges); the other two were found wearing jewelry (Ramos and Moore).

12. Two of the victims were disposed of outside (Ramos and Hodges); one was disposed of indoors (Moore). Pictured below: L-R, Ramos, Hodges, and then Moore.

13. One of the victims was posed after death in a manner and location so as to be found (Ramos); two were not posed, and were left in such a manner as to hide them from sight and delay discovery (Hodges and Moore).

14. One of the victims was covered after death by the offender (Moore); two were left open to the elements (Ramos and Hodges).

Please do not hesitate to contact me with any questions

Brent E. Turvey, MS

REFERENCES

Atchereley, L. (1913) *Modus Operandi: Criminal Investigation and Detection.* Leeds: Chorley & Pickersgill, Ltd.

Black, H. C. (Ed.). (1990) ***Black's Law Dictionary***, St. Paul, MN: West Publishing.

Burgess, A. N., Burgess, A. W., Douglas, J., & Ressler, R. (Eds.). (1992) *Crime Classification Manual,* New York: Lexington Books.

Chisum, J. & Turvey, B. (2011) *Crime Reconstruction*, 2nd Ed., San Diego: Elsevier Science.

Depue, R., Douglas, J., Hazelwood, R., & Ressler, R. (1995) "Criminal Investigative Analysis: An Overview," in Burgess, A., Hazelwood, R. (Eds.) *Practical Aspects of Rape Investigation, 2nd Ed.*, Boca Raton: CRC Press.

Groth, A.N. (1979) *Men Who Rape*, New York: Plenum Press.

Gross, H. (1924) *Criminal Investigation*, London: Sweet & Maxwell.

Hazelwood, R. "Analyzing the Rape and Profiling the Offender," (1995) Burgess, A., Hazelwood, R. (Eds.) *Practical Aspects of Rape Investigation, 2nd Ed.*, Boca Raton: CRC Press.

Hazelwood, R., and Warren, J. (2003) "Linkage Analysis: Modus Operandi, Ritual, and Signature in Serial Sexual Crime," *Aggression and Violent Behavior*, 8, pp. 587–598.

Kirk, P. (1953) *Crime Investigation*, New York: Interscience.

Money, J. (1988) *Lovemaps: Clinical Concepts of Sexual/Erotic Health and Pathology, Paraphilia, and Gender Transposition in Childhood, Adolescence, and Maturity*, New York: Prometheus Books.

Petherick, W. & Turvey, B. (2010) "Forensic Criminological Assessments" in Ferguson, C., Petherick, W. & Turvey, B. (Eds) *Forensic Criminology.* San Diego: Elsevier Science.

Petherick, W. & Turvey, B. (2009) *Forensic Victimology.* San Diego: Elsevier Science.

People of the Philippines v. Rodrigo Loteyro Aguinaldo, GR No. 130784, Oct. 13, 1999.

Saferstein, R. (1998) *Criminalistics: An Introduction to Forensic Science,* 6th Ed., New York: Prentice Hall.

Salfati, C.G. and Taylor, P. (2006) "Differentiating sexual violence: A comparison of sexual homicide and rape," *Psychology, Crime and Law*, Vol. 12(2): pp. 107-125.

Thornton, J. I. (1997) "The General Assumptions and Rationale of Forensic Identification," in D.L. Faigman, D. H. Kaye, M. J. Saks, & J. Sanders (Eds.) *Modern Scientific Evidence: The Law and Science of Expert Testimony,* vol. 2, West Publishing.

Savino, J. & Turvey, B. (2011) *Rape Investigation Handbook*, 2nd Ed. San Diego: Elsevier Science.

Turvey, B. (2001) "Sexual Homicide: Research Review and Findings, Part 1," *Journal of Behavioral Profiling*, December, Vol. 2, No. 2.

Turvey B. (2011) *Criminal Profiling: An Introduction to Behavioral Evidence Analysis, 4rd Ed.,* London: Elsevier Science.

Weston, P., and Wells, K. (1974) *Criminal Investigation: Basic Perspectives*, 2nd ed., Englewood Cliffs, NJ: Prentice-Hall.

REFERENCES

DeForest, P., 2005. Crime scene investigation. In: Rosen, M., Sullivan, L. (Eds.), Encyclopedia of Law Enforcement. State and Local, vol. 1. Sage Publications, Thousand Oaks, CA, pp. 112–116.

Turvey, B., 2011. Criminal Profiling: An Introduction to Behavioral Evidence Analysis, fourth ed. Elsevier Science, London.

CHAPTER

Examining Allegations of Sexual Assault

14

B.E. Turvey

Forensic Solutions LLC, Sitka, Alaska, United States; Institute of Forensic Investigation and Criminal Profiling, Juarez, Mexico

M. McGrath

Unity Healthy Systems, Rochester, NY, United States

J. Freeman

Forensic Solutions LLC, Sitka, Alaska, United States; University of Western Ontario, London, ON, Canada

CHAPTER OUTLINE

Allegations of sexual assault are just that. Consequently, until there has been an investigation and a criminal conviction, the person making the allegation may only be referred to as a complainant. Referring to them as a "victim" prior to this is biased, from a forensic perspective and violates the function of a criminal trial. This is because using the term victim assumes that a crime has happened and that the allegation is true. Otherwise why have a trial at all.

Victim's advocates will balk at this notion, and they should. But they should also understand that the forensic examiner has a very specific role in court proceedings. In these proceedings, it is not scientifically acceptable to presume the very thing meant to be demonstrated. That is called circular reasoning, and it prevents unbiased inquiry. So while they balk and keep everyone honest, they must not be allowed to diminish the only value of the forensic examiner to court proceedings and that is the forensic examiner's objectivity.

The purpose of this chapter is to demonstrate the value of objective forensic examinations in cases of alleged sexual assault and to reveal the importance of maintaining

Behavioral Evidence Analysis. http://dx.doi.org/10.1016/B978-0-12-800607-8.00014-8

professional objectivity in the face of those who seek politically preferred outcomes as opposed to those based in reliable scientific evidence.

THE PILLARS

As discussed in Freeman et al. (2012), there are five pillars supporting a solid sex crimes investigation: the victim's statement, the victim's sexual assault exam, the crime scene evidence, the suspect's statement, and the suspect's sexual assault examination. If any of these pillars is weak or absent, then the certainty regarding the events that took place is reduced.

Pillar weakness manifests itself in a variety of forms. In some cases, the complainant's statement has been accepted uncritically, with little investigation of suspect evidence or the crime scene. In other cases, the complainant has been entirely ignored out of apathy and laziness.

Very often when this author is called upon to examine a complaint of sexual assault, or a series of related complaints, the breakdowns are obvious and consistent. Evidence, such as the rape kit, will be untested or even uncollected; those charged with the examination of evidence are untrained, negligent, or heavily biased; and politics will have given way to reason. In other words, nobody is sure what has actually happened because too many people have interfered or will not have done their job correctly.

LOCATING CRIME SCENES

Key to the search and examination of any crime scene and related evidence is first locating it and all of its satellites. The crime scene may not be completely evident. The investigator may have to look for it. This is in fact one of the most common problems in cases of sexual assault—the inability of complainants to properly identify the crime scenes associated with their alleged attack and the failure of investigators to seek them out.

To that end, in the case of a rape or sexual assault, understand that the following interactions must or may occur, and not necessarily in the same location.

1. The offender will have approached the victim.
2. The offender will have attacked the victim.
3. The offender may have moved the victim to a secluded location for privacy during the attack.
4. The offender may have moved the victim to a secluded location for storage before or after the attack.
5. The offender may have moved the victim to a secluded or public location for disposal.
6. The offender may have transported the victim in a vehicle.
7. The offender will have departed from the scene.
8. The victim may have fled to a safe/neutral location.
9. The victim may have left clothing or other items at the safe/neutral location.
10. The offender may have preselected/targeted and conducted surveillance of the victim prior to the sexual assault.

Each of these events may represent a different crime scene that the offender and victim must enter and exit. In locating all points of entry, all the points of exit, and the routes between each, the investigator may find evidence of the victim's or offender's passing. This may come in the form of patterns or traces left behind as either one came into contact with objects in each scene or it may come in the form of items that either one discarded or dropped incidentally along the way.

FALSE REPORTS

Almost without exception, it is a crime to lie to a police officer or any other mandated reporter, with respect to involvement in, or the occurrence of, criminal activity. Many criminal statutes address these kinds of lies. Depending on the circumstances, false reports may be charged as misdemeanor or felony violations. Examples of criminal statutes that may apply include

- Obstruction of justice: Obstructing, delaying, or preventing the communication of information relating to a violation of any criminal statute by any person to a criminal investigator by any means (eg, bribery, intimidation, and false statements).
- False swearing: A false statement, oral or written, made under oath or penalty of perjury.
- Perjury: A lie communicated under oath or penalty of perjury about a material fact in a criminal matter. This is a particular kind of false swearing.
- False reporting: The false report, conveyance, or circulation of an alleged or impending criminal offense.

For purposes of this work, a false report (or false allegation) refers to any untruthful statement, accusation, or complaint to authorities asserting that a crime did or will occur. A false reporter is one who makes false allegations or reports. False reporting is generally a crime, even when reports are made indirectly to authorities by a third party, such as a friend, intimate partner, spouse, employer, counselor, or medical professional.

The reality is that such false reports occur with enough frequency that investigative failure to consider the possibility is actually a due process violation (McGrath and Turvey, 2012[a]). This responsibility falls, at least initially, on law enforcement investigators. As explained in Sexual Assault Task Force (2009):

> *Law enforcement is responsible for determining whether reports of sexual assault meet the criteria of a criminal offense as determined by the state criminal code. This responsibility includes determining the credibility and, ultimately, the investigative outcome of sexual assault reports….*
>
> *Identifying a false report of sexual assault requires a thorough investigation that factually proves that a criminal sexual offense neither occurred nor was attempted.*

In order to determine the credibility of a complaint, both the complainant and the victim must have the right to be heard, and to be believed, until contradicted by the results of an impartial investigation of the evidence.

[a] This section has been adapted from McGrath and Turvey (2012).

Motives for false reporting include anger/revenge; profit; crime concealment; concealment of illicit activities; mitigation of responsibility; and mental defect (such as drug use, intoxication, or mental illness—as a contributing factor).

RED FLAGS

The following is a list of investigative red flags that have been helpful to the authors in identifying potential false reports of sexual assault.

1. Initiation of the report, or pressure to report, by someone other than the complainant herself (eg, spouse, parents, intimate partner, friend, coworker, supervisor, hospital staff) unless the victim is unable to report or is too young to represent himself/herself.
2. The complainant is unable to say where the sexual assault occurred, or locate it when pressed, when nothing would appear to prevent her from being able to do so (eg, no blindfold, no drugs or alcohol to impair memory).
3. A vague description of the attacker is provided, when descriptions of other parts of the crime are more detailed.
4. While able to discuss details before and after the alleged sexual assault, the complainant avoids answering specific questions about the attack by crying hysterically, becoming angry without provocation, or engaging in other deflective behavior.
5. The complainant appears to be interested in something other than reporting the sexual assault (eg, change in housing, disability payments, attention, lawsuit).
6. The report of a sexual assault serves to provide an alibi of some kind.
7. Reconstruction of the physical evidence is at odds with the story of the victim (eg, a lack of defensive injury when a significant struggle is reported; the attacker is reported to have broken in through windows that are screwed or painted shut; damage or evidence transfer to complainant clothing is not consistent with the reports of pulling, dragging, or tearing).
8. Injuries sustained by the complainant are consistent with known patterns of self-inflicted injuries.
9. The complainant's details are similar to information seen commonly in movies and on television (eg, abduction on a busy street by masked suspects in a van).

It is important to remember that these red flags are not conclusive evidence that a false report of sexual assault has been made. They should be used as a guide. Their existence suggests that further investigation is needed. Until any red flags have been explained, no conclusion about the merits of the complaint may be formed either way.

GEORGIA v. JESSIE L. ARNOLD

Consider the case of *Georgia v. Jessie L. Arnold*, from the author's files. In late 1999, Mr. Arnold was tried and convicted for an alleged sexual attack in January of that same year. He was found guilty of aggravated sexual assault and other related offenses. This occurred despite overwhelming evidence of his innocence, and despite the recantation of the complainant.

In this case, the expert used by the state was a fraud, the evidence in its custody was lost, the investigation by the police was negligent, and the complainant recanted her allegations multiple times, to police, admitting that she lied about being raped in order to punish Mr. Arnold for infidelity.

In 2014, author Turvey was retained by Attorney Joseph King of Atlanta to examine the evidence and material related to the conviction of Mr. Arnold. Significant findings related to the issues already mentioned are detailed in the following affidavit, which was submitted to the court in 2014:

AFFIDAVIT OF BRENT E. TURVEY, PHD

STATE OF ALASKA)
)
CITY & BOROUGH OF SITKA)

Before me, the undersigned authority, personally appeared Brent E. Turvey, who after being duly cautioned and sworn states under oath as follows:

1. My name is Brent E. Turvey. I am over the age of eighteen; of sound mind; capable of making this affidavit; and personally acquainted with all of the facts stated herein.

2. I am a Forensic Scientist and Crime Reconstructionist, practicing since 1996.

3. I hold a PhD in Criminology and a Master of Science in Forensic Science.

4. I have written extensively on the issue of sex crimes investigation in peer reviewed publications.

5. I have extensive experience conducting investigative and forensic work in criminal cases for both law enforcement agencies and attorneys worldwide related to sex crimes.

6. I have provided expert analysis and testimony in numerous cases of reported sexual assault, in both State and Federal Court.

7. I have been qualified in State and Federal Court as an expert in the areas of Forensic Science, Crime Reconstruction, Crime Scene Analysis, Crime Scene Investigation, Sex Crimes Investigation, and False Allegations of Sexual Assault.

8. I have previously qualified as an expert and given expert testimony in crime reconstruction and crime scene investigation in the state of Georgia.

9. I have authored and co-authored numerous textbooks on these and related subjects, including the *Rape Investigation Handbook, 2nd Edition (2012)*, with Detective John O. Savino of the New York City Police Department's Manhattan Special Victim Squad (ret.); and *Forensic Fraud (2013)*, an empirical study of fraudulent forensic examiners and their testimony over a ten year period (2000-2010).

10. I have been contacted by Attorney Joseph King to examine the evidence and material related to *Georgia v. Jessie L. Arnold.*

11. I was provided with case material, post-conviction, that included a police investigative report from Det. Moore; trial transcripts; the affidavit of Richard Sullivan, MD; Houston Medical Center records relating to the reported sexual assault of Janice Moore; Texas State Board of Medical Examiners Temporary Suspension Order for Theodore Bowles JR., D.O.; Final order on Dr. Bowles from the State of Maryland; Georgia State Board of Medical Examiners Initial Decision and Order of Summary Suspension of Dr. Bowles; Expert letter and affidavit from Edward Friedlander, MD; the affidavit from Peter Boyd, MD; Expert Affidavit of Adel Shaker, MD; the affidavit of Todd Antin, MD; Letters and sworn statements of Janice Moore; the affidavit of Theodore A. Bowles, D.O.; and CHAPTER 24, SEXUAL ASSAULT PROTOCOL, Sec. 15-24-1 & 15-24-2 of the Georgia Code;

12. As part of my efforts, I also referenced National Institute of Justice (2004) *A National Protocol for Sexual Assault Medical Forensic Examinations*, Washington, DC: U.S. Department of Justice, Office on Violence Against Women, NCJ 206554, September. These are the national standards and protocols for sexual assault investigation.

13. After a careful examination of the facts, information, and evidence provided to my office, it is my expert opinion that the evidence is sufficiently reliable to support Conclusions 1-4 outlined in this affidavit.

14. **Conclusion #1:** Theodore A. Bowles, D.O., an expert witness for the prosecution in the area of sexual assault examinations, gave false and misleading testimony during the trial of of Jessie Arnold. In this examiner's opinion, the false and misleading testimony with respect to Dr. Bowles' findings and expertise amounts to forensic fraud. This is based on the fallowing facts and information:

15. Dr. Bowles had a history of drug addiction and abuse which he failed to disclose before or during the trial of Mr. Arnold, misleading the court and the trier of fact as to his reliability, perception and cognitive faculties. The prosecution also failed in it's duty to discover and disclose this impeachment (aka *Brady*) material to the defense;

16. Dr. Bowles had a history of getting his license to practice medicine suspended in multiple states which he failed to disclose before or during the trial of Mr. Arnold, misleading the court and the trier of fact as to his reliability and fitness

to practice medicine. The prosecution also failed in it's duty to discover and disclose this impeachment material to the defense;

17. Dr. Bowles was practicing medicine without a valid license at the time of his involvement in the examination of the complainant in this case, and during his expert testimony. He failed to disclose this to both his employer and to the court before or during the trial of Mr. Arnold, misleading the court and the trier of fact as to his reliability and fitness to practice medicine. The prosecution also failed in it's duty to discover and disclose this impeachment material to the defense;

18. On p. 343 of his sworn testimony, Dr. Bowles states "I see about six to 7,000 patients a year in the emergency room". This number is not supportable. With 365 days in a year, Dr. Bowles would need to see 20 patients a day. Excluding weekends, he would need to see approximately 24 per day. However, according to the Affidavit of Dr. Sullivan, Dr. Bowles worked only 624 hours at the Houston Medical Center during the year in question. This would be less than 16 full time weeks (at 40 hour per week). Given that Dr. Bowles testified that he needs about 30 minutes per victim to perform an examination (which sounds quite hurried to this examiner), at most he could have seen 1,248 patients in that year. And then only if he did not spend any time doing paperwork, which would be malpractice. In short, Dr. Bowles' testimony that he sees 6,000 or 7,000 patients a year was a false statement intended to improperly bolster his experience and subsequent credibility;

19. On p.341-342 of his sworn testimony, Dr. Bowles states the following: "I would say maybe 30 to 40 percent at the time, you can be --- you can be reasonably

sure that the patient --- you can be reasonably sure of whether the patient has or has not been raped, and I would say probably 30 percent of the time." He claims this ability is based on his ability to assess complainant demeanor, physical marks, the presence of semen, and injury to sexual organs like the vagina. There is no scientific or empirical basis for this specific statistic. This false testimony is a statistical fabrication with no support in the known scientific literature;

20. All scientists must adhere to ethical guidelines and practice standards intended to fulfill and maintain what is referred to as "scientific integrity"; and they must also avoid intentional violations of that integrity. Scientific integrity must be earned at all junctures and not presumed. When weaknesses exist, they must be acknowledged, considered, and then reported as a function of limits set against any reliable interpretation.

21. *Cherry-Picking* results, which is a violation of scientific integrity, refers to selectively reporting (and thereby emphasizing) only desired results or information rather than the entirety of examinations performed and results achieved. It is a form of scientific misconduct that can generally only be identified during the objective peer review process. This has been considered a form of scientific misconduct since at least the 1830s.

22. The literature is clear that there is no such thing as a typical or expected reaction for a victim of a violent crime, including rape. Therefore any complainant demeanor is consistent with sexual assault. Failing to be clear about this during

sworn testimony is highly misleading, bordering on false testimony. It may also be described as a form of scientific misconduct that is referred to as *Cherry-Picking*;

23. On pp.365-366 of his sworn testimony, Dr. Bowles states that the absence of complainant genital injury is consistent with rape. However, he fails to make it clear that the absence of genital injury is also consistent with consensual sexual penetration. Failing to be clear about this during sworn testimony in sexual assault trial is highly misleading, bordering on false testimony. It may also be described as a form of scientific misconduct that is referred to as *Cherry-Picking*;

24. In his 2014 affidavit, Dr. Bowles states of his sworn testimony at trial: "I told the District Attorney that I could not say Ms. Moore was raped. And I did not say Ms. Moore was raped during my testimony." This assertion is false. Any reasonable read of the trial transcript makes it clear Dr. Bowles testified that not only does he have a special ability to detect sexual assault victims based on how they act; but that the complainant's presentation to him was consistent with having been sexually assaulted. He clarifies this multiple times during his trial testimony, leaving no doubt as to his meaning. The statements in this 2014 affidavit are therefore false;

25. **Conclusion #2:** There were numerous red flags for false reporting in this case which should have resulted in further investigation by law enforcement and not the arrest of the defendant. This is based on the fallowing facts and information (consistent with red flags discussed in the *Rape Investigation Handbook, 2nd Ed.*):

26. The complainant made her report to another party first (her mother), and not to law enforcement;

27. The complainant appeared to be compelled to report to law enforcement by a third party (her mother), and not necessarily of her own independent volition;

28. The complainant had a clear revenge motivation for false reporting (suspicion of infidelity), which she admitted to police investigators;

29. The complainant recanted her allegations multiple times, to police and to the defendant; she admitted to lying to police about being raped in order to punish Mr. Arnold for infidelity;

30. The complainant admitted under oath that she tried to set up the defendant on multiple occasions;

31. The complainant signed notarized documents recanting her allegations and asserting her desire not to have Mr. Arnold prosecuted;

32. There is apparently no direct physical evidence in this case of sexual assault (e.g., genital injury or damaged victim clothing).

33. **Conclusion #3:** There were multiple investigative failures in this case, resulting in an incomplete and inadequate record of the physical evidence. In turn this precluded an adequate understanding of the facts of the case and prevented an adequate defense. This is based on the fallowing facts and information:

34. Sec. 15-24-1 & 15-24-2 of the Georgia Code requires that a written sexual assault protocol be developed by a committee and adhered to, in order to facilitate interagency coordination and cooperation (and presumably due process);

35. According to the District Attorney's Office, there is no sexual assault protocol committee, in violation of this code. This is evidence of bad faith;

36. According to the District Attorney's Office, no written sexual assault protocol appears to exist, and therefore it could not have been followed, in violation of this code. This is evidence of bad faith;

37. The bloody tampons in the trash mentioned by the complainant were not collected, nor is there any evidence that they actually existed. These should have been collected and tested to verify or refute the complainant's initial accusations of sexual assault as part of the police investigation;

38. The knife alleged to have been used by the defendant in this case was collected, but there is no physical evidence that is was used by the defendant in relation to any criminal activity. Subsequently, this item of evidence has apparently been lost by authorities, precluding post conviction examination and testing efforts;

39. The bedsheets alleged to have been associated with a sexual assault in this case were collected but apparently not examined or tested. Consequently, there is no related physical evidence to support or refute the complainant's claims. Subsequently, this item of evidence has apparently been lost by authorities, precluding post conviction examination and testing efforts;

40. The complainant's clothes were apparently not collected as evidence, in violation of national practice standards (NIJ, 2004);

41. No photographs were apparently taken of the complainant's genital injuries, or lack thereof, in violation of national practice standards (NIJ, 2004);

42. No photographs were apparently taken of damage or evidence transfer to the complainant's clothing, or lack thereof, in violation of national practice standards (NIJ, 2004);

43. The apparent semen that was collected from the victim was not submitted for DNA testing, which is paradoxical to the notion of semen evidence collection. In other words, this sample is from an unknown donor and has not been linked to the defendant. Failure to do so represents an investigative failure to seek out, identify and/or exclude suspects in this case. Subsequently, this sample has apparently been lost by the authorities.

44. **Conclusion #4:** There are multiple IAC issues in this case, resulting from incompetent and inadequate forensic efforts by defense counsel. This is based on the fallowing facts and information:

45. The defense failed in its due diligence to investigate Dr. Bowles' credentials for the impeachment material described in Conclusion #1;

46. The defense failed to cross-examine Dr. Bowles about his background and expertise for the impeachment information material described in Conclusion #1;

47. The defense failed to call an expert to evaluate Dr. Bowles' unsupported findings and implausible experience, described in Conclusion #1;

48. The defense failed to call an expert to rebut Dr. Bowles' clearly false testimony, described in Conclusion #1;

49. The defense failed to request the apparent semen collected in the rape kit be tested for DNA an compared to Mr. Arnold for exclusionary purposes.

50. I am available and willing to testify under oath to any of the facts and opinions provided in the Forensic Examination Report.

I declare under penalty of perjury that the foregoing is true and correct.

Brent E. Turvey, PhD

STATE OF Alaska)
)
CITY & BOROUGH OF Sitka)

Brent E. Turvey, after first being duly sworn according to law, makes oath that he has read the foregoing Affidavit, and that the facts set forth therein are true to the best of his knowledge, information and belief.

Sworn and subscribed before me this 9th day of May, 2014.

JULI AUDETTE NOTARY PUBLIC STATE OF ALASKA

Notary Public

My commission expires: 03·29·2016

At this writing (October of 2015), Mr. Arnold's appeal awaits a hearing which is to be scheduled sometime in December of 2015.

COLORADO v. MARIO RAXON

Consider also the report prepared in case of *Colorado v. Mario Raxon*. It involves a complaint of sexual assault against Mario Raxon (Male, 23) and his codefendant, Keenan Miller (Male, 23). The complainant was their mutual friend, a 15-year-old girl named Savannah, who often spent time at their apartment. They had all known each other for about a year. This complaint rises from events that are alleged to have taken place in Colorado Springs on the evening of February 6, 2012.

Significant investigative, forensic, and victimological findings were discovered in this case and detailed in the following report:

Forensic Examination Report

Forensic Examiner
Brent E. Turvey, PhD
Forensic Solutions, LLC
Sitka, Alaska
www.forensic-science.com
bturvey@forensic-science.com

Date of Report
September 25, 2013

Report for
Jeff Barker & Josh Tolini, Barker & Tolini, P.C.
720 S. Tejon Street
Colorado Springs, CO 80903
(719) 227-0230

In Re
Colorado v. Mario D. Raxon, Case #D0212012CR000521

Purpose

Colorado v. Mario Raxon involves a complaint of sexual assault against Mario Raxon (Male, 23) and his co-defendant, Keenan Miller (Male, 23), by their mutual friend Savannah Pasierb (Female, 15). They had known each other for about a year. This complaint arises from events that are alleged to have taken place at 265 Rim View Drive, Apt. F, in Colorado Springs; in the defendant's vehicle (a silver Ford Taurus); and at an unknown location on Rampart Range Road. These events are alleged to have occurred on the evening of February 6, 2012.

The purpose of this report is to present this examiner's reconstruction-oriented findings regarding the forensic investigation, physical evidence, wound patterns and behavioral evidence relevant to the complaint.

Crime Reconstruction

Crime reconstruction is the determination of the actions and events surrounding the commission of a crime. Reconstructions must be based on reliably established facts and evidence (Chisum and Turvey, 2011).

The uncritical acceptance of any witness or suspect statement as fact is not permissible scientific practice. This is the case for at least two reasons. First, forensic examiners are required to use the scientific method when performing their analyses. This means the development, investigation, and consideration of alternate hypothesis for any observations and events. As explained in Chisum and Turvey (2011; p.95-96)[1]:

> A reconstruction of events is not as simple as observation and conclusion based on experience. There are steps in between that must be followed to ensure a measure of reliability and accuracy. A reconstruction must be a conclusion regarding what has occurred, or not, based on a consideration of the forensic sciences, the scientific method, and analytical logic. Anything offered without this foundation is a guess, no matter how many years of experience one stacks beneath it for support.

For example, when presented with a witness statement, objective science requires equal consideration of truthfulness and falsity on the part of the witness. Both possibilities must be considered without prejudice. This is especially true in a forensic context when there is an accusation of rape. As explained in Gross (2009) "failing to consider the accuser may be intentionally lying effectively eradicates the presumption of innocence."

Second, forensic examiners are not allowed to assume facts for the purposes of analysis: facts must be established.[2] This may seem redundant, as *facts* are

---

[1] See Chisum & Turvey (2011; p.108): "Reconstructionists must demonstrate an understanding of science, forensic science, and the scientific method… It has been said, and it is true, that "if there is no science, there can be no forensic science" (Thornton, 1997; p. 17).

[2] See Chisum & Turvey (2011; p.109): "7. Reconstruction conclusions must be based on established facts. Facts may not be assumed for the purpose of analysis."

generally defined as verifiable and indisputable circumstances or information. However, it is not uncommon for investigative assumptions or theories to be treated as facts and remain unexamined. The uncritical acceptance of any statement or theory, without an assessment of its internal integrity or evidentiary corroboration, provides an insufficient basis for the reliable scientific reconstruction of events.

Materials Examined

This examiner arrived the conclusions in this report based on a careful examination of case material requested from and provided by attorneys Jeff Barker & Josh Tolini in August and September of 2013. That material included, but was not limited to, the following:

1. Police investigative reports, interviews and affidavits;
2. SANE reports and notes;
3. Forensic reports (e.g., crime lab);
4. Crime scene photos;
5. Complainant injury photos;
6. Suspect injury photos;
7. Suspect vehicle photos;
8. Defense investigator interview with Joey Dumont.

Summary of Findings

This section provides a summary of major reconstruction findings in this report. Supporting evidence is provided in the *Discussion of Findings* section.

1. **Law enforcement investigators and the SANE in this case had a duty of care with respect to truth-seeking in general and evidence in specific.**

2. **The investigative and forensic efforts of law enforcement with respect to the Apartment scene were inadequate. This prevented the recognition, preservation, collection, and testing specific items of evidence. This also is likely to have caused an untold volume of evidence to be missed entirely.**

3. **The investigative and forensic efforts of law enforcement with respect to the Rampart Range Road crime scene were inadequate rising to the level of *abandonment*[3]. This has prevented the recognition, preservation, collection, and testing specific items of evidence. This also is likely to have caused an untold volume of evidence to be missed entirely.**

[3] As discussed in Crowder and Turvey (2013), and Gershman (1997), professional *abandonment* refers to incompetence and negligence to the point of effective professional absence causing harm to the client. It also refers to the abandonment of one's professional duty of care.

4. **The forensic efforts related to the Sexual Assault Examination of the complainant was inadequate, violating local and national protocols. This prevented the recognition, preservation, collection, and testing specific items of evidence. This also is likely to have caused an untold volume of evidence to be missed entirely.**

5. **The physical and behavioral evidence in this case is inconsistent with multiple prosecution theories.**

6. **The physical and behavioral evidence in this case evidences multiple investigative "red flags" consistent with false allegations of sexual assault.**

Discussion of Findings

This section provides supporting evidence for the findings summarized in the previous sections.

1. **Law enforcement investigators and the SANE in this case had a duty of care with respect to truth-seeking in general and evidence in specific:**

The investigation of reported crime is the statutory and jurisdictional province of various local, state, and federal law enforcement agencies (Sullivan, 1977). The specific agencies responding to a criminal complaint, and ultimately in charge, depend on which laws have been reported to be broken and where. Whichever agency takes charge of a criminal complaint, they have the legal authority to respond to the scene, interview witnesses and suspects, collect evidence, and make arrests[4].

Any responding law enforcement agency, along with those they employ, has a corresponding professional *duty of care*. This refers to the professional and legal obligation to be competent custodians of any victims that are encountered; any criminal investigations that are initiated; any evidence that supports or refutes allegations of criminal activity against accused suspects; and any suspects that they take into custody (see Bopp and Schultz, 1972; Gross, 1924; Hansen and Culley, 1973; Kappeler, 2006; SATF, 2009; and Savino and Turvey, 2011). Very often this duty of care is a matter of explicit statute and agency policy, wherein law enforcement officers are not allowed to turn a blind eye to crime and must respond to protect life and property. It is also commonly made part of the formal oath they take when being sworn in. If an agency, or its officers and investigators, do not hold or perceive a professional duty of care to their community, then they are not fit to serve it (Gross, 1924); let alone respond to criminal complaints and assume the responsibilities associated with the collection and testing of physical evidence.

[4] The section is adapted from Crowder and Turvey (2013).

The primary responsibilities of law enforcement, when responding to a criminal complaint, include (adapted from basic criminal investigation and crime scene processing guidelines found in Gross, 1924; O'Connell and Soderman, 1936; Rau, 2000; Snyder, 1944; Wade, 1999; and Weston and Wells, 1974):

1. Protect themselves; call for back-up when needed.
2. Establish who is involved.
3. Ensure that everyone involved is safe.
4. Get medical assistance for those that need it.
5. Determine what happened.
6. Establish who made the complaint and what it is about.
7. Identify any witnesses.
8. Seek out, identify, collect, and protect any physical evidence.
9. Ensure the objective forensic examination of all relevant evidence.
10. Determine whether or not a crime has taken place.
11. Identify any legitimate criminal suspects.
12. Establish whether probable cause exists for an arrest.
13. Arrest any criminal perpetrators.

These tactical issues also reflect an ethical responsibility. Investigators may not assume what happened based on the statements of one party. They may not assume that any crime has actually occurred until the facts have been established by a thorough investigation. They must be sufficiently educated to understand what the elements of each crime are and the what probable cause is. They must also impartially place the cuffs on anyone they determine has broken the law. For example, as explained in Bryden and Lengnick (1997; pp. 1230–1231):

> As with all crimes, the police decide whether a reported rape actually occurred, and attempt to determine who committed it. If they want the case to go forward, they "found" the complaint and transmit the file to the prosecutor's office... The police must investigate, a task that cannot easily be combined with offering the emotional support that the victim needs. The detective presumably wishes to avoid an injustice to a wrongly accused individual. In addition, for reasons of professional pride, he does his best to avoid looking naive by falling for a story that turns out to be false.

Meeting these responsibilities is best accomplished with a thorough, diligent, and comprehensive investigation. By comprehensive investigation, the examiner means a detailed review of the complainant and their statements; the careful consideration of witness and suspect statements; and the diligent collection and examination of any related physical evidence to confirm or refute case theory. All of this must be attended prior to making final determinations regarding whether a crime has been committed and whether probable cause exists to arrest any suspects. See generally Bopp and Schultz (1972); Gross (1924); Kappeler (2006); Leonard (1969); O'Connell and Soderman (1936); Sullivan (1977); Savino and Turvey (2011); and Weston and Wells (1974).

2. The investigative and forensic efforts of law enforcement with respect to the Apartment scene were inadequate. This prevented the recognition, preservation, collection, and testing specific items of evidence. This also is likely to have caused an untold volume of evidence to be missed entirely.

This finding is based on at least the following facts and evidence:

A. The apartment crime scene does not appear to have been secured, to provide for scene integrity, in any reasonable or effective fashion.

B. There is no crime scene security log to indicate who entered and exited the scene, when, and their respective responsibilities.

C. The photographs of the apartment crime scene provided to this examiner are random, sometimes quite blurry, and lack sufficient context to be meaningful beyond documenting a limited inventory and general sense of the location interior. There is also no clear photo log.

D. The photographs of the apartment crime scene provided to this examiner lack evidence measurements or identification markers/indicators.

E. Using the photos provided, it is not clear where each of specific items of evidence were found in the apartment, or their relationship to other items.

F. This examiner was not provided with a basic crime scene sketch to indicate the location of all items of evidence that were discovered and collected.

G. There are reports requesting forensic examinations of specific evidence items. However, there are no clear overall photos of these items, with measurements, before, during or after forensic examination. This prevents later examination or consideration of the evidence should specific questions or theories arise. This also fails to provide for a reliable chain of custody.

These investigative and forensic failures on the part of law enforcement investigators prevent reliable confirmation of related case theory, secondary examination, and any reliable reconstruction of related events.

3. The investigative and forensic efforts of law enforcement with respect to the Rampart Range Road crime scene were inadequate rising to the level

of *abandonment*[5]. This has prevented the recognition, preservation, collection, and testing specific items of evidence. This also is likely to have caused an untold volume of evidence to be missed entirely.

This finding is based on at least the following facts and evidence:

A. It is alleged that the complainant, 15yo Savannah Pasierb, was abducted to a location somewhere on Rampart Range Road in defendant Raxon's Ford Taurus.

B. There is no evidence that the Rampart Range Road crime scene was precisely located and confirmed by law enforcement investigators.

C. There is no evidence that law enforcement investigators processed the Rampart Range Road crime scene in terms of taking photographs, even in general.

D. There is no evidence that law enforcement investigators processed the Rampart Range Road crime scene in terms of searching for and documenting expended shotgun shells, tire treads and footwear impressions (the complainant was reportedly not wearing anything from the waist down; she reportedly fled the vehicle at that location and was subsequently forced back inside the vehicle at gunpoint after the shotgun was discharged multiple times).

E. It is alleged that the complainant was ultimately dropped off at Soda Springs Park by the defendants, naked from the waist down, and that she walked from that location to a friend's house. According to Det. Huddleston's report (February 7, 2012; p.3): "The friend she had intended to see was Tyler O'Brien (all other identifying information was refused) but discovered he no longer lived at this residence. His ex-roommate, Karen (last name and other identifying information refused) still lived there and Karen was the person who answered the door. Karen allowed Savannah to call Tyler and Tyler responded to the house and picked her up."

F. There is no evidence that law enforcement investigators identified, travelled, documented and otherwise confirmed the complainant's alleged route from Soda Springs Park to her friends house. This would include a search for documentary evidence (e.g. video surveillance cameras), witnesses and lost evidence along that route (e.g., the

[5] As discussed in Crowder and Turvey (2013), and Gershman (1997), professional *abandonment* refers to incompetence and negligence to the point of effective professional absence causing harm to the client. It also refers to the abandonment of one's professional duty of care.

complainant's underwear and phone, both of which she reports missing).

These investigative and forensic failures prevent investigation and confirmation of related case theory, as well as a reliable reconstruction of related events.

4. **The forensic efforts related to the Sexual Assault Examination of the complainant was inadequate, violating local and national protocols. This prevented the recognition, preservation, collection, and testing specific items of evidence. This also is likely to have caused an untold volume of evidence to be missed entirely.**

This is based on at least the following facts and evidence:

A. The Nursing Practice Council/ Policy Committee's guidelines, provided in discovery, under the section titled "Policy" dictate: "After appropriate treatment has been rendered, the SANE will obtain a history, conduct a head to toe exam, perform a detailed genital exam, and collect forensic specimens for evidence." This comports with national standards (NIJ, 1999; NIJ, 2004).

B. There is no evidence of head to toe documentation as required by NIJ sexual assault examination guidelines. That is to say, photos provided of the complainant during the sexual assault examination are apparently focused on certain specific areas of possible related injury - many of which are poorly photographed, unclear, or in a state of healing. There are also no overall body photos, and only a few context photos for certain injuries (e.g., front and back).

C. There are no photos intended to provide negative documentation as required in forensic protocols (e.g., absence of injury). This suggests poor or limited forensic training.

D. Multiple photos taken during sexual assault examination, and then provided to this examiner, have been blacked out. These blacked out areas conceal pertinent locations on the complainant's body where evidence of injury is naturally investigated in a sexual assault. This is unacceptable in a forensic context, and prevents competent or informed forensic examination of those areas.

E. There are no photos of the complainant's genital areas (e.g., breasts, vaginal area, buttocks, or anus) or mouth. This prevents competent or informed forensic examination of those sites. This violates basic forensic protocol.

F. There are no photos of the complainant's neck despite reports of strangulation. This hampers competent or informed forensic examination and interpretation of injuries (or their absence) at this site (e.g., there should be fingermark injuries consistent with strangulation).

G. There are no photos of the complainant's feet despite reports of walking an undetermined distance, half naked and without shoes, to a private residence. This hampers competent or informed forensic examination and interpretation of injuries (or their absence) to these areas (e.g., there should be injuries or wear to the complainant's feet).

H. The Nursing Practice Council/ Policy Committee's guidelines, provided in discovery, explain that collection of victim history is crucial to treatment and forensic efforts. Specifically: "The history should be detailed enough to focus the examiner's effort on the area of injury or evidence." This comports with national standards (NIJ, 1999; NIJ, 2004).

I. As explained in Jamerson (2009; p.114): "...intake and history information is necessary to competently inform and prioritize the physical examination... Each patient is unique; any treatment and forensic efforts should be individually crafted to his or her particular condition and history." Jamerson (2009) further explains that SANE history collection efforts specifically include (p.117-120) "recent consensual sexual activity", "post-assault activities", "history of drug abuse", history of mental health and behavioral problems, and history of STDs (aka, STIs).

J. The SANE did ask the complainant whether or not she had consumed any alcohol that evening, and the answer was yes.

K. There is no evidence or documentation that the SANE established the complainant's "recent consensual sexual activity", "post-assault activities", or any "history of drug abuse".

L. There is no evidence or documentation that the SANE took a complete medical history of the complainant.

M. There is no evidence or documentation that the SANE took a complete mental health history of the complainant.

N. There is no evidence or documentation that the SANE established whether the complainant was currently under the care of a counselor or physician.

O. There is no evidence or documentation that the SANE established whether the complainant was taking any prescription medications that might interfere, or be synergistic, with additional medications to be administered during the exam or the alcohol that she consumed that evening (e.g., pain meds, birth control, or psychotropics).

P. The Nursing Practice Council/ Policy Committee's guidelines, provided in discovery, under the section titled "Drug Facilitated Sexual Assault" explain: "Testing for the presence of drugs and /or alcohol should be considered part of the evidence collection and significant to the investigation of the sexual assault." This comports with national standards (NIJ, 1999; NIJ, 2004).

Q. There is clear evidence that this was a drug-related event (e.g., complainant acknowledged drinking alcohol that night; drug paraphernalia was found at the defendants apartment; there were reports that the complainant was snorting psychotropic medication that evening with the defendants). However, the SANE nurse intentionally failed to perform a toxicological examination of the complainant. This omission is both serious and troubling, from a forensic perspective.

These forensic failures prevent investigation and confirmation of related case theory, as well as a reliable reconstruction of related events. They also hamper a fully informed assessment of the complainant's ability to sense, perceive, ambulate, and think rationally on the evening of the alleged attack - for investigative and forensic purposes.

5. **The physical evidence in this case is inconsistent with multiple prosecution theories.**

This finding is based on at least the following facts and evidence:

A. The SANE documents multiple areas of slight bruising and scratches to the complainant. However, the connection of these injuries to an attack committed by the defendants is presumed. It is not reconstructed or confirmed by a forensic analysis. For example, a number of these injuries are in various stages of healing and therefore not necessarily connected to events within the prior 24 hrs. This is not mentioned, explained or even explored.

B. There is no forensic report confirming evidence of complainant blood on the sheets or bedding at the defendant's apartment. The absence of such injury is inconsistent with theories suggesting that there was sexual activity on the bed subsequent to victim injury. This owing to *Locard's Exchange Principle* (see Chisum and Turvey, 2011; and Thornton, 1997[6]).

C. There is no forensic report confirming evidence of complainant injury, struggle, or sexual activity in the defendant's vehicle. The absence of such injury is inconsistent with theories suggesting that there was such activity in the defendant's vehicle. This owing to *Locard's Exchange Principle* (see Chisum and Turvey, 2011; and Thornton, 1997).

D. According to the affidavit by Det. Huddleston, in describing an injury to the complainant, he asserts: "The lower back abrasion appeared in a round circle similar to the end of a shotgun barrel".

E. This examiner is not aware of a circular abrasion to the complainant's back, and no such injury appears in the SANE photos of that region.

F. In the SANE photos provided, this examiner observed a square compression abrasion on the complainant's lower back. It is not possible that this abrasion was produced by a shotgun barrel. Rather, it appears to be a compression pattern from a belt buckle or something similar. This is consistent with its square shape and the centrally oriented horizontal mark that could have easily been produced by a buckle post. A shotgun barrel is round, and would leave a round compression pattern. It would also not have a central horizontal compression line across the center (See discovery photo: DSC_0086.jpg).

G. According to the affidavit by Det. Huddleston: "Ms. Pasierb [the complainant] described she was lying on her back and Miller grabbed her by the wrists and held her down. She further described that Miller held her wrists on either side of her head with his hands."

H. As previously suggested, there is no physical evidence that the complainant was restrained in this manner. Specifically, the absence of documentation or reporting by the SANE regarding bruises from hands or fingers on her arms or wrists is inconsistent with being forcibly grabbed by the wrists and held down. The related failure of the SANE to document these areas with photographs, given the account of the attack, is problematic at best.

I. According to the affidavit by Det. Huddleston: "Ms. Pasierb also had a raspy voice and complained of pain to her neck from being strangled." This

[6] Thornton (1997) explains "Forensic scientists have almost universally accepted the *Locard Exchange Principle*. This doctrine was enunciated early in the 20th Century Edmund Locard, the director of the first crime laboratory, in Lyon, France. Locard's Exchange Principle states that with contact between two items, there will be an exchange of microscopic material."

suggests that Det. Huddleston agrees the complainant was strangled as reported.

J. As previously suggested, there is no physical evidence that the victim was manually strangled, or strangled with a ligature. Specifically, the absence of documentation or reporting by the SANE regarding bruises from hands or fingers on her neck, the absence of ligature marks to her neck, and the absence of any photos taken of the neck is inconsistent with such an attack. The related failure of the SANE to document these areas with photographs, given the account of the attack, is problematic at best.

6. **The physical and behavioral evidence in this case evidences multiple investigative "red flags" consistent with false allegations of sexual assault[7].**

This is based on at least the following facts and evidence:

A. *Initiation of the report, or pressure to report, by someone other than the complainant*: The complainant did not seek to report the attack to law enforcement. Nor did the friends that she told about the attack. Rather, she was compelled to report by her mother, who took her to the police the next day.

B. *The report of a sexual assault serves to provide an alibi*: The complainant was a minor engaged in illicit activity with age inappropriate friends. She was also unsupervised and in the immediate vicinity of illegal drug illegal use prior to the alleged attack - if not possibly engaged in illegal drug use herself. She was also at a location other than where she was supposed to be.

C. According to the interview of Jonathan Tyler O'Brien by Investigator Philip Donner of DA's Office on 8/28/2012: "Mr. O'Brien said he was texting Ms. Pasierb through out the night. Mr. O'Brien said Ms. Pasierb texted that she was drinking with Mario Raxon and Keenan Miller at the apartment. Mr. O'Brien said later he got a text that they were going up to Rampart Range Road. Mr. O'Brien said Ms. Pasierb stopped texting when she said she was going to Rampart Range Road. Mr. O'Brien said the text message stopped after that and he did not hear from Ms. Pasierb for 2-4 hours, Mr. O'Brien did not recall the exact time period."

D. *Reconstruction of the physical evidence is at odds with the story of the complainant*: There is no indication in Mr. O'Brien's account that the complainant was in fear of her life and safety prior to going up to Rampart Range Road with the defendants. The fact that she was freely texting with

---

[7] For common red flags, see discussions in Savino and Turvey (2011).

him "through out the night", and the fact that Mr O'Brien did not contact authorities himself, suggests the opposite. Curiously, this examiner is not aware that police collected these texts from Mr. O'Brien.

E. *Reconstruction of the physical evidence is at odds with the story of the complainant*: Mr. O'Brien's account conflicts with accounts suggesting that this was part of a spontaneous unplanned abduction and suggests the need for further investigation.

F. *Reconstruction of the physical evidence is at odds with the story of the complainant*: The fact that the complainant was able to use her cellphone to text Mr. O'Brien prior to going up to Rampart Range Road conflicts with accounts that the complainant lost her cellphone, or cellphone battery, prior to her abduction. This inconsistency suggests the need for further investigation.

G. *Recent severe personal problems*: Law enforcement investigators learned that the complainant was being home schooled. Specifically, According to the affidavit by Det. Huddleston: "she used to attend Manitou Springs High School until recently. Ms. Pasierb said she currently takes online classes and no longer sees her friends as much as in the past." The reasons and consequences related to this major life change appear to have gone uninvestigated by law enforcement.

H. *History of false statements or drug abuse*: According to the complainant's ex-boyfriend, he broke up with her because of her tendency to be manipulative, her tendency to make untrue statements, and her drug abuse.

I. History of false reporting: According to the complainant's ex-boyfriend, she falsely reported to him that she was abducted and sexually assaulted to explain being late one night.

The occurrence of one or two red flags in a single case is not uncommon, though each should be investigated in order to allow for an acceptable case resolution. However, the occurrence of so many unattended and unexplained red flags in a single case comprises an unacceptable remainder. Ultimately, it suggests a lack of overall reliability with respect to the certainty of any investigative of forensic conclusions, and the need for further investigation.

Brent E. Turvey, PhD

REFERENCES

Aiken, M., Burgess, A., and Hazelwood, R. (1995) "False Rape Allegations" in Burgess, A., and Hazelwood, R. (Eds.), *Practical Aspects of Rape Investigation: A Multidisciplinary Approach*, New York: CRC Press.

Bopp, W. and Schultz, D. (1972) *Principles of American Law Enforcement and Criminal Justice*, Charles C. Thomas, Springfield, IL.

Chisum, J. & Turvey, B. (2011) *Crime Reconstruction*, 2nd Ed., San Diego: Elsevier Science.

Crowder, S. and Turvey, B. (2013) *Ethical Justice: Applied Issues for Criminal Justice Students and Professionals*, San Diego: Elsevier Science.

Gershman, B. (1997) *Trial Error and Misconduct*, Lexis Law, Charlottesville, VA.

Gross, H. (1924) *Criminal Investigation,* 3rd ed., London: Sweet and Maxwell.

Gross, B. (2009) "False rape allegations: an assault on justice." *The Forensic Examiner,* Spring, 18(1); pp.66-70.

Hansen, D. and Culley, T. (1973) *The Police Training Officer*, Charles C. Thomas, Springfield, IL.

Jamerson, C. (2009) "Forensic Nursing: Approaching the Victim as a Crime Scene," in Petherick, W. and Turvey, B. (Eds) *Forensic Victimology*, San Diego: Elsevier Science.

Kappeler, V. (2006) *Critical Issues in Police Civil Liability, 4th ed.*, Waveland Press, Long Grove, IL.

Kennedy, D. and Witkowski, M. (2000) "False allegations of rape revisited: A replication of the Kanin study," *Journal of Security Administration*, June, 23 (1); pp.41-48

Leonard, V. (1969) *The Police, The Judiciary, and the Criminal*, Charles C. Thomas, Springfield, IL.

National Institute of Justice (1999) *Death Investigation: A Guide for the Scene Investigator*, Research Report NCJ 167568, Washington, DC: NIJ.

National Institute of Justice (2004) *A National Protocol for Sexual Assault Medical Forensic Examinations,* Washington, DC: U.S. Department of Justice, Office on Violence Against Women, NCJ 206554, September.

O'Connell, J. and Soderman, H. (1936) *Modern Criminal Investigation,* New York: Funk & Wagnalls.

Rau, R. (2000) *Crime Scene Investigation: A Guide for Law Enforcement*, Washington DC: National Institute of Justice, Technical Working Group on Crime Scene Investigation, NCJ 178280, January.

Savino, J. and Turvey, B. (2011) *Rape Investigation Handbook*, 2nd Ed., San Diego: Elsevier Science.

SATF (2009) "False reports and case unfounding," *Attorney General's Sexual Assault Task Force*, State of Oregon, Position Paper, January 22.

Snyder, L. (1944) *Homicide Investigation,* Springfield, IL: Charles C. Thomas.

Sullivan, J. (1977) *Introduction to Police Science*, *3rd ed.*, McGraw-Hill, , New York.

Thornton, J. I. (1997) "*The General Assumptions and Rationale of Forensic Identification*," in D.L. Faigman, D. H. Kaye, M. J. Saks, & J. Sanders (Eds.) *Modern Scientific Evidence: The Law and Science of Expert Testimony,* vol. 2, West Publishing.

Wade, C. (1999) *Handbook of Forensic Services,* Washington, DC: U.S. Department of Justice, Federal Bureau of Investigation.

Weston, P., and Wells, K. (1974) *Criminal Investigation: Basic Perspectives, 2nd ed.*, Englewood Cliffs, NJ: Prentice-Hall.

The author (Turvey) gave expert forensic testimony in this case for the defense at trial, detailing the issues outlined without significant rebuttal from the state. However, during closing arguments, the prosecution introduced previously undisclosed text messages implicating the defendants in the sexual assault.

One jury found Keenan Miller guilty of first degree kidnapping while failing to find him guilty of sexual assault; and anther jury found Mario Raxon guilty of second degree kidnapping and sexual assault. While this outcome is not what the defense would have preferred, in both cases the prosecution was able to completely prove their case. And both cases are currently under appeal.

REFERENCES

Freeman, J., Savino, J., Turvey, B., 2012. Crime scene investigation in sexual assaults. In: Savino, J., Turvey, B. (Eds.), Rape Investigation Handbook. Elsevier, San Diego.

McGrath, M., Turvey, B., 2012. In: Savino, J., Turvey, B. (Eds.), Rape Investigation Handbook, second ed. Elseiver, San Diego.

Sexual Assault Task Force, January 22, 2009. False Reports and Case Unfounding: Recommendations for Law Enforcement Response. Position Paper on Best Practice, Attorney General's Sexual Assault Task Force. Criminal Justice Committee, Salem, Oregon.

CHAPTER

Examining Sexual Homicides

15

B.E. Turvey

Forensic Solutions LLC, Sitka, Alaska, United States;
Institute of Forensic Investigation and Criminal Profiling, Juarez, Mexico

J. Freeman

Forensic Solutions LLC, Sitka, Alaska, United States;
University of Western Ontario, London, ON, Canada

CHAPTER OUTLINE

The term *sexual homicide* is a broad classification. It can be accurately used to describe any homicide that evidences one or more of the following: sexual activity, a sexual component, or a sexual aspect. Examples of these include evidence of sexual activity between the offender and the victim, victim nudity—full or partial to include the exposure of the breasts or genitals, a sexual motive or theme, and/or the presence of sexual material (eg, nude photos, pornography, erotic literature) or devices (eg, sex toys, bondage-related restraints, or masks associated with sexual activity) in the crime scene.

Television, film, and so-called "true crime" material, which are for the most part produced by criminology ingenues, have led pretty much everyone to believe that sexual homicide is associated almost exclusively with stranger crime. In specific, that it is a product of serial murder. This is a dangerously misinformed perspective and has led to a nearly continuous misunderstanding of the phenomenon.

Behavioral Evidence Analysis. http://dx.doi.org/10.1016/B978-0-12-800607-8.00015-X

FREQUENCY

Rape in concert with homicide comprises only a small percentage of murders nationwide (rape–homicide is only one type of sexual homicide, but it is the easiest to recognize). According to some studies, that number is between 0.5% and 1.1% (Myers et al., 1998; Crocker, 2001). However, it is important to point out that the statistics surrounding the precise number of sexual homicides are problematic at best. Revitch & Schlesinger (1983) make the following argument (p. 206): "Highly accurate statistics are actually impossible to obtain because the classification of sex murder or assault is not made only on physical evidence of the crime, but on intrapsychic motives as well." This and other arguments regarding "spuriously low" figures of sexual homicide are provided in Burgess et al. (1986), Grubin (1994) and Myers et al. (1998).

Furthermore, it is quite possible that there are more unrecognized sexual homicides occurring than those which are commonly regarded. Sexual homicide is often reported as a crime that most frequently occurs between strangers. An examination of the data regarding motivations for domestic violence and domestic homicides could potentially change that view. According to Coker (1992), on the subject of domestic violence complaints:

> *Sexuality figures prominently in most of these complaints: she's not sexually responsive enough; she is--or desires to be--sexually unfaithful. The women, in turn, describe abusive partners or expartners as extremely possessive, suspicious, and jealous and clinicians describe the men as "pathologically" jealous. The control of the woman's sexuality also extends to sexual abuse--abuse that may become extreme such as rape, forced sex with animals or other men, and physical attacks on the woman's sex organs or breasts.*

This is supported in Grubin (1994) and also in Palmer and Thornhill (2000, p. 43), which states that:

> *Male sexual jealousy is a major factor in wife beating and homicide in all human societies for which data exists. Males in many cultures often use violence and the threat of violence in attempts to control the sexual behavior of their mates.*

So the argument may be made that at least a portion of domestic homicides have a sexual motivation; are motivated by power, sexuality, and jealousy; or involve sexually symbolic behavior. That is to say, at least a portion of domestic homicides may in fact be unrecognized sexual homicides, depending on the definition one uses. So while we do not know how many sexual homicides there are, we do know that they are poorly understood and therefore vastly underestimated.

BASIC TYPES OF SEXUAL HOMICIDE

The following basic types of sexual homicide are known to exist:

Rape–Homicide: Homicide in association with forcible or coerced sexual penetration. This is a generic classification, nonspecific to victim–offender relationship, or whether there is a serial or even a ritual nature to the crimes. Not all sexual homicides are rape–homicides though this is an assumption often made. Moreover, each of the following types of sexual homicide *may or may not be* a rape–homicide.

Intimate (aka domestic) offender: Sexual homicide committed by a current or former intimate partner, family member, or member of the victim's household. This involves cumulative fantasy or rage with respect to a specific victim over time. The victim is targeted by the offender; the specific motive is a product of a preexisting relationship; and risk to the offender is higher because they can be more quickly identified by investigators.

Proximal offender: Sexual homicide committed by an offender with proximity to the victim, but no real relationship. They are either a stranger or barely an acquaintance. The victim is targeted by the offender; the specific motive is a product of obsession and fantasy; and risk to the offender is mild because they are not easily identified by investigators.

Environmental offender: Sexual homicide committed by an offender who is trolling specific locations or location types for a particular class of victims. In these cases, there is no direct connection between the victim and the offender. Rather, the victims are available because of their presence at a particular "watering hole" where potentially certain types are known to gather (eg, a jogging park, a college dormitory, a prayer group, a bar, a mall parking lot, or an area frequented by prostitutes). In these cases, the act is imagined as part of an offender's fantasy (eg, power, degradation, sadism). Committing the act, a sexual homicide, fuels the satisfaction and/or evolution of the fantasy. This genesis is the reason that this type of sexual homicide is most commonly associated with serial murder. The cycle involved is akin to that suffered by an addict. Though it is quite a bit less predictable in terms of time frames. The interval between attacks may be days, weeks, months, or even years. This all depends on the needs, the pressures, and the patience (or lack thereof) suffered by the offender.

A BRIEF LITERATURE REVIEW

Sexual homicide is defined variously as fatal battery in association with "normal sexual motivation or with abnormal ('perverted' or 'unnatural') sexual behavior," (Adelson, 1974, p. 663); the killing of a person in the context of power, sexuality, and brutality (Burgess et al., 1988, p. 1); and murder in tandem with either an overt sexual assault or sexually symbolic behavior (Myers et al., 1998; Myers, 2001). These are not the only definitions, but they are the most prevalent among researchers who choose to both use the term and define it. The definition provided in Myers (2001) most closely fits the definition provided at the beginning of this chapter, and was obviously expounded upon to assist utility in application.

Consider the findings presented in the following published studies relating to sexual homicides:

DEMING, MITTLEMAN & WELTI (1983)

Medical examiner Charles Wetli, MD, along with two colleagues, published a study of 41 female victims of proven fatal-sexual assault from Dade County, Florida

(Deming et al., 1983). Their aim was to examine the crime scene characteristics from this type of sexual homicide in order to develop a working crime scene profile for use by investigators and forensic examiners. The cases in this study evidenced the following:[a]

- The bodies of younger women, averaging 31 years, were most often found in canals, fields, or vacant lots.
- The bodies of older women, averaging 51 years, were found most often in their residences.
- Death usually resulted from mechanical asphyxiation, and the use of firearms was infrequent.
- Various instruments used to harm, restrain, or kill the victim were most often obtained at the scene of death and reflected the emotionality and impulsivity of the incident.
- Ligature bindings, torn clothing, varying degrees of disrobing, and bite marks were not infrequent.
- Alcohol was found in the blood of 40% of the victims and averaged 0.14%.
- Black victims were represented more frequently than their racial distribution in this community.

The study concluded that the scene and autopsy findings of the average female sexual assault victim form a characteristic profile that should direct further investigation on a particular case (Deming et al., 1983). For example, according to the testimony of Dr. Wetli in Florida v. Julio Ortiz (2000), this study supported a high probability that a deceased woman found in an isolated field, disrobed, with her clothing down her legs, and with her vaginal area exposed, would likely have been the victim of strangulation and sexual assault.

However, it must be noted that sexual homicides may have few if any of the characteristics reported in Deming et al. (1983). It must also be noted that some or all of these characteristics may be evident in a nonsexual homicide. So while the findings in Deming et al. (1983) support the likelihood of a possibility, and even a good investigative hypothesis, they are not conclusive. What these findings provide are indicators or "red flags" for investigators and forensic scientists that highlight the possibility of a sexual homicide. That is to say, the existence of any or all of these crime scene characteristics suggests an inductive hypothesis of sexual homicide that requires verification through investigation, examination, and reconstruction.

MacCULLOCH, SNOWDEN, WOOD, & MILLS (1983)

Published by a group of forensic psychiatrists from Park Lane Hospital in Maghull, Liverpool, England (except Dr. Wood, who was associated with Lynfield Mount

[a] There will be no shortage of poorly trained criminologists and attorneys who will read this and think that it is a list of features that may be generalized to identify sexual homicides. That is not how research findings work, and using them in such a fashion is disingenuous at best. At worst, it is a deliberate deception. The findings describe the sample studied, nothing more.

Hospital in Bradford), this study examined the offenses of 16 male hospital patients convicted of a "clear sexual offense" or an offense with "sexual connotations" (MacCulloch et al., 1983). While not a study of homicide offenses, seven of those patients were actually convicted of what may be defined as sexual homicides.

Of those offenders convicted of sexual homicides, the crime scene characteristics and offender history yielded the following results:

- Five cases (71%) involved women victims, two cases involved male-child victims.
- Six cases (86%) involved the victim suffering multiple stab wounds.
- Three cases (45%) involved the victim suffering from strangulation.
- Two cases (29%) involved the victim suffering a blow from a brick.
- One case (14%) involved necrophilia.
- None of the cases involved torture.
- Three cases (45%) involved an offender with prior burglary convictions.
- Two cases (29%) involved an offender with a prior sex crime conviction.
- Two cases (29%) involved an offender with no prior criminal convictions.

BURGESS, DOUGLAS & RESSLER (1988)

The FBI's Criminal Profiling Project involved the study of 36 incarcerated sexually oriented murderers and their 118 victims (mostly women) from 1979 to 1983 (Burgess et al., 1988; pp. x–xi). This study was conducted to determine whether there were "significant behavioral differences at the crime scene between crimes committed by organized sexual murderers and those committed by disorganized sexual murderers," (Burgess et al., 1988; pp. x). In other words, it was intended to validate the FBI's organized/disorganized classification system as an aid in apprehending sexually oriented murderers. All of the offenders were male, most were white, and 29 of them had killed multiple victims. The remaining seven offenders had killed only one victim each. This makes it a study of serial murderers mixed with a study of single-sexual homicides.

Regarding the data collected by FBI agents for inclusion in the Criminal Profiling Project, Burgess et al. (1988, p. xi) is fairly clear: "...the information collected mainly reflects events as recalled by offenders."

The use of such information without corroboration amounts to an uncritical reliance upon offender interviews as a source of data, worthy of study. Given that criminals lie, and anyone claiming to be a human lie detector suffers from arrogant presumption or delusion, the results of research conducted in this manner are at best questionable. What one has gathered as data is not necessarily what occurred in the crime scene, but what the offender wanted the interviewer to think occurred in the crime scene. Sometimes these are one and the same; sometimes they are not. A thorough reconstruction of the crime using physical evidence is the only reliable method for corroborating such statements.

The FBI's Criminal Profiling Project was formalized in 1982 with a National Institute of Justice (NIJ) grant (Burgess et al., 1988, p. x). Upon compiling their data and preparing a research paper, their study was presented to the NIJ for publication.

According to Nobile (1989), "the Justice Department rejected the study for government publication after outside reviewers flayed its statistics and methodology." This concern was repeated by James Lange and K. DeWitt Jr., who gave a paper at the Metropolitan Washington Mensa Regional Gathering in Arlington, Virginia in February of 1990, titled "What the FBI Doesn't Know About Serial Killers and Why." According to Rossmo (1995): "Lange and DeWitt Jr. (1990) state that the 36 sexual murderer sample used in this research was woefully inadequate for any extrapolation purposes, and the database so flawed the US Department of Justice cut off the project's funding after an external review."

For example, aside from the enormous problem of uncritical reliance on offender interviews, there was no baseline data for comparison to give the data meaning, and the database used was stocked with information from newspaper articles. When one adds these circumstances up, it is difficult to disagree with the concerns raised by the external review.

Despite this set back, FBI agents sought publication in Ressler et al. (1986), and then in Burgess et al. (1988). No significant changes were made to the paper (same sample size, same database, same methodology, etc.). This "research" was also used as the basis for some of the classifications provided in Burgess et al. (1992).

As of this writing, this invalidated 36-offender study, published in Burgess et al. (1988), remains the basis for FBI profiling assumptions, methods, and related expert testimony.

GRUBIN (1994)

Dr. Don Grubin, a forensic psychiatrist from England practicing at Newcastle City Health Trust, published the first detailed study in the United Kingdom designed to examine the sexual murder of women. According to Grubin (1994), in this study: "21 men who murdered women in the course of a sexual attack and 121 men convicted of rape were interviewed in six prisons. Victim statements were obtained in 103 cases (73%)."

Of those offenders convicted of sexual homicides, one had murdered twice, and six others (29%) had a previous conviction for rape (Grubin, 1994). The study yielded the following results:

- Nine (43%) of the offenders were diagnosed with alcohol dependence.
- Nine (43%) of the offenders evidenced paraphilic behavior in their crimes.
- Eight (38%) of the offenders had previous contact with psychiatric services.
- Twelve (57%) of the offenders had used alcohol in the hours prior to the offense.
- Seven (33%) of the offenders had intercourse with unconscious or dead victims (six of whom had used alcohol in the hours prior to the offense).
- Five of the murdered women were over 60 years of age.
- In 29% of the murder–rapes, access was gained to the victim by breaking into her home in the course of a burglary.

- In 29% of the murder–rapes, access was gained to the victim by stalking her on the street.
- Weapons, usually knives, were present in eight (38%) of the offenses.
- Fourteen (67%) of the victims were strangled.
- Two (10%) of the victims were stabbed.
- A gun was involved in only one offense.

This study involved the use of a baseline comparison group of 121 nonhomicidal rapists. Additionally, the operational definition of the term "sexual murder" was made clear in the method of sample selection as a murder "in which a sexual assault was likely to have occurred, though this need not have involved penetration" (Grubin, 1994). The *n* in this study is commensurate to or greater than other studies, the baseline group is appropriate and informative, and the definition is consistent with the literature.

In regards to the data itself, it involves 90-minute offender interviews augmented by law enforcement and court records. As described in Grubin (1994): "Information was gathered from prison files, and victim statements were obtained in 103 cases (73%); where these were not available, as in cases of murder, police and prosecution summaries provided a description of the offense." These data sources are certainly of sufficient quality for use.

MYERS, BURGESS & NELSON (1998)

Forensic psychiatrist Wade Myers, MD of the University of Florida, along with Dr. Ann Burgess and Jamie Nelson (a PhD candidate in psychology), published a study (Myers et al., 1998) of 14 incarcerated juveniles with 12 female victims. Each offender had entered the prison system between January 1990 and December 1996. Additionally, each had simultaneously committed sexual assault and homicide or attempted homicide while being under 18 years of age (Myers et al., 1998).

The purpose of this study was to provide a descriptive systematic study on the criminal and behavioral characteristics of juveniles who commit sexual homicides. In essence, the authors were aiming for an inductive profile of juveniles who commit sexual homicide. To achieve this, the results of Myers et al. (1998) were discussed in the context of prior FBI (NCAVC) research and theories regarding sexual homicide and crime classification methods (Burgess et al., 1992; Burgess et al., 1988; Dietz et al., 1995; Ressler et al., 1986).

Myers et al. (1998) presents the following results, among many others:

- Seven (50%) of the offenders were white; seven (50%) of the offenders were black.
- Eight (67%) of the victims were known by the offender.
- Six (43%) of the victims were an acquaintance of the offender.
- Four (33%) of the victims were strangers.
- All of the victims lived in the same city or town as the offender.

- Seven (58%) of the victims lived in the same neighborhood as the offender.
- Three (25%) of the victims lived next door to the offender.
- Three (25%) of the victims were at high risk; nine (75%) of the victims were at low risk.
- Thirteen (93%) of the offenders had acted violently toward others in the past.
- Twelve (86%) of the offenders had a prior arrest.
- Seven (50%) of the offenders had a prior arrest for burglary or theft.
- Four (19%) of the offenders had a prior arrest for assault and/or battery.
- Three (21%) of the offenders had a prior arrest for trespassing.
- Two (14%) of the offenders had a prior arrest for robbery.
- One (1%) of the offenders had a prior arrest for sexual battery.
- Vaginal sexual assault occurred in eight (67%) of the attacks.
- Weapons were used in eleven (92%) of the attacks.
- Knives were used in nine (75%) of the attacks.
- Strangulation occurred in four (33%) of the attacks.
- Guns were used in two (17%) of the attacks.

The data in this study involved the examination of psychiatric, law enforcement, and court records. As described in Myers et al. (1998) determinations were made based on correctional files (presentencing evaluations, crime descriptions, psychological evaluations, prior arrest sheets, and other offense-related data). They were not based on data collected from NCAVC referrals.

CASE REPORTS

Consider the following case reports prepared in two separate consultations: the sexual homicide of Leanne Holland (a child) and Armita Wiltsey (an adult female). Both reports are full-fledged threshold assessments with some profiling inferences based on available evidence.

With respect to utility, the author consulted on the Graham Stafford case (in the sexual homicide of Leanne Holland) for the defense in postconviction, examining physical evidence issues as well as performing a crime scene analysis. A host of problems were uncovered, including highly misleading DNA testimony by the state's key witness. It took a number of years, but Mr. Stafford finally got a hearing and his convictions were vacated in 2009. The state, recognizing its error, did not seek a retrial.

APPENDIX IV

THRESHOLD ASSESSMENT: THE QUEEN v. GRAHAM STAFFORD (The homicide of Leanne S. Holland)

Body found: Thursday, 1:45 p.m., September 26, 1991

Investigating Agency: Queensland Police Department, Queensland, Australia

Report by:
Brent E. Turvey, MS Forensic Science
Forensic Scientist & Criminal Profiler
Knowledge Solutions, LLC
1961 Main Street, PMB 221
Watsonville, CA 95076
(831) 786-9238; bturvey@corpus-delicti.com

For:
Dr. Paul Wilson, Criminologist
Graeme Crowley, Private Enquiry Agent

After reviewing the case materials detailed below, a determination was made by this examiner that insufficient investigation and forensic analysis have been performed in this case. That is to say, many of the suggested events and circumstances in this case remain *inductive hypotheses* awaiting verification through testing rather than *deductive conclusions* (Thornton, 1997) upon which reliable let alone probative inferences about crime related activity and behavior can be made. To assist the successful investigation and forensic analysis of the materials and evidence in this case, this examiner has prepared a *Threshold Assessment*.

A *Threshold Assessment* is an investigative report that reviews the *initial* physical evidence of crime-related behavior, victimology, and crime scene characteristics for a particular unsolved crime, or a series of potentially related unsolved crimes, in order to provide immediate investigative direction (Baeza *et al.*, 2000). It involves the employment of scientific principles and knowledge, including Locard's Exchange Principle, critical thinking, analytical logic, and evidence dynamics.

Locard's Exchange Principle, a cornerstone of the forensic sciences, states that when an offender comes in contact with a location or another person an exchange of evidence occurs (Saferstein, 1998). As a result of this exchange, the offender both leaves something of themselves behind, and takes something of that person or place away with them when they leave.

Critical thinking may be described as the process of actively and skillfully conceptualizing, applying, analyzing, synthesizing, and/or evaluating information gathered from, or generated by, observation, experience, reflection, reasoning, or communication, as a guide to belief and action (Turvey, 1999). In terms of forensic analysis, it involves the evaluation of the real merits and limitations of physical evidence, and the results of subsequent tests performed on that evidence, as opposed to taking a position because it is agreeable to one's personal beliefs on an issue.

Analytical logic involves the ability to study a crime scene, and any subsequent documentation, and arrive at logical, well-reasoned conclusions. This ideally involves the formation of hypotheses that can be tested against the established facts of the case. The end result of this process is that conclusions may be drawn that follow naturally from the evidence that is present. Such conclusions may be referred to as deductions (Thornton, 1997).

Evidence Dynamics refers to any influence that changes, relocates, obscures, or obliterates physical evidence, regardless of intent. It can occur during the interval that begins as evidence is being transferred and ends when the case is ultimately adjudicated (Chisum and Turvey, 2000).

EXAMINATIONS PERFORMED

The examiner made this *Threshold Assessment* of the above case based upon, but not limited to, a careful examination of the following case material:

- Various media accounts relating to the disappearance of Leanne Hollánd
- Various media accounts relating to the court activity of Graham Stafford
- Queensland Police Department Running Sheet Re: Disappearance of Leanne Sarah Holland
- Various Queensland Police Department Major Incident Job Logs
- Various Queensland Police Department Crime Investigation Logs
- Various photographs of the victim's home
- Various crime scene photos
- Various autopsy photos
- Post Mortem Examination Report by Dr. Rosemary R. Ashby, Institute of Forensic Pathology, Brisbane dated Nov. 5, 1991
- Statutory Declaration of Dr. Rosemary R. Ashby, Institute of Forensic Pathology, Brisbane dated November 5, 1991

- Statutory Declaration of Dr. Kristine Bently, Institute of Forensic Pathology, Brisbane dated November 25, 1991
- Statutory Declaration of Christine Lawrence, former bar attendant, Kerwick Hotel, Redbank, dated May 18, 1995
- Statutory Declaration of Elizabeth Reimers of Collingwood Park, mother of Leanne Holland's friend, Sarah, dated June 15, 1995
- Statutory Declaration of Dr. Anthony Ansford of the John Tonge Centre for Forensic Sciences, Coopers Plains, Brisbane, dated July 17, 1996
- Statutory Declaration of Leo Freney of the John Tonge Centre for Forensic Sciences, Coopers Plains, Brisbane, dated July 26, 1996
- Petition for Exercise of the Royal Prerogative for Mercy, by Neil Macgroarty, Barrister-at-law, dated September 18, 1996
- Outline of Submissions on Behalf of the Crown, Court of Appeals, Supreme Court of Queensland, The Queen v. Graham Stuart Stafford
- Reasons for Judgement, Court of Appeals, Supreme Court of Queensland, The Queen v. Graham Stuart Stafford by P. Fitzgerald, dated September 23, 1997
- Reasons for Judgement, Court of Appeals, Supreme Court of Queensland, The Queen v. Graham Stuart Stafford by J.A. Davies, dated September 23, 1997
- Reasons for Judgement, Court of Appeals, Supreme Court of Queensland, The Queen v. Graham Stuart Stafford by J.A. McPherson, dated September 23, 1997

BACKGROUND/TIME LINE

According to statements made by Melissa Holland, Leanne's older sister, she last saw Leanne Sunday evening, September 22, 1991. Leanne was reportedly watching television. Melissa further stated that she went to bed that evening and then left for work at **7:45 a.m.** Monday morning. There is no mention of her seeing Leanne, who was on the first day of her school holidays, that morning.

According to a statement made by 14-year-old Jason Farrell, he spoke with Leanne in the front yard of her home, at 70A Alice Street, Goodna, on Monday, **7:55 a.m.,** September 23, 1991. She was reportedly of normal mood and appearance, and her hair was its normal blondish color.

According to a statement made by Shane Cuthway of the Cecil Hotel, he saw Leanne on the veranda of her home at approximately **8:30 a.m.** on Monday, September 23, 1991.

According to statements made by Terrence Holland and Graham Stafford,

Leanne was last seen at her home at, **9:30 a.m.** on Monday, September 23, 1991 when she left to meet a friend at the shopping center. Mr. Holland was Leanne Holland's father. He stated that Graham Stafford was the last person to see Leanne at their home. Graham Stafford is the live-in boyfriend of Leanne's older sister, Melissa Holland.

According to a statement made by Peter Edgecumbe of the Cecil Hotel, he saw Leanne walking towards the St. Ives Shopping Center, alone, between **9–9:30 a.m.** on Monday, September 23, 1991.

According to the Queensland Police Department Running Sheet Re: Disappearance of Leanne Sarah Holland, a 15-year-old witness whose name has been withheld saw Leanne at the St. Ives Shopping Center. This witness saw Leanne at **9:50 a.m.** on Monday, September 23, 1991 "carrying a white plastic shopping bag and talking to a Male person wearing a black AC/DC T/shirt and black jeans. Male person had blonde hair and shoulder lexngth [sic]. Slim build approx. 16–17yrs old." This witness is described as Leanne's ex-boyfriend.

According to statements made by Kylie Stark, owner of the Goodna Convenience Foodstore located at 24 Queen St. in Goodna, Leanne came into her store twice on Monday, September 23, 1991. Stark first saw Leanne leaving the store alone and in a good mood at approximately **3:05 p.m.,** when she arrived to take over for her husband. Stark saw Leanne again between **3:30–4:00 p.m.** when she came in, alone, to buy chips.

According to a statement made by Robert Baker of 9 Fitch Street, Goodna, he saw Leanne entering the Private Bar of the Cecil Hotel at **8:30 p.m.** on Monday, September 23, 1991.

According to the Queensland Police Department Running Sheet Re: Disappearance of Leanne Sarah Holland, Terrance Holland filed a missing persons report with that agency on September 24, 1991 at **5:45 p.m.** . The family apparently did not realize that Leanne was missing until approximately this time.

According to investigative and autopsy reports, the body of Leanne S. Holland was found by Trail Bike Units searching the areas around Redbank Plains Road at **1:45 p.m.** on Thursday, September 26, 1991. She was found in bushland several yards west of the intersection of Greenwood Village and Redbank Plains Roads.

Graham Stafford was quickly developed as a suspect in this case due to the fact that he was alleged to be the last person at the Holland home to see Leanne Holland alive. Many of the investigative tips and leads in the Queensland Police Department Major Incident Job Log were not investigated subsequent to his arrest. Notations beneath many of these tips and leads read simply "This information is no longer relevant to the Holland murder as Graham Stuart Stafford has been arrested for the Murder of Leanne Holland." Tips and leads that were not further investigated include a 40-year-old neighborhood male, previously convicted of sex offenses, who was allegedly approaching neighborhood girls. They also include a report man with blood on his hands and jeans that entered a shop on September 25, 1991 asking for money. This becomes significant upon consideration of the weak circumstantial evidence that provided the foundation for Mr. Stafford's arrest.

Despite the lack of any evidence of Leanne's death at her home, and the lack of any conclusive evidence of, or witnesses to, Graham Stafford's presence at the disposal scene or involvement in the crime, Graham Stafford was tried and convicted of Leanne Holland's murder on March 25, 1992. This conviction was appealed. On August 25, 1992 the Court of Appeals dismissed the appeal. However the Court did find that part of the evidence given by Dr. Rosemary Ashby, the forensic pathologist in this case, was wrongfully admitted.

On September 18, 1996, another appeal was prepared which detailed the misinformed interpretations of forensic evidence in this case. The Court of Appeals of the Supreme Court of Queensland ruled by a vote of 2–1, on September 23, 1997, to uphold the conviction of Graham Stafford.

Judge P. Fitzgerald wrote a 27-page opinion calling for the dismissal of the conviction on September 23, 1997, in which he concluded:

> The foundation of the prosecution 'scenario' has been substantially eroded by the evidence of Mr. Freney, Professor Ansford, and Ms. Morris, and the scenario was wrong in critical respects. It seems to me impossible to avoid the conclusion that the jury convicted the appellant on the basis of evidence which presented a significantly mistaken version of events . . .
>
> I would allow the appeal, quash the conviction and order that the appellant be retried.

Judge J. A. Davies wrote a 15-page opinion calling for the dismissal of the appeal on September 23, 1997, in which he concluded:

> Apart from unreliable evidence of sightings of Leanne on or after the afternoon of 23 September 1991 there remains no evidence casting doubt on the opportunity which the appellant had to kill Leanne that afternoon . . . Although the new evidence may make it unlikely that the appellant killed Leanne in the house and left her body in the boot of his car for two days I am satisfied that there is no significant possibility that a jury acting reasonably, even with that evidence before it, would have doubted that he killed her.
>
> . . .
>
> I would therefore dismiss the appeal.

Judge J. A. McPherson, who apparently collaborated with Judge J. A. Davies, wrote a 2-page opinion calling for the dismissal of the appeal on September 23, 1997, in which he concluded:

> I have read and agree with the reasons of Davies J.A. for dismissing this appeal.
>
> . . . the question is not, and never has been, whether the hypothesis or explanation suggested by the prosecution at the trial was established beyond a reasonable doubt . . .
>
> In the present case it is possible on the evidence before the jury at the trial and before the Court to arrive at more than one possible explanation or theory of how the appellant might have murdered the girl and disposed of her body. In reaching their verdict the jury may have been drawn to any one or more of such hypothesis.

So, indeed, The Court of Appeals of the Supreme Court of Queensland agreed that the prosecutions scenario and evidence were deeply flawed. However, two of three judges determined that the prosecution's scenario did not have to be proven beyond a reasonable doubt. These judges were further of the opinion that the jury on this case may have convicted Mr. Stafford based on the consideration of an entirely different scenario. The following should be noted: No alternate scenario suggesting Mr. Stafford's guilt was presented at trial. No alternate scenario suggesting Mr. Stafford's guilt was presented by the Court of Appeals in its reasons for judgement. The jury was not asked to describe the specific scenario that they had convicted Mr. Stafford of.

VICTIMOLOGY

Victimology is a thorough study of all available victim information. This includes items such as sex, age, height, weight, family, friends, acquaintances, education, employment, residence, and neighborhood. This also includes background information on the history and lifestyle of the victim such as overall personal habits, hobbies, criminal history, and medical histories. Establishing victimology is a necessary part of determining the context of some crimes (Baeza *et al.*, 2000). Furthermore, it is generally accepted that the decedent's social, medical, and mental health history can provide insight into the behavior/state of mind of an individual, focus further investigation, and produce clues that will aid in establishing the cause, manner, and circumstances of a death (NMRP, 1999).

Name: Leanne Sarah Holland

Race: Caucasian

Sex: Female

DOB: 10/1/78

Age: 12

Height: Less than 5′

Weight: 41 kg (90 lbs)

Hair: Blonde

Residence location: 70A Alice Street, Goodna, QLD

Occupation: Student at Redbank Plains Highschool

Relationship Status: According to investigative reports, Leanne did have an ex-boyfriend; however, little information was provided to this examiner about this individual other than he was 15 years old and arguably age-inappropriate. Leanne was also, according to her sister, receiving regular phone-calls from an age-inappropriate (19-year-old) male.

Social history: According to investigative findings of the Queensland Police, Leanne had a history of sexual promiscuity with neighborhood boys. She also had a history of getting into cars with strangers, and specifically of hitch-hiking.

Family history: According to investigative findings of the Queensland Police, Leanne lived with her father (Terence), her sister (Melissa), and her sister's boyfriend (Graham Stafford). Her mother and grandmother do not live in the area, and have not seen her in some time. According to interviews with Leanne's friends, Leanne experienced tension with her older sister Melissa, as Terrence Holland left Leanne in Melissa's care when he was away. This is reported to have occurred frequently. Leanne was known to spend a great deal of her time away for her home, outside of adult supervision.

Medical and mental health history: Unknown.

Lifestyle risk: This term refers to the overall risk present by virtue of an individual's personality, and their personal, professional, and social environments. The belief is that certain circumstances, habits, or activities tend to increase the likelihood that an individual will suffer harm or loss (Turvey, 1999). Based even on the limited information available to this examiner,

Leanne Holland was at a high overall lifestyle risk of being the victim of a violent crime. This given the following circumstances:

- History of socializing with age-inappropriate males
- History of sexual promiscuity
- History of hitch-hiking and related activities
- History of getting into vehicles with strangers
- Lived in an area with known sex offender
- History of spending time away from home unsupervised

Incident risk: This term is used to refer to the risk present at the time of the victim's death by virtue of their state of mind and hazards in their immediate environment. Based even on the limited information available to this examiner, Leanne Holland was at a high overall incident risk of being the victim of a violent crime. This given the following circumstances:

- Known to be away from home unsupervised on September 23, 1997
- Witnessed hitch-hiking and/or related activities (walking alone along roadside) on September 23, 1997
- Witnessed at St. Ives Shopping Center on September 23, 1997
- Witnessed socializing with age-inappropriate males on September 23, 1997
- Witnessed entering a bar on September 23, 1997

EQUIVOCAL ANALYSIS OF AUTOPSY FINDINGS

Dr. Rosemary R. Ashby of the Institute of Forensic Pathology, Brisbane prepared the autopsy report of Leanne Holland, on Nov. 5, 1991. I have some concern for the crime reconstruction theories that this report puts forward. My opinion is based upon consideration of the following crime reconstruction issues:

1. **Contact Burn Evidence**: There is mention of burn injuries by prosecutors, judges and the news media in this case. However, the findings at autopsy are equivocal and incomplete on this issue. That is to say, the autopsy report does not confirm conclusively that there are burn marks on this victim's body. On page 4, the report states:

   > There were a number of dark red/brown crusty marks suggestive of abrasion marks or dried out burn marks though none of these were surrounded by an obvious vital reaction.

This is in reference to an injury on the left buttock, two injuries behind the left knee, and a circular injury on the right thigh. The autopsy report goes on to conclude on page 6 that:

> Right Thigh Mark – Shows charring and heat effect of the epidermis and dermis consistent with a burn. There is a slight vital reaction.
>
> Left Buttock Mark – Similar appearances including a blister bulla. There is a slight vital reaction.
>
> Left Knee Marks – Similar appearances but no obvious vital reaction.

The language "consistent with" is a qualifier used to suggest a lack of certainty and the possibility of alternate explanations. Given the alternate explanation provided in this report (abrasion marks), the decomposing state of the body, and the equivocal language provided in the above quoted section of the autopsy report, it is evident that there is a significant question as to whether or not these injuries are actually burn marks.

Furthermore, even if it were established that these were burn injuries, there is no mention by the forensic pathologist in her report of attempts to distinguish between deliberate and accidental infliction. This is a difficult task requiring a thorough investigation of the circumstances of the burn injury. According to Pelteir *et al.* (1997):

> Children are burned for different reasons . . . A detailed history, including previous trauma, presence of recent illnesses, immunization status, and the status of routine medical care, is critical, as is careful documentation of the scene of the injury, including photographs and drawings.
>
> . . .
>
> Purposely inflicted "branding" injuries usually mirror the objects that caused the burn (such as cigarette lighters and curling irons), and are much deeper than the superficial and random burns caused by accidentally touching these objects. Most accidental injuries with hot steam or curling irons occur when the hot item is grasped or falls. These are usually second-degree injuries and randomly placed, as might happen when a hot iron strikes the skin in multiple places as it falls.
>
> . . .
>
> Key questions in this area are:

- Where is the burn injury and could the child reach the area unassisted?
- Does the child normally have access to the item (such as a cigarette lighter) that caused the injury?
- How heavy is the item and how strong is the child? For instance, is the steam iron a small travel-size one that a small child could lift or a full-size home model that might be too heavy?
- Is there any sparing that would be significant to the injury?
- How was the item heated and how long did it take to heat it to cause the injury?
- Is the injury clean and crisp, with a distinctive pattern of the object, or is it shallow or irregular, as from a glancing blow?
- Several cleanly defined injuries, especially on an older child, could indicate that the child was held motionless by a second perpetrator while the first perpetrator carefully branded the child.
- Are there multiple burns or other healed burns?
- Has the child been punished before for playing with or being too close to the hot object?

Monteleone (1996) is in agreement with these guidelines, stating "Intentional cigarette burns are usually deeper and scar more extensively."

Additionally, there is no attempt to classify the burn injuries as either first, second, third, fourth, or fifth degree in nature for the benefit of clarity in presenting findings.

There is no evidence that any of these crucial issues were paid more than a small amount of attention in the evaluation of these alleged burn injuries, and certainly no mention of the victim history that is requisite for the nature of the findings offered. This lack of investigation, consideration and classification on the part of the forensic pathologist makes a reliable determination of accidental versus intentional infliction with regards to the alleged burn injuries impossible.

It is furthermore clear to this examiner that the failure on the part of the forensic pathologist to even discuss the issue of accidental versus intentional infliction is good evidence that she assumed the intentional nature of the injuries rather than established it. Basing conclusive statements on unqualified assumptions is not a legitimate forensic practice.

2. **Peri-Anal Wound**: There is a description of a peri-anal injury on the victim. The autopsy report, on page 3, states:

> In the region of the anus, the anal margin itself is not torn and it did not appear very likely that full anal intercourse had taken place . . . it could be seen that there was a wound just to the left of the anal margin in the natal cleft , 2–2.5 cm long with well defined margins allowing for decomposition and with one end slightly more pointed than the other.

The Statutory Declaration of Dr. Rosemary R. Ashby further states, regarding the same injury, that:

> The appearances of the peri-anal wound suggests that this may have been done with a rather blunt knife.

There is no discussion in the autopsy report relating to whether or not this injury is a laceration (a torn or jagged wound, which tends to have abraded and contused edges), a sharp force or incise injury (a stab, cut, or chop), or an artifact of decomposition (for a discussion, see DiMiao and DiMiao, 1993; Turvey, 1999). As such the injury is unexplained until the time of the statutory declaration. Even then, Dr. Ashby refuses to classify the injury, and states only that it might be the work of a dull knife. This interpretation assumes that a knife was used to cause the injury in the first place, and then that it must have been dull because it did not leave behind the characteristics associated with a sharp force injury. This manner of inquiry is reductive, working backwards from an assumption of a weapon type to establish a theory, rather than establishing the facts of the injury and then discussing potential weapons.

Furthermore, the language "may have been" is a qualifier used to suggest a lack of certainty and the possibility of alternate explanations. In fact, the amount of insect activity and decomposition in and around the injury suggest that this may be a natural result of the decomposition process and not an intentionally inflicted wound at all. Given this alternate explanation of the circumstances of the wound, the failure of Dr. Ashby to investigate alternate possibilities, and the equivocal language used by Dr. Ashby to describe the injury, it is evident that there is significant question as to whether or not this injury is actually the result of a dull knife.

3. **Evidence of "Lustmurder"**: According to the Statutory Declaration of Dr. Rosemary R. Ashby:

> This type of death might fall into a lust killing or sadomasochistic killing with distorted sexual drive. In such cases, cuts or fine scratches in patterns may be

> found upon the skin, known as picqueres. In this case, they appear to have been done after death and outlined with blood.

This conclusion is rendered without any substantial foundation. First, the evidence dynamics relating to the environment and body decomposition have not been ruled out as contributing to these injuries and patterns. According to Chisum and Turvey (2000):

> The failure to consider *Evidence Dynamics* as a part of any crime reconstruction process has the potential to provide for misinterpretations of physical evidence, and inaccurate or incomplete crime reconstructions. Any subsequent use of the reconstruction for investigations, trial or behavioral analysis would have a diminished foundation and relevance, compounding the harm in legal, investigative and academic venues. It is the responsibility of the forensic scientist to perform reconstructions of the circumstances and behaviors involved in a crime with care, and to be aware of the possibility of *Evidence Dynamics*, in order that opinions regarding reconstruction of the crime reflect the most informed and accurate rendering of the evidence.

Second, the inflammatory descriptor "Lustmurder" used by Richard von Kraft-Ebing is a nonspecific and intentionally inclusive term that describes almost all sexually motivated crimes that involve homicide, arguably no different than the term "sexual homicide" (Baeza and Turvey, 1999). It is also not synonymous with a sadistic killing. More to the point, evidence of sadistic behavior at the crime scene requires that the following three circumstances be present: a conscious victim, a period of time indicated by repeated nonlethal injury, and evidence of sexual gratification by the offender (Baeza and Turvey, 1999). As the victim was dead when the injuries in question were inflicted, and sexual gratification on the part of the offender may only be assumed (there is a lack of injury to sexual regions of the body, no evidence of sexual penetration, and equivocal evidence relating to anal injury as described above), there is no foundation for either classification.

A discussion of this issue is provided in the literature review of sadistic behavior prepared by Baeza and Turvey (1999), who explain that:

> Interpreting necrophilic behavior as sadistic ignores, again, the requisite victim suffering to sexually arouse the offender. The dead cannot suffer. Perhaps one of the most helpful and informed renderings of sadism, however, can be found in Dietz *et al.* (1995):

> Sexual Sadism is a persistent pattern of becoming sexually excited in response to another's suffering . . . Inflicting pain is a means to create suffering and to elicit the desired responses of obedience, submission, humiliation, fear, and terror.

In summary, it is apparent to this examiner that the opinions relating to crime reconstruction and crime classification offered by Dr. Rosemary R. Ashby are equivocal, reductive, incomplete, and under-informed. They are subsequently not based on hypothesis testing, consideration/investigation of alternate theories, or other reasonable means of forensic inquiry.

SCENE CHARACTERISTICS

Location and scene types: A *primary scene* is the location where the offender engaged in the majority of their attack or assault upon their victim or victims. A *disposal scene* or dumpsite is the place where a body is found (Turvey, 1999). The outdoor location where the body of Leanne Holland was found is undeniably a disposal site. The death scene, or primary scene, however, has not been reliably established. This examiner has not seen any documentation of a search of the area surrounding this disposal site sufficient to exclude a potential primary scene proximate to the body. This examiner has also not seen documentation of evidence from other locations sufficient to include them as a potential primary or secondary scene with respect to this crime.

Note: The trunk of Mr. Stafford's car is put forth as a secondary scene in this case. This is based upon the finding of a single maggot and blood on a blanket, a chux cloth, and bag contained therein. The maggot is only one in number and therefore its presence is conspicuous. It has not, however, been individuated by virtue of DNA testing as being associated with the victim's body in this crime. The items spotted with blood that were found in the trunk also have not been individuated by virtue of DNA testing as being associated with the victim in this crime. Additionally, sloughed hair or tissue was found in the trunk of this vehicle, which would be expected given the decomposition that was said to have taken place. And finally, Mr. Freney's report states that the blood on the bag was conspicuously fresh, and not decomposed. Having said all of this, it is clear that none of the judges who ruled on this case believed that the victim's body was actually placed in the trunk of this vehicle.

Point of contact: This is defined as the location where an offender first approaches or acquires a victim (Turvey, 1999). The lack of certain evidence and the nature of the victim's activities, as witnessed by those who knew her, do not provide for a reliable determination of the point of contact at this time.

Note: Authorities did not find the victim's shoes, socks, backpack, or shopping bag. If either item were found at her home, this would suggest that she came home and would effect the timeline. If these items were not found at her home, their presence at another location would be highly suggestive of a *primary scene* or *point of contact.*

Use of weapons: A blunt object of some kind was most certainly used to inflict the injuries to the victim's head; however, no such object has been located which has been reliably associated with this crime. There is no other reliable evidence of the use of a weapon in this crime.

Victim resistance: This refers to the amount and type of opposition or non-compliance offered by the victim during an attack (Turvey, 1999). There is evidence of victim resistance by virtue of the defensive bruising present on the back of the victim's hands. It is most likely that these injuries were received while the victim was covering her head, in an effort to protect herself from oncoming blows.

Method of approach: This term refers to the offender's strategy for getting close to a victim (Turvey, 1999). The lack of certain evidence and the nature of the victim's activities, as witnessed by those who knew her, do not provide for a reliable determination of the offender's method of approach at this time.

Method of attack: This term refers to the offender's mechanism for initially overpowering a victim once they have made their approach. It is appropriate to describe a method of attack in terms of the weapon, and the nature of the force involved (Turvey, 1999). It is evident that at some point during the attack the offender used a blunt object to inflict *punishment oriented force* while the victim was unrestrained. This given the severe, repeated injuries to the victim's head in concert with the defensive bruising present on the back of the victim's hands. According to Turvey (1999), *punishment oriented force* is defined as "Brutal and short-lived levels of force that are reflected in extensive, severe wound patterns. In cases where brutal force is used, it is not uncommon for the victim to require hospitalization, or to die, as a result of the injuries inflicted. It must be made clear that homicide is not necessarily the desired result in such cases."

There is also evidence that the attack involved physically aggressive offender behavior that is intended to manipulate, regulate, restrain, and subdue victim behavior, or *control oriented force* (Turvey, 1999) detailed below.

Methods of control: This term refers to the means used by an offender to manipulate, regulate, restrain, and subdue victim behavior of any kind throughout the duration of an offense (Turvey, 1999). Methods of control in this case appear to include manual, in the form of finger mark bruising to the victim's left forearm and neck. Asphyxiation is not listed as a contributing cause of death in the autopsy report. There is no other evidence that suggests the use of other methods of control in this case.

Sexual acts: Evident in the crime scene photos and consistent with the autopsy report (except where discussed above in relation to the victim's peri-anal injury), there is no evidence of sexual activity in this case.

Note: The body of the victim was found partially nude at the scene, with her lower back, buttocks, legs, and feet exposed. This may be partially explained by dragging. There is no evidence to suggest that this is related to sexual activity or sexual attack, however.

Verbal behavior: Unknown.

Evidence of planning and precautionary acts: Precautionary acts are offender choices made before, during, or after an offense that are consciously intended to confuse, hamper, or defeat investigative or forensic efforts for the purposes of concealing their identity, their connection to the crime, or the crime itself (Turvey, 1999). Their existence may be used to suggest planning or knowledge during various phases of a crime. Without a precise determination of the primary scene in this case, it is not possible to make a reliable determination regarding the precautionary acts that may be evident in this case.

Note: If the area surrounding the disposal site were reliably excluded as containing the primary scene, the disposal of the body in a location dissociating it from the primary scene would be considered a precautionary act. Additionally, the victim's hair was determined to have been dyed red or auburn. Unless the possibility that the victim dyed her own hair can be reliably excluded, and the possibility that the offender dyed the hair as a punishment also reliably excluded, this act cannot be reliably considered a precautionary act committed to conceal the victim's identity.

Motivational aspects: This term is used to refer to the emotional or psychological themes or needs that offenders satisfy when they commit offense behaviors. The time, effort, and brutal levels of force evident in this attack support the conclusion that anger, or a desire for retaliation primarily motivated this offense. An anger-retaliatory motivation is evidenced by a convergence of behaviors that are expressions of rage, either towards a specific person, group, institution, or a symbol of either. This expression will often take the overt form of excessive or brutal force aggression. (Turvey, 1999). Motivational behaviors in this case include, but may not be limited to:

- Severe, repeated blows to the victim's head.

In this examiner's opinion, the anger and desire for punishment evidenced by these acts is not necessarily directed specifically at Leanne Holland. It may be the result of cumulative rage unrelated to the victim.

Note: It is unknown how the underpants and skirt of the victim were torn. They may be the result of transport, dragging, or a struggle with the offender. It is further unknown as to how the victim came to rest at the scene as she was found. If the victim were purposefully left at the scene with her lower half exposed, this would be considered a motivationally oriented behavior. However, this may simply be a result of the offender being interrupted or in a hurry when disposing of the victim's body.

OFFENDER CHARACTERISTICS

Offender characteristics include any attributes that may be ascribed specifically to the unknown person or persons responsible for the commission of particular criminal acts, including those that are physical, psychological, social, geographical, or relational (Baeza *et al.*, 2000).

Sex: Investigative assumptions in this case to date have apparently included the preconceived theories (treated as fact) that there was but one offender involved in this crime, and that this offender must be male. The first part of this assumption may not be correct. There is evidence of two different types of footwear impressions in soil near the body. The second part of this assumption, while an interesting hypothesis, can be neither completely supported nor completely falsified by the physical evidence in this case. This rests on the consideration of two issues:

- There is no reliable evidence of sexual assault. Even if the anal tearing were associated with an attack to the anus by the offender (which has not been established), this would not be definitive proof of a male attacker.
- The rage and punishment oriented force evidenced in this case are just as likely the work of a female attacker as they are a male attacker. Moreover, given these things in concert with the age of the victim, investigators should wish to vigorously work to exclude all custodial figures.

Knowledge of/familiarity with location: The use of this location as a disposal site suggests an offender(s) with a high degree of knowledge of, and familiarity with, the surrounding area. It should be noted, however, that this location is very public in terms of its near visual proximity to Redbank Plains Road. It is well used and subsequently well known by the residents and visitors to and from neighboring towns.

Skill level: Despite the precautionary acts evident in this case, the offenders left a great deal of physical evidence behind at the scene. They also exposed themselves to the risk of discovery and association with the crime by leaving the body at the essentially public location where it was discovered. This examiner would characterize offender actions related to planning and precautionary acts as having low homicide-related skill.

Knowledge of/familiarity with victim: The facts and circumstances of this case discussed in the victim risk and motivational aspect sections of this report suggest the involvement of an offender(s) that need not have any prior familiarity with the victim. Though that possibility is certainly not excluded, given the amount of rage that is evident.

INVESTIGATIVE SUGGESTIONS

The following is a list of suggestions for further investigating and establishing the facts of this case:

1. Reference is made in the *Outline of Submissions on Behalf of the Crown* to DNA testing. Kristine Bentley makes further reference to blood tests performed on items of evidence in her report dated July 26, 1996. However, this examiner has seen no report that explains either of these references in detail. There appears to be some conspicuous confusion as to what tests where performed, precisely, and what the results where for those tests for each individual item of evidence. This confusion may have contributed to an overemphasis of the blood evidence by both the jury and the judges presiding over the appeal. This examiner strongly recommends that the precise nature of all blood testing be ascertained and reviewed by an independent forensic serologist. In any event, STR DNA tests should be run on all blood associated with items of evidence.
2. In the victim's home the baseboard of the bathroom vanity should be removed and the area examined for any bloodstains.
3. An unknown hair was found in the trunk of Graham Stafford's car. This item should be examined and compared to known sample's of victim

hair by a hair and fiber expert. Additionally, suitability for STR DNA analysis on any root material should be determined. In addition to this, mitochondrial DNA testing is possible using the hair shaft if all else fails.

4. A maggot was found in the trunk of Graham Stafford's car. It should be tested using STR DNA analysis and compared to the victim's known STR DNA profile for individuation.
5. A single short, nonpubic hair can be visualized on the victim's buttocks, just to the right of the ruler in place to measure other injuries. It should be determined if this hair was recognized and collected. If so, this item should be examined and compared to known sample's of victim hair by a hair and fiber expert. Additionally, suitability for STR DNA analysis on any root material should be determined.
6. There is no mention in the case materials provided to this examiner of fingernail clippings being tested in this case, though they were collected and sent to Kristine Bentley. They should be examined for tissue. If tissue is present, STR DNA analysis should be performed.
7. A clump of hair was found in the bathroom bin in the victim's home. There is no mention of analysis performed on this hair. This item should be examined and compared to known samples of victim hair by a hair and fiber expert. It should be determined whether or not this hair was dyed, and if so, what color. Additionally, suitability for STR DNA analysis on any root material should be determined. In addition to this, mitochondrial DNA testing is possible using the hair shaft if all else fails.
8. Plastic bags were found both underneath the victim's body. This can and should be tested for latent fingerprints using the technique known as Vacuum Metal Deposition. It should also be compared to any unused bags in the victim's home. Not only for brand, size, and type, but for individuating characteristics such as the rifling of the plastic as it passes through the machine. Bags that have been torn apart may be reliably connected in sequence from the same roll using this manner of examination.
9. A bloodstain pattern expert should be employed to review all the blood evidence in this case, specifically the blood found on items in Graham Stafford's vehicle. Was blood dripped onto these items? Was the blood smeared onto these items? Was this fresh blood with no decomposition? How could this blood have gotten where it was found? Determine plausibility of the "no blood on clothes theory" put forth by the prosecution.
10. A forensic entomologist should be employed to examine the insect evidence in this case. What can the insects tell us about the location(s) of the body? Time of death estimates? Examine the maggot found in

the trunk of Stafford's vehicle and attempt to determine its age and how long the victim would have been dead for the maggot to develop as it did. If a time range is possible, determine who had access to the car during that particular time period.

11. There is some disagreement as to whether or not the victim's underwear and skirt were torn or cut. Cutting would suggest the use of a weapon. Tearing suggests a possible struggle. Photographs of these items should be obtained to determine which is the case.
12. The victim's former boyfriend is a witness in this case, who provided potential suspect and timeline information. A firm timeline of his activities from Monday, September 23 to Thursday, September 26, 1991 needs to be established, and corroborating witnesses interviewed.
13. According to statements made by Terrence Holland and Graham Stafford, Leanne left home at 9:30 a.m. to meet a friend at the shopping center. While some effort was made to interview female friends of the victim to determine whom she was meeting with, very little effort was made to interview or locate age-inappropriate male friends that the victim was known to socialize with. A list of her known male friends should be made and interviewed as suspects in this case.
14. A serious inquiry into which friend the victim may have been meeting at the shopping center on Monday should be made with Graham Stafford, Terence Holland, and Melissa Holland.
15. Another twelve-year-old girl was killed in this area subsequent to the arrest of Graham Stafford. The details of that murder should be obtained and compared with the findings to this case.
16. The victim's diary should be reviewed to develop a suspect pool as well as to obtain further victimological information.
17. Incoming and outgoing calls (MUDs and LUDs) to the victim's residence for the period before and during her disappearance should be reviewed from phone company records, if possible, to develop a suspect pool.
18. Check police records for anyone stopped and questioned for any reason in the vicinity of the victim's home, the locations where she was observed, the routes she would have walked, and the location near where her body was found for all of the dates during her disappearance. These individuals should be included in the suspect pool.
19. Check police records to ascertain if any traffic summonses (parking or moving violations) were issued in the same areas listed in action item #17. These individuals should be included in the suspect pool.

A FORENSIC SCIENTIST'S RESPONSE TO THE DISMISSAL OF THIS APPEAL

In this examiner's opinion, it is clear that both dissenting Judges, J.A. Davies and J.A. McPherson, believed that Mr. Stafford was guilty, and therefore did not warrant a new trial. Their belief was based upon the consideration of the following evidence: (1) the small amount of blood found in Mr. Stafford's vehicle, which they apparently believe is the victim's blood. *Note:* this blood was not sufficiently tested to individuate its source using modern DNA testing, and the conditions of transfer not reliably established. Therefore this blood has not been reliably associated with the victim or the crime; (2) the small amount of blood found in the common bathroom of the victim's home, which they apparently believe is the victim's blood. *Note:* this blood was not sufficiently tested to individuate it's source using modern DNA testing, and the conditions of transfer not reliably established. Therefore this blood has not been reliably associated with the victim or the crime; (3) the maggot found in Mr. Stafford's vehicle, which they apparently believe is associated with the victim's body. *Note:* this maggot was not sufficiently tested to individuate its source using modern DNA testing, therefore it has not been reliably associated with the victim or the crime.

It is clear to this examiner, given the irrational reliance on these items of evidence as certain indications of guilt, that the two dissenting judges in this case have not been given an explanation of the difference between the concept of forensic identification (class characteristics) and forensic individuation (individual characteristics). This may have to do with quality of the testimony provided by the forensic scientists testifying for the prosecution in this case. The problem identity is discussed thoroughly by Kirk (1974), who mentions the following relevant concern:

> The inept or biased witness may readily testify to an identity, or to a type of identity, that does not actually exist. This can come about because of his confusion as to the nature of identity, his inability to evaluate the results of his observations, or because his general technical deficiencies preclude meaningful results.

Thornton (1997) provides the most useful explanation of this all too important forensic issue that this examiner has come across, and it bears repeating here:

> **§ 20-2.1 Class and Individual Characteristics**
> In the comparison of physical evidence, it is often helpful to make use of the concepts of class characteristics and individual characteristics. Class characteristics are general characteristics that separate a group of objects from a universe of diverse objects. In a

> comparison process, class characteristics serve the very useful purpose of screening a large number of items by eliminating from consideration those items that do not share the characteristics common to all of the members of that group. Class characteristics do not, and cannot, establish uniqueness. Individual characteristics, on the other band, are those exceptional characteristics that may establish the uniqueness of an object. It should be recognized that an individual characteristic, taken in isolation, may not in itself be unique The uniqueness of an object may be established by an ensemble of individual characteristics. A scratch on the surface of a bullet, for example, is not a unique event; it is the arrangement of the scratches on the bullet that may mark it as unique.
>
> An example of a class characteristic is "red." The characteristic "red" separates red items from those of all other colors. Class characteristics may be chained together to further refine the screening or elimination process. "Red Buick" will instantly exclude from consideration any other vehicle, but will not distinguish among a sub-population of red Buicks. There is a fundamental mathematical foundation to this type of elimination, which resides in the "either/or" logic of Boolean algebra. Any vehicle that is not a red Buick may he eliminated because it is "either" of another manufacturer "or" it is of some other color.
>
> An example of an individual characteristic would be the VIN number of the vehicle. The license plate number might be an individual characteristic, but the possibility exists that there would be some duplication of license plate numbers among different states and possibly between different countries.

To be clear, blood evidence, unless it has been analyzed using STR or RFLP techniques is not typically considered individuating (Saferstein, 1998). Hair evidence, again, unless it has been analyzed using STR or RFLP techniques is also not typically considered individuating. They are considered class evidence (Saferstein, 1998). Any statement about their ultimate origin absent these individuating tests is a hypothesis or a theory, not a conclusion. The apparent failure of forensic scientists employed by the prosecution to didactically explain the limitations of the class evidence in this case to the court, and the jury, with regards to this issue is appalling.

Furthermore, the suggestion by the two dissenting judges that the prosecution's scenario, and the individual facts upon which it was based, did not need to be proven beyond a reasonable doubt is an affront to justice. This reasoning has an impact that is two-fold. First, it single-handedly alleviates the prosecution of the burden proof by virtue of removing the requirement of accuracy, in that it allows the presentation of scenarios to the judge and jury that are known even by the court to be nonfactual and unsound. Second, it alleviates the court's need for forensic scientists, and any other professionals who may testify as to the interpretation of physical evidence by suggesting that the jury may be trusted to interpret and reconstruct complex physical evidence without any reliable expert forensic guidance. A rational argument cannot be made in support of either circumstance.

It is appropriate to close this response with a quote from a learned forensic scientist and colleague who has written succinctly and rationally on this subject (Chisum, 1999):

> The prosecutor seeks to convict the defendant by making the crime more heinous in nature. The defense seeks to exonerate the defendant. Both theorize about how the crime occurred with different objectives. Both cannot be correct and, lacking a reconstruction, both are probably wrong. The theories are alternatives and should be examined against the evidence.

Brent E. Turvey
Forensic Scientist

ADDENDUM

Figure App. IV.1a–c Leanne Holland body and outdoor disposal scene as photographed by authorities

REFERENCES

Baeza, J., Chisum, W.J., Chamberlin, T.M., McGrath, M., and Turvey, B. (2000) "Academy of Behavioral Profiling: Criminal Profiling Guidelines," *Journal of Behavioral Profiling*, **1** (1, January).

Baeza, J. and Turvey, B. (1999) "Sadistic Behavior: A Literature Review," *Knowledge Solutions Library*, Electronic Publication, URL: http://www.corpus-delicti.com/sadistic_behavior.html, May, 1999.

Chisum J. (1999) "An Introduction to Crime Reconstruction" in Turvey B. *Criminal Profiling: An Introduction to Behavioral Evidence Analysis*, London: Academic Press.

Chisum, W. J. and Turvey, B. (2000) "Evidence Dynamics: Locard's Exchange Principle and Crime Reconstruction," *Journal of Behavioral Profiling*, **1**(1, January).

Dietz, P., Hazelwood, R., and Warren, J. (1995) "The Criminal Sexual Sadist," in Burgess, A. W. and Hazelwood, R. (Eds.) *Practical Aspects of Rape Investigation: A Multi-disciplinary Approach*, 2nd ed., New York: CRC Press.

DiMaio D. and DiMaio V. (1993) *Forensic Pathology*, New York: CRC Press.

Kirk, P. (1974) *Criminal Investigation*, 2nd ed., New York: John Wiley & Sons.

Monteleone, J. (1996) *Recognition of Child Abuse for the Mandated Reporter*, 2nd ed., St. Louis: GW Medical Publishing Inc.

NMRP (National Medicolegal Review Panel) (1999) *Death Investigation: A Guide for the Scene Investigator*, Washington, DC: National Institute of Justice.

Pelteir, P., Purdue, G., and Shepard, J. (1997) *Burn Injuries in Child Abuse*, Washington, DC: Office of Juvenile Justice and Delinquency Prevention (OJJDP), National Institute of Justice.

Saferstein, R. (1998) *Criminalistics: An Introduction to Forensic Science*, 6th ed., Upper Saddle River, NJ: Prentice Hall.

Thornton, J.I. (1997) "The General Assumptions and Rationale of Forensic Identification," in Faigman, D., Kaye, D., Saks, M., and Sanders, J. (Eds.), *Modern Scientific Evidence: The Law and Science of Expert Testimony*, Vol. 2, St. Paul, MN: West Publishing Co.

Turvey, B. (1999) *Criminal Profiling: An Introduction to Behavioral Evidence Analysis*, London: Academic Press.

APPENDIX

Threshold Assessment

Homicide of Armida Wiltsey

Body Found: Tuesday, November 14, 1978, at approximately 10:15 p.m. by Roy English, East Bay MUD Ranger.
Investigating Agency: Contra Costa County Sheriff's Department.

Report by:
Jodi Freeman, MCrim
Date: September, 20, 2010
jodi.freeman@rogers.com
Report for:
Brent Turvey
Forensic Solutions LLC
bturvey@corpus-delicti.com

PURPOSE

After reviewing the case materials, a determination was made by the examiner that insufficient investigation and forensic analysis have been performed in this case to warrant the rendering of a criminal profile. The purpose of this report is to provide investigative suggestions by means of a threshold assessment. A *threshold assessment* is an investigative report that reviews the initial physical evidence of crime scene related behavior, victimology, and crime scene characteristics for a particular unsolved crime, or a series of potentially related unsolved crimes, in order to provide immediate investigative direction (Turvey, 2008). A threshold assessment involves the employment of scientific principles and knowledge, including Locard's exchange principle, critical thinking, analytical logic, and evidence dynamics (Turvey, 2008).

Locard's exchange principle, a cornerstone of the forensic sciences, states that when an offender comes in contact with a location or another person, an exchange of evidence occurs (Saferstein, 1998).
Critical thinking may be described as the process of actively and skillfully conceptualizing, applying, analyzing, synthesizing, or evaluating information gathered from, or generated by, observation, experience, reflection, reasoning, or communication, as a guide to belief and action (Turvey, 2008).

Criminal Profiling: An Introduction to Behavioral Evidence Analysis, Fourth Edition

Analytical logic involves the ability to study a crime scene and any subsequent documentation and arrive at logical, well-reasoned conclusions. This ideally involves the formation of hypotheses that can be tested against the established facts of the case. The end result of this process is that conclusions may be drawn that follow naturally from the evidence that is present. Such conclusions may be referred to as deductions (Thornton, 1997).

Evidence dynamics refers to any influence that changes, relocates, obscures, or obliterates physical evidence, regardless of intent. Evidence dynamics are at work even before the crime happens and also during the interval that begins as physical evidence is being transferred or created (Chisum and Turvey, 2007).

This threshold assessment is limited to the assumption that the evidence and investigative reports at the time of examination were correct. As the evidence changes, so will the results provided in this report. Should any new information be provided, the findings in this threshold assessment must be reconsidered.

CASE MATERIALS

The examiner rendered this threshold assessment based on a careful examination of case evidence. This evidence included, but was not limited to, the following:

- Contra Costa County police interviews
- Contra Costa County police reports and evidence examination reports
- Contra Costa County witness statements and line-ups
- Contra Costa County crime scene photos
- Contra Costa County crime scene sketches
- Contra Costa County bloodhound tracking report
- Autopsy report and photos of Armida Wiltsey
- Lafayette Reservoir map and brochure
- Media report "Jogger is Strangled, Raped at Reservoir"

BACKGROUND

According to the Contra Costa County police reports, the body of Armida Wiltsey (40, WF) was found laying in the southeast corner of the Lafayette Reservoir, at approximately 10:15 p.m. on Tuesday, November 14, 1978, by Roy English, an East Bay MUD ranger.

The victim was found 40 yards off of the main jogging trail, lying in a brushy area.

Crime scene photos indicate that the victim was found partially clothed, lying on her left side in a curled-up position. The victim was wearing a blue jogging shirt and blue jogging shoes. Her blue jogging pants and white underwear were found lying partially on top of the victim and partially to her side and her jogging shirt was lifted up, exposing her breasts. Crime scene and autopsy photos evidence fecal matter on the victim's buttocks and clothing. Abrasion marks on the victim's face are also evident, along with pressure marks on her neck and wrists. According to Armida Wiltsey's autopsy report, the cause of death was asphyxiation due to neck trauma.

According to police interviews and victimological inquires, Armida Wiltsey was a dedicated mother who spent the majority of her time with her family and involved with her son's school. On the day of the homicide, the victim left her residence at some point before 9:00 a.m. and was reported missing by her neighbor,

Larry Busboom, at approximately 7:00 p.m. after she failed to pick up her son from school. The victim's vehicle was subsequently located across the street from the main entrance of the Lafayette Reservoir, commencing a search of the area. Armida Wiltsey's body was discovered at approximately 10:15 p.m. with the assistance of three dog-handlers.

TIMELINE

The following timeline information was taken from Contra Costa County police interviews and reports.

Tuesday, November 14, 1978

At some point before 9:00 a.m., Armida Wiltsey helped her husband, Boyd Wiltsey, pack for a business trip. That morning, she told her husband that she was concerned about taking their son to school. Armida Wiltsey left her residence and dropped her son off at school before driving to the Lafayette Reservoir to go for a jog.

At approximately 9:00 a.m., Armida Wiltsey's vehicle, a 1975 Datsun, was seen by Gail Overra across the street from the Lafayette Reservoir, where it was eventually discovered. It is estimated from police interviews with witnesses in the area that the victim was "pulled into the bushes" between 9:30 a.m. and 9:45 a.m.

At 12:00 p.m., Armida Wiltsey failed to pick up her son from school, which was routine for her to do. At 7:00 p.m., the victim was reported missing by her neighbor, Larry Busboom. At some point between 7:00 p.m. and 9:50 p.m., police discovered the victim's vehicle across the road from the Lafayette Reservoir. At 9:50 p.m., a search of the reservoir commenced, involving a search by foot, vehicle, helicopter and bloodhounds. At approximately 10:15 p.m., the body of Armida Wiltsey was found by Roy English, an East Bay MUD Ranger.

Wednesday, November 15, 1978

At approximately 12:30 a.m., police met the victim's husband, Boyd Wiltsey, at the airport to inform him that his wife was dead.

VICTIMOLOGY

Victimology is the process of investigating, establishing and evaluating victim traits and history: learning everything there is to know about victims, who they were, where and how they spent their time, and how they lived their life (Petherick and Turvey, 2009). A victimology requires an extensive examination of the victim's lifestyle exposure and situational exposure, as well as knowledge of the underlying sociological theories that contribute to these exposures.

Name: Armida Wiltsey
Race: Caucasian
Ethnicity: Hispanic
Sex: Female
D.O.B: October 29, 1938
Age: 40
Height: 62 inches
Weight: 105 lbs.

Eye Color: Brown
Hair Color: Black
Family legend:
Armida Wiltsey: Victim (40)
Boyd Wiltsey: Victim's husband
Name Unknown: Victim's biological son (10)
Daniel Boyd Wiltsey: Victim's stepson (19)
Michael Wiltsey: Victim's stepson (23)
Residence location: 4169 Cora Lee Lane, Lafayette, Contra Costa, California. USA.
Residence type and description: Armida Wiltsey lived with her husband Boyd Wiltsey, and their 10-year-old son at their residence located at 4169 Cora Lee Lane in Lafayette, California. The residence type is unknown but police interviews suggest that the Wiltseys lived in an upper-middle class residence. This is evident by the employment of a live-in nanny, Julie Doherty (18, WF), who lived with the family at their residence, providing light housework and babysitting for their 10-year-old son.

The criminal history of the residence and surrounding neighborhood is unknown.

Family history: Armida Wiltsey was married to Boyd Wiltsey. The length of their marriage is unknown. According to the police interview with Boyd Wiltsey, he had no problems with his wife and they had no history of major arguments or disagreements. The last time he saw Armida Wiltsey was on the morning of the homicide, before he left for his business trip. Boyd Wiltsey frequently traveled for business.

Armida Wiltsey and Boyd Wiltsey had a 10-year-old son together. Boyd Wiltsey also had two sons from a pervious marriage, Daniel Boyd Wiltsey and Michael Wiltsey. Michael Wiltsey was living in Oregon at the time of the homicide. It is unknown where Daniel Boyd Wiltsey was residing. According to the police interview with Julie Doherty, Daniel Wiltsey had a drug problem. The extent of his drug problem is unknown.

Social history: Armida Wiltsey was a homemaker. She did not work outside of the home and according to Julie Doherty, her life was devoted to her family and spending time with friends in the area. Her activities included participating in the P.T.A at her son's school and volunteering for the school library.

Armida Wiltsey jogged 3–5 mornings a week at the Lafayette Reservoir. She had been jogging for approximately 3–4 months prior to the homicide and had started her jogging program gradually.

According to police interviews with Julie Doherty, Susan Todd, Gail Overra, Sandy Busboom, and Kim DeStPaer, Armida Wiltsey had no male friends other than her husband and no problems in her marriage to Boyd Wiltsey. However, an anonymous letter received by the Oakland Police Department stated that Guy Icalaolle had an affair with Armida Wiltsey and was responsible for the homicide.

Criminal history: Armida Wiltsey's criminal history is unknown.

Drug and alcohol use: There is no known evidence of drug or alcohol use by the victim. According to Armida Wiltsey's autopsy report, there were no substances in the victim's body at the time of the homicide.

According to Julie Doherty, Daniel Wiltsey had a drug problem. The extent of his drug problem is unknown.

Medical and mental health history: Armida Wiltsey's autopsy report indicates that she was generally in good health and her body was well developed and nourished. According to the victim's neighbor, Larry Busboom, she was seeing a doctor for "female problems." According to the victim's medical records, she had last seen her physician two weeks prior to the homicide for a vaginal infection.

Armida Wiltsey had no known mental health issues.

VICTIM EXPOSURE

Victim lifestyle exposure: *Lifestyle exposure* refers to the frequency of potentially harmful elements that exist in a victim's everyday life as a consequence of biological and environmental factors, as well as past choices (adapted from Petherick and Turvey, 2009).

Armida Wiltsey was a *low-exposure victim* who was rarely exposed to the possibility of suffering harm or loss (adapted from Petherick and Turvey, 2009). This is due to the following circumstances:

1. The victim's daily routine revolved around her family, specifically her son. There is no evidence to suggest that she engaged in activities outside of her family interests, except for her routine jogging.
2. The victim's family and friends knew her daily jogging routine and she was accountable to her husband, son, friends, and live-in babysitter. These individuals acted as capable guardians who would have noticed if she had gone missing (Petherick and Turvey, 2009).
3. The victim's autopsy report reveals that she was healthy, well nourished and not suffering from any underlying medical issues.
4. The victim did not have any issues with anyone around her. There is evidence to suggest that she may have had an affair but the validity of this information has not been established.
5. The victim's stepson, Daniel Boyd Wiltsey, had a drug problem at the time of the homicide. However, it is unknown whether the victim was routinely exposed to this behavior. This factor would increase the lifestyle exposure of the victim.

Victim situational exposure: *Situational exposure* refers to the amount of actual exposure or vulnerability experienced by the victim to harm, resulting from the environment and personal traits, at the time of victimization (Petherick and Turvey, 2009).

Armida Wiltsey was a *low-medium exposure victim* who was vulnerable to some harm or loss immediately prior to victimization (adapted from Petherick and Turvey, 2009). This is due to the following circumstances:

1. The homicide occurred during daylight hours and the reservoir was populated with joggers.
2. The victim did not have auditory interference and was alert to her surroundings.
3. The victim's autopsy report reveals that she tested negative for alcohol and drugs. The victim was not under the influence of substances at the time of the homicide.
4. The reservoir was located in a secluded area with dense shrubbery. This environment increased the victim's situational exposure but did not completely remove the capable guardianship of other joggers in the area (Petherick and Turvey, 2009). This is evident in police interviews that state that other joggers witnessed individuals in the bushes on the day of the homicide.
5. The victim was jogging alone at the time of the homicide. This factor increased the situational exposure of the victim.
6. There were no security features at the park and the entry gate was left open. This factor increased the situational exposure of the victim.

CRIME RECONSTRUCTION

A *crime reconstruction* is the determination of the actions and events surrounding the commission of a crime. A reconstruction may be accomplished by using the statements of witnesses, the confession of a suspect, the statement of a living victim, or by the examination and interpretation of physical evidence (Chisum and Turvey, 2007).

Findings

The available physical evidence supports the following sequence of events that occurred on Tuesday, November 14, 1978. Should any new information be provided, this sequence of events and the subsequent findings must be reconsidered.

1. At some point before 9:00 a.m., Armida Wiltsey left her residence and drove to the Lafayette Reservoir.
2. At some point before the attack on Armida Wiltsey, the evidence suggests that the victim walked by the portable toilets at the Lafayette Reservoir.
3. At some point after 9:00 a.m., the offender acquired the victim and immediately covered her mouth with his hand.
4. At some point after the offender acquired the victim, she engaged in physical resistance.
5. At some point after the victim resisted, the offender manually strangled the victim, causing her to lose consciousness and die. It is unknown whether the victim died immediately after the strangulation. The evidence suggests that this attack occurred in an area between the jogging path and the disposal site.
6. At some point after the victim was unconscious, her hands were bound.
7. At some point after the victim was unconscious, she was anally penetrated. The evidence suggests that the offender removed the victim's pants and underwear, pulled up the victim's shirt, and anally penetrated the victim while she was lying on her left side.
8. At some point after the offender penetrated the victim, the offender wiped off the object used in the penetration.
9. At some point after the attack, the offender removed the ligatures.
10. At some point after the offender removed the ligatures, the evidence suggests that the offender took the ligatures from the crime scene.
11. At some point after the attack, the offender carried the body of the victim to the disposal site and placed her there.

Discussion

1. At some point before 9:00 a.m., Armida Wiltsey left her residence and drove to the Lafayette Reservoir. This is supported by the following facts:
   a) According to the police interview with Boyd Wiltsey, Armida Wiltsey was at home that morning.
   b) According to the police interview with Gail Overra, Armida Wiltsey's vehicle was seen across from the Lafayette Reservoir at approximately 9:00 a.m.
2. At some point before the attack on Armida Wiltsey, the evidence suggests that the victim walked by the portable toilets at the Lafayette Reservoir. This is supported by the following facts:
   a) The bloodhound search for the victim started at the victim's car and proceeded to the portable toilets before locating the victim's body.
   b) Crime scene photos reveal sand on the bottom of the victim's shoes and footprints in the sand near the portable toilets at the reservoir. The footprints match the pattern of the victim's shoes. This suggests that the victim walked in this area, however, the footprints cannot be individuated (Chisum and Turvey, 2007). It is unknown whether the footprints were left on the day of the homicide.
3. At some point after 9:00 a.m., the offender acquired the victim and immediately covered her mouth with his hand. This is supported by the following facts:
   a) According to police interviews, witnesses at the Lafayette Reservoir did not report hearing any screams or unusual noises. This suggests the offender immediately covered the victim's mouth to functionally prevent her from screaming.

  b) Autopsy photos reveal injuries to the victim's mouth that are consistent with control-oriented force. They also reveal a contusion on the victim's lower lip in the shape of a finger. This injury indicates that the victim was struggling with the offender upon the initial application of force.

4. At some point after the offender acquired the victim, she engaged in physical resistance. This is supported by the following fact:
   a) Criminalistic reports and autopsy photos reveal debris, including fibers, tissue and traces of blood, under the victim's fingernails. This evidence suggests that that victim scratched the offender.
5. At some point after the victim resisted, the offender manually strangled the victim, causing her to lose consciousness and die. It is unknown whether the victim died immediately after the strangulation. The evidence suggests that this attack occurred in an area between the jogging path and the disposal site. This is supported by the following facts:
   a) The offender manually strangled the victim, causing her to lose consciousness and die.
      i. The victim's autopsy report reveals that the cause of death was asphyxiation due to neck trauma.
      ii. Autopsy photos evidence hand marks on the victim neck.
      iii. Autopsy photos reveal that the victim's blood was not pumping after the strangulation, indicating that she did not regain consciousness.
   b) The evidence suggests that the attack occurred in an area between the path and the disposal site.
      i. The reservoir was populated with joggers on the day of the homicide but the crime was not witnessed. This suggests that the attack did not occur on the jogging path.
      ii. The victim was moved to the disposal site after the attack (See *Crime reconstruction section 11* of report).
6. At some point after the victim was unconscious, her hands were bound. This is supported by the following facts:
   a) Autopsy photos reveal ligature marks on the victim's wrists.
   b) Autopsy photos reveal that the ligature marks do not contain tearing of the skin. This indicates that the victim was unconscious (or deceased) at the time she was bound.
7. At some point after the victim was unconscious, she was anally penetrated. The evidence suggests that the offender removed the victim's pants and underwear, pulled up the victim's shirt and anally penetrated the victim while she was lying on her left side. This is supported by the following facts:
   a) The offender removed the victim's pants and underwear.
      i. Crime scene photos evidence the victim naked from the waist down and partially covered with her jogging pants and underwear.
   b) The victim was anally penetrated.
      i. The victim was found naked from the waist down. This suggests that a sexual act took place.
      ii. Police reports and crime scene photos evidence fecal matter at the crime scene, on both the victim's buttocks and clothing. The presence and location of the fecal matter indicate anal penetration occurred.
      iii. The autopsy report reveals a linear tear of the victim's perineum. This injury is consistent with anal penetration.
   c) The evidence suggests that the victim was lying on her left side at the time she was penetrated.
      i. Autopsy photos evidence scratch marks and abrasions on the victim's left side. There is an absence of similar injuries anywhere else on the victim's body.
8. At some point after the offender penetrated the victim, the offender wiped off the object used in the penetration. This is supported by the following fact:
   a) Crime scene photos evidence fecal matter on the clothing of the victim. This suggests that the offender wiped off the material from the object used to penetrate the victim.

9. At some point after the attack, the offender removed the ligatures. This is supported by the following fact:
   a) Crime scene and autopsy photos evidence the victim without ligatures.
10. At some point after the offender removed the ligatures, the evidence suggests that the offender took the ligatures from the crime scene. However, this cannot be concluded until the twine found at the crime scene is further examined.
11. At some point after the attack, the offender carried the body of the victim to the disposal site and placed her there. This is supported by the following facts:
   a) Crime scene photos evidence the victim in a heavily bushed area that would significantly minimize the ability of the offender to sexually assault her in this location. The victim's autopsy report also reveals injuries that are inconsistent with the assault occurring at the disposal site. The victim would have injuries present on both sides of her body.
   b) The victim's injuries, including multiple scratch-type abrasions, are consistent with the victim being carried through the bushes to the disposal site.
   c) Crime scene photos reveal the victim's pants were caught above her on a branch, suggesting the victim was placed at the disposal site.
   d) Crime scene photos reveal a lack of drag marks or transfer material present on the victim's clothing, hair, and body, eliminating the possibility that she was dragged to the disposal site.

CRIME SCENE CHARACTERISTICS

Location type: The crime scene existed in an outdoor environment. The victim's body was found outside in a brushy area, exposed to the elements of nature. This is evident in crime scene photos, police sketches and police investigative reports.

Location of the scene: The crime scene in this case was in the southeast corner of the Lafayette Reservoir, located at 3949 Mount Diablo Road in Costa County, California. According to police reports, the victim's body was found 40 yards from the jogging path on the hillside, enclosed in brushy vegetation. The path was frequently used by joggers and had multiple access points, including foot trails from the parking lot and jeep trails from residential neighborhoods. The temperature on the evening of the homicide was 40–50 degrees Fahrenheit, as evidenced in the police reports and crime scene photos that reveal frost on the ground. The criminal history of the location is unknown.

Crime scene type: The known crime scene in this case was the *disposal site*[1] of the body. Crime scene and autopsy photos strongly suggest that the victim was moved to this location (see *Crime reconstruction* section of report). The location of the *primary crime scene*[2] is unknown. The primary crime scene cannot be established without a further search for evidence. This search should focus on reviewing the crime scene photos in an attempt to locate transfer evidence or fecal matter in the surrounding area, as well as clothing or other evidence that indicate the victim's presence in a specific location. The investigation should also focus on the victim's clothing in an attempt to locate transfer evidence that may suggest that she was assaulted in another location.

1 *Disposal site* is used to describe a crime scene where a body is found (Turvey, 2008).
2 *Primary crime scene* is the location where the offender engaged in the majority of his or her attack/assault upon the victim or victims (Turvey, 2008).

Victim selection: *Victim selection* refers to the process by which an offender intentionally chooses or targets a victim (Turvey, 2008). In this case, the evidence and location of the crime suggest that a prior relationship between the victim and offender was not necessary for the commission of the crime (see *Knowledge of victim* section of this report). The victim was an *opportunistic victim,* chosen based on availability and opportunity.

Victim location: *Victim location* refers to the characteristics of the victim's location prior to the *point of contact*. In this case, the victim location shares the same characteristics as the location of the scene (see *Location of the scene* section of report).

Point of contact: *Point of contact* refers to the precise location where the offender first approached or acquired the victim (Turvey, 2008). The point of contact in this case is unknown. Further investigation into the location of the primary crime scene may provide investigators with knowledge of where the victim was first contacted (refer to *Crime scene type* section of report).

Method of approach: *Method of approach* refers to the offender's strategy for getting close to a victim (Turvey, 2008). In this case, it is unknown whether the offender approached the victim with a surprise approach or a con approach. Crime scene photos suggest that the brushy area around the jogging trail may have provided the offender with the opportunity to surprise the victim at a moment of vulnerability. However, the offender may have also gained the victim's trust by use of deception. The method of approach cannot be inferred from the available evidence.

Method of attack: *Method of attack* refers to the offender's mechanism for initially overpowering a victim after making the approach. It is appropriate to describe a method of attack in terms of the weapon and the nature of the force involved (Turvey, 2008). In this case, the offender initially overpowered the victim by applying control-oriented force to her mouth (see *Use of force* section of report). Armida Wiltsey's autopsy photos evidence injuries to her mouth, consistent with force used to prevent the victim from screaming. A contusion is also evident near her lip that indicates she was struggling during this initial application of force.

Use of force: *Use of force* refers to the amount of force used by the offender during an attack(Turvey, 2008). The amount of force used against the victim in this case may be characterized as *lethal-force.*[3] The strangulation of the victim involved physically aggressive behavior that was sufficient to kill the victim. The strangulation may also be referred to as *control-oriented force,*[4] used to restrict the victim's movements by rendering her unconscious. The offender also engaged in control-oriented force by binding the victim's hands together to prevent movement and delay her escape. Control-oriented force was also applied to the victim's mouth to prevent her from screaming, and further used to move the victim from the initial point of contact to the location at which the attack occurred. It is the opinion of the examiner that the control-oriented behavior of the offender was functional.

Methods of control: *Method of control* refers to the means an offender uses to manipulate, regulate, restrain, and subdue victim behavior of any kind throughout the offense (Turvey, 2008). The offender applied multiple levels of control-oriented force to the victim during the commission of the offense (see *Use of force* section of report).

3 *Lethal force* is a term used to describe physically aggressive behavior that is sufficient to kill. It includes the intentional infliction of injuries to vital areas such as the head, heart, or neck. It may involve a weapon, chemical, or bare hands (Turvey, 2008).

4 *Control-oriented force* is a term used to describe the physically aggressive behavior that is intended to restrict victim movement.

Use of weapons: According to Armida Wiltsey's autopsy report, the victim died of asphyxiation due to neck trauma. The absences of gunshot wounds or other sharp force injuries indicate that no weapons were used in the commission of this crime.

Victim response: *Victim response* refers to the victim's reaction to offender behavior (adapted from Turvey, 2008). The criminalist report suggests that the victim engaged in physical resistance by scratching the offender. Traces of blood and debris found under the victim's fingernails were noted in the report and material under the victim's fingernails is also visible in autopsy photos. The contusion under the victim's mouth also suggests that the victim resisted the offender at the time her mouth was covered.

Verbal behavior: The injuries to the victim's mouth indicate that the offender applied control-oriented force to prevent her from screaming. This suggests that the verbal behavior of the victim was limited. The extent of the verbal behavior of the offender is unknown but police reports state that witnesses did not hear voices or unusual noises in the area.

Sexual acts: A *sexual act* is any offender behavior involving sexual organs, sexual apparatus, or sexualized objects (Turvey, 2008). Crime scene photos reveal that the victim was found naked from the waist down, suggesting that the offender engaged in a sexual act during the commission of the crime. The fecal matter found on the victim's clothing and buttocks indicates that the victim was anally penetrated (see *Crime reconstruction* section of report).

Time: The exact amount of time the offender spent with the victim is unknown.

Multiple offenders: There is no evidence in this case to suggest that multiple offenders were involved in the commission of this crime.

Evidence of planning: The extent of offender *planning* may be determined by assessing whether or not the offender possessed the means for the commission of the crime (Turvey, 2008). In this case, it is the opinion of the examiner that the offense was planned. This is supported by the fact that the offender chose a location which he or she knew would contain potential victims, the offender chose a location in which an offense could be carried out in a hidden area, the offender brought ligatures to the crime scene and the area itself was secluded and required offender knowledge (see *Knowledge of crime scene* section of report).

Opportunistic elements: *Opportunistic elements* refer to any unplanned elements that the offender seized on for inclusion in an offense (Turvey, 2008). The examiner found no evidence of the use of opportunistic elements in the commission of this crime, except the victim (see *Knowledge of victim* section of report).

Precautionary acts: *Precautionary acts* refer to behaviors that an offender commits before, during, or after an offense that are consciously intended to confuse, hamper, or defeat investigative or forensic efforts for the purpose of concealing the offender's identity, connection to the crime, or the crime itself (Turvey, 2008). It is the opinion of the examiner that the offender committed precautionary acts during the commission of the crime. This opinion is supported by the following facts:

1. The body of the victim was moved after she was attacked (see *Crime reconstruction* section of report). This suggests that the offender wanted to delay the investigative effort to find the body and draw investigative efforts away from the primary crime scene.
2. The offender removed the ligatures on the hands of the victim (see *Crime reconstruction* section of report). This suggests that the offender removed evidence that would link him or her to the crime scene.
3. The offender took the object used to penetrate the victim (see *Crime reconstruction* section of report).

4. The offender engaged in control-oriented force to prevent victim resistance. These behaviors intended to conceal the offender's identity by preventing individuals in the area from witnessing the crime. These behaviors included the manual strangulation of the victim to render her unconscious, the force applied to the victim's mouth to prevent her from screaming, and the ligatures used to bind the victim's hands to delay her escape.

Missing items: The only known items taken from the crime scene were the ligatures used to bind the victim's hands and the object that the offender used to penetrate the victim with (unless the offender's penis was used to penetrate the victim). It is the opinion of the examiner that the ligatures, and possible object, were evidentiary items, taken as a precautionary act.

The body: The body of the victim was carried to the disposal site at some point after the attack (see *Crime reconstruction* section of report).

Evidence of staging: *Staging* refers to a crime scene in which the offender has purposely altered evidence so as to mislead authorities or redirect the investigation (Turvey, 2008). It is the opinion of the examiner that there is no evidence to indicate that the offender attempted to stage this crime scene.

MOTIVATION

It is the opinion of the examiner that there are crime scene behaviors that support both a *power-reassurance* and *power-assertive* motivation. The basis for this opinion resides in the consideration of the following:

1. A *power-reassurance* motive is evidenced by crime scene behaviors that are intended to restore the offender's self-confidence or self-worth through the use of low-aggression means (Turvey, 2008).
   a. The lack of victim injuries is consistent with a power-reassurance motive.
   b. The placement of the victim in the disposal site is consistent with a power-reassurance motive.
2. A *power-assertive* motive is evidenced by crime scene behaviors that intend to restore the offender's self-confidence or self-worth through the use of moderate to high aggression means (Turvey, 2008).
   a. The sexual behavior the offender engaged in with the victim reflects a power-assertive motive.
   b. The victim was unconscious and therefore not involved in the sexual act. The offender forced the victim to submit to the offender's sexual behavior. This behavior is consistent with a power-assertive motive.
3. The examiner can eliminate the possibility of an *anger retaliatory*[5] motivation. The crime scene behaviors and victim injuries lack consistency with this motivation. The victim's injures would have evidenced high levels of force and *overkill*[6] and the crime scene behaviors would have evidenced anger.
4. The examiner can eliminate the possibility of a *sadistic motivation.*[7] This can be supported by the fact that there was a lack of torture inflicted on the victim. The autopsy photos reveal a lack of injuries consistent with torture and the victim was unconscious at the time of the sexual attack, eliminating a necessary component of sadism (Turvey, 2008). The crime also lacked a controlled environment. The reservoir was populated with joggers who would have witnessed elements of torture, including verbal resistance of the victim. The amount of time the offender would have to engage in sadistic behavior would be minimal at that location.

5 *Anger retaliatory* motive is evidenced by crime scene behaviors that indicate a great deal of rage, either toward a specific person, group, or institution, or a symbol of either (Turvey, 2008).

6 *Overkill* is injury beyond that needed to cause death. It involves the repeated infliction of injury subsequent to the application of lethal force (Turvey, 2008).

7 *Sadistic* crime scene behaviors are those that evidence offender sexual gratification from victim pain and suffering (Turvey, 2008).

5. The examiner can eliminate the possibility of a *profit motivation*.[8] This can be supported by the fact that the offender did not take any items of value from the victim. Police reports reveal the victim was found with her ring, earrings, and car keys.

OFFENDER CHARACTERISTICS

Knowledge of Crim Scenee

It is the opinion of the examiner that the offender had knowledge of the crime scene prior to the homicide. Local knowledge of the crime scene was not required, but the evidence suggests that the offender had, at the very minimum, knowledge of the existence of the location. This is supported by the fact that the Lafayette Reservoir is not a location that can be seen from the open road, suggesting that the offender had knowledge of the location and engaged in pre-surveillance. The level of planning associated with this offense suggests that it is unlikely that it was opportunistic or accidental (see *Evidence of planning* section of report).

A series of *contradictory acts* were also evident that increased the offender's likelihood of drawing the attention of the authorities and being identified during or subsequent to the crime (Turvey, 2008). The following contradictory acts were present:

1. The offense took place during daylight hours, increasing the likelihood that the victim or other witnesses in the area would identify the offender.
2. The offender acquired the victim while she was out for a routine jog. The victim was accountable to her capable guardians who would have noticed if she was gone for an extended period of time.

Familiarity with the crime scene increased the confidence level of the offender to the point at which the offender was comfortable enough to increase the level of risk associated with the crime, as evidenced by the offender's contradictory acts.

Knowledge of Victim

It is the opinion of the examiner that a prior relationship between the offender and the victim was not necessary for the commission of this crime. The crime took place in an area that was routinely populated with individuals, increasing the number of accessible victims. There is no further evidence to suggest that pre-surveillance of the victim occurred prior to the homicide.

Knowledge of Methods and Materials

It is the opinion of the examiner that the offender had both knowledge of the methods and materials that were used in the commission of this crime. Knowledge of materials was demonstrated by the fact that the offender brought the ligatures to the crime scene and possessed the physical ability and confidence to use them. However, no special skills or abilities were required to commit this crime (see *Evidence of criminal skill* section of report). Knowledge of methods is demonstrated by the fact that the offender knew how to control the victim and carry out the offense.

---

8 *Profit-oriented* behaviors include those that service material or personal gain (Turvey, 2008).

Evidence of Criminal Skill

Criminal skill may be thought of as a function of the offender's *planning* and their *precautionary acts* (Turvey, 2008). It is the opinion of the examiner that the offender had a *medium level of criminal skill*. This is demonstrated by the fact that the offender was skilled in the victim takedown, which resulted in little injury to the victim, suggesting that the offender had engaged in this type of behavior previously. The offender also possessed the criminal skill necessary to move the body to a hidden location and remove the ligatures on the victim's wrists.

The examiner cannot conclude the offender *lacked forensic awareness* because there is no evidence to indicate that the twine found at the crime scene was left by the offender. If the twine found at the scene was used in the crime, this may indicate a lack of forensic awareness or interruption. If the twine was not used in the crime, this may indicate forensic awareness because the offender took the ligatures from the crime scene to remove evidence that may have linked the offender to the crime. No other evidence was found that addressed the issue of forensic awareness.

Physical Characteristics

It is the opinion of the examiner that the offender possessed a level of physical strength necessary to carry the victim's body. The evidence indicates that the body of the victim was placed at the disposal site at some point after the attack (see *Crime reconstruction* section of report).

INVESTIGATIVE SUGGESTIONS

The following is a list of suggestions for further investigating and establishing the facts of this case:

1. A thorough examination of the crime scene photos and the photos of the surrounding area should be conducted in an attempt to locate the primary crime scene. Investigators should focus their attention on the photos in an attempt to locate possible fecal matter, transfer evidence, or other evidence that may indicate victim–offender interaction occurred. This should include:
   a. Photos of the location where the victim's earring was discovered.
   b. Photos of the area surrounding the portable toilets. According to the police reports, the bloodhounds traveled from the victim's car to portable toilets in the reservoir before locating the victim's body. This evidence coupled with the footprints in the area suggests that the victim was in this area prior to the attack. This may provide evidence that will assist in the location of the primary crime scene or the point of contact.
   c. The tissues found in the victim's vehicle should be tested in comparison to the tissues found in the reservoir.
2. The clothing of the victim should be examined in an attempt to locate transfer evidence that may suggest the location at which the offender acquired or assaulted the victim.
3. Thorough interviews should be conducted with the family and friends of the victim to establish a more thorough victimology. Victimological inquiries should include the following:
   a. The nature of the victim's relationships with other males.
   b. The nature of Daniel Wiltsey's drug problem.
   c. The reason why the victim was worried about taking her 10-year-old son to school on the day of the homicide.
   d. The criminal and mental history of Armida Wiltsey.

598 APPENDIX: **Threshold Assessment**

4. DNA tests should be conducted on the victim's fingernails clippings. John Patty examined fingernail clippings from the victim's hands and noted debris, including fibers and tissue. On two of the fingernails from the victim's right hand, he saw a very thin trace of blood.
5. DNA test should be conducted on the hairs found on the victim's clothing.
6. The vaginal and anal swabs of the victim should be tested for epithelial cells to indicate whether the victim was penetrated with a penis.
7. The fecal matter on the victim's clothing should be tested for transfer evidence and DNA.
8. Tests should be conducted on the twine found at the crime scene to determine whether the twine was used in the commission of the crime. This includes testing the twine for the victim's DNA and establishing whether the twine matches the victim's injuries evidenced in the autopsy photos.
9. Crime statistics from the Lafayette Reservoir and other parks in the area should be reviewed.
10. Offenders with a similar *modus operandi*[9] should be reviewed. These crimes include, but are not limited to, kidnapping, sexual assaults, and muggings.

The examiner is available for discussion of these suggestions.

Jodi Freeman, MCrim

REFERENCES

Chisum, J., Turvey, B., 2007. Crime Reconstruction. Elsevier, San Diego, CA.

Petherick, W., Turvey, B., 2009. Forensic Victimology. Elsevier, San Diego, CA.

Saferstein, R., 1998. Criminalistics: An Introduction to Forensic Science, sixth edition. Prentice-Hall, New York, NY.

Thornton, J.I., 1997. The General Assumptions and Rationale of Forensic Identification. In: Faigman, D.L., Kaye, D.H., Saks, M.J., Sanders, J. (Eds.), Modern Scientific Evidence: The Law and Science of Expert Testimony, vol. 2. West, St. Paul, MN.

Turvey, B., 2008. Criminal Profiling: An Introduction to Behavioral Evidence Analysis, third edition. Academic Press, London, England.

[9] *Modus operandi* is the offender's method of operation, consisting of their habits, techniques, and peculiarities of behavior (Turvey, 2008).

REFERENCES

Adelson, L., 1974. The Pathology of Homicide. Charles C. Thomas Publisher, Springfield, IL.

Burgess, A., Burgess, A., Douglas, J., Ressler, R., 1992. Crime Classification Manual. Lexington Books, New York.

Burgess, A., Douglas, J., Ressler, R., 1988. Sexual Homicide: Patterns and Motives. Lexington Books, New York.

Burgess, A.W., Ressler, R.K., et al., 1986. Sexual homicide: a motivational model. Journal of Interpersonal Violence 1 (3), 251–272.

Coker, D., Fall 1992. Heat of passion and wife killing: men who batter/men who kill. Southern California Review of Law and Women's Studies.

Crocker, P., 2001. Is the death penalty good for women? Buffalo Criminal Law Review 917.

Deming, J.E., Mittleman, R.E., Wetli, C.V., July 1983. Forensic science aspects of fatal sexual assaults on women. Journal of Forensic Sciences 28 (3), 572–576.

Dietz, P., Hazelwood, R., Warren, J., 1995. The criminal sexual sadist. In: Burgess, A.W., Hazelwood, R. (Eds.), Practical Aspects of Rape Investigation: A Multidisciplinary Approach, second ed. CRC Press, New York.

Florida v. Julio Ortiz., 2000. No. 3D99-2761, Aug. 23, 2000 (766 So.2d 1137).

Grubin, D., November 1994. Sexual murder. British Journal of Psychiatry 165 (5), 624–629.

MacCulloch, M.J., Snowden, P.R., Wood, P.J.W., Mills, H.E., 1983. Sadistic fantasy. Sadistic behavior and offending. British Journal of Psychiatry 143, 20–29.

Myers, W.C., 2001. Juvenile Sexual Homicide. Academic Press, London.

Myers, W.C., Burgess, A.W., Nelson, J.A., March 1998. Criminal and behavioral aspects of juvenile sexual homicide. Journal of Forensic Sciences 43 (2), 340–347.

Nobile, P., July 1989. The making of a monster. Playboy.

Palmer, C., Thornhill, R., 2000. A Natural History of Rape. MIT Press, Cambridge.

Ressler, R., Burgess, A., Douglas, J., Hartman, C., D'Agostino, R., September 1986. Sexual killers and their victims: identifying patterns through crime scene analysis. Journal of Interpersonal Violence 1 (3), 288–307.

Revitch, E., Schlesinger, L., 1983. Sexual dynamics in homicide and sexual assault. In: Revitch, E., Schlesinger, L. (Eds.), Sexual Dynamics of Anti-social Behavior. Charles C. Thomas Publisher, Springfield, IL.

Rossmo, D.K., 1995. Geographic Profiling: Target Patterns of Serial Murderers (Dissertation). Simon Frasier University.

CHAPTER

Applied Case Linkage Analysis

16

B.E. Turvey

Forensic Solutions LLC, Sitka, Alaska, United States; Institute of Forensic Investigation and Criminal Profiling, Juarez, Mexico

J. Freeman

Forensic Solutions LLC, Sitka, Alaska, United States; University of Western Ontario, London, ON, Canada

CHAPTER OUTLINE

One of the most important functions that can be served by crime scene analysis efforts is case linkage. As discussed in Turvey (2011), *case linkage*, also referred to as linkage analysis, is the process of determining whether there are discrete connections, or distinctive behavioral factors, that associate two or more previously unrelated cases by means of crime scene analysis. It involves establishing and comparing the physical evidence, victimology, crime scene characteristics, motivation, modus operandi (MO), and signature behaviors of each of the cases under review. It also requires consideration of both behavioral similarities and dissimilarities.

Case linkage is used in two separate and very different contexts: *investigative* and *forensic*.

With respect to investigative contexts, case linkage is used to assist law enforcement by helping to establish whether and when to apply investigative resources (eg, identifying serial or pattern cases, or closing cases by exceptional means). The linkage need not be very strong or certain to favor such a decision. This is because public safety is at issue, and the investigation is considered ongoing. Therefore, it is expected that more information may come later that changes these findings.

In forensic (a.k.a. legal) contexts, case linkage is employed to assist the court with determining whether or not there is sufficiently distinctive behavioral evidence

Behavioral Evidence Analysis. http://dx.doi.org/10.1016/B978-0-12-800607-8.00016-1

to connect crimes together in their commission. This determination can be used to help decide specific forensic issues, such as whether similar crimes may be tried together or whether similar past crimes may be brought in as evidence at trial. The legal threshold for a probative link is necessarily high and must involve the identification of a unique or distinctive pattern of behavioral factors (MO and signature alike) across all cases determined to be linked.

MAJOR ISSUES

There are a number of major issues to consider when conducting a linkage analysis.

First, it is an evaluation of offender MO and signature behaviors to include factors in victim selection and offender motivation. This means that it may or may not be pertinent to consider physical evidence depending on whether this is at issue. In many cases, linkage analysis will be used in court as a substitute for physical evidence—because it is absent. In this way, the prosecution may seek to use behavior to connect offenses with the same confidence as with DNA or fingerprint analysis.

Second, linkage analysis is a form of forensic examination resulting in an expert forensic opinion. It is not something that lawyers or the court should be determining on their own without expert assistance. There is, in some jurisdictions, case law to support this. However this does not stop those without any relevant education or training in the area from wading in and giving uniformed opinions.

Linkage analysis, just like any other form of forensic examination, is the domain of properly educated and trained forensic experts. When the court considers related opinions from any other source, it invites misunderstanding, confusion, and error. The courts have an obligation to ensure that they do not consider similar fact evidence and its introduction unless it comes from a credible expert source.

The final major issue here is that legitimate expertise in serial crime (and case linkage analysis) is rare. In fact, there is no shortage of experts who are willing to pretend (or wrongfully believe themselves) to be experts in this area. Further still, there are forensic examiners qualified in other unrelated areas who have no problem venturing into linkage analysis and giving expert opinions, all the while admitting their lack of expertise, and the court is quite willing to accept their testimony as evidence.

This convergence of these realities is a serious problem for not only the profession of criminal profiling, but also for the cause of actual justice as well. Forensic examiners have an ethical obligation to refrain from giving expert opinions when they are ignorant in a given subject, despite how helpful they think they are being. At the same time, the court has an obligation to bar such testimony when it comes from those who are either unqualified or trumpeting their lack of knowledge.

CASE REPORTS

Consider the following case reports prepared by this examiner for three different cases. In each case, forensic examiners can be found falsely reporting similarities as differences, cherry-picking findings, and giving expert opinions while admitting a lack of actual expertise:

Linkage Analysis: Washington v. Robert L. Yates (2002)

Robert Lee Yates, Jr. defied many of the inductive predictions that are frequently offered regarding serial murderers—he was married, had a good job, a nice home, many close friends, did not abuse drugs or alcohol, and had a devoted family. He was caught because of an old tip that finally made its way into the investigative forefront. As explained in Hornblower (2000)[a]:

Jennifer Joseph, 16, was a runaway, reported to be engaged in prostitution, from Spanaway. She was shot to death. Her body was found northeast of Spokane August 26, 1997.

> *It was the slick, shiny, vintage Corvette that ultimately led investigators to the suspect. A prostitute told police she had seen the killer's youngest victim, Jennifer Joseph, in the car nine days before her body was found. Joseph, a striking Asian-American teenager from Tacoma, had dropped out of high school only three months earlier. The hair of a Caucasian male was found on a towel near her decomposed corpse. Working through 6000 tips associated with more than*

[a]Excepted from Hornblower, M. "The Spokane Murders" *Time Magazine*, July 17, 2000, Vol. 156.

a dozen victims, police eventually compiled a database of all Corvette owners in Washington and Idaho and another of all Corvettes stopped by police checks. They tracked a car that had recently been sold and matched its carpet fibers to those on Joseph's shoes. Seizing the vehicle, they found bloodstains similar in genetic makeup to that of Joseph's parents. And they found a mother-of-pearl button identical to one on Joseph's blouse. They then tracked the car's previous owner.

On April 18, sheriff's deputies arrested Robert Lee Yates Jr., 47, on his way to work. His Honda Civic carried a bumper sticker saying WHY MUST I BE SURROUNDED BY FRICKIN' IDIOTS? Forensic experts found his fingerprint on one of the plastic bags tied around a victim's head, and Yates' genetic profile, from blood drawn after his arrest, matched semen found on the corpses. Says Sheriff Mark Sterk: "There's no doubt in my mind we're going to convict this guy." But at Yates' arraignment, the mother of one of the victims looked in disbelief at the accused killer, a balding father of five in a navy blue suit and wire-rimmed spectacles. "He looks like a little mouse," she said.

There's the wife of 23 years, the religious upbringing, the military career as a respected helicopter pilot, the new job as a $13.75-an-hour crane operator, the split-level home with forsythia bushes and a backyard barbecue. Yates sent out Christmas cards and won Army medals for meritorious service. "Bobby is a loving, caring, sensitive son; a fun-loving and giving brother; an understanding, generous and dedicated father who enjoys playing ball, fishing and camping with his kids," the Yates family said in their only statement to date. "Bobby is the type of person you would want to have as your best friend."

Yates grew up in Oak Harbor, Wash., a small town on picturesque Puget Sound, where his father was an inventory specialist at Whidbey Naval Air Station. His Seventh-Day Adventist family observed the Sabbath, avoided alcohol and pork and never used four-letter words. When their Oak Harbor church was destroyed in a fire, Yates Sr. and Jr. chipped in to reconstruct it. In high school Yates pitched for the baseball team, sang in the choir and picked vegetables in the summer. A "solid guy" and "Joe Average" is how classmates remember him.

After two years of premed at Walla Walla College, Yates married Linda Brewer, daughter of a prison guard, and at 25 enlisted in the Army. By the end of his 18-year career, Yates was a master aviator, instructing other pilots on how to teach flying. He was quiet, methodical and extraordinarily patient. Only one incident from his military record stands out: while on assignment in Somalia, Yates and his fellow soldiers spied a wild pig from their helicopter. Weary of Army rations, they shot it, swooped down and brought it back to cook in camp. The breach of discipline had no serious consequences.

Like many soldiers, Yates was a defender of the National Rifle Association, writing to a Watertown, N.Y., newspaper in 1994 and declaring, "If we seek answers to the crime problem, let's look to the criminal and focus on enforcement of existing laws, stiffer penalties, more prison space and deterrents to criminal activities."

Home videotapes of his possessions, seized after his arrest, show five handguns, among them two of the type used to kill the victims.

Yates did not retire from the military and move back to Washington until 1996, but police believe they can link him to several of the murders through his frequent vacations before then. In June 1996, three months after the Yateses moved to South Hill, a tony section of Spokane, a prostitute turned up dead. That fall, Linda Yates would later tell investigators, her husband failed to return home one night and showed up the next morning with blood all over the back of his van. He claimed he had run over a dog and transported the animal and its owner to a veterinarian.

She believed him. "Bells and lights would normally go off," says Sterk. "But this guy hid everything from his family. I'm convinced his wife and daughters didn't have a clue." But there were also signs of domestic trouble. He was charged with a misdemeanor when his daughter Amber, 19, filed a complaint that he had hit her.

The case was still pending when he was arrested on more serious charges. It was not until September 1999 when sheriff's deputies, working their way through Corvette owners, called in Yates. He had sold his Corvette in 1998, but before that he had been stopped twice in it for traffic violations, once near East Sprague, once near the burial site of a victim. Yates told investigators he had not patronized prostitutes in Spokane, but they noted in their report that he was "sweating profusely." He refused to provide DNA samples. Several weeks later, police pulled him over as he was driving a Honda Civic with a known prostitute in the passenger seat. He was not charged with a crime until, a few months later, a crime lab analyzed fibers from the Corvette he had owned.

On May 31 Yates was arraigned on charges of murdering eight women, all allegedly engaged in prostitution and drug use. He was also charged with robbing and attempting to kill Christine Smith. Hands folded before him, Yates looked more like a solemn insurance adjuster than a criminal. He pleaded not guilty on all counts.

In 2000, Yates pleaded guilty to killing 10 women, mostly prostitutes and/or drug addicts, and the attempted murder of another woman in Spokane County from 1996 to 1998. He also admitted killing a young couple picnicking near Walla Walla in 1975, when he was a guard at the Washington State Penitentiary and he confessed killing a 23-year-old Seattle woman, Stacy Elizabeth Hawn, in Skagit County in December 1988. Consequently, a judge sentenced him to 408 years in prison. He made these confessions as part of a plea arrangement to avoid the death penalty.

However, not every concerned jurisdiction in Washington state signed on to the deal. In a move that is the basis for an unresolved appeal filed in late 2006, the Pierce County prosecutor's office, acting on their own, filed charges of first-degree murder against Yates. They wanted him to get the death penalty for murdering Melinda Mercer, 24, in 1997 and Connie LaFontaine Ellis, 35, in 1998.

In order to prove Yates' guilt in the two Pierce County cases, prosecutors relied in part on behaviorally linking those crimes to the killings he had already confessed to. They brought in two experts whose testimony they could all but guarantee; Robert Keppel, PhD (a former homicide detective and retired chief investigator for the Washington State Attorney General's Office) and FBI profiler Mark Safarik. They got in line to testify that the crimes had a signature and that the same person must have committed them, even though they disagreed on some points.

The author was hired by the defense to peer review their methods and conclusions. Subsequent to the submission of the report below, Robert Keppel was barred from giving testimony and Mark Safarik's expertise in the area of linkage analysis was revealed to the court as sorely lacking. The trial judge learned that Safarik was not an expert on the subject. But the prosecution needed him. The judge, in a rare move, qualified Safarik to testify in Yates as an "expert by proxy"—because he ostensibly hung out with agents at the FBI who possessed this expertise, some of it must have rubbed off.

Yates was convicted, sentenced to death, and the case is currently under appeal.

CASE REPORT

May 28, 2002
Re: Washington v. Robert L. Yates—Linkage Analysis

Mary Kay High, an attorney representing Robert Yates, asked this examiner, Brent E. Turvey, MS of Sitka, Alaska to evaluate the nature, methodology, and content relating to conclusions provided in a "*Criminal Investigative Analysis*" report dated February 7, 2002 prepared by FBI SSA Mark Safarik, as well as the "*Modus Operandi and Signature Analysis*" report dated March 26, 2002 by Robert D. Keppel, PhD.

In order to complete this particular task, I was provided with, and examined, the following case material:

1. Professional Resume of FBI SSA Mark E. Safarik
2. Criminal Investigative Analysis report dated 2/7/02 by FBI SSA Mark Safarik
3. Professional Resume of Robert D. Keppel, PhD
4. Modus Operandi and Signature Analysis report dated 3/26/02 by Robert D. Keppel, PhD
5. Material related to the operation of the HITS (Homicide Investigation and Tracking System) database (manual, guidelines, policies, personnel background, etc.)
6. Individual victim HITS forms
7. Memo from John Turner, Chief Criminal Investigator of HITS to Mary Kay High, Attorney for Robert L. Yates, dated April 30, 2002.

CONCLUSIONS

Conclusion #1—It is the opinion of this examiner that the conclusions rendered in the "Criminal Investigative Analysis" report dated February 7, 2002 prepared by FBI SSA Mark Safarik are not supported by the evidence and reasoning provided and are based on flawed methodology.

Conclusion #2—It is the opinion of this examiner that the conclusions rendered in the "Modus Operandi and Signature Analysis" report dated March 26, 2002 by Robert D. Keppel, PhD are deficient as they stand unsupported by the evidence cited and are based on an unreliable database.

CONCLUSION #1

FBI SSA Mark Safarik was contacted by the Tacoma Police Department and the Pierce County District Attorney's office to perform a behavioral review of the following homicide cases to determine linkage: Melinda Mercer, Connie Ellis, Shannon Zielinski, Jennifer Joseph, Heather Hernandez, Darla Scott, Shawn Johnson, Lauri Wason, Sunny Oster, Linda Maybin, Michelyn Derning, Melody Murfin, Patrick Oliver, and Susan Savage. Also reviewed was the attempted homicide of Christine Smith (15 victims in total).

It is the opinion of this examiner that the conclusions rendered in the "Criminal Investigative Analysis" report dated February 7, 2002 prepared by FBI SSA Mark Safarik are not supported by the evidence and reasoning provided.

The basis for this opinion is the consideration of the following facts:

1. The supported conclusions are not distinctive.
2. The report makes extensive assumptions about offense-related behavior and circumstances that are not entirely supported by the existing evidence.
3. The report paradoxically argues that clear differences are actually similarities.
4. The conclusions of the report rely upon a deficient method that has been roundly criticized, as well as a cause for reversal, in recent court cases.
5. The report is provided without the strongly worded disclaimer that appears in the investigative reports prepared by this agency.

Nondistinctive Conclusions

The conclusions in this report that can be supported are not distinctive.

A. The "Criminal Investigative Analysis" report concludes, "The offender targeted specific areas where prostitutes could be found." While this appears to be a true statement, it is hardly distinctive. Areas frequented by prostitutes are a draw for all manner of violent crimes and violent criminals. Prostitutes themselves are a nexus for criminal activity, often both the perpetrators and victims of violent crime.
B. The "Criminal Investigative Analysis" report concludes, "All of the victims died from handgun gunshot wounds." While true, this is hardly distinctive. Many people die from handgun gunshot wounds.

C. The "Criminal Investigative Analysis" report concludes, "All of the victims except for Oliver were shot in the head." While true, this is hardly distinctive. Many people who are shot and killed are shot in the head.

D. The "Criminal Investigative Analysis" report concludes, "All of the victims except Smith (survived) had been transported from the location where they were killed to a dump site." While possibly true, this would not be distinctive. It is common for victims of homicide to be transported to a disposal site to (1) facilitate their discovery, (2) dissociate the offender from the offense, and/or (3) conceal the location of the actual offense and related evidence.

E. The "Criminal Investigative Analysis" report concludes, "The disposition of all the murdered victims bodies except Murfin (for obvious reasons) would be described as dumped with minimal effort to prevent discovery." This conclusion is not a fact; rather it is a matter of opinion. Minimal effort to prevent discovery suggests that the body was left in plain view with few precautionary acts. In any case, this conclusion is hardly distinctive, and given the broad continuum of disposal behavior evidence in these cases, this conclusion hardly represents a theme.

F. The "Criminal Investigative Analysis" report concludes, "All the body dumps except Savage and Oliver were adjacent to roadways." This conclusion is hardly distinctive. Many bodies are disposed of adjacent to roadways. Also, given the broad continuum of disposal behavior evidence in these cases, this conclusion hardly represents a theme.

G. The "Criminal Investigative Analysis" report concludes, "All the female victims were either sexually assaulted or exhibited evidence of a sexual assault component to the crime." While this may be true, it is hardly distinctive. Female victims of homicide are regularly the victims of a sexual assault. However, this conclusion may not be true—this examiner is not willing to concede that all of the victims exhibited evidence of a "sexual assault component" until such time as this term is carefully defined in use. The more inclusive the term, the less distinctive it is.

Assumptions About Offense Behavior

The report makes extensive assumptions about offense-related behavior and circumstances that are not entirely supported by the existing evidence. This is not a legitimate forensic practice.

A. The "Criminal Investigative Analysis" concludes, "All of the victims except Savage and Oliver were prostitutes with drug abuse histories." This conclusion is partially an assumption. To this examiner's knowledge, the drug use history of every victim has not been established and confirmed by the physical evidence. In some cases, the physical evidence was not available to make that determination due to advanced decomposition (Zielinski, Joseph, Henandez, Murfin, and Ellis).

Furthermore, this conclusion does not help support the notion of a single offender. It suggests the possibility of the opposite. It is accepted that high-risk activity (such as drug use and prostitution) actually increases the potential suspect pool dramatically.

B. The "Criminal Investigative Analysis" report concludes, "All of the victims except Savage and Oliver disappeared while engaged in prostitution." This conclusion is actually an assumption. To this examiner's knowledge, the precise activity of the victims prior to their disappearance has not been reliably established. The report itself explains this on p. 4, when it states that each victim "was believed to be engaged in prostitution. In other words, there was nothing to suggest that any of the victims disappeared while engaged in other activities not involved in prostitution." There is also nothing to definitively show that they must have been engaging in prostitution. What an examiner believes and what the evidence can prove are significantly different issues. This speaks to the difference between an investigative opinion and a forensic (court-worthy) opinion.

C. The "Criminal Investigative Analysis" report concludes, "All of the victims, although fitting a similar victim type appear to have been victims of opportunity." This is an assumption. Since there has been no definitive evidence of the precise activities of all of the victims at the time of the attacks, it cannot be reliably established how the victims were acquired. That is to say, we cannot know for certain whether victims were preselected and surveilled by an offender or not. This is an uninformed speculation (a blanket crime reconstruction) built on the assumption that each victim was attacked by someone employing them as a prostitute.

D. The "Criminal Investigative Analysis" report concludes, "With all of the victims there was a noted absence of any other serious injury except the gunshot wounds." This is an assumption. In several cases, decomposition precluded a conclusive finding by obscuring areas of potential physical injury: absence of evidence is not evidence of absence—it is inconclusive.

The report deals with this on p. 17 by using phrases like "it appears that" and "it is common" and "typically" rather than talking about the inconclusive nature of the findings in these cases. In short, those cases where a finding is inconclusive must be excluded from the linkage. To assume the absence of injury under such a circumstance is not a legitimate forensic practice.

E. The "Criminal Investigative Analysis" report concludes, "None of the victims sustained observable defensive injuries." This is not only an assumption; it is redundant of the previous conclusion. Again, decomposition precluded a conclusive finding by obscuring areas of potential physical injury in several cases; absence of evidence is not evidence of absence—it is inconclusive. Those cases where the findings of injury are inconclusive must be excluded from the linkage. To assume the absence of injury under such a circumstance is not a legitimate forensic practice.

F. The "Criminal Investigative Analysis" report concludes, "The lack of identifiable injury, which suggests they were captured by force and the nature of the interaction between prostitutes and their customers strongly suggests that the offender gained the trust and cooperation of all the victims through the use of a ruse." This is an uninformed speculation (a blanket crime reconstruction).

G. The "Criminal Investigative Analysis" report concludes, "Ten of the female victims including Mercer and Ellis had personal items to include jewelry and or clothing taken." According to Chisum & Turvey (2000):

> *The general term* Evidence Dynamics *has been developed by the authors to refer to any influence that changes, relocates, obscures, or obliterates physical evidence, regardless of intent.*

Given evidence dynamics, it is not reasonable to assume that items missing from a crime scene were taken, let alone taken by an offender. They may have simply gone undetected at the scene, for starters, or animals may have moved them. In any case, what happened to the items has not been reliably established, and remains a matter of speculation only.

Differences Reported as Similarities

The report paradoxically argues that clear differences are actually similarities. This is not a legitimate forensic practice.

A. The "Criminal Investigative Analysis" report concludes, "The targeted victim group was consistent; female, white or light skinned, and late 20s to late 30s." This conclusion demonstrates dissimilarity. The report tries to explain away these dissimilarities on p. 16, but only highlights them further by stating that some were older than the range and some were younger than the range, and ultimately chronological age is problematic in this group because of the hard lifestyle of the victims. In any case, the report describes the victim selection criteria as "generalized victim criteria" rather than specific. All of this amounts to the fact that the victims were of varying ages and of varying races. This is subsequently not a thematic or distinctive issue.

B. The "Criminal Investigative Analysis" report concludes, "Twelve of the fifteen victims were shot *only* in the head." This conclusion demonstrates dissimilarity. 12 of 15 victims were shot only in the head. 3 of 15 were not. In any case, as previously discussed, this is hardly distinctive. Many people who are shot and killed are shot in the head.

C. The "Criminal Investigative Analysis" report concludes, "All of the victims except Savage, Oliver, and Joseph were shot with a .25 caliber handgun. Joseph was shot with a .22 caliber. Savage and Oliver were shot with a large caliber. Although the offender changed weapons with Murfin's murder, he still chose a Raven Arms Inc. .25 caliber handgun. This suggests that the offender was comfortable with this weapon, it performed the way he wanted it to, and he saw no need to change what had proven to be successful for him." This conclusion demonstrates dissimilarity in the caliber of weapon used for various offenses. Different offenses involved different weapons. Moreover, .25 caliber handguns are not distinctive—they are a common street weapon among pimps, prostitutes, and drug dealers/users because they are inexpensive and easy to conceal.

D. The "Criminal Investigative Analysis" report concludes, "Johnson, Wason, Oster, Maybin, and Mercer were all linked by exact matches from Magtech .25 caliber bullets. Hernandez's bullets came from the same gun for investigative purposes but could not be identified as an exact match. Zielinski matched the same brand of bullets as all .25 caliber victims. The holes in Scott's skull indicated a .25 caliber round." This conclusion not only demonstrates dissimilarity in the caliber of weapon used for various offenses, but also inclusiveness related to the weapons used where the caliber does appear to match. Either the item is consistent across the cases or it is not consistent. If it is not, then the cases do not show a linkage and must be excluded.

E. The "Criminal Investigative Analysis" report concludes, "Seven victims had their heads covered in plastic bags including Mercer and Ellis. One had plastic bags associated with her body. Two had towels associated with their bodies. Three and possibly four were outdoor scenes with no need for plastic bags. One victim survived." This conclusion demonstrates the great dissimilarity in specific disposal activities. Its inclusion seems at odds with proving behavioral similarities or a theme across all of the cases.

F. The "Criminal Investigative Analysis" report concludes, "Six of the victims including Mercer exhibit evidence of postmortem sexual assault." This conclusion demonstrates dissimilarity. 6 of 15 victims exhibit evidence of postmortem sexual assault. 9 of 15 do not. Either the item is consistent across the cases or it is not consistent. If it is not, then the cases do not show a linkage and must be excluded.

G. The "Criminal Investigative Analysis" report concludes, "Ten of the female victims including Mercer and Ellis had personal items to include jewelry and or clothing taken." Aside from being a great assumption, as previously discussed, this conclusion demonstrates dissimilarity. 5 of 15 victims did not show that jewelry and or clothing had apparently been taken. Either the item is consistent across the cases or it is not. If it is not, then the cases do not show a linkage and must be excluded.

Deficient Method

The conclusions in this report rely upon a profiling method developed and taught by the Federal Bureau of Investigation referred to as *linkage analysis* or *Link-Analysis*. This method has been roundly criticized by the court in New Jersey v. Steven Fortin (2000) and Pennsylvania v. Christopher Distefano (1999). For a detailed review of these cases and the related offender identification issues, please see Turvey (2000), included with this affidavit.

Absence of Disclaimer

According to Hazelwood (1995, pp. 176–177), a criminal profile, aka—Criminal Investigative Analysis (Depue et al., 1995, p. 115 and *Cooper and King*, 2001, p. 10), is an investigative tool only. As such, the following disclaimer precedes each such report prepared by members of the FBI's BSU (Behavioral Science Unit).

> *It should be noted that the attached analysis is not a substitute for a thorough and well-planned investigation and should not be considered all inclusive. The information provided is based upon reviewing, analyzing, and researching criminal cases similar to the case submitted by the requesting agency. The final analysis is based upon probabilities. Note, however, that no two criminal acts or criminal personalities are exactly alike and, therefore, the offender may not always fit the profile in every category.*

This caution indicated by the disclaimer is explained in Depue et al. (1995, p. 125), where it is stated that:

> *CIA [Criminal Investigative Analysis] and profiling should be used to augment proven investigative techniques and must not be allowed to replace those methods; to do so would be counterproductive to the goal of identifying the unknown offender.*

This examiner has read this disclaimer on similar reports drawn up by FBI BSU personnel when reviewing their investigative reports. However, this examiner has made note that this disclaimer is absent from reports submitted by BSU personnel during a trial, when expert testimony may be needed. It could be argued that the inclusion of such a disclaimer at trial might tend to hamper admissibility because it addresses the issue of limited reliability. It seems significant, however, as the conclusions are based on the same methodology as reports prepared by the BSU during an investigation.

CONCLUSION #2

Robert D. Keppel, PhD was contacted by the Tacoma Police Department and the Pierce County District Attorney's office to perform a behavioral review of the following homicide cases to determine linkage: Melinda Mercer, Connie Ellis, Shannon Zielinski, Jennifer Joseph, Heather Hernandez, Darla Scott, Shawn Johnson, Lauri Wason, Sunny Oster, Linda Maybin, Michelyn Derning, and Melody Murfin (12 victims in total).

It is the opinion of this examiner that the conclusions rendered in the "Modus Operandi and Signature Analysis" report dated March 26, 2002 by Robert D. Keppel, PhD are deficient as they stand, unsupported by the evidence cited, and are based on an unreliable database.

The basis for this opinion is the consideration of the following facts.

1. The report makes assumptions about pertinent offense-related behavior and circumstances that are not entirely supported by the existing evidence.
2. The "Linking of Cases by Crime Laboratory Analyses and Results: Firearm Evidence" section explains that clear limitations exist in the firearms evidence. This shows a negative total linkage.
3. The "Linking of Cases by Crime Laboratory Analyses and Results: DNA Evidence" section explains that clear limitations exist in the DNA evidence. This shows a negative total linkage.

4. The "Modus Operandi" section paradoxically argues that the MO changed from one case to the next. This shows a negative total linkage.
5. The "Signature Analyses" section includes highly emotional, speculative, and unsupported opinions about the offender's specific state of mind during specific acts.
6. The data in the HITS case database are unreliable.
7. The case linkage error rate for HITS is unknown.
8. The false negative case linkage rate for the HITS database is unknown.
9. The false positive case linkage rate for the HITS database is unknown.

Assumptions About Offense Behavior/Unsupported Conclusions

The report makes extensive assumptions about offense-related behavior and circumstances that are not entirely supported by the existing evidence. This is not a legitimate forensic practice.

A. According to the "Modus Operandi and Signature Analysis" report (p. 15), the offender preselected his weapon in all of the offenses and all of the offenses were sexually oriented. The offender apparently preselected different weapons, showing variation and not similarity. Furthermore, there is no explanation of evidence provided to support the statement that these are sexually oriented offenses.
B. According to the "Modus Operandi and Signature Analysis" report (p. 15), most sexually oriented murders involve hands on killing such as strangulation, bludgeoning, or stabbing. Furthermore, "Evidence of these types of injuries from such types of killings was absent in all of the cases." This is an assumption. Additionally, this statement could be used to argue against the report's previous conclusion that these were sexually oriented killings (ie,if most sexually oriented murders have these elements, and these elements are absent, the evidence is less consistent with a sexually oriented offense, especially when evidence of sexual activity is absent).
C. According to the "Modus Operandi and Signature Analysis" report (p. 15), "the placement of gunshots to the head of each victim is a signature element of this killer." If this is indeed true, why was this not true in each case, and why did the number of shots vary? Also, why did the weapon vary? Given these variances, it is difficult to view the headshots as truly signature oriented or "unchanging." This conclusion appears unsupported. It should be noted that this is the only behavior referred to as a "signature element."

Firearms Evidence Differences Presented as Similarities

The "Linking of Cases by Crime Laboratory Analyses and Results: Firearm Evidence" section paradoxically presents clear differences and limited reliable linkage across the cases. While there are some similarities and linkages within the firearms evidence, there are serious limitations inherent in the evidence as well, which this section explores. This is evidence of a negative total linkage.

This examiner is at a loss as to why this section is relevant to the opinion that the same person must have committed all of the offenses.

DNA Differences Presented as Similarities

The "Linking of Cases by Crime Laboratory Analyses and Results: DNA Evidence" section paradoxically presents clear differences and limited reliable linkage across the cases using the available DNA evidence. While there are apparently reliable linkages within the DNA evidence, there are serious limitations as well because of negative findings in the Zielinski, Hernandez, Joseph, and Ellis cases, which this section explains. This is evidence of a negative total case linkage.

This examiner is at a loss as to why this section is relevant to the opinion that the same person must have committed all of the offenses.

MO Changed From One Murder to the Next

The "Modus Operandi" section states that the offender's MO "changed from one murder to the next." This includes elements such as victim age, race, time of day, and disposal sites. This would seem to contradict the Criminal Investigative Analysis report dated 2/7/02 by FBI SSA Mark Safarik. This is also evidence of a negative total case linkage.

Emotional, Speculative, and Unsupported Opinions About State of Mind

The "signature analyses" section is primarily comprised of highly emotional, speculative, and unsupported opinions about the offender's specific state of mind during specific acts. Little room is made for alternative, functional (MO-oriented) explanations of offense-related behavior in this section. While certainly entertaining, and the type of material one expects in a true crime novel, this examiner is of the professional opinion that critiquing this section of the report would have the unfortunate effect of raising it to a level that it does not deserve.

It can be said that the statistics provided in this section relevant to issues of behavioral rarity are not cited as part of any published study in the report. Furthermore, rarity is not the same as distinctiveness. A discussion of this difference is avoided in the report.

Unreliable Homicide Investigation and Tracking System Data

The data in the HITS case database are unreliable (and subsequent conclusions drawn from the data are equally unreliable) for the following reasons:

A. HITS data uncritically rely on information and opinions provided by the requesting agency as reliable (according to the Memo from John Turner, Chief Criminal Investigator of HITS to Mary Kay High dated April 30, 2002, p. 2, Q11).

B. Many of the HITS form fields involve providing crime reconstruction opinions that may be beyond the ken of a given criminal investigator.

C. Many of the HITS form fields involve subjectively derived profiling-oriented, legal, and psychiatric opinions rather than objective facts (motive, psychopathy, victim risk, face covering, symbolic artifacts, offender anger, and offender lifestyle). It should also be noted that the HITS Coding manual uses the term "Crazy People" to define the mental/insane category and inaccurately defines psychopathic as someone who commits psychotic offenses.

D. The HITS database is apparently populated by case information at various levels of verification and reliability.

E. The HITS database is populated by an unknown number of unverified cases drawn from media/newspaper accounts (according to HITS SOP, Newspaper Descriptions dated 9/5/95 as well as the Memo from John Turner, Chief Criminal Investigator of HITS to Mary Kay High dated April 30, 2002, p. 2, Q6).

Unknown Case Linkage Error Rate

The case linkage error rate for HITS or those using HITS results is unknown.

A. According to job description information provided in relation to HITS, Tamara Matheny (a HITS crime analyst) maintains a monthly log of all positive investigative analyses. I have not seen this log in the discovery material provided.

B. According to the Memo from John Turner, Chief Criminal Investigator of HITS to Mary Kay High dated April 30, 2002 (p. 3, Q17), asking for a showing of the error rate of HITS is too vague. This answer seems evasive. It is apparently not known how often probabilistic HITS linkages are right and how often they are wrong.

Without this information, the reliability of HITS query results must remain in question.

False Negatives

The false negative case linkage rate for the HITS database is unknown. That is to say, it is not known how often HITS results, or the interpretation of HITS results, have unlinked a known offender and their known offense. This is stated in the memo from John Turner, Chief Criminal Investigator of HITS to Mary Kay High dated April 30, 2002 (p. 3, Q19). Without this information, the reliability of HITS query results must remain in question.

False Positives

The false positive case linkage rate for the HITS database is unknown. That is to say, it is not known how often HITS results, or the interpretation of HITS results, have linked a known offender and an offense known to have been committed by another offender. This is stated in the Memo from John Turner, Chief Criminal Investigator of HITS to Mary Kay High dated April 30, 2002 (p. 3, Q20). Without this information, the reliability of HITS query results must remain in question.

Brent E. Turvey, MS.

REFERENCES

Chisum, W.J., Turvey, B., January 2000. Evidence dynamics: Locard's exchange principle & crime reconstruction. Journal of Behavioral Profiling 1 (1).

Depue, R., Douglas, J., Hazelwood, R., Ressler, R., 1995. Criminal investigative analysis: an overview. In: Burgess, A., Hazelwood, R. (Eds.), Practical Aspects of Rape Investigation, second ed. CRC Press, Boca Raton.

Hazelwood, R., 1995. Analyzing the rape and profiling the offender. In: Burgess, A., Hazelwood, R. (Eds.), Practical Aspects of Rape Investigation, second ed. CRC Press, Boca Raton.

New Jersey v. Steven Fortin, No.A-95/96–98, Supreme Court of New Jersey, 2000.

Pennsylvania v. Christopher Distefano, Case No. 99–0640, 1999.

Turvey, B., May 2000. Criminal profiling and the problem of forensic individuation. Journal of Behavioral Profiling 1 (2).

SUPPLEMENTAL REPORT - DRAFT

Forensic Examiner
Brent E. Turvey, MS, Forensic Criminologist
Forensic Solutions, LLC
Sitka, Alaska
www.forensic-science.com
bturvey@forensic-science.com

Date of Report
November 29, 2011

Report for
Dana-Marie Forbes, LLB, Senior Procurator Fiscal Depute
Frank Mulholland, QC, Solicitor-General
Crown Office and Procurator Fiscal Service (COPFS)
Edinburgh, Scotland
http://www.copfs.gov.uk

In Re: *Thomas R. Young v. HM Advocate*

Purpose

On September 27, 2010, this examiner submitted a Linkage Analysis report regarding this matter which, in large part, examined similarities and differences between the following murders: Mary Gallacher, Frances Barker, Anna Kenny, Hilda McAulay, Christine Eadie, Helen Scott and Agnes Cooney. That report revealed (p.13)" "significant behavioral and motivational dissimilarities that refute any suggestion of a probative link" between those cases. That report also revealed (p.13): "no behavioral evidence" that those cases "share behavioral factors unique enough to suggest that a single offender must be responsible."

The purpose of this supplemental report is to assess specific elements of the record and address their impact on the findings in this examiners original Linkage Analysis report. Specifically, the trial of Thomas Ross Young in 1977; the first "BEHAVIOURAL INVESTIGATIVE ADVISOR'S REPORT" by Lee Rainbow, dated June 4, 2004; and the second "BEHAVIOURAL INVESTIGATIVE ADVISOR'S REPORT" by Lee Rainbow, dated May 28, 2010.

Materials

The conclusions in this report are based on an examination of the following evidence:

- *H.M. Advocate v. Thomas Ross Young*, re: Frances Barker, trial transcripts, October 19-21 & 24, 1977;

- The "BEHAVIOURAL INVESTIGATIVE ADVISOR'S REPORT" by Lee Rainbow, dated June 4, 2004;

- The "BEHAVIOURAL INVESTIGATIVE ADVISOR'S REPORT" by Lee Rainbow, dated May 28, 2010.

Findings

1. ***H.M. Advocate v. Thomas Ross Young*, re: Frances Barker, trial transcripts, October 19-21 & 24, 1977**

   An examination of the trial transcripts in *H.M. Advocate v. Thomas Ross Young* (1977) does not reveal any evidence that conflicts with the findings provided in this examiner's Linkage Analysis report dated September 27, 2010. This is based on at least the following facts:

   A. This examiner relied on the testimony provided in these transcripts, in part, when rendering Section VII: "CRIME ANALYSIS – Frances Barker".

B. The guilty verdict in this case was based on physical evidence associating the victim and the defendant, who were strangers at the time, with no indication of malfeasance or tampering.

C. The guilty verdict in this case is in alignment with this examiner's Linkage Analysis report, in that there is no behavioral evidence to suggest that the person who was convicted of the murder Frances Barker must also have been responsible for the other murders under consideration.

2. **BEHAVIOURAL INVESTIGATIVE ADVISOR'S REPORT by Lee Rainbow, dated June 4, 2004**

The "BEHAVIOURAL INVESTIGATIVE ADVISOR'S REPORT" by Lee Rainbow, dated June 4, 2004 provides opinions that conflict with this examiner's Linkage Analysis report dated September 27, 2010. However, a careful examination of Mr. Rainbow's 2004 report does not reveal evidence or information that would cause this examiner to alter those 2010 findings. This is based on at least the following facts:

A. Mr. Rainbow's 2004 report is offered as investigative, not forensic (aka not sufficiently reliable for judicial use).

B. The caveats listed on p.1 of Mr. Rainbow's 2004 report signal a lack of reliability and confidence in the findings.

C. P.1, item 1 of Mr. Rainbow's 2004 report provides that the report "… does not constitute a statement of expert evidence."

D. P.1, item 4 Mr. Rainbow's 2004 report provides that findings presented are locked into information examined to date, and that "further information that comes to the investigators notice should be discussed with the BIA."

E. Mr. Rainbow's 2004 report indicates that the case material was received on May 27, 2004. The report was written on June 4, 2004. Based on this examiner's direct knowledge of the case material examined, this insufficient time to examine that material, deliberate over findings, and prepare a written report of those findings.

F. P.4 of Mr. Rainbow's 2004 report offers a caveat in bold, signalling an overall lack of confidence and reliability: "This report should be viewed as a preliminary report and not a definitive statement regarding linkage. It is emphasized that this report should be viewed as the first stage in an ongoing process and has not been written, nor should it be viewed as suitable for judicial purposes at this stage."

G. P.5 of Mr. Rainbow's 2004 report provides that this is not an objective report with impartial goals. Rather, it was written to "Assist the prosecution case".

H. P.6 of Mr. Rainbow's 2004 report provides a chart based on assumptions and reconstruction attempts well beyond the expertise of the analyst. That is to say, Mr. Rainbow is a police officer with no offering of a formal education or training in the forensic sciences or crime reconstruction. Crime reconstruction is required in order to establish the behaviors that occurred in the cases under consideration, not assumptions and inexpert surmise.

I. The chart on p.6 of Mr. Rainbow's 2004 report identifies major differences across the 8 cases under evaluation. It is also significant that this chart indicates no two cases share precisely the same behavioral indicators.

J. Mr. Rainbow's 2004 report concludes that no firm conclusions may be reached, other than further investigative work needs to be done before firm conclusions may be reached.

3. BEHAVIOURAL INVESTIGATIVE ADVISOR'S REPORT by Lee Rainbow, dated May 28, 2010.

The "BEHAVIOURAL INVESTIGATIVE ADVISOR'S REPORT" by Lee Rainbow, dated May 28, 2010 provides opinions that conflict with this examiner's Linkage Analysis report dated September 27, 2010. However, a careful examination of Mr. Rainbow's 2004 report does not reveal evidence or information that would cause this examiner to alter those 2010 findings. This is based on at least the following facts:

A. Mr. Rainbow's 2010 report is deeply conflicted regarding its purpose, reliability, and utility. It purports to present (p.2) "opinions and conclusions in a clear, unambiguous manner, with explicit supporting rationale, suitable for judicial scrutiny." Then it goes on to argue that the methods used to arrive at the findings in the report are not reliable enough to stand on their own in a judicial setting (p.9): "The purpose of this report is to furnish the Court with information regarding behavioural consistency and the potential implications for case linkage in a very specific set of circumstances... Analysis employed to identify potential linked offences can aid investigative efforts through resource allocation and intelligence sharing, but cannot in itself be used to support similar fact considerations within any related judicial process."

B. Mr. Rainbow's 2010 report warns that (p.5): "It should be noted that although the author has made significant contributions to behavioural analysis methodology through pioneering development of an enhanced prioritisation technique for familial DNA search results utilising Likelihood Ratio methodology, he has no formal mathematical or statistical qualifications and should not be considered an 'expert' in the field of probability or statistics." This warning is vital, given Mr. Rainbow's lack of qualification in this area. It is also misleading, as Mr. Rainbow goes on to violate this admonition by offering opinions and advice based almost entirely on his interpretation of statistical analysis that alone has performed, in a report designated specifically for judicial consideration. See pp.15-16; "6.5.2 Statistical Considerations"; see also pp. 29-32; "7.4.5 Points of Similarity – Coincidence"; see also pp. 32; "7.4.6 Summary of Points of Similarity – Coincidence".

C. Mr. Rainbow's 2010 report explains: "the basic premise of investigating potential links between cases is to demonstrate not only behavioural similarity between them, but also to consider the frequency of those behaviours in general." This narrow methodology is focused on similarities and not dissimilarities, which essentially enables what is referred to as *confirmation bias*. This is a bias identified by cognitive psychologists in which examiners seek the proofs of their preconceived theories (.e.g., those rendered without sufficient investigation in Mr. Rainbow's 2004 report), while excluding evidence that might tend to refute them.

D. Mr. Rainbow's 2010 report dismisses the importance of obvious behavioral dissimilarity in his findings with a brief statistically oriented remark (p.36): "Although the formal application of similar probabilistic analyses as utilised for the similarities has not been employed, similar thresholds of acceptance regarding significance in consistency have been adopted. These, in combination with a richer behavioural interpretation have highlighted that the differences observed between the cases under consideration do not undermine the hypothesis of a single offender, and represent expected or acceptable levels of deviance from a consistent and 'scripted' offence." Without a clear showing of precisely what constitutes "acceptable levels of deviance", which is absent, this statement has no meaning. This also, again, begs consideration of Mr. Rainbow's warning regarding his lack of statistical expertise.

E. The essential findings in Mr. Rainbow's 2010 report are based on statistical probabilities that he admits lacking sufficient education, training, and expertise to derive, using a database of comprised of known offenses that has no known error rate. That Mr. Rainbow was willing to offer what are meant to be court worthy opinions of any kind, in an area that he admits is beyond his expertise, is inexplicable.

F. Mr. Rainbow's 2010 report concludes (p.40): "Based on the above analyses and considerations of all the known facts, viewed with reference to the available research literature and experiential knowledge gained through over a decade of behavioural analysis, it is the author's opinion that all six cases under consideration can be attributed to the same individual and hence represent the linked cases of a serial offender." Given the uncertainty regarding accepted methodology cited in the report, and the lack of empirical research specific to serial homicide case linkage cited, with an 80% rate of accuracy (unacceptable in any forensic setting), the certainty of this opinion is not supported by the body of the report.

G. The conclusion of Mr. Rainbow's 2010 report violates its own prohibition against confusion, by failing to make clear the qualifying language that is evident. It states "all six cases under consideration can be attributed to the same individual". However, "can" is not the same as "must be" or "to the exclusion of all other possibilities". Without more clear language on this issue, the conclusion of this report, given its lack of internal support, makes very little sense to this examiner.

Linkage Analysis Report

Forensic Examiner
Brent E. Turvey, MS, PhD
Forensic Solutions, LLC
Sitka, Alaska
www.forensic-science.com
bturvey@forensic-science.com

Date of Report
April 21, 2015

Report for
Attorneys Robert Motta Sr., Robert Motta Jr., and Alison Motta
Motta & Motta, LLC
559 W. Galena Blvd., Aurora, IL 60506
218 N Jefferson St., suite 300 Chicago, IL 60661
Office: (630) 844-2766, Cell: (630) 779-8381

In Re: *Nebraska v. Anthony Garcia*

Purpose

The purpose of this forensic report is to answer the following questions, at the request of Attorney Alison Motta:

1. What are the nature, scope and limits of Linkage Analysis?

2. Is the report prepared by Tom Bevel based on sound and reliable methodology, and are the conclusions sound?

3. Is there a common scheme or plan, or a distinctive pattern of similarities, between the Hunter-Sherman double homicides (2008) and the Brumback double homicides (2013), sufficient to suggest that the same person committed both crimes?

Linkage Analysis - Methodology

Linkage analysis refers to the process of determining whether or not there are discrete connections, or behavioral commonalities, between two or more previously unrelated cases through *Crime Analysis* (aka, *Crime Scene Analysis*) (Petherick and Turvey, 2010). As explained in Turvey (2011), it is most often employed to serve one of two purposes: (1) to assist law enforcement with the application of its resources by helping to direct investigative efforts; and (2) to assist the court in determining whether or not there is sufficient behavioral evidence to suggest a common scheme or plan in order to address forensic issues, such as whether similar crimes may be tried together or whether other crimes may be presented as evidence (Hazelwood and Warren, 2003).

It is also understood that there are very different thresholds of evidence for *investigative* and *forensic* (aka, court-worthy) conclusions.

Modus Operandi

Modus operandi (MO) is a Latin term that means *method of operating*. It has been in wide use for more than a hundred years by investigators and scholars alike. A criminal's modus operandi is comprised of choices and behaviors that are intended to assist in the completion of a crime (Atcherley, 1913; Dienstein, 1995; Gross, 1924; Turvey, 2011; Weston and Wells, 1974). *Black's Law Dictionary* (Black, 1990, p. 1004) translates the phrase *modus operandi* as "method of operation or doing things," and states that it is "used by police and criminal investigators to describe the particular method of a criminal's activity."

The literature is clear that not all criminals have a particular MO, but some can develop and maintain similar enough methods to justify law enforcement linking suspected cases *investigatively*.

MO is adaptive, changing sharply based on the flexible state of the offender (e.g. mood, substance abuse, mental illness), the victim (e.g. mood, substance abuse, fear response), and the crime scene (e.g. day/night, weather, witnesses). Therefore, while investigatively helpful, is not considered a sufficiently reliable mechanism for linking or unlinking cases in a forensic (aka legal) context.

Offender Signature

An offender's crime scene *signature* is a pattern evidenced by an accumulation of signature behaviors. *Signature behaviors* are individual acts committed by an offender that are not necessary to commit the crime but that suggest the psychological or emotional needs of that offender (Burgess, Burgess, Douglas, and Ressler, 1992; Hazelwood and Warren, 2003; Salfati and Taylor, 2006; Turvey, 2013). Unlike MO, signature can be more stable over the lifetime of an offender, as it is reflective of more enduring psychological motives and themes.

Investigative v. Forensic analyses

Investigative and *forensic* analyses are different. An investigative analysis is completed during an investigation, while facts are still being established and before a complete picture of the case is understood. It is conducted to move the case forward and lead investigators towards additional evidence and suspects. It is also subject to rapid change as new evidence and information are constantly being gathered. Investigative tools and their results are not necessarily designed or even intended for courtroom use and, therefore, must be offered and regarded with humility.

A forensic analysis is conducted in accordance with legal guidelines in order to achieve admissibility in court. It is based on the facts and evidence that are brought forth to make a legal finding, and therefore less subordinate rapid changes of fact and evidence. Because a forensic analysis is meant to be court worthy and have impact on court rulings, a higher standard competency must be evident in examiner education and training, as well as in their findings. In other words, forensic examinations are no place for assumptions or unsupported, inexpert supposition presented with inappropriate levels of certainty and without the appropriate scientific humility.

In a forensic context, a linkage analysis is conducted to identify whether the behavioral evidence in a given set of cases is sufficient to suggest the identity of the offender. This by virtue of demonstrating whether a common scheme or plan can be identified in the MOs and signatures that are present. These findings can be used to explain whether the behavioral uniqueness requirement set forth in governing regional case law has been met.

This is why, as provided in *NJ v. Sterling* (2011), only qualified forensic experts may opine on the issue of case linkage or linkage analysis - it is complex forensic discipline that is open to abuse and misunderstanding by those without sufficient education or training.

Limitations

This examiner admonishes readers of this linkage analysis report to understand the following limitations:

The accuracy of the findings provided in this report are dependent on the accuracy of the findings and the quality of the materials examined. While best efforts have been made to assess to the quality of materials examined, and that quality appears sufficient, it is not possible for this examiner to vouch for the accuracy of every investigative and forensic report provided. Therefore, should any major inaccuracies be identified in the materials provided, the findings in this case linkage analysis must be re-evaluated.

Should any additional or new evidence or findings be provided to this examiner subsequent to this report, the findings in this case linkage analysis must be re-evaluated.

Materials Examined

This examiner rendered the crime analysis and linkage analysis findings in this report based on a careful examination of case material requested from and provided by attorney Alison Motta. That case evidence included, but was not limited to, the following:

1. Police investigative reports,affidavits, and warrants re: the homicides of re: Shirlee Sherman, Thomas Hunter, Roger Brumback, and Mary Brumback;

2. Douglas County Coroner's Office - Autopsy reports, photos and notes re: Shirlee Sherman, Thomas Hunter, Roger Brumback, and Mary Brumback;

3. Homicide crime scene photos re: Shirlee Sherman, Thomas Hunter, Roger Brumback, and Mary Brumback;

4. Crime lab reports related to the homicides of Shirlee Sherman, Thomas Hunter, Roger Brumback, and Mary Brumback;

5. Report of opinions by Tom Bevel re: State v. Anthony Garcia, dated July 16, 2014.

Summary of Findings

1. **The report prepared by Tom Bevel violates basic guidelines for linkage analysis set forth in *The Crime Classification Manual* (Burgess, Burgess, Douglas, and Ressler, 1992).**

2. **The report prepared by Tom Bevel is based on non-scientific and inaccurately rendered methodology. Moreover, the conclusions offered in the report are uninformed, misleading, and without foundation.**

3. **Linkage Analysis: While there is a general investigative link between the double homicide cases, there is significant behavioral dissimilarity to distinguish them. Consequently, these crimes do not share a common scheme, or any pattern, of behavioral factors distinctive enough to suggest that a single offender must be responsible.**

Discussion of Findings

1. **The report prepared by Tom Bevel violates basic guidelines for linkage analysis set forth in *The Crime Classification Manual* (Burgess, Burgess, Douglas, and Ressler, 1992).**

   This finding is based, primarily, on the fallowing facts and evidence:

   A. The Crime Classification Manual (CCM) explains that linking cases is a comprehensive process (p.260), and stresses the importance of assessing victimology, modus operandi, and offender signature in linkage analysis efforts.

B. As will be discussed in conclusion #3, significant victimological differences are ignored or glossed over in Mr. Bevel's analysis and reported findings.

C. Mr. Bevel's report is prepared in such a manner as to avoid comparing victimology in any fashion. This avoids highlighting the significant differences in victim age and their respective relationships.

D. The CCM prescribes the importance of distinguishing between modus operandi and signature behaviors when linking cases (e.g., "MO should not be the only criterion used to connect crimes, especially with the repeat offender who alters the MO through experience and learning… However, the signature aspect remains the same… The signature aspect should also receive greater consideration than the victim similarities…"; pp.262).

E. Mr. Bevel's analysis does not identify or discriminate between offender modus operandi behaviors and offender signature behaviors found at the crime scenes under consideration. These foundational concepts, universally held as necessary for viable linkage analysis efforts, are not mentioned at all in Mr. Bevel's written report. Only the generic (non-specific) terms "similarities" and "dissimilarities" are used.

F. Mr. Bevel's testimony at deposition is essentially an admission that he does not know what the terms modus operandi and offender signature mean in specific. Rather his definitions are vague and inaccurate (e.g., he believes the concepts originated with the FBI). Ultimately, his testimony can only be read as an admission that he did not (and could not) consider these foundational concepts in his analysis or findings.

G. As will be discussed in conclusion #3, significant signature differences between the crime scenes are ignored or glossed over in Mr. Bevel's findings.

2. **The report prepared by Tom Bevel is based on non-scientific and inaccurately rendered methodology. Moreover, the conclusions offered in the report are uninformed, misleading and without foundation.**

This finding is based, primarily, on the fallowing facts and evidence:

A. Mr. Bevel is not a forensic expert in the areas of examining offender modus operandi, offender signature, or linkage analysis. He holds no behavioral science education or training. He has not published in this area. Furthermore, he has conceded his lack of knowledge and expertise on these subjects in his deposition for this case[1].

B. Mr. Bevel's report is offered without reference to standardized terms, language, or underlying methodology. In fact it is offered without operationalized terms or references of any kind.

C. Mr. Bevel's report promises to offer "a physical evidence review and scene analysis". However, there is no showing of a physical evidence review or a scene analysis of any kind in this report. Rather, it is a series of highly speculative reconstruction opinions provided within two lists. The first list is labelled "Similarities and dis-similarities between three separate crimes". The second list is labelled "Connections between three separate crimes and defendant Anthony Garcia".

D. The reconstruction opinions expressed in the aforementioned lists are provided without explanation. There is no discussion of the underlying logic or scientific. This is not an acceptable scientific practice.

E. Mr. Bevel's report acknowledges the fact that he does not intend to demonstrate how his reconstruction opinions were generated in his report, stating: "While all events and segments may not be explained, those that are explained reflect the best explanation of event(s) sequence based upon the known facts." In reality, none of the "events and segments" in this report are explained to any degree. Again, they are provided without scientific foundation within lists of assumed "facts".

F. Mr. Bevel's report concludes with the caveat that "Additional study will be required to conduct a complete reconstruction for specific actions and events for each victim's attack." This is an acknowledgement that the actions and events described in the report are not based on a complete reconstruction of the evidence. This is not a legitimate scientific practice.

G. Mr. Bevel's report focuses on comparing selected variables from three different crime scenes: the Hunter-Sherman double homicide in 2008; the Brumback double homicide in 2013; and the "attempted entry" into Dr. Chhanda Bewtra's house in 2013. It focuses on similarities, and it does not address the significance of major dissimilarities even when acknowledged. This is referred to as "cherry-picking" the data. It is not an acceptable scientific practice because it produces biased and

[1] It is worth noting that it is a violation of professional ethics to offer forensic services and opinions outside of one's areas of education, knowledge and competence.

misleading results. These omissions will be discussed in the next section.

H. In the first list, Mr. Bevel's report states at item 3: "Knives belonging to each residence were used and left at the respective scenes." This is referred to as *use of available materials*. This is not a similarity as reported, but rather a dissimilarity in context. To be clear, in each case of homicide a different knife of no particular meaning to the offender was used. Superficially, one could argue that there is an investigative link with the use of available materials in these two crimes (modus operandi); however, upon close analysis this choice does not indicate a meaningful signature behavior. Close analysis in context reveals that different knives were used in each crime to differing signature effect.

I. In the third case, no knife was used because there was no attack and no subsequent homicide. The absence of a killing with a corresponding weapon makes this case all the more different from the others. In this instance, it is a difference reported improperly as a similarity. This inappropriately boosts the certainty the overall finding.

J. In the first list, Mr. Bevel's report states at item 4: "A hand gun was used in the Brumback scene". This mention of the handgun fails to explain that the handgun was used in the Brumback scene to to kill Roger Brumback. This is a significant behavioral dissimilarity, as the use of multiple weapons during a crime can be an indication of multiple offenders.

K. Mr. Bevel's report is prepared in such a manner as to avoid comparing the specific methods of killing in each case. This avoids highlighting the use a firearm in the Brumback case against the use of knives and the absence of any killing in the other cases.

L. In the first list, Mr. Bevel's report states at item 5 that knives were left in the necks of the victims at the Hunter-Sherman crime scene (reported as a similarity), and that stab wounds without knives are found in the necks of the Brumbacks (reported as a dissimilarity). This is confusing, because deliberately leaving a knife in both necks at one crime scene is a significant signature behavior that is absent from the other homicide scene. The report seems to acknowledge this major dissimilarity, but the ultimate findings do not.

M. This report of a similarity at item 5 becomes even more confusing when one considers that it appears in a table intended to present similarities across all three cases (as the title of this list makes clear). This finding fails to address the fact that no knife at all was used to inflict injuries of any kind at the Bewtra crime scene. This finding is not a similarity across either of the homicide scene.

N. In the first list, Mr. Bevel's report states at item 16: "Two deceased victims, Thomas Hunter and Mary Brumback's attack are consistent with responding to the attack on the first victim at their respective scenes". The report comments: "Mary responds to gunshots fired at front door,"; and "Hunter responds to attack noise, possibly scream(s) from Sherman". These reconstruction opinions are very specific, and offered without any supporting evidence or argumentation. In fact, they are more speculative than anything else, offering possibilities and not certainties. Unfortunately, Mr. Bevel's report immediately treats these possibilities as certainties in his linkage analysis. This is not a legitimate forensic practice.

O. It the second list prepared by Mr. Bevel, he attempts to connect Mr. Garcia directly to each of the crimes. He does so while also purporting to find no "disconnectors". This highly prejudicial exercise does not attempt to define what disconnectors are, or how they might be qualified.

P. Mr. Bevel's report fails to mention a major behavioral dissimilarity: that only one of the victims, Thomas Hunter, is a pre-teen male child. The rest are aged adults. This omission is significant.

Q. Mr. Bevel's report fails to mention a major behavioral dissimilarity: that one of the victims, Mary Brumback, suffered 20 cutting wounds to the hands and arms. These injuries are consistent with time taken at the scene to inflict torture. She is the only victim to suffer such injuries. This omission is significant.

R. The rest of the items not mentioned above, but detailed in the aforementioned report by Mr. Bevel, are sufficiently generic to homicides involving knife wounds that they do not rise to the level of distinct, let alone unique.

S. It bears mentioning that Mr. Bevel concludes his report with the following: "In my analysis, I find a solid foundation of similarities and connectors that identify the best explanation as a common attacker(s) associated to all three crimes in question. The connectors identify the defendant, Anthony Garcia, as the attacker for the murders and for the attempted break in on Dr. Chanda Bewtra's residence." This succession of findings, which violates the ultimate issue, is far over the line for any forensic examiner, let alone being unwarranted given the evidence ignored in Mr. Bevel's report.

T. There is no physical evidence connecting any of the cases in Mr. Bevel's report to each other or to the defendant. This would include consideration of the absence of evidence such as firearms, ballistics, fingerprints, DNA, and any other form of trace evidence. The absence of physical evidence connecting these cases to each other, or to the defendant, makes the Mr. Bevel's conclusions all the more troubling.

3. Linkage Analysis: While there is an investigative link between the double homicide cases, there is significant behavioral dissimilarity to distinguish them. Consequently, these crimes do not share a common scheme, or any pattern, of behavioral factors distinctive enough to suggest that a single offender must be responsible.

This analysis will only consider the Hunter-Sherman double homicide and the Brumback double homicide. This is because the Bewtra case did not involve a physical attack of any kind. As such the Bewtra case is immediately and necessarily excluded, behaviorally, from any legitimate case linkage effort involving a homicide, let alone a double homicide.

Similarities
The relevant similarities between the Hunter-Sherman double homicide and the Brumback double homicide include, primarily, the following:

A. Both cases involve double homicides.

B. Both cases involve one male victim and one female victim.

C. Both cases involve fatal sharp force injuries to the victims' necks.

D. Both cases involve residential home invasions during daylight hours with only two people at home.

E. Neither case involves a sexual assault or aspect (e.g., sexual themes or nudity).

F. Nothing of financial value appears to have been taken from either location.

Dissimilarities
There are significant behavioral dissimilarities between the Hunter-Sherman double homicide and the Brumback double homicide. These include primarily the following:

A. In the Brumback case, the victims were married and of the same age; in the Hunter-Sherman case, they were unrelated and of vastly different ages, sizes, and maturity. From a victim selection standpoint, this is a significant difference.

B. Only one of the victims, Thomas Hunter, was an 11 year old male child. The rest were aged adults. Criminologically, killing a child is distinct from killing an adult with respect to offender capability, disposition and motivation. This significantly distinguishes the Hunter-Sherman case.

C. One of the victims, Mary Brumback, suffered 20 cutting wounds to the hands and arms. The majority of these are consistent with defensive injury. However, four of these injuries are consistent with time taken at the scene to inflict torture. These are described in the autopsy report as "four clustered superficial punctate cuts" (p.6). Mary Brumback was the only victim to suffer such injuries. This significantly distinguishes the Brumback case.

D. Roger Brumback was shot three times, which directly contributed to his cause of death. He was the only victim to suffer such injuries. This significantly distinguishes the Brumback case.

E. Roger Brumback was stabbed in the face, which directly contributed to his cause of death. He was the only victim to suffer such an injury. This significantly distinguishes the Brumback case.

F. The Brumback case involved multiple weapons used against a single victim (a gun and sharp force injury, re Roger Brumback). This tends to suggest multiple offenders.

G. Given the evidence of time taken to torture Mary Brumback, along with the use of a gun as a method of killing with the other, this further suggests the possibility of two offenders in that scene. There is no evidence of multiple offenders in the Hunter-Sherman case. This significantly distinguishes the Brumback case.

H. The specific motive for the torture of Mary Brumback is unknown - though it is consistent with a profit motivation (e.g., torturing a victim to get information on the location of valuables or for security passwords/ codes). In any case, it is known that torture is a relatively rare signature behavior. The absence of torture in the Hunter-Sherman case is therefore strong evidence that the motives for those killings were not at all similar. In other words, the offender did not not demonstrate a desire to spend time with, or inflict pain and suffering on, the victims in the Hunter-Sherman case. Torture is a major signature behavior relevant to motive, and it significantly distinguishes the Brumback case.

I. In the Brumback case, the victims are stabbed in the neck. In the Hunter-Sherman case, the victims are also stabbed in the neck. However, in the Hunter-Sherman case, both knives are left in place to the hilt. This is a major signature behavior, and significantly distinguishes these cases.

J. In the Hunter-Sherman case, Shirlee Sherman suffered 18 stab wounds to the neck in generally the same clustered location. This is evidence of what is referred to as *overkill*. It is suggestive of intense offender rage - associated with direct personal anger with the victim, offender mental illness, or offender substance abuse. Thomas Hunter suffered 8 clustered stab wounds to the neck, which could be interpreted as overkill, especially where a child victim is concerned - as they are not generally able to fight back. This is distinct from the stab wounds to the neck in the Brumback case (Roger Brumback suffered 4 stab wounds to the neck in different areas, and Mary suffered 6 to the neck in different areas).

Key behavioral factors, and dissimilarities, are expressed in the Table below: "Distinctive Modus Operandi & Signature Behaviors". It should be noted that while the motive for the the Brumback case cannot be establish with certainty by the behavioral evidence, it is not consistent with overkill/ anger, and there is indicia of a profit motivation by virtue of the torture of Mary Brumback.

Distinctive Modus Operandi & Signature Behaviors

	(2008) Sherman - Hunter	(2013) Brumback	Behavioral Dissimilarity
1 Double Homicide	Yes	Yes	No
2 Home invasion/ Daylight hours	Yes	Yes	No
3 Victims in a custodial relationship	Yes	No	Yes
4 Child Victim	Yes	No	Yes
5 Method of Killing: Sharp Force	Yes	Yes	No
6 Knives left in Neck of victim	Yes	No	Yes
7 Method of Killing: Gunshot Wound	No	Yes	Yes
8 Multiple methods of killing	No	Yes	Yes
9 Evidence of Torture	No	Yes	Yes
10 Evidence of Multiple Offenders	No	Yes	Yes
11 Overkill/ clustered stabs to neck	Yes	No	Yes
12 Motive	Anger	Unknown (Profit)	Yes

Please do not hesitate to contact me with any questions

Brent E. Turvey, MS, PhD

REFERENCES

Atchereley, L. (1913) *Modus Operandi: Criminal Investigation and Detection*. Leeds: Chorley & Pickersgill, Ltd.

Black, H. C. (Ed.). (1990) ***Black's Law Dictionary***, St. Paul, MN: West Publishing.

Burgess, A.N., Burgess, A.W., Douglas, J., and Ressler, R. (1992) *Crime Classification Manual,* Lexington Books, New York, NY.

Dienstein, W. (1995) "Criminal Investigation" in Bailey, W. (Ed.) *The Encyclopedia of Police Science, 2nd Ed.*, Garland, New York.

Gross, H. (1924) *Criminal Investigation*, London: Sweet & Maxwell.

Hazelwood, R., and Warren, J. (2003) "Linkage Analysis: Modus Operandi, Ritual, and Signature in Serial Sexual Crime," *Aggression and Violent Behavior*, 8, pp. 587–598.

New Jersey v. Bruce Sterling (2011) Superior Court of New Jersey, Appellate Division, Case No. A-5579-06T4, A-0048-08T4.

Petherick, W. & Turvey, B. (2010) "Forensic Criminological Assessments" in Ferguson, C., Petherick, W. & Turvey, B. (Eds) *Forensic Criminology.* San Diego: Elsevier Science.

Salfati, C.G. and Taylor, P. (2006) "Differentiating sexual violence: A comparison of sexual homicide and rape," *Psychology, Crime and Law*, Vol. 12(2): pp. 107-125.

Turvey, B. (2001) "Sexual Homicide: Research Review and Findings, Part 1," *Journal of Behavioral Profiling*, December, Vol. 2, No. 2.

Turvey B. (2011) *Criminal Profiling: An Introduction to Behavioral Evidence Analysis, 4rd Ed.,* London: Elsevier Science.

Turvey, B. (2013) "Offender Signature," in Houck, M., Saukko, P., & Seigal, J. (Eds.) Encyclopedia of Forensic Science, 2nd Ed., London: Academic Press.

Weston, P., and Wells, K. (1974) *Criminal Investigation: Basic Perspectives*, 2nd ed., Englewood Cliffs, NJ: Prentice-Hall.

REFERENCES

Hornblower, M., July 17, 2000. The Spokane Murders, vol. 156. Time Magazine.
Turvey, B., 2011. Criminal Profiling: An Introduction to Behavioral Evidence Analysis, fourth ed. Academic Press, San Diego.

CHAPTER

Criminal Profiling and Crime Scene Analysis in Postconviction Review

17

B.E. Turvey

Forensic Solutions LLC, Sitka, Alaska, United States;

Institute of Forensic Investigation and Criminal Profiling, Juarez, Mexico

CHAPTER OUTLINE

Postconviction review refers to examination of cases subsequent to a criminal conviction. By definition, these cases are somewhere in the appellate process. That is to say, there has already been a trial, there has already been a conviction, and the defendant is seeking relief.

In some cases, the defendant will be claiming actual innocence, and this may or may not be a case. This consideration should actually be irrelevant to the objective forensic examiner. Their role is to examine the facts and the evidence, not make legal determinations—though some are eager to do so in what can only be described as a confusion of their role as an expert. The role of the forensic expert is to educate investigators, attorneys, and the courts so that they can make better arguments and findings in legal proceedings (Crowder and Turvey, 2013). In these kinds of cases, where innocence is being claimed, the forensic examiner may or may not be able to identify evidence that supports or refutes this claim. But they cannot know until they have done their examination.

In other cases, the defendant will be seeking relief from a wrongful conviction that involves some kind of culpability on their part. That is to say, they admit to being involved in the crime, or connected to it in some fashion, but they feel the charges and punishment are excessive. For example, they may have been convicted of first degree murder, perhaps even a capital crime, when in fact they are claiming self-defense.

In these cases it is preferable to work directly for the attorney representing the defendant. However, it is not a strict requirement. Oftentimes the forensic examiner

Behavioral Evidence Analysis. http://dx.doi.org/10.1016/B978-0-12-800607-8.00017-3

will be contacted by an advocacy group, the defendant's family, or the defendants themselves. This is because they are indigent, or because defense attorneys have drained them of all resources without providing adequate representation. Whichever the case may be, the forensic examiner must decide whether to take the case and whether the defendant is in a position to make use of the findings.

In extreme cases involving indigent defendants or issues of public interest, it may be in the examiner's interests to examine the case for a reduced fee or even pro bono (for expenses only; no expert fees). This is not unusual, as attorneys and forensic experts do it all the time as a public service. However, it is only advised in the rarest of situations, not as a rule, because those who do not pay for services do not tend to value them, and because the examiner runs the risk of being branded a crusader on a mission rather than an objective advocate of the evidence.

Postconviction review is an important function of the independent forensic examiner, as very often there is no money for expert examination by the defense at trial. Either because the defense is negligent; because the defense has no money and the court would not approve public funds for their experts; or because the defense is ignorant regarding how to procure public funds for experts in indigent cases. The best defense attorneys always seek experts to review the forensic work of the state, and failure to do so essentially invites a wrongful conviction of some kind (Cooley and Turvey, 2014).

Those who oppose the notion of postconviction review by private forensic experts are either ignorant of how the judicial system works, or fear that something untoward may be uncovered. To quote the English poet Samuel Johnson (1709–84): "Fraud and falsehood only dread examination. Truth invites it." This becomes even more important in light of a recent study from the University of Michigan which shows that the number of wrongful convictions being identified in the United States, which often boasts the fairest justice system in the world, is dramatically rising each year (McCay, 2015). This is likely due to the awareness of wrongful convictions and increased public and private funding to examine the issue.

OKLAHOMA v. KARL FONTENOT

Consider the conviction of Karl Fontenot for the abduction and murder of Donna "Denice" Haraway. As explained in Cosgrove (2013):

> *Chris Ross is the only person left in his office who was there when Donna Denice Haraway went missing. Haraway's murder was one of the first murder trials he worked on as a 27-year-old prosecutor.*
>
> *Almost 30 years later, Ross serves as the district attorney for Pontotoc, Hughes and Seminole counties. And almost 30 years later, nothing has changed his mind on who killed Haraway.*
>
> *Meanwhile, efforts are underway to free Karl Fontenot and Tommy Ward from prison, the two men convicted of the 1984 killing of the 24-year-old Ada woman. The Oklahoma Innocence Project, an initiative based out of Oklahoma City University's law school, filed a brief in support of application for post-conviction relief on July 24 that outlines why the organization's legal staff believes Fontenot should be released from prison.*

"There were many inconsistencies throughout the investigation into Ms. Haraway's disappearance, many of which help our case for post-conviction relief for Karl," Tiffany Murphy, the Oklahoma Innocence Project director, said during the July 24 news conference. "We firmly believe an innocent man has been in prison for nearly 30 years for a crime he did not commit." And Ward, also convicted of Haraway's murder, awaits a similar brief to be filed.

His attorney Mark Barrett said he has been working on Ward's case for several years and anticipates that a brief will be filed for Ward. It will outline issues similar to what can be found in the Oklahoma Innocence Project brief, although it won't likely be identical. Barrett said he believes that Ward and Fontenot are both innocent. "You can expect something that will be filed on Tommy Wards' behalf not too far in the distant future," Barrett said. "Exactly when, we're not sure."

...

Fontenot and Ward were tried in court in September 1985. Both men were found guilty and sentenced to death. They were scheduled to die in January 1986. Fontenot's case was appealed, and he was granted a new trial.

During the time span of Fontenot's appeal, Haraway's remains were found about 30 miles east of Ada. In 1988, Fontenot was retried, convicted and sentenced to death a second time. His sentence was later commuted to life in prison without the possibility of parole, according to the Oklahoma Innocence Project.

THE VICTIM

Donna "Denice" Haraway (24, White Female [WF]) was considered to be an attractive woman, though shy and a bit awkward, by those who knew her. She was 8 months into her marriage with Steven Haraway at the time of her abduction from McAnally's convenience store. She had been employed there, working the counter, for about 9 months.

THE ADA EVENING NEWS

Missing

Local clerk abducted

Nigh asks disaster aid

Donna "Denice" Haraway.

By all accounts, Haraway was a dedicated student, in addition to being a wife and holding down a job. She was enrolled at a local college, working toward a teaching degree. She would even study at the store, behind the counter, when things were slow. However, she had also been receiving harassing phone calls while work. And only while at work. This caused her a great deal of concern for her safety, as she often worked alone.

THE ABDUCTION

According to law enforcement reports, Haraway was seen last at McAnally's convenience store around 8:30 pm on Saturday, April 28, 1984. She was the lone clerk on duty that evening. This was not uncommon.

In relation to Haraway's disappearance, a regular customer, Gene Whelchel, made three calls that evening: first, he called Mr. McAnally, the owner of the store; second, he called the store manager, Monroe Atkeson; and third, he called the Ada (Oklahoma) Police Department. Mr. Whelchel explained that when he arrived at the store, the clerk was not there and the cash register drawer was open.

Mr. Atkeson, the store manager, drove from his home to the store. Additionally, Ada PD responded to the scene.

Other relevant background is taken directly from the court's decision in Fontenot v. State (1988):

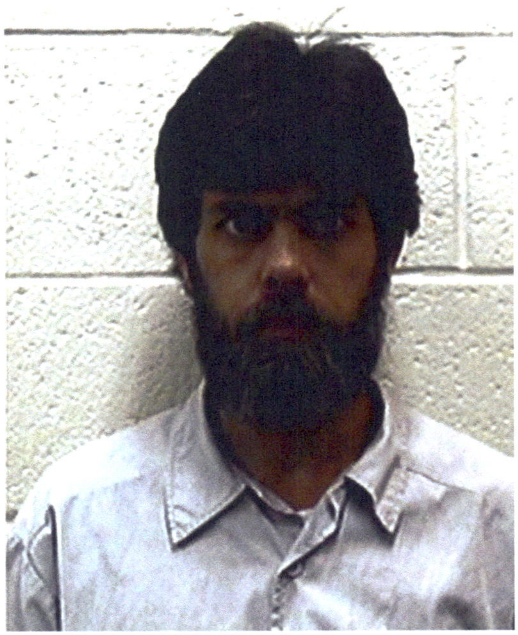

Karl Fontenot around the time of his arrest.

[Karl Fontenot] and Tommy Ward were tried for the crimes during September, 1985. In October of 1984, Tommy Ward made a statement to law enforcement officers which inculpated Fontenot, an individual named Odell Titsworth, and to a slighter degree, himself. Fontenot and Titsworth were arrested as a result and Fontenot gave a statement substantially in agreement with Ward's except that it more clearly inculpated Ward. In each Ward's and Fontenot's statements, the instigator and ringleader in the criminal acts was said to be Titsworth. However, Titsworth was eliminated as a suspect within a few days of his arrest because of clear proof the police had that he had not been an accomplice.

According to the statements of Ward and Fontenot, Haraway was robbed of approximately $150.00, abducted, and taken to the grounds behind a power plant in Ada where she was raped. According to [Fontenot's] version, she was then taken to an abandoned house behind the plant where Titsworth stabbed her to death. She was then burned along with the house. When Haraway's remains were found in Hughes County, there was no evidence of charring or of stab wounds, and there was a single bullet wound to the skull.

It is helpful to understand that Karl Fontenot and Tommy Ward were convicted of abducting and murdering Ms. Hawaray, 5 months before her body was actually found.

THE MURDER

On Monday, January 20, 1986, a trapper found the partial skeletal remains of Denice Haraway; these were later identified through her dental records. The remains were located approximately 1 mile south and 3½ miles west, of Gerty, Oklahoma off a county road. The remains were found scattered in a wooded area.

The few crime scene photographs that were taken depict a skull, various scattered bones, and a conspicuous pile of bones placed on a rock. Bits and pieces of clothing and jewelry were also found at the scene, but not photographed or otherwise documented. According to Mrs. Haraway's autopsy report, a gunshot wound to the head was reported as the probable cause of death. There was no evidence that the victim was stabbed, burned, or sexually assaulted.

In short, every detail alleged to be provided by Fontenot and Ward to investigators about the abduction and murder of Denice Haraway turned out to be either unsubstantiated or completely false.

POSTCONVICTION REVIEW

In late 2012, the author (Brent E. Turvey, PhD) was retained by attorney Tiffany Murphy to conduct a postconviction review of the facts and evidence related to the abduction and murder of Donna "Denice" Haraway, and the conviction of Karl A. Fontenot (Fontenot v. State, 1988). He was then asked to provide a professional assessment of the quality, competence, and thoroughness of the investigative- and forensic-efforts in this case. This assessment was conducted with the intent of determining whether sufficient investigative- and forensic-efforts have been undertaken to establish the facts of the case for use in related court proceedings.

There were four major findings, the last of which is perhaps the most significant. They are detailed in the following report:

Investigative and Forensic Assessment

Abduction and Homicide of Donna "Denice" Haraway

Last Seen:
McAnally's convenience store (her place of work);
Saturday, April 28th, 1984, at approximately 8:30 P.M.

Skeletonized Remains Found:
West of Gerty off a county road;
Monday, January 20th, 1986;
Approx. 5:00 P.M. by Allan Tatum, Trapper

Investigating Agencies:
Ada Police Department, Oklahoma
Pontoc County Sheriff's Office
Oklahoma State Highway Patrol
Oklahoma State Bureau of Investigation

Report by:
Brent E. Turvey, Ph.D; Forensic Scientist
Forensic Solutions LLC
(907) 738-5121

Date: June 2nd, 2013

Report for:
Tiffany R. Murphy, JD; Director, Oklahoma Innocence Project
Oklahoma City University School of Law
2501 N. Blackwelder
Oklahoma City, OK 73106
(405) 208-6805

Purpose

This examiner (Turvey) was retained by Tiffany Murphy, JD, to conduct a post conviction review of the facts and evidence related to the abduction and murder of Donna "Denice" Haraway, and the conviction of Karl A. Fontenot (*Fontenot v. State*, 1988). He was then asked to provide a professional assessment of the quality, competence, and thoroughness of the investigative and forensic efforts in this case. This assessment was conducted with the intent of determining whether sufficient investigative and forensic efforts have been undertaken to establish the facts of the case for use in related court proceedings.

Turvey Report
Haraway case: Page 1 of 13

Duty of Care

The investigation of reported crime is the statutory and jurisdictional province of various local, state, and federal law enforcement agencies (Sullivan, 1977). The specific agencies responding to a criminal complaint, and ultimately in charge, depend on which laws have been reported to be broken and where. Whichever agency takes charge of a criminal complaint, they have the legal authority to respond to the scene, interview witnesses and suspects, collect evidence, and make arrests[1].

Any responding law enforcement agency also has a professional *duty of care*. This refers to the professional and legal obligation to be competent custodians of any victims that are encountered; any criminal investigations that are initiated; any evidence that supports or refutes allegations of criminal activity against accused suspects; and any suspects that they take into custody (see Bopp and Schultz, 1972; Gross, 1924; Hansen and Culley, 1973; Kappeler, 2006; SATF, 2009; and Savino and Turvey, 2011). Very often this duty of care is a matter of explicit statute and agency policy, wherein law enforcement officers are not allowed to turn a blind eye to crime and must respond to protect life and property. Very often it is also made part of the formal oath they take when being sworn in. If an agency, or its officers and investigators, do not hold or perceive a professional duty of care to their community, then they are not fit to serve it (Gross, 1924); let alone respond to criminal complaints and assume the responsibilities associated with the collection and testing of physical evidence.

The primary responsibilities of law enforcement, when responding to a criminal complaint, include (adapted from basic criminal investigation and crime scene processing guidelines found in Gross, 1924; O'Connell and Soderman, 1936; Rau, 2000; Snyder, 1944; Wade, 1999; and Weston and Wells, 1974):

1. Protect themselves; call for back-up when needed.
2. Establish who is involved.
3. Ensure that everyone involved is safe.
4. Get medical assistance for those that need it.
5. Determine what happened.
6. Establish who made the complaint and what it is about.
7. Identify any witnesses.
8. Seek out, identify, collect, and protect any physical evidence.
9. Ensure the objective forensic examination of all relevant evidence.
10. Determine whether or not a crime has taken place.
11. Identify any legitimate criminal suspects.
12. Establish whether probable cause exists for an arrest.
13. Arrest any criminal perpetrators.

---

[1] The section is adapted from Crowder and Turvey (2013).

These tactical issues also reflect an ethical responsibility. Investigators may not assume what happened based on the statements of one party. They may not assume that any crime has actually occurred until the facts have been established by a thorough investigation. They must be sufficiently educated to understand what the elements of each crime are and the what probable cause is. They must also impartially place the cuffs on anyone they determine has broken the law. For example, as explained in Bryden and Lengnick (1997; pp. 1230–1231):

> As with all crimes, the police decide whether a reported rape actually occurred, and attempt to determine who committed it. If they want the case to go forward, they "found" the complaint and transmit the file to the prosecutor's office... The police must investigate, a task that cannot easily be combined with offering the emotional support that the victim needs. The detective presumably wishes to avoid an injustice to a wrongly accused individual. In addition, for reasons of professional pride, he does his best to avoid looking naive by falling for a story that turns out to be false.

Meeting these responsibilities is best accomplished with a thorough, diligent, and comprehensive investigation. By comprehensive investigation, the examiner means a detailed review of the complainant and their statements; the careful consideration of witness and suspect statements; and the diligent collection and examination of any physical evidence. All of this must be attended prior to making final determinations regarding whether a crime has been committed and whether probable cause exists to arrest any suspects. See generally Bopp and Schultz (1972); Gross (1924); Kappeler (2006); Leonard (1969); O'Connell and Soderman (1936); Sullivan (1977); Savino and Turvey (2011); and Weston and Wells (1974).

Materials Examined

This examiner made a directed request for all available investigative and forensic materials (e.g., police reports, forensic reports, witness reports, and court testimony) related to this case to the Office of Tiffany Murphy. Materials were provided as they became available up until the time that this report was written. The relevant case materials included, but were not limited to, the following:

1. Various Oklahoma State Bureau of Investigation (OSBI) investigative reports, e.g.;
    - Inv. Hogan Report dated May 7, 1984;
    - Inv. Featherstone Report dated January 31, 1986;
2. Various Oklahoma State Bureau of Investigation evidence examination reports;
3. Various Medical Examiner reports and logs (e.g., Larry Balding, MD - Deceased);
4. Report from Richard McWilliams, Phd, Forensic Anthropologist, January 23, 1986;
5. APD crime scene photos of McAnally's convenience store (exterior only);
6. APD crime scene photos re: skeletonized remains of Haraway;
7. Richard Kerner's report of Investigation, May 19, 1988 (K-Mar Legal Investigations, Inc.);
8. "Haraway Case, Background on Haraway" report from Mr. Ross, Prosecutor;
9. Testimony from various investigators and witnesses from original trials, e.g.
    - Monroe Atkeson, Manager, McAnally's convenience store (Haraway's boss);
    - Witness Lenny Timmons;
    - Witness Gene Welchel;
    - Chief of Detectives Dennis Smith, APD;
    - Det. Mike Baskin, APD;
    - Officer harvey Phillips, APD;
    - Inv. Gary Rogers, OSBI;
    - David Dixon, Criminologist, OSBI;

- Ann Reed, Criminologist, OSBI;
- DA's Investigator Bruce Johnson;
- DA's Investigator George Bond;

10. Investigator Dan Grothaus interview report: Wesley Edens, January 25, 2013;
11. Investigator Dan Grothaus interview report: Jess Stott, May 10, 2013;
12. Signed affidavit of Vickey Jenkins re: Karen Wise;
13. Gene Geitzen, Forensic Consulting, LLC, Report dated April 3, 2013;
14. Gene Geitzen photos of evidence exhibits from Box labelled "88-571; Fontenot v. State".

Background

According to police interviews and victimology based on the above-cited reports and evidence, Donna Denice Haraway was eight months into her marriage with Steven Haraway. She was considered a very attractive woman, though shy and a bit awkward. By all accounts she was also a dedicated student who was working towards a teaching degree at a local college. She had been employed at McAnally's for approximately nine months prior to her abduction. She was known to study at the store, behind the counter, when things were slow. She had also been receiving harassing phone calls while work. There is also one report that she talked about acquiring a firearm out of concern for her personal safety.

According to law enforcement reports, Donna "Denice" Haraway (24, WF) was last seen at her place of work, McAnally's convenience store, at approximately 8:30 P.M. on Saturday, April 28th, 1984. Haraway was the lone clerk on duty that evening.

A customer, Gene Whelchel, made three calls that evening: first to Mr. McAnally, the owner of the store; second, he notified the store manager, Monroe Atkeson; and third, he notified the Ada Police Department. Mr. Whelchel explained that the clerk was not in the store and that the cash register drawer was open. The manager then drove from his home to the store. Additionally, Ada PD responded to the scene.

Other relevant background is taken directly from the court's decision in *Fontenot v. State* (1988):

> [Karl Fontenot] and Tommy Ward were tried for the crimes during September, 1985. In October of 1984, Tommy Ward made a statement to law enforcement officers which inculpated Fontenot, an individual named Odell Titsworth, and to a slighter degree, himself. Fontenot and Titsworth were arrested as a result and Fontenot gave a statement substantially in agreement with Ward's except that it more clearly inculpated Ward. In each Ward's and Fontenot's statements, the instigator and ringleader in the criminal acts was said to be Titsworth. However, Titsworth was eliminated as a suspect within a few days of his arrest because of clear proof the police had that he had not been an accomplice.
>
> According to the statements of Ward and Fontenot, Haraway was robbed of approximately $150.00, abducted, and taken to the grounds behind a power plant in Ada where she was raped. According to appellant's version, she was then taken to an abandoned house behind the plant where Titsworth stabbed her to death. She was then burned along with the house. When Haraway's remains were found in Hughes County, there was no evidence of charring or of stab wounds, and there was a single bullet wound to the skull.

On Monday, January 20th, 1986, a trapper found partial skeletal remains of Denice Haraway; these were later identified through her dental records. The remains were located approximately 1 mile south, and 3 ½ miles west, of Gerty, Oklahoma off a county road. The remains were found scattered in a wooded area.

The few crime scene photographs that were taken depict a skull, various scattered bones, and a conspicuous pile of bones placed on a rock. Bits and pieces of clothing and jewelry were also found at the scene, but not photographed or otherwise documented. According to Mrs. Haraway's autopsy report, a gunshot wound to the head was reported as the probable cause of death. There was no evidence that the victim was stabbed, burned, or sexually assaulted. In short, every detail alleged to be provided by Fontenot and Ward to investigators about the abduction and murder of Denice Haraway turned out to be either unsubstantiated or completely false.

Findings - Summary

The following is a summary of major findings related to this assessment.

1. The investigative and forensic efforts of law enforcement at the location of Haraway's abduction (McAnally's convenience store; April 28, 1984) were inadequate rising to the level of *abandonment*[2]. This prevented the recognition, preservation, collection, and testing specific items of evidence, as well as an untold volume of evidence that would have been missed.

2. The investigative efforts of law enforcement subsequent to Haraway's abduction were inadequate rising to the level of abandonment.

3. The investigative and forensic efforts of law enforcement at the location where Haraway's remains were found (West of Gerty, off a county road; Monday, January 20th, 1986) were inadequate rising to the level of abandonment. This prevented the recognition, preservation, collection, and testing specific items of evidence, as well as an untold volume of evidence that would have been missed.

4. It is unclear from the case record that anyone, whether prosecution or defense, fully understood that the victim had given birth to at least one child, and what that must have meant for the investigation. There is no evidence whatsoever that they focused on or followed up on this forensic finding, which is perhaps the single most important finding in this case.

Findings - Discussion

The following is a discussion of the major findings related to this assessment, already summarized in the previous section.

1. The investigative and forensic efforts of law enforcement at the location of Haraway's abduction (McAnally's convenience store; April 28, 1984) were inadequate rising to the level of abandonment. This prevented the recognition, preservation, collection, and testing specific items of evidence, as well as an untold volume of evidence that would have been missed. This is based

[2] As discussed in Crowder and Turvey (2013), and Gershman (1997), professional *abandonment* refers to incompetence and negligence to the point of effective professional absence causing harm to the client. In effect, it also refers to the abandonment of one's professional duty of care.

on at least the following facts and evidence (see testimony of officers and investigators from Ada PD):

A. The First Officer on site did not secure crime scene or provide for scene integrity in any reasonable or effective fashion.
- No security tape deployed.
- No security log kept re: personnel/witnesses/ patrons entering and exiting the scene.
- Did not keep the manager out of the scene.
- Did not shut down McAnally's to business (e.g., continued to sell gas).
- This is further demonstrated by the register tape, which shows customers paying for items in the store after law enforcement arrived on scene.

B. The responding investigators failed to secure, investigate, and collect potential evidence at the crime scene.
- Once on scene, they did not immediately address and correct the lack of security.
- No efforts were made to preserve the physical evidence.
- Investigators did not instruct anyone to engage in crime scene processing efforts.
- No independent count of the money present at the scene was conducted; investigators relied on the manager for this information.
- Investigators failed to collect Haraway's purse from the crime scene.
- Haraway's driver's license was provided that evening to investigators from her purse by the manager.
- The manager gave Haraway's purse to her husband, Steve; Steve Haraway apparently gave the purse to police investigators a year later, in May of 1985, violating any reasonable or effective chain of custody.
- While the investigators were on scene, the manager disposed of a cigarette butt that he found burning in an ashtray on the counter and an open beer can which is believed to be the last item purchased, preventing their collection as evidence.
- Law enforcement investigators left the scene unsecured and allowed the manager lock up in their absence.

C. The responding investigators failed to identify, secure, investigate, and collect potential evidence from Ms. Haraway's vehicle, which was reported to be parked at the crime scene that evening. They did acknowledge it existed at the scene, as this was pointed out by the manager, but it was not opened, the registration was not verified, and potential evidence relating to potential suspects could easily have been missed.

2. The investigative efforts of law enforcement subsequent to Haraway's abduction were inadequate rising to the level of abandonment. This is based on at least the following facts and evidence:

A. Missing person report was filed by Haraway's sister, mother, and step-father containing detailed descriptive information.

B. A telex was sent out by law enforcement investigators with no description of victim clothing because they thought clothing was not important. This is investigatively unsound.

C. Law enforcement investigators sent out Haraway's dental records to other agencies, in lieu of a physical description. This suggests that they presumed she was actually dead (this would be the only reason other agencies would need or have use for dental records). Such an assumption so early on, with no indication of violence or injury at the scene, is investigatively irresponsible.

D. Basic investigative procedure in a missing persons case would dictate getting witness statements of the victim's description, and victim photos from the family, for regional distribution. There is no evidence that this was done.

E. Basic investigative procedure in a missing persons case would dictate running the victim's name and home address through criminal databases to establish any history of criminal activity by the victim, any known criminal associates, or any prior victimization. There is no evidence that this was done.

F. Basic investigative procedure in a missing persons case requires interviews with immediate family (e.g., husband, mother, sister, and stepfather) for pertinent background and potential suspect information or development. There is no evidence that this was done, other than a single interview with the mother by the OSBI.

G. Basic investigative procedure in any felony crime scene would require checking phone records of incoming and outgoing calls with respect to the scene itself (e.g., McAnally's), the victim's home, and any friends or family. There is no evidence that this was done.

H. Basic investigative procedure in a missing persons case requires interviews with recent romantic or sexual partners (e.g., ex-husbands and ex-boyfriends) for pertinent background and potential suspect information or development. There is no evidence that this was done.

I. Defense investigator interview efforts revealed information regarding Wes Weissinger, Haraway's jealous and reportedly drug-addicted ex-fiancé with whom she lived with for a time. They further have revealed that Haraway became apparently pregnant while engaged to Weissinger, and had at least one abortion, all prior to her marriage with Steve Haraway. The police and prosecution knew of Haraway's prior relationship with Weissinger, but there is no evidence that they followed up on or investigated the extent of it - let alone any potential relevance to her abduction.

Turvey Report
Haraway case: Page 7 of 13

J. Basic investigative procedure in a missing persons case requires interviews with close personal friends for pertinent background and potential suspect information or development. There is no evidence that this was done.

K. A defense investigator interview with Karen Wise, Haraway's best friend at the time, revealed that Haraway was believed to be pregnant at the time of her abduction. The police and prosecution should have been aware of this, as Karen Wise testified at trial and there was ample opportunity to elicit this and other related information.

L. The prosecution misplaced a box of exhibits labelled "88-571; Fontenot v. State". This box was recently discovered by accident in a closet at a Sheriff's Office. It contained, among other things, a gray shirt, long sleeved; a brown leather purse, labeled "purse belonging to Denice Haraway, given to D. Smith by Steve Haraway, 5-24-85" - State's Exhibit 61 (the purse contained numerous items, not all of which are mentioned here); a piece of blue jean material from the zipper area of a pair of jeans (found inside the purse); An "Office of the State's Medical Examiner" envelope labeled "Metal fragment found in skull of Donna Haraway, State's Exhibit 15B"; a small blue manila envelope labeled "Blue jean material found 25' NW of skull"; an unsealed evidence bag, labelled "strand of hair" State's Exhibit 17; the victim's earrings; a blue and white pocket book; a SW Bell calling card for Donna Haraway, no. 405-332-8957 - loose in the box; rolled up adding machine tape from the McAnally's register, State's Exhibit 60; a cigarette butt, loose in the box; a blue card with a "Family Planning Clinic" appoint time and date: "November 16, @ 1P.M."; microscope slide with hair, loose in the box; a piece of paper with a name a phone number on it; and the victim's driver's license, loose in the box.

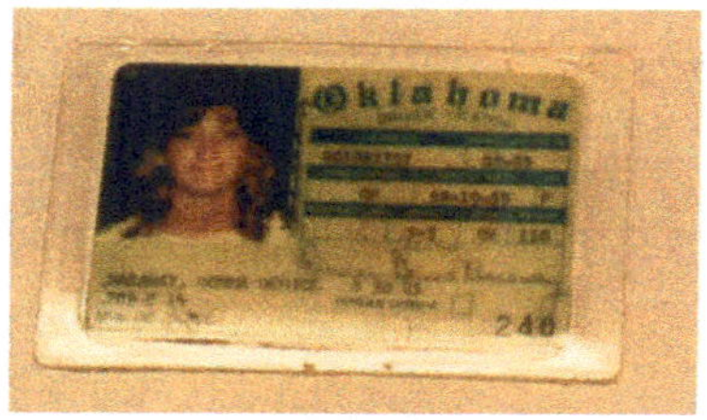

M. The cash register tape did not appear to have been previously unravelled or examined subsequent to being collected and boxed by law enforcement investigators. Unravelling it revealed that it had been used by law enforcement investigators to associate and record the names of customers who purchased items at McAnally's on the night of of Haraway's abduction. There is no evidence that these customers were interviewed by law enforcement investigators.

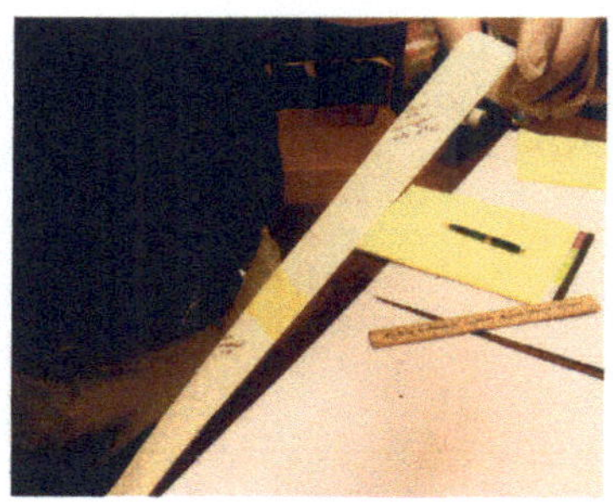

N. There is no evidence that law enforcement investigators researched the calls associated with the SW Bell calling card for Donna Haraway.

O. There is no evidence that police investigators followed up on the blue card with a "Family Planning Clinic" appoint time and date: "November 16, @ 1P.M." from Haraway's purse. This becomes investigatively relevant with respect to her reported history of abortion, reported pregnancy, and the finding that she gave birth subsequent to her abduction (see finding No. 4 in this report).

3. The investigative and forensic efforts of law enforcement at the location where Haraway's remains were found (West of Gerty, off a county road; Monday, January 20th, 1986) were inadequate rising to the level of abandonment. This prevented the recognition, preservation, collection, and testing specific items of evidence, as well as an untold volume of evidence that would have been missed. This is based on at least the following facts and evidence:

A. The First Officer on site did not secure crime scene or provide for scene integrity in any reasonable or effective fashion. This is standard practice even when remains have been in place for extended periods of time, to prevent further evidence loss, damage, or obliteration (Chisum and Turvey, 2011).
- No security tape deployed.
- No security log kept re: personnel/witnesses/ patrons entering and exiting the scene.

B. It is unclear from the record whether scene was "processed" on 1/20/86 or 1/21/86

C. Scene photos lacked sufficient quantity, quality, context and measurements.

D. Some bones appeared to be improperly piled together for photos, and were then packaged together in a sack.

E. There is no written investigative or forensic report on who found what or where at the scene.

F. There is no scene diagram

G. There was no directed or deliberate forensic excavation for other evidence concealed by brush or beneath soil.

H. According to a supplemental MEs report, some victim bones and a watch were found in a rat's nest by a farmer some 30' away from the original site on 1-30-96. There is no evidence that the watch put under a clear chain of custody or submitted for forensic analysis (e.g., fingerprinting; now DNA testing).

Turvey Report
Haraway case: Page 9 of 13

I. Additionally, there is no evidence that anyone in authority investigated or confirmed whether the watch or the earrings found with these remains actually belonged to the victim.

J. The ME's office was not notified; bones were therefore removed without proper legal authority by the police, the OSBI and the Sheriff's Department.

K. The scene was vacated and left unsecured before investigators returned on 1/24/86: the OSBI, the prosecutor, the sheriff and the ME went out there and found more bones.

L. In late February of 1986, law enforcement investigators returned to search this scene with both ECU college students and victim family members. Either group being involved with formal search efforts at this scene is highly inappropriate.

M. There were, in effect, multiple searches on multiples dates by multiples agencies with no reports of search activity or chain of custody regarding evidence collected.

N. Based on a review of the documentation, it is likely that evidence still exists at that location, to include more bones and perhaps even the victim's engagement ring, which was not recovered.

4. It is unclear from the case record that anyone, whether prosecution or defense, fully understood that the victim had given birth to at least one child, and what that must have meant for the investigation. There is no evidence whatsoever that they focused on or followed up on this forensic finding, which is perhaps the single most important finding in this case. This is based on at least the following facts and evidence:

A. There is no evidence that the victim gave birth prior to her abduction.

B. There is strong forensic evidence that the remains found, which are conclusively identified as those of Donna "Denice" Haraway, belong to an adult female that has given birth to at least one child through her birth canal. As stated in the Report from Richard McWilliams, Phd, Consulting Forensic Anthropologist to the ME's Office, January 23, 1986: "Marks on the pelvis indicate she had given birth to at least one child."

C. There is no evidence that investigators, prosecutors, or the defense understood the significance of this information: the victim would need to have been held in captivity for up to as many as nine months in order to give birth. Any suspects generated would need to be physically capable of this. In addition, this means there would necessarily be another crime scene where the victim was held - which has yet to be acknowledged let alone identified by law enforcement efforts.

D. No skeletal remains of an infant were found in association with the remains of Donna "Denice" Haraway. This means that either scene search efforts were inadequate to the task of finding them; that the child was killed subsequent to its birth and disposed cf elsewhere; or that the child was not killed and may yet be alive. None of these possibilities have been investigated, or excluded, by investigative efforts to date.

Please do not hesitate to contact me with any questions regarding these findings.

Brent E. Turvey, PhD
Forensic Scientist

References

Bopp, W. and Schultz, D. (1972) *Principles of American Law Enforcement and Criminal Justice*, Charles C. Thomas, Springfield, IL.

Bryden, D. and Lengnick, S. (1997) "Rape in the criminal justice system," *The Journal of Criminal Law and Criminology*, Vol. 87, Summer; 1194–1384.

Chisum, J. and Turvey, B. (2011) *Crime Reconstruction, 2nd ed.*, San Diego: Elsevier Science.

Crowder, S. and Turvey, B. (2013) *Ethical Justice: Applied Issues for Criminal Justice Students and Professionals*, San Diego: Elsevier Science.

Fontenot v. State (1988) OK CR 170, 742 P.2d 31, Case Number: F-85-769.

Gershman, B. (1997) *Trial Error and Misconduct*, Lexis Law, Charlottesville, VA.

Gross, H. (1924) *Criminal Investigation*, London: Sweet & Maxwell.

Hansen, D. and Culley, T. (1973) *The Police Training Officer*, Charles C. Thomas, Springfield, IL.

Kappeler, V. (2006) *Critical Issues in Police Civil Liability, 4th ed.*, Waveland Press, Long Grove, IL.

Leonard, V. (1969) *The Police, The Judiciary, and the Criminal*, Charles C. Thomas, Springfield, IL.

O'Connell, J. and Soderman, H. (1936) *Modern Criminal Investigation*, New York: Funk & Wagnalls.

Rau, R. (2000) *Crime Scene Investigation: A Guide for Law Enforcement*, Washington DC: National Institute of Justice, Technical Working Group on Crime Scene Investigation, NCJ 178280, January.

Savino, J. and Turvey, B. (2011) *Rape Investigation Handbook, 2nd ed.*, Elsevier, San Diego, CA.

SATF (2009) "False reports and case unfounding," *Attorney General's Sexual Assault Task Force*, State of Oregon, Position Paper, January 22.

Snyder, L. (1944) *Homicide Investigation*, Springfield, IL: Charles C. Thomas.

Sullivan, J. (1977) *Introduction to Police Science, 3rd ed.*, McGraw-Hill, , New York.

Wade, C. (1999) *Handbook of Forensic Services,* Washington, DC: U.S. Department of Justice, Federal Bureau of Investigation.

Weston, P., and Wells, K. (1974) *Criminal Investigation: Basic Perspectives, 2nd ed.*, Englewood Cliffs, NJ: Prentice-Hall.

A MISSING CHILD

Everyone agrees that Donna Haraway had not given birth prior to her abduction. However, her remains tell a different story. The remains found west of Gerty, which are conclusively identified as those of Donna "Denice" Haraway, belong to an adult female who has given birth to at least one child through her birth canal. As stated clearly in the Report from Richard McWilliams, PhD, Consulting Forensic Anthropologist to the medical examiner (ME)'s office, dated January 23, 1986: "Marks on the pelvis indicate she had given birth to at least one child."

This finding means that the victim would need to have been held in captivity for up to as many as nine months in order to have given birth. Consequently, any suspects generated would need to be capable of physically holding her. They would need a place to do it, and they would need to be available to keep her alive while she was captive. This means another crime scene.

Additionally, no skeletal remains of an infant were found in association with the remains of Donna "Denice" Haraway. This means that either those scene search efforts were inadequate to the task of finding them; that the child was killed subsequent to its birth and disposed of elsewhere; or that the child was not killed and may yet be alive. None of these possibilities have been investigated, or excluded, by investigative efforts to date.

This leads to the author's final conclusion in this case, which is: It is unclear from the case record that anyone, whether prosecution or defense, fully understood that forensic reports indicated that the victim had given birth to at least one child. Moreover, nobody involved seemed to understand what this meant for the investigation and prosecution of Karl Fontenot. There is no evidence whatsoever that anyone focused on or followed up on this forensic finding, which is perhaps the single most important finding in this case.

In a case that already involves significant volumes of evidence (eg, investigative reports and physical evidence) withheld from the defense and investigative shortcomings across the board, the failure to grasp and follow up on this issue is not a surprise. However, this does not make it less important. Those interested in seeking the truth in this case, with the duty of care to do so, have an obligation to find out whether this child, born subsequent to Ms. Harway's captivity was killed or perhaps remains alive to this day. The answer to that question is likely the answer to the entire case.

THE APPEAL

The appeal filed by Fontenot's attorney, Tiffany Murphy, cites numerous problems with the original conviction, explaining (Murphy, 2013, p. 2): "The jury's conviction is invalid due to a plethora of Brady evidence withheld from defense and appellate counsel, ineffective assistance of counsel, the admission of false evidence by the prosecution, and police misconduct." The appeal goes on to explain the following (pp. 2–3):

> *Newly discovered evidence not presented during Mr. Fontenot's trial establishes his innocence. Much of this evidence remained in the State's custody throughout the investigation and prosecution of Mr. Fontenot through both of his trials without being disclosed to any of his defense counsel in violation of several constitutional rights. The focal point of Mr. Fontenot's innocence claim rests on evidence showing that Mrs. Haraway was being harassed and stalked by a man in the months and weeks leading up to her disappearance. Further, the withheld ME report shows not only a botched handling of the crime scene, a pattern in this case, but more importantly that Mrs. Haraway gave birth to a child sometime before her death.*
>
> *Documents showing Mr. Fontenot's alibi were also within the 860 pages of undisclosed Oklahoma State Bureau of Investigation (OSBI) reports along with other evidence. Additionally, the sole eyewitness placing Mr. Fontenot in McAnally's recanted his identification. Finally, Karen Wise, the convenience store clerk at JP's explained the pressure both the police and prosecution placed on her to change her description of men seen at JP's convenience store to fit the police theory of the crime. The totality of this newly discovered evidence establishes not only Mr. Fontenot's innocence but the specific actions by the State to manufacture a case against him on the flimsiest evidence.*

So not only were a substantial volume of pertinent reports and evidence withheld by the state during the trial, and not only was the investigation negligent to the point of abandonment, but the state's only real evidence, an eyewitness, has recanted her identification. If ever there were a case that begged for a new trial this would be it.

However, in early 2015, as reported in Palmer (2015):

> *A quest to overturn the murder conviction of a man a legal defense group claims is innocent was denied by a Pontotoc County judge just before he retired.*
>
> *An appeal was filed Thursday in the state Court of Criminal Appeals by attorneys for the Oklahoma Innocence Project. The group represents Karl Fontenot, whose story was featured in the book "The Dreams of Ada" and was mentioned by John Grisham in his nonfiction book "The Innocent Man." Fontenot was convicted of the 1984 murder, robbery and kidnapping of Ada store clerk Donna Denice Haraway.*
>
> *"Both Karl and his legal team were disappointed with the judge's ruling," said his attorney, Tiffany Murphy. "We'll continue to litigate on Karl's innocence."*

What this means is that the appeals in this case will continue. And eventually an impartial judge will read the case, do the math with the evidence, and then realize that a new trial is warranted. They will also join other jurists in the 21st century who hold that misconduct by the state is only encouraged in future cases by not holding its agents accountable for what has been done in the past. However long that takes, and it can be decades in the experience of this examiner, the important thing is for objective forensic analysts to make the record clear so that attorneys and jurists have all the tools they need to eventually craft justice.

REFERENCES

Cooley, C., Turvey, B., 2014. Miscarriages of Justice. Elsevier Science, San Diego.

Cosgrove, J., August 4, 2013. Report Sparks Debate Over Innocence of Karl Fontenot. The Oklahoman.url: http://newsok.com/report-sparks-debate-over-innocence-of-karl-fontenot/article/3868927.

Crowder, S., Turvey, B., 2013. Ethical Justice: Applied Issues for Criminal Justice Students and Professionals. Elsevier Science, San Diego.

Fontenot v. State, 1988. OK CR 170, 742 P.2d 31, Case Number: F-85-769. See Also: Karl Fontenot v. District Court of Pontotoc County State of Oklahoma, State of Oklahoma. No. CR-88-43. Brief in Support of Application for Post-Conviction Relief.

McCay, T., January 27, 2015. More Prisoners Were Found Wrongfully Convicted in 2014 Than Ever Before. news.mic.com. url: http://mic.com/articles/109286/more-prisoners-were-found-innocent-in-2014-than-ever-before-and-we-re-barely-even-looking.

Murphy, T.R., 2013. Karl Fontenot v. State of Oklahoma, District Court of Pontotoc County State of Oklahoma, No. CR-88–43. Brief in Support of Application for Post-Conviction Relief. url: http://works.bepress.com/tiffany_murphy/5.

Palmer, J., February 1, 2015. Innocence Project's Quest to Free Karl Fontenot From Prison Denied by Ada Judge. The Oklahoman. url: http://newsok.com/article/5389314.

Index

Note: Page numbers followed by "f" indicate figures, and "b" indicate boxes.

D

E

T

U

V

W

Y

Kolibri 360 GmbH
Ferdinand-Jühlke-Straße 7
99095 Erfurt, Deutschland
produktsicherheit@kolibri360.de